CW00765058

An Illustrated History of the Rod

First published 1865 by William Reeves, London.

This Edition 2000 © AKS Books Ltd.
PO Box 39, Bexhill-on-Sea,
East Sussex TN40 1WR, England.

Please write for full list.

All rights reserved

ISBN 1 899861 20 3

Printed and bound in Great Britain
by Antony Rowe Ltd, Chippenham, Wiltshire

FOREWORD

by EDWARD ANTHONY

T**HE** H*ISTORY of the Rod*, by the Reverend Wm. Cooper, BA, was first published in England in 1865, and is entirely typical of most "objective" works on the subject of corporal punishment of that or any era in that (a) its declared purpose is altogether different from its actual purpose, and (b) that the author published it under a false name. Given (a), (b) is hardly surprising, but in fact the author of this vast treatise (the original edition ran to 550 pages) was even more of an authority than most of his readers realised. His real name was James G. Bertram and, among other works, he is known to be the author of one of the most famous (and elegant) pieces of flagellant fiction of the Victorian Era, *Personal Recollections of the Use of the Rod*, otherwise known as *The Merry Order of St. Bridget*, which was first published some three years after *The History of the Rod*, though actually claiming to have been written in the later eighteenth century. Bertram chose the name Margaret Anson for *The Merry Order* but for the earlier book he did as others had done before him and employed a good, solid-sounding ecclesiastical *nom-de-fouet*.

In my 1995 book *Thy Rod and Staff* I described the real purpose of this general class of work as: "Primarily that of exciting and arousing, while maintaining, at least superficially, and whenever the author remembers to invoke it, a veneer of condemnation—the classic facing-both-ways posture, implemented to differing levels of success depending on the author's self-control (or self-delusion)." I also described it as "flawed as a work of scholarship—few direct references

are supplied... though in a list of sources the author demonstrates his
own very wide reading." These might seem somewhat damning com-
ments, except that the book's sheer size—and Bertram's audacity in
presenting it as a "straight" work of scholarship—must endear it to
any connoisseur; while many of its brighter inventions have since
passed into the Flagellants' public domain, with anecdotes and related
incidents appearing and re-appearing in anthologies and other collections without any of the anthologisers seeming to realise that they
were first concocted by James G. Bertram and first published in *The
History of the Rod*. Flawed or not, it is therefore a major Source.

And fiction a great deal of it is also, although there is no reason to
doubt the general veracity of the anecdotes and snippets that Bertram
deploys throughout the book, especially its first half, when he is
attempting to establish the volume's credentials. One senses, however,
that in dutifully writing about Discipline Among the Carthusians and
Carmelites and Flogging in Africa he is being just that—dutiful. His
real interest centres closely around the (for him) contemporary application of physical discipline to young ladies—the core subject of this
book beyond doubt, while some of its (fictional, though purporting to
be otherwise) chapters on this particular sub-genre of Disciplinary
Writing can clearly be seen as prototypes for the more fully developed
Merry Order. It is also more than possible that Bertram himself supplied more than one of the (now famous) readers' contributions to
journals like *Family Herald*, *Queen* and the *Englishwoman's Domestic
Magazine*, many of which he quotes in this book with (it seems to me)
more than the usual tongue in cheek. If so, he was surely amongst the
most prolific flagellationist writers of all time, and certainly one of the
most influential. For a few years at least, he appears to have been a
one-man industry.

For some reason I see him as rather Pickwickian—bald head, fluffy
side-whiskers, gleaming pince-nez, chuckling as he flits between his
racks of books by candlelight, saying "Ha!" as he discovers a faded cutting... a sip of port... the scratch-scratch of his quill pen...another sip
of port... and so the night wears on. Fancy? Possibly.

Certainly he appears to have kept his *nom-de-plume* safe for some years. In 1870 "Edgar Markham" (actually St. George H. Stock, known to be the author of *The Romance of Chastisement*) wrote to the "Rev. W.M. Cooper M. A." (which is slightly odd in itself, since "Cooper" only claimed a Bachelor's degree on the frontispiece of his book) praising the work and offering to open a correspondence. It is not known if a reply was sent. The copy that Australian composer Percy Grainger purchased in 1909 must have been seriously second-hand: nevertheless he liked it enough to eulogise it in a letter to his lady friend Karen Holten. Grainger at least was under no illusions about the book's purpose: "Seldom in my life have I gone through such a lecherous day... my head ached, my eyes burnt, my body shook, of the excitement of reading..."

Perhaps the most poignant possible reader of *The History of the Rod*, however—and I stress this is only conjecture—is the psychoanalyst Henry Havelock Ellis's single most famous patient, the educated flagellomane "Florrie". In part of her long deposition, which Havelock Ellis quotes in full, she relates how her fantasies (of girls' school whippings) were fuelled by a book she found which lovingly described how the young ladies sentenced to the birch were first dressed in degrading costume and then horsed on the back of a maid. "This," she remembered, "was the source of much extra shame" [in her fantasy]. Descriptions just such as these may certainly be found in the latter half of *The History of the Rod* (and indeed also in *The Merry Order.)* Were one or both of these books to blame for inflaming "Florrie's" passion? If so, they surely fulfilled their creator's intention.

THE BEAUTIFUL MADAME LAPUCHIN
Knouted by Order of Elizabeth, Empress of Russia

FLAGELLATION & THE
FLAGELLANTS.

A HISTORY OF THE ROD

IN ALL COUNTRIES

FROM THE EARLIEST PERIOD TO THE PRESENT TIME

By The Rev. Wm. M. COOPER, BA

Britannia scourged by Pitt

WITH NUMEROUS ILLUSTRATIONS;

A NEW EDITION, REVISED AND CORRECTED

AKS
BOOKS
LIMITED

ILLUSTRATIONS.

CONTENTS

CONTENTS

PRELIMINARY.

THE WRITER, now that his work is concluded, is not inclined to dwell on the difficulties under which he laboured in the preparation of the present volume. Although this History of the Rod may be regarded as "a compilation," still the task required more than an ordinary expenditure of time and trouble. The facts and anecdotes brought together in the following pages were found to be very widely scattered, and frequently accompanied by details which on no possible pretence could now be openly published—

> *Est et fidelli tuta silentio*
> *Merces*—HOR.

Indeed, it would have been simply impossible to have given the chronicle of Conventual and Monastic Discipline entire: the coarseness, the brutality, the refined cruelty often exercised, were of a character so objectionable, that no good end could have been accomplished by giving every circumstance and every detail narrated in these old records. The writer's aim has been to lay before the student interested in the progress of civilisation as full an account of the use of the Rod as propriety on the one hand and as history on the other demanded.

No apology is offered for what is recorded in this book: it was neither compiled for the prurient nor the prudish, the writer's sole aim being to give (to the best of his ability) a true History of the Rod as an instrument for correctional purposes in the Church, the State, and the Family.

W. M. C

INTRODUCTION

IT is recorded of an old-fashioned schoolmaster that in the course of fifty years he administered to his pupils nearly half-a-million canings, and a hundred and twenty-four thousand proper floggings! This pedagogue, who in the days of Solomon would have been a man after that wise king's own heart may be taken as the type of a class of teachers who flourished "in the good old days" —rigid disciplinarians who never spared the rod nor spoiled the child. Happy schoolboys of the present day have but a faint notion of those times, or of the severities undergone at school by their fathers and grandfathers. Flagellation, except for garrotters, has gone nearly out of fashion in this country, and the birch of to-day is but the ghost of what it was a hundred years since, and the rod even of that period was only a faint shadow of the terrible whips and scourges of a much earlier age.

Nor was the Rod in early times confined to schoolboys; it had, from small beginnings, become a symbol of authority at which even bearded men trembled, and, as any one may read, was wielded with tyrannical power by the kings and conquerors of antiquity; for the practice of flagellating the human body dates from the earliest ages of mankind, and has been chronicled by the most ancient authors. Without doubt, the destinies of mankind have been greatly influenced by the scourge, and the curiosities of flagellation form an interesting chapter in the progress of human civilisation.

Records of various kinds of corporal chastisement inflicted during the most remote pagan ages are still extant, the heathens having made a most industrious use of the scourge, frequently practising with relentless severity on the backs of their unfortunate captives. The extended use of the whip, however, is due to more Christian times. The ancient Persians were familiar with the Rod: the nobles of the kingdom even were not spared when flagellations were going the round, whilst a satirical custom prevailed then, as it does even yet in some eastern countries, of the punished having to return grateful thanks for the punishment—an observance of etiquette which at a not

very remote period, we believe, was insisted upon by hard-hearted
lady teachers—

"Flick-em, flap-em, over the knee,
  Say, Thank you, good dame, for whipping of me."

After a time, in Persia, nobles were spared the indignity of a personal application of the scourge, it being arranged in the case of such
grandees that future punishments should be inflicted on their clothes
instead of their bare bodies, thus rendering the whipping in their case
much pleasanter than it would otherwise have been, leading to the
belief that it was at that time the proverb originated, of one law for the
rich and another for the poor.

Before the foundation of Rome the whip was the daily portion of
the slave, and the ancient Romans became adepts in the use of the
scourge. In the satires of Juvenal, and in the writings of other authors,
there are numerous examples of severe flagellations bestowed upon
slaves. The judges of the period were surrounded by a variety of whips
and scourges: in order to strike evil-doers with terror, they were
shown in the courts of law in profusion. These instruments of torture
had each a particular name; for mild punishments there was the *ferula*, and for degrees of greater severity there were harsher instruments
of correction, the severest of all being the terrible *flagellum*. The
Roman judges had unlimited power over the culprits who were
brought before them, while masters and mistresses held the lives of
their slaves so cheap that it was no uncommon matter for some of
them to be whipped to death; and, as all who are versed in the manners and customs of ancient Italy know, the retainers of a first-rate
Roman household were so numerous that some of them were sure to
be in disgrace. In accounts of Roman life which we have read, some
unfortunate slave was generally found asking the feasting guests to
intercede with the master and save him from being flogged. In an elaborate description of Trimalchios' banquet we have an example of this.
Indeed, the practice of whipping slaves was often indulged in as an
excellent mode of amusing guests, either during dinner or after the

feast had terminated. The ladies were, however, far more severe and ingenious in their disciplines than the men, and the waiting-maids of these fair despots led in consequence a very unpleasant life. A lady's dressing-room is said to have been as well furnished with scourges as a court of law. The Roman ladies required a perfect army of female attendants, each having a particular duty to perform connected with the house or the toilette; those performing duties in the dressing-room were made to attend their mistress in a partially nude state, in order that there should be no impediment to an immediate whipping if any thing displeased the lady. One way of punishing male slaves was to suspend them by their hands to a strong beam, and attach to their feet a heavy weight, in order that they might not kick the person who flogged them. Ladies used to whip their maids while suspended to the beam, a slight difference, however, being made in the mode of suspension—these victims of the incensed fair being hung up by their hair, a piece of cruel ingenuity that has never been tried in later times, although many persons have been punished for cruelty to their servants. It is not long since a lady in Scotland was imprisoned for thirty days for slapping her servant's face! whilst another mistress who had chastised her servant-maid in the old orthodox fashion, with the household taws, had to pay damages to the young woman in consequence; and we lately read, in the assize intelligence, that a straw plait manufacturer at Luton was sentenced to six months' imprisonment for birching one of his female workers.

It would appear that at a very early period school masters learned to use rods upon the backs of their disciples. There are numerous anecdotes extant of flogging schoolmasters of ancient times; and there are stories also of preceptors who were flogged by their pupils!

The greatest of all the curiosities of flagellation were those voluntary scourgings which were performed by the Spartan youths of Lacedemonia. Plutarch alludes to the whipping customs of Sparta in the character of an eye-witness. Boys delighted in being whipped for a whole day before the altar of Diana, at the annual contest of flagellations. The "gamest" boy, if we may use the word, was he who could endure the greatest number of stripes—he carried off the prize, or, at

any rate, became victor in the contest. These exhibitions were conducted before the parents of the children, who eloquently exhorted
their youths to bear the pain with fortitude. Priests were appointed to
witness the ceremony, examine the wounds and predict the future
career of the heroes. The example of these youths raised up other sects
of flagellants—philosophers who cultivated birch and used whip-cord
with a zeal worthy of a better cause. In the course of time these sects
of whipping zealots began to spread (not, however, without being
ridiculed) into different countries, giving rise to a great number of
anecdotes connected with customs of flagellation, which will be found
in the body of this work, and need not be further alluded to here than
to mention that at a later date there was founded on these Spartan
exhibitions the rather disgusting festival of the Lupercalia, a curious
example of the kind of voluntary flagellations once so common.

It was long debated whether flagellation as a punishment or flagellation as a penance was the more ancient of the two kinds of whipping;
but there need be little doubt about the matter, corporal punishment
being as old as sin. The voluntary flagellations, no doubt, resulted in
imitation of the punishment: in other words, persons had the strength
of mind to punish themselves for such sins as they knew they had committed—and so this practice became in time a portion of the daily life
of persons who were more devout than others. Damian, the Cardinal
Bishop of Ostia, is the first historian of these voluntary flagellations,
and he tells us about the extraordinary vigour with which some of the
more zealous of the religious of early days used to flog themselves.

Voluntary flagellation of the kind alluded to dates from a far back
period: about the fifth century of the Christian era. The progress of
flagellation among the Christians was at first very slow, but, after a
time, spread so rapidly as to attract the attention of all Christendom,
a large body having sprung up, who practised the art with great industry and severity "The Flagellants," as they were called, began their
career in Italy, but soon extended into Germany and even into
England in a small degree; and to operators of those days used to wield
the scourge as if it was a prime social enjoyment. These flagellating
bodies originated in superstition, and their acts may be classed

amongst the greatest of all the curiosities connected with the use of the whip. One sect of the Flagellants originated in fear of the plague, which was raging at the time, it being thought that only by severe penance could the divine wrath be turned away.

Various modifications of the system in time arose, as, for instance, in Spain, where Flagellants imparted a tone of gallantry to their discipline, by undergoing their self-inflicted punishment under windows in the presence of their mistresses. Indeed, to such an extent was the practice carried that there arose persons who taught the polite art of flagellation, perhaps like the art of writing, in half-a-dozen lessons! The ladies were doubtless delighted with the homage paid to them, and rewarded youthful martyrs by lifting their veils for a brief moment. As the author of Hudibras says:-

> Why may not whipping have as good
> A grace, performed in time and mood,
> With comely movement, and by art,
> Raise passion in a lady's heart?

Private and family flagellation rapidly extended. In the houses of the great nobility, and in the palaces of kings, flogging had become very prevalent. Stories are still extant of queens—Catherine de' Medicis is a motherly example—who, placing their maids of honour over their knees, whipped them like little children; and ladies of quality living at court, whether in the immediate suite of the Queen or not, were not exempt, when they became naughty, from chastisement of the same kind. Pages in the palaces were frequently to be found on the flogging-block—indeed, at one time, the flagellation of a page excited no notice. We read of pages who were whipped for mocking the priests of a household. Others of the King's retainers had frequently to submit to similar discipline; in fact, the oft-recurring administration of corporal punishment was a portion of the every-day life of that period. The place selected for carrying out these disciplines, in the palaces of the kings or the nobility, was the kitchen. Persons of quality, however, were not flogged there; but it was there that flagellations were administered to drunken priests, pert maid-servants, or forward pages, and where generally the lower retainers suffered chastisement. Ladies of rank and persons of condition would, in all probability, be whipped in a much more private place, where they would not be exposed to the gibes and insults of the menial servants. There are instances on record of queens being flogged: a favourite sultana has before now been made to endure the whip, and among female slaves in the great seraglios the birch is still very familiar. In such romances and tales as depict the manners and customs of those remote times, there may be found various anecdotes of disciplines inflicted at court. As an instance, the story of the poet Clopinel, which illustrates court life of a certain period, is elsewhere related. Among the great people who have been flogged we find the names of more than one king.

There is another phase of flagellation equally curious, and of great antiquity—viz., those practices of discipline which were incidental to life in convents and monasteries. Some of the monkish orders were particularly severe in their discipline, and many curious stories are still extant regarding the whipping customs of these devout classes. So far back as the time of the Vestals, we have notices of the severe punishments inflicted for breaches of the rules laid down for the guidance of those virgins who tended the sacred fire. Although these young ladies were persons of great importance, it is on record that several of them were whipped. Having been previously covered over with a thin veil, they were compelled to suffer punishment in a dark room by the hands of a priest.

In convents long ago (and at present [?]), it was the rule that the punishments awarded to erring sisters should be inflicted by a woman that was elderly and severe in her nature; while the flagellations awarded to those of the sterner sex were ordained to be given by a morose brother; and strict rules were laid down as to the modesty with which all punishments were to be inflicted. There was, however, a time in the Church when this virtue of modesty was not so highly prized—in fact, at one period, in some of the monasteries, nakedness was held very cheap: delinquent brothers, being made to strip, were flogged, not only in the sight of their own congregation, but before the public as well! By an act of the Constitution of the Abbey of Cluny, it was ordained that brethren guilty of certain faults should be striped naked, and be tied up and flogged in a street or public place, so that all might see them. Voluntary flagellations, or those not inflicted by the law of the Order, were, of course, inflicted at the will of the individual. Many monks and nuns have been celebrated for the immense number of blows with which they chastised themselves.

There was one priest, in particular, who, in these old times, was celebrated for his zeal in laying on the discipline. His name was Cornelius Adriansen, and he was distinguished by having his particular mode of whipping named after him, so that a Cornelian discipline meant a flagellation *supra dorsum nudum*. Another person in holy orders became at one time very notorious for his style of discipline: this was Father Girard, the trial of whom, for flagellating and otherwise abusing Miss Cadière made at the time a great noise. This *cause célèbre* was published in a folio volume, which gave full details of the doings of the supposed sorcerer.

Throughout the period which we have indicated flagellation, public and private, was as nearly as possible universal; it was in such general repute, especially with monastic bodies, that nuns were recommended to flagellate themselves before proceeding to the election of a lady superior. The instruments in use for the purposes of monastic flagellation have been various. Father Dominic used a besom (i.e., a birch-rod.). Other saints have been more eccentric, and employed whatever instrument came in their way, whether the thongs or a stick. Again, some have used bunches of nettles, whilst others have preferred thistles; and one very devotional lady used a bunch of feathers. St. Bridget beat herself with a bunch of keys; and other ladies of simpler imaginations have made use of their hands.

Flagellation has its romantic and comic side, although it is quite possible that Eton pupils and other schoolboys may fail to see any fun in birch. Schoolboys of the present day who find themselves in "the bill" have generally but a very dim idea of the humour that has at various times been associated with the Rod. In corroboration of what we assert, there is told, on another page, numerous stories connected with the house of St. Lazare, which at one period existed in Paris, known as the seminary of the good boys, and kept by certain pious monks who carried on a *roaring* trade in flagellations.

In a medical point of view, flagellation was at one time in repute; it was thought to be, if we may use a simile, but another way of blistering the skin; and as a remedy for certain complaints, the birch held a distinguished place. The ancients also reverted to it as a moral agent, and a remnant of this idea prevailed till a comparatively recent period, as exemplified in the flagellation of maniacs and others. The doctors held that a smart whipping re-animated the torpid circulation of the cutaneous vessels, and led to an increase of muscular energy. Physicians used to prescribe a liberal amount of slapping for some of their patients; and there is on record an anecdote of a great lady who ordered her servants to give her physician a dose of birch of great strength, as she was under the impression that the learned gentleman was in the habit of betraying the secrets of the prison-house.

Enough is chronicled in the following pages to show how prevalent the use of the Rod has been in all ages and in all countries. Advancing civilisation has happily banished the frequent use of the scourge from among us, and it is admitted that the country does not suffer much from its absence. It is not yet "sixty years since" the birch was wielded with terrible severity both in the public and private schools of our own country, and also in the domestic circle. Masters and mistresses frequently corrected their servants, and parents their children, with the birch or the whip. Apprentices were often chastised. Mrs. Brownrigg flogged some of her girls to death, for which crime she was executed. A century ago, neither sex nor age formed a boundary to the administration of corporal chastisement. Even grown women had to bow submissive before the Rod. Dr. Johnson tells of a lady in Leicestershire who used to birch her grown-up daughters. In Russia, flogging, although greatly on the wane, still prevails; in that country the stick and the knout form a part of the penal law. We need not wonder, therefore, that the birch is the portion of disobedient ballet-girls, and that ladies of quality have been occasionally flogged at the police bureau for the good of their moral health. Stories of the knout are common.

To return again to our own country, we may remind our readers of the time when criminals were flogged through the streets—a custom that may again be revived in the case of garrotters; naughty women were whipped in Bridewell, and parties of fashionables used to be made up to go witness the sight! Some ladies of rank once had the mortification—it was their own choice—to be flagellated by a milliner for theft; and it is recorded that two gentlewomen were birched for stealing caudle-cups from the Royal Palace. Long ago, too, another quaint flagellating custom was exceedingly prevalent in this country. On the occasion of an execution taking place, all the younger branches of a family were thoroughly birched, in order that they might the better recollect the awful event. Perhaps the oddest case of flagellation referring to our own country is that of a clergyman who insisted on whipping his housemaid, "after the manner of a schoolboy," and who rushed into print to defend his conduct when it was impugned. A curious practice also prevailed in some of our village schools: a naughty boy would be strapped down to a desk at the door, and, being partially undressed, it fell to every pupil to administer a blow to the delinquent as he or she left the school. Except at some of the large public schools of England, the rod is now seldom used, and even at Eton and Harrow it is not so often resorted to as formerly. The birch was at one time immoderately used in schools for young ladies, and naughty pupils, of all ages, had to submit, often with many humiliating ceremonies—ceremonies said to have been borrowed from the convent schools of foreign countries—to "elegant flagellation."

In a well-known penny periodical, an attempt was made, about twelve years ago, to persuade the public that corporal chastisement was still inflicted in some of the ladies' schools of this country, but the whole story must have been a pure invention, as no one whom we have consulted seems to know a school in England where such practices are tolerated. A great controversy was lately carried on in the pages of a popular magazine about the whipping of girls. The details which were given of various punishments excited a "sensation" and were hotly denied—it being asserted that such punishments were too immodest and brutal for the present age of refinement; but that the kind of discipline described is reviving in the domestic circle is certain, and, as it has been more than once recommended by ladies of quality, may again become fashionable. *Apropos* of the whipping of young ladies, a girl of the period, aged seventeen, lately asked, through the columns of Public Opinion, if she could not raise an action of damages against her governess for having whipped her as if she were a child!

In various foreign countries the Rod is still the badge of power. In Austria soldiers are made to run the terrible gauntlet. Russia has not yet abolished the knout, and the ladies of Poland have been openly scourged by Russian soldiers! China has still the great bamboo; Turkey governs with the stick; the Siamese have their nightly birches; and in Africa there is "mumbo jumbo." Grown young ladies are still whipped in some of the American schools, and it was reserved for the Americans to make a trade of flogging, they having invented, in the days of slavery, a machine for whipping niggers!

The birch has been celebrated in poetry. Many allusions have been made to the Rod by the poets and there are various serious, sentimental, and satirical poems—whippiads, rodiads, birchiads, &c.—extant; but, unfortunately, they are too coarse for "the general reader." The children's toy-books of forty years ago dealt largely in birch. We have preserved one of these, giving a history of two naughty boys, who never did "nothing at all." Mamma punished them at last, as is related by the poet:-

> Then down both their trousers she took,
> While each stroke made them furiously squall.
> "Oh, why, mamma, what are you at?"
> "My dears, I'm at 'nothing at all'"

Shenstone's and Crabbe's poetical works have also numerous allusions to the punishment of the Rod; and there are likewise poems on the subject which, although they were not considered indelicate or vulgar by our grandfathers and grandmothers, are at the present day totally unfit to be reproduced, notwithstanding some of them are very witty and well written.

Plate II.   THE ROD IN EGYPT

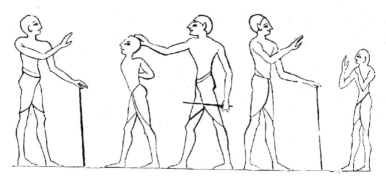

THE GENERAL USE OF THE BASTINADO.

—Beni Hassan

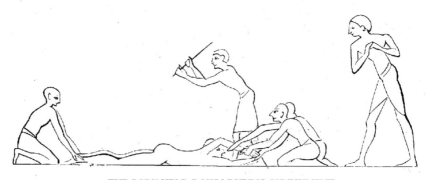

THE BODY HELD DOWN DURING PUNISHMENT.

—Beni Hassan

LABOURERS BEATEN BY TASKMASTERS.

—Pyramids

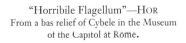

"Horribile Flagellum"—Hor
From a bas relief of Cybele in the Museum
of the Capitol at Rome.

Gladiators fighting with
Flagella
From a coin

CHAPTER I

A LEARNED CONTROVERSY TO BEGIN WITH

THE origin and progress of flagellation is involved in obscurity, and it is unnecessary to say that no means exist of tracing out the first whipping that was inflicted, or the name and address of him or her who administered or received it; but it may be shrewdly guessed that the population of the world would not be very numerous when the practice was instituted. We shall not venture here on an inquiry into antediluvian discipline, preferring to confine ourselves, in the meantime, to the subject in its comparatively modern aspect.

A tremendous dispute agitated the learned world at one period as to whether whipping as a penance or whipping as a punishment was first introduced. One author contended for one view of the case, and his opponent fought to establish an opposite theory. The facts related by the old controversialists are so lost in words, and hidden in Latin quotations, or so frittered away in notes and commentaries, as to make it a task of no small difficulty to separate the corn from the chaff. Whipping, as a penance, has at any rate made its mark on language. The various methods of doing penance were at first all comprehended under the term *disciplines*; but so great was the prominence awarded to flagellation (*disciplina flagelli*, "the discipline of the whip"), that in process of time *discipline* was used to express that kind of penance alone. Indeed, in French, we find that word appropriated to designate the instrument of religious flagellation: for example, in Molière's play of "Tartuffe; or, The Hypocrite," Tartuffe says to his valet:-

> "Laurent, serrez ma haire avec ma discipline,
> Et priez que toujours le Ciel vous illumine."
>
> *Tartuffe*, ac. iii., sc. a.

"Laurent, lock up my haircloth and *discipline*, and pray that Heaven may always enlighten you." Disciplines thus mean voluntary flagellations inflicted on themselves by penitents with scourges, whips, or rods. But the controversy need not be further alluded to than to say, that all the probabilities are in favour of "punishment" as first giving occasion for the use of the rod.

Other two points connected with flagellation that have also formed a subject of controversy, and been the theme of many writers, may be illustrated before going farther. The proper place of the body on which to inflict a discipline gave rise to great differences of opinion: some writers were in favour of bestowing the blows on the back and shoulders, which was called "the upper discipline" —sursum disciplina: others, again, advocated deorsum disciplina, "the lower discipline," as being the proper whipping.

According to the most learned of the controversialists, the upper discipline was highly disapproved of, because of its tendency to hurt the eyes and the breasts of the penitents; such, indeed, is the danger of wounding these sensitive parts, that at this day, when a woman is flogged in Sweden—a frequent occurrence for some offences—she is laid in a copper sheath, which fits the front part of her person with so much nicety as to leave only the hips or back exposed to the lash. A celebrated medical journal lately observed, in commenting on the flogging of a party of garrotters, that heavy punishments ought to be given by instalments of ten or a dozen stripes at a time, and that a lower discipline would be, by far, the most effective as a deterrent from crime.

Father Gretzer, a very ancient disciplinarian, was much troubled in his mind as to the proper part on which to lay the stripes, and obtained the following opinion from a learned doctor:- "The vulgar opinion that lashes applied to the back are apt to hurt the eyes is not well grounded. It is true that the great loss of blood injures the brain, and consequently the eyes, which are called by some the sprouts of it; and these it affects by the diminution it causes of the vital heat. But there does not arise from disciplines such a great loss of blood as that the brain may thereby suffer any considerable deperdition of its heat; on the contrary, since scarifications on the back are often employed with success for the cure of disorders in the eyes, why should bad consequences to them be feared from a few stripes? Those, therefore, alone, who are of a weakly habit of body the exercise in question can hurt, but not persons of a good constitution; and when disciplines are so moderately inflicted as to cause no loss of blood, and barely to affect the colour of the skin, no detriment certainly ought to be feared from them."

Such was the decision of an excellent physician, and to it Father Gretzer adds that he willingly and readily subscribes.

"Physicians and anatomists say," writes another author on this part of the subject of flagellation, "that the secret or open communion between all parts of the human body is such, that it is impossible to do any material and continual injury to one part without the other parts being also sooner or later affected. Hence it follows that those persons who execute disciplines upon themselves with great severity fall in process of time into serious distempers of some kind or other, so as at length to find themselves disabled from continuing those practices by which they intended to procure the improvement of their morals."

All physicians, however, do not agree with the authorities just quoted. Some have delivered different opinions concerning the harmlessness of discipline with respect to the eyes; and whether it was that the Capuchin Friars thought the advice of these latter of greatest weight, or that they intended their zeal should be unrestrained by any apprehension, they adopted the use of the lower discipline; and the generality of nuns did the same, from the like intention of securing their eyesight. "Determined thereto by the advice of able physicians and pious persons, they gave up flagellating themselves on their shoulders, in order to belabour and slash their loins with knotted small cords and hardened rods."

There was still another point to be considered in this matter. By most of the ancient monastic rules, religious persons were forbidden to inspect any part of their naked bodies, lest such indulgence might give rise to wicked thoughts. "If such disciplines," it has been argued, "cannot be performed in secret without danger, is it prudent to execute them in the presence of witnesses?" Tertullian observes, that "Nature has made either fear or shame the attendants on every evil action. What man or woman then could, without shame, execute a lower discipline in company with other persons?". Shakespeare says:-

"The chariest maid is prodigal enough
If she unmask her charms to the moon."

This amusing and very learned controversy lasted a long time, and ended, like many others, by the adherents of each system thinking their own the best. The wrangle described, naturally enough, led to another interesting inquiry, which is summarised in the next chapter for the benefit of the curious reader.

CHAPTER II

A BRIEF SUMMARY OF ANOTHER CURIOUS CONTROVERSY.

D E LOLME—in reality the Abbé Boileau, brother of the poet— assures us that the part upon which mankind sits is extremely deserving of esteem. It is, in the first place, a characteristic part of humanity: it is formed by the expansion of muscles which, anatomists inform us, are proper to the human species, and exist in no other animal.

Nor do these parts confer upon man a distinction from animals that is of an honorary kind merely. Like the faculty of walking erect, which, as Ovid remarks, enables him to behold the sun or the stars, as he goes forward, it puts him in a condition to promote the liberal arts and sciences, as well as the mechanical arts and manufactures. By the power of *assiduity* it confers upon man, it is so useful to him in the study of the law, that it has been looked upon as being as good as the head itself, with which it has, in that respect, been put upon a par; and it is a common saying in the universities, that, in order to succeed in that study, a man must have an *iron head*, and *leaden posteriors*; to which they add, *a golden purse*, to buy books with.

This part of the human frame not only serves to make man learned and industrious; it contributes as well to the beauty of the species, being itself capable of a great degree of beauty.

Without mentioning the opinions held by different savage nations, who take pains to paint and adorn that part, we know that the Greeks, who were a cultivated and polite people, entertained high notions of its beauty. They seem to have thought that it had the advantage, in that respect, of all the other parts of the human body; for, though we do not find that they ever erected altars to fine arms, fine legs, fine eyes, or even to a handsome face, yet they did that honour to the part mentioned, and expressly erected a temple to Venus, under the appellation of *Venus Callipyge*. The above temple was built, as some say, on the occasion of a quarrel that arose between two sisters, who contended which of the two was most elegantly shaped in that part of the body.

The Latins entertained the same notions as to the beauty of that part, or those parts, on which man sits as the Greeks. Horace bestows upon them the appellation of *fair:* and he declares it is as his opinion, that for a woman to be defective in this part of the body is one of the greatest blemishes she can have—a defect equal to having a flat nose or a long foot.

Among the moderns, notions of the same kind have prevailed. Rabelais, a well-known writer, La Fontaine, and the celebrated poet Rousseau, all allude to the subject; the latter, in one of his epigrams, speaks of the above-mentioned Grecian temple erected to Venus, and declares that it would have been that temple which he would have most assiduously frequented.

Other persons have thought, that, besides the above advantages, the part mentioned was, moreover, capable of dignity, and partook of the importance of its owners. This is an opinion which the poet Scarron expressed, in a copy of verses written to a certain lady, whose husband having lately been made a duke, had thereby conferred on her the right to be seated in the Queen's assembly: "she had been given the *tabouret*" (a stool). Favourable sentiments of the kind just mentioned seem also to have been entertained by Lord Bolingbroke, whose distinguished character as a statesman, a politican, and a philosopher, render him extremely fit to be quoted in this place.

Other writers have carried their notions still farther, and have thought that the part in question was capable, not only of being beautiful, but even of being endowed with dignity and splendour. Thus, M.

Pavillon, a French *bel esprit* under the reign of Louis XIV, who filled the office of King's General Advocate at Metz, was a member of the French Academy, and nephew of a bishop, wrote some verses which he inserted in the collection of his works, entitled, *Métamorphose du Cu d'Iris en Astre.*

On the other hand, we find that part of the body—which has been thought by some to possess so many beauties, and has accordingly become the subject of respect and admiration—has been made by others the object of scoffs, and a chosen place to insult. The prevailing vulgar practice, in cases of provocation, of threatening, or even serving, the part in question with kicks, might be alluded to, but it is better to observe generally, that among all nations it has been deemed the proper place for beatings, lashings, and slappings.

That this notion prevailed among the Romans, we are informed by passages from Plautus, and by St Jerome. The same practice was also adopted by the Greeks, as will be proved by the instance of the philosopher Peregrinus. And under the reign of the Emperors, when the two nations (the Greek and Roman) had, as it were, merged into one, similar notions concerning the fitness of the same part to bear verberations and insults continued to prevail. Of this we have a singular instance in the manner in which the statue of the Emperor Constantine was treated, at the time of the revolt of the town of Edessa: the inhabitants, not satisfied with pulling that statue down, in order to aggravate the insult, flagellated it on the part alluded to. Among the French, similar notions prevail. We may cite proofs of this from their language itself, in which the verb that is derived from the word by which the part here alluded to is expressed signifies of itself, and without the addition of any other word, to beat or verberate it: thus, Voltaire supposes his Princess Cunegonde to say to Candide— *Tantdis qu'on vous fessoit, mon cher Candide.* From the above French word *fesser* has been again derived the noun *fessade*, signifying a verberation on the same part; the same as the word *claque*, which originally meant a slap in general, now signifies a slap on what has been called "the seat of honour." Among the Italians, the practice of verberating the same part also obtains, if we are to trust to proofs likewise derived from their language; and from the word *chiappa* they make *chiappata*, the meaning of which is the same as the French word *claque*.

We find the practice generally prevalent throughout Europe. It was certainly adopted in Denmark, and even in the court of that country, towards the latter part of the 17th century, as we are informed by Lord Molesworth, in his "Account of Denmark." It was the custom, his lordship says, at the end of every hunting match at court, that, in order to conclude the entertainment with as much festivity as it had begun, a proclamation was made—if any could inform against persons who had infringed the known laws of hunting, let him stand forth and accuse. As soon as the contravention was ascertained, the culprit was made to kneel down between the horns of the stag that had been hunted; two of the gentlemen removed the skirts of his coat; when the king, taking a small long wand in his hand, laid a certain number of blows, which was proportioned to the greatness of the offence, on the culprit's breech; whilst, in the meantime, the huntsmen with their brass horns, and the dogs with their loud mouthings, proclaimed the king's justice, and the criminal's punishment: the scene affording great diversion to the queen and those of the court who were present at the ceremony.

In Turkey, a verberation on the breech was the common chastisement inflicted either on the Janissaries or Spahis. In Poland, a lower discipline was the penance constantly inflicted upon certain offenders, previously to tying them together by the bond of matrimony; or, indeed, some time after they had been married. In England, castigations of the same kind were at an early period adopted among the respectable part of the nation. Among the Spaniards, they so generally consider the part of the human body of which we are treating here as the fittest to bear ill usage and mortification, that in every place there is commonly some good friar who makes himself answerable for the sins of the whole parish; and who, according as he has been fee'd for that purpose, flogs himself, or at least tells his customers he has done so: hence the common Spanish saying:- "I am as badly off as the friar's —;" which is said by persons who think that they are made to pay, or suffer, for advantages they are not admitted to share.

A serious flagellation on that part is the punishment which was established at the Cape of Good Hope among the Dutch, as Kolben informs us, for those found smoking tobacco in the streets: a practice which was frequently the cause of houses taking fire. Among the Persians, punishments of the same kind are also established; and we find in Chardin an instance of a captain of the outward gate of the king's seraglio who was served with it, for having suffered a stranger to stop before that gate and look through it. The Chinese use a like method of chastisement, and inflict it with a wooden instrument, shaped like a large solid rounded spoon. In the "Arabian Nights' Entertainment," which, no doubt, is faithful to the manners of the time, we see, from the story of the cobbler Bakbarah, that they viewed the matter in a similar light. This cobbler having fallen in love with a beautiful lady belonging to some wealthy man, whom he had seen through the window of her house, would afterwards keep for whole hours every day staring at that window. The lady, who proposed to make game of him, one day sent a female slave to introduce him to her, and then gave him to understand, that if he could overtake her by running after her through the apartments of her house, she would accept him as her sweetheart: he was besides told, that in order to run more nimbly he must strip to his shirt. To all this Bakbarah agreed; and after a number of turns, up and down the house, he was at last enticed into a long, dark, and narrow passage, at the farthest extremity of which an open door was to be perceived; he made to it as fast as he could, and when he had reached it, rushed headlong through it; when, to his no small astonishment, the door instantly shut upon him, and he found himself in the middle of a public street of Bagdad, which was chiefly inhabited by curriers. A number of these latter, struck by the sudden and strange appearance of the unfortunate Bakbarah, who, besides stripping to his shirt, had suffered his eye-brows to be shaved, laid hold of him, and soundly lashed the softest part of his person with their straps. To complete his misfortunes, the judge of police sentenced him to receive a hundred strokes on the soles of his feet, and to be banished from the city.

As will be seen throughout the following pages, the custom of whipping was at one period universal; and in those countries where flogging is still practised in schools or prisons, it is generally the rule to bestow the flagellation on that part of the body which mankind are wont to sit upon.

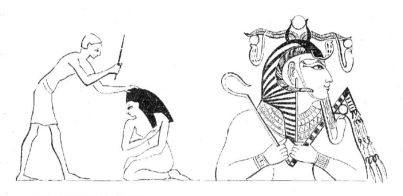

WOMAN BASTINADOED.

—*Beni Hassan*

KING HOLDING A WHIP

—*Thebes*

ASSYRIAN PUBLIC WORKS. SLAVES DRAGGING A COLOSSAL FIGURE.

—*Koujunjik Gallery, Brit. Mus.*

CHAPTER III

FLAGELLATION AMONG THE JEWS

FLAGELLATION is undoubtedly a very ancient mode of coercive punishment. The earliest record of it occurs in the fifth chapter of Exodus, where the sacred historian informs us that Pharaoh flagellated the Israelites. He required them to furnish a certain quantity of bricks every day, and when the specified number was not made up the officers were beaten. The words of the Vulgate are in verse 14 *"flagellati sunt,"* and in verse 16 *"flagellis cædimur,"* and both expressions signify, were lashed with rods or whips. Further on in the Old Testament we find that flagellation was the punishment awarded under the old law, as delivered to Moses, to those who were found guilty of particular sins: "And whosoever lies with a woman that is a bond maid, betrothed to an husband, and not at all redeemed, nor freedom given her: she *shall be scourged*: they shall not be put to death, because she was not free." The Mosaic Law likewise prescribed the number of lashes to be administered to criminals: "And it shall be, if the wicked man be worthy to be beaten, that the judge shall cause him to lie down, and to be beaten before his face according to his fault by a certain number. Forty stripes he may give him, and not exceed: lest if he should exceed, and beat him above with these many stripes, then thy brother should seem vile unto thee." —Deut., ch. xxv., ver. 2, 3. The writers of the New Testament make frequent mention of flagellation. They all notice the circumstance that Jesus Christ was scourged before his crucifixion. In John, ch. ii., v. 15, we are told that Christ himself made a scourge of small cords, and drove the money-changers from the Temple. In the Acts, ch. v., v. 40, it is narrated that the apostles were beaten with scourges. Saint Paul, in enumerating the persecutions and sufferings he underwent for the sake of the Gospel, says, "Of the Jews five times received I forty stripes save one;" and "Thrice was I beaten with rods, once was I stoned, thrice I suffered shipwreck: a night and a day I have been in the deep;" and again, "And others had trials of cruel mockings and scourgings; yea, moreover, of bonds and imprisonments."

The passages which we have quoted from the Scriptures refer only to flagellation as a punishment, and afford no justification of voluntary flagellation, still less of the excessive use of the lash practised and recommended by monks of later days, who often lashed themselves with knotted cords, and sometimes with whips armed with spikes or sharp points. The Law of Moses expressly limited the number of stripes that might be inflicted to forty. In no case might this number be exceeded. Thus, even to the convicted criminal, justice was tempered with mercy, and excessive scourging was forbidden. In practice among the Jews the number of blows inflicted was in fact limited to thirty-nine, lest, by any accident in counting, the criminal should receive more than the legal number. There was another reason still for limiting it to thirty-nine, and this was the peculiar manner in which the punishment of stripes was inflicted. The scourge was of leather, and had three thongs—one very long, going round the body at every blow, and the other two much shorter—and this was struck thirteen times, making thirty-nine, whereas an additional blow would have brought the number to forty-two.

The advocates of religious whipping have been extremely desirous to support their position by the authority of Scripture, and have ransacked the Bible for that purpose, but with indifferent success. Besides the passages already quoted, there are only two more referring to flagellation, and these are held by some to prove that flagellation is a scriptural and meritorious exercise. In Psalm lxxiii., v. 14, David exclaims, "For all day long have I been plagued and *chastened* every morning." The words of the Vulgate are "*fui flagellatus*," "I have been whipped;" and taken in a literal sense, may mean that the Psalmist was in the practice of lashing himself every day. The majority of writers are of opinion that the words are to be understood in a figurative and not a literal sense: that the stripes were only the misfortunes and troubles which are so frequently the lot of good men in this world.

The last passage on this point occurs in St. Paul's Epistle to the Corinthians, and has been the subject of much learned controversy. St. Paul there says (1 Cor. ch. ix., ver. 27), "I chastise my body and keep it under subjection." Several writers of great authority assert that the Apostle here means to say that it was his practice to lash himself in order to overcome his vicious inclinations. James Gretzer, one of the Jesuit fathers, affirms that the Greek words in the text literally signify, "I imprint on my own body the stripes or marks of the whip, and render it livid by dint of blows," and his opinion is followed by other theologians. Apart from these authorities, and considering the meaning of the Greek word in dispute, it cannot be held to signify voluntary flagellation. It occurs only in this passage and in the parable of "the importunate widow," as given by Luke, ch. xviii., ver. 5, "Lest by her continual coming she *weary* me." The word means properly to strike under the eye either with the fist or cestus, so as to render the part livid, or as we say 'black and blue'; in common phrase, to give any one a black eye. The word is derived from the Grecian games, of which the Apostle has just been speaking. Its secondary meaning then comes to be, to treat any one with harshness, severity, or cruelty; and thence also so to treat any civil inclinations or dispositions, or to subject one's self to mortification, or self-denial, or to a severe and rigid discipline, that all corrupt passions might be removed. Add to this the fact that Paul, when he has occasion to speak of actual stripes, nowhere uses this expression. Most of the Greek and Latin fathers favour the opinion that Paul did not practise self-flagellation, and that in this particular passage he expressed himself in a figurative manner.

After the compilation of the *Talmud* or *unwritten law* of the Jews, about 500 years after Christ (so named in distinction to the law of Moses or *written* law), containing their traditions, it appears that a kind of voluntary discipline was practised among them. In the third chapter of "Malkos" we are informed that the Jews, after they had finished their prayers and confessed their sins (which were exercises they derived from their ancestors), used to lash one another with scourges. Buxtorf, who is considered a good authority, thus describes the practice in his "Judaic Synagogue," published in 1661—"That there are constantly two men in every Jewish School, who withdraw from the rest of the company, and retire into a particular place of the room, where they are met; that one lays himself flat on the ground with his

THE ARMY OF ASSHER BAM-PAL FLOGGING CAPTIVES TAKEN IN A BATTLE WITH THE SUSIANS. —*Koujunjik Gallery, Brit. Mus.*

A SKETCH FROM "ISRAEL IN EGYPT" BY

E. J. Poynter, R.A.

head turned to the north and his feet to the south (or his head to the south and his feet to the north); and that the other, who remains standing, gives him thirty-nine blows upon his back with a strap or thong of ox leather. In the meanwhile, the man who is lashed recites three times over the thirty-eighth verse of the 78th Psalm. This verse in the Hebrew language contains just thirteen words; at every word the patient recites, he receives a lash from the other man, which, when he has recited the whole verse three times over, makes up the pre-scribed number thirty-nine; and at every time he says the last word, he strikes his own breast with his fist. This operation being concluded, the *operator* in his turn becomes the *patient*, and places himself in the same situation as the other had done, who then uses him in the same brotherly manner in which the former had used him, and they thus mutually chastise each other for their sins, and *rub one another* as the learned author observes, *like asses*. This practice of flogging among the Hebrews will be found described in a novel called "Count Teleki; a Story of Modern Jewish Life and Customs."

CHAPTER IV

FLAGELLATION AMONG THE ROMANS, ETC.

THE ancient Romans carried the practice of flagellation farther, perhaps, than any other nation; and there are several authors who refer to their use of the scourge. Flagellatic emblems were common in every house; and the judges of the nation were surrounded with an array of whips, scourges, and leather straps, in order to terrify offenders and bring them to a sense of duty; but a great number of instruments of flagellation, besides those mentioned above, were successfully brought into use for punishing slaves. Among those were particular kinds of cords, manufactured in Spain. The scourges had all different names: there was the *ferula*, a flat strap of leather, which was the mildest of all; then came the *scutica*, an instrument of twisted parchment, which was a degree more severe than the first named; after that there was the *flagella* and the terrible *flagellum*, the severest of all, which was composed of plaited thongs of ox leather. In the third Satire of the first book of Horace, there is an account of the gradation in severity between the above-mentioned instruments of whipping. Horace lays down the rules which he thinks a judge ought to follow in the discharge of his office. He also addresses himself, somewhat ironically, to persons who, adopting the principles of the stoics affected much severity in their opinions, and pretended that all crimes being equal, they ought to be punished in the same manner. "Make such a rule of conduct to yourself," says Horace, "that you may always proportion the chastisement you inflict to the magnitude of the offence; and when the offender only deserves to be chastised with the whip of twisted parchment, do not expose him to the lash of the horrid leather scourge; that you should only inflict the punishment of the flat strap on him who deserves a more severe lashing, is what I am by no means afraid of." There were other instruments of punishment still more terrible than the flagellum, such as balls of metal stuck full of small sharp points, and fastened to the end of long whips. So prevalent did the practice of whipping slaves become, that in course of time these unfortunates came to be named by the wits after the particular kind of flagellation they were made to undergo, as *Restiones*, *Bucœdæ*, *Verberones*, *Flagriones*, &c. The scourge was looked upon by the Romans as characteristic of dominion; and the master or mistress of a Roman household often exercised their terrible powers with unrelenting severity, the poor slaves being frequently scourged to death from a mere caprice.

It is evident that the flagellation of slaves, or the fear they entertained of incurring punishment, frequently provided Plautus with incidents for the conduct of his plots; thus in his *Epidicus*, a slave who is the principal character in the play concludes, upon a certain occasion, that his master has discovered his whole scheme, because he has spied him, in the morning, purchasing a new scourge, at the shop in which they were sold, Moreover, those same fagellations have in general formed an inexhaustible fund of pleasantry for Plautus: in one place, for instance, a slave, intending to laugh at a fellow slave, asks him how much he thinks he weighs, when he is suspended naked, by his hands, to the fatal beam, with an hundred weight (centupondium) tied to his feet; which was a precaution taken, as commentators inform us, in order to prevent the slave who was flagellated from kicking the man (virgator) whose office it was to perform the operation: and in another place, Plautus, alluding to the thongs of ox leather with which whips were commonly made, introduces a slave engaged in deep reflection on the surprising circumstance of "dead bullocks, that make incursions upon living men."

Vivos homines mortui incursantboves!

There are many other customs of the ancient Romans which might be quoted to illustrate the universal prevalence of flagellation. For

CRIMINALS BEATEN TO PRISON

—Harleian MS. 4374.

WASHING AND SCOURGING

instance, whipping and lashing were so generally considered among the Romans as the lot of slaves, that a whip or scourge became the emblem of their condition. Of this there is an instance in the singular custom, mentioned by Camerarius, which prevailed at one time, of placing in the triumphal car, behind the triumpher; a man with a whip in his hand; the meaning of which was to shew, that it was no impossible thing for a person to fall from the height of glory into the most abject condition.

It was quite a sufficient excuse among the Roman ladies to whip a slave if, as Juvenal expresses it, their nose displeased them; in other words, if they were not satisfied with the state of their own charms. Their wantonness of power was carried still farther. It was a customary thing with some of them, when they proposed having their hair dressed with both nicety and expedition, to have the dressing-maid stripped to the waist, ready for flagellation, should she be guilty of any fault or mistake in performing her task. The fair termagants at last carried these cruelties to such a pitch, that in the beginning of the empire it was found necessary to restrain their licence. During the reign of the Emperor Adrian, a lady was banished for five years for inflicting undue cruelties on her female slaves. The smallest faults, such as breaking glasses or over-seasoning dishes, exposed these wretched serfs to grievous whippings, which were sometimes inflicted in presence of guests who happened to be entertained at table, as a means of affording a little diversion. The following is a literal translation of a passage from Juvenal in which he describes the way an angry woman treats her slaves, upon an occasion when her husband has slighted her: "Woe to her waiting woman: the dressing maids lay down their tunics, the errand slave is charged with having returned too late, the straps break on the back of some; others redden under the lash of the leather scourge, and others of the twisted parchment"

With reference to the banishment of the lady mentioned above, it may be stated that in the course of time the severity of mistresses towards their female slaves became so marked that a provision was made in the Council of Elvira to restrain it; in this act it was ordained, that if any mistress caused her slave to be whipped with so much cruelty that she should die, the lady should be suspended from communion for a certain number of years. The following are the terms of the above ordinance, in the fifth canon: "if a mistress, in a fit of anger and madness, shall lash her female slave or cause her to be lashed, in such a manner that she expires before the third day, by reason of the torture she has undergone; inasmuch as it is doubtful whether it has designedly happened, or by chance; if it has designedly happened, the mistress shall be excommunicated for seven years; if by chance, she shall be excommunicated for five years only; though, if she shall fall into sickness, she may receive the communion."

Ladies having a very large establishment would not themselves condescend, except in a moment of passion, to chastise their slaves. Some great woman had been satirised for doing so:

"I hate a vixen that her maid assails,
And scratches with her bodkin or her nails;
While the poor girl ill blood or tears must mourn,
And her heart curses what her hands adorn,"

says Ovid. Particular slaves were kept (*lorarii*) for scourging their fellow-slaves. The public flagellators (*carnifices*) were also occasionally employed. Indeed, it was a favour which called for the slaves' gratitude when they received their chastisement from the hand of the Domina. Far more cruel was the punishment when, in her anger, she directed it to be inflicted on the wretched culprit by a female brought up to such employment, and kept for that particular purpose. In this case they were immediately seized, without mercy, and bound, by their twisted hair, to a door-post or a pillar, and lashed on their bare backs with thongs cut from ox-hides, or knotted cords, till the mistress pronounced the word "enough!" or "go!"

But it was not upon their slaves only that Roman masters or mistresses inflicted the punishment of flagellation, for they often served in the same manner young men of position who came into their house upon errands of love. The favourite disguise on the occasion of such adventures was a slave's dress, because a man so habited was able to get into the house and to go about without being noticed; but when the husband either noticed the stranger or had been told by his faithful wife of the visit, he would feign to mistake the man for a runaway or other strange slave, who had entered his house with a felonious intention, and treat him accordingly. The opportunity, indeed, was a favourable one for revenge, and if to this consideration be added the severe temper of the Romans and their jealous disposition, it is easy to conclude that such an opportunity, when obtained, was seldom suffered to escape, and that many a Roman spark caught in disguise, engaged perhaps in the then fashionable pursuit of seducing his neighbour's wife, has, with a *centupondium* clapped to his feet, been sadly rewarded for his ingenuity. These flagellations gave, as may be supposed, great delight to the real slaves. Many adventurers obtained access to Roman houses without being discovered, because of the slaves being so numerous. Sallust, the celebrated historian, having gone to court the wife of Milo, Faustina the daughter of Tullia, was found out and severely flogged! He was also compelled to pay a considerable sum of money.

Besides the employment of the whip in the cause of good morals, the Romans introduced whipping into their religious ceremonies, and especially into the festival of the *Lupercalia*, performed in honour of the god Pan. The word comes from Lupercal, the name of a place under the Palatine Mount, where the sacrifices were performed. The *Lupercalia* were celebrated on the 15th of the Kalends of March—that is, on the 15th of February, or, as Ovid observes, on the 3rd day after the Ides. They are supposed to have been established by Evander. Virgil speaks of the dancing *Salii* and naked *Luperci*, and the commentators explain that these last were men who, upon particular solemnities, used to strip themselves stark naked, and who ran about the streets, carrying straps of goat's leather in their hands, with which they struck such women as they met in their way. Nor did those women run away; on the contrary, they willingly presented the palms of their hands to them in order to receive the strokes, imagining that these blows, whether applied to their hands or to other parts of their body, had the power of rendering them fruitful or procuring them an

A PRIEST WITH THE FLAGELLARIUM
From the original Brass preserved in the Church of Sawbrey, All Saints,
Huntingdonshire. Date, about 1380

GAMES IN A SAXON AMPHITHEATRE
It will be observed from the Illustration that the same Instrument—the birch—was used
for a performing bear as for the slave represented in Plate V.

easy delivery.

The Luperci were in very early times formed into two bands, named after the most distinguished families in Rome, *Quintiliani* and *Fabiani;* and to these was afterwards added a third band, named *Juliani*, from Julius Cæsar. Marc Antony did not scruple to run as one of the *Luperci*, having once harangued the people in that condition. This feast was established in the time of Augustus, but afterwards restored and continued to the time of Anastasius. The festival was celebrated so late as the year 496, long after the establishment of Christianity. Members of noble families ran for a long time among the *Luperci*, and a great improvement (!) was moreover made in the ceremony. The ladies, no longer contented with being slapped on the palms of their hands as formerly, began to strip themselves also, in order to give a fuller scope to the *Lupercus*, and allow him to display the vigour and agility of his arm. It is wickedly said that the ladies became in time completely fascinated with this kind of "diversion," and that the ceremony being brought to a degree of perfection was so well relished by all parties, that it existed long after many of the other rites of paganism were abolished; and when Pope Gelasius at length put an end to it, he met with so much opposition that he was obliged to write an apology.

Whipping ceremonies were common among various other nations of antiquity. The practice is believed to have originated with the Egyptians. Herodotus, the historian, relates that, at the annual festival held at Busiris, in honour of their goddess Isis, "while the sacrifice is performing, the whole assembly, amounting to several thousands of both men and woman, beat one another." The Syrians thought that the gods might upon particular occasions be appeased by using scourges and whips, and their priests lashed themselves with an instrument made of twisted woollen cords armed with small bones.

At Lacedæmon there was an annual festival held called the *Day of Flagellations*, the chief ceremony being the whipping of boys before the altar of Diana. Several ancient authors have given a description of this festival, and all agree in stating that the Spartan youths were lashed in the presence of their parents and friends. These boys, called

Bomonicæ, were originally free-born Spartans, but afterwards they were of mean birth, and generally of a servile origin. This operation was performed by an officer in a severe and unfeeling manner, and that no compassion should be raised, the priest stood near the altar with a small light statue of the goddess, which suddenly became heavy and insupportable if the lash of the whip was more lenient or less rigorous than necessary. The parents of the children attended the ceremony, and exhorted them not to make any signs that might be unworthy of Laconian education. These flagellations were often so severe that the blood gushed profusely from the wounds, and many expired under the lash without uttering a groan, or betraying any marks of fear. Such a death was reckoned very honourable: the corpse was buried with much solemnity, and a garland of flowers was placed on its head. The origin of this festival is unknown. Some suppose that Lycurgus first instituted it in order to inure the youth of Lacedæmon to bear labour and fatigue, and to render them insensible to pain and wounds. Others maintain that it is a mitigation of an oracle which ordered that human blood should be shed on Diana's altar, and, according to their opinion, Orestes first introduced the custom after he had brought the statue of Diana Taurica into Greece. There is another tradition which mentions that Pausanias, as he was offering up prayers and sacrifices to the gods before he engaged Mardonius, was suddenly attacked by a number of Lydians who disturbed the sacrifice, and were at last repelled with staves and stones, the only weapons with which the Lacedæmonians were provided at that moment. In commemoration of this, therefore, the whipping of boys was instituted at Sparta. The festival was regarded with much favour, and continued to be held throughout many political changes in the Spartan republic. Of the Thracians, another ancient nation, it is related that young men of noble families were on certain occasions cruelly lashed.

CHAPTER V

FLAGELLATION IN MONASTERIES AND CONVENTS

THERE is little or no evidence that self-flagellations prevailed in the first monastic institutions. The code of rules prepared by their founders does not mention the voluntary use of thongs and whips. Indeed, the chief kind of flagellation alluded to by the writers of those times is that bestowed on the ancient saints by the "Father of Lies" himself, who was doubtless moved to anger by the exceeding sanctity of those holy men. St Anthony, the founder of monastic life, was particularly favoured in this respect. The devil paid him many personal visits, subjected his virtue to divers trials and temptations, and frequently set upon and lashed him. Other saints might be mentioned who were also treated in the same way. Although self-flagellation was not enjoined by the ancient monastic rules, yet those statutes appointed flagellation as the means of correction, and vested the power of inflicting it in the hands of the superiors of such establishments. Even before the erection of monasteries, we are told that the bishops among the early Christians assumed such a power, and exercised it upon their own flocks, and also on those who were not of their Churches.

With regard to flagellation in monasteries, the abbot not only had the power of correction, but he was allowed *carte blanche* in his use of it. For example, it was ordained with respect to a monk convicted of being a liar, thief, or striker, "that if, after having been warned by the elder monks, he neglects to mend his manners, he shall on the third time be exhorted in the presence of all the brethren to leave off his bad practices. If he still neglects to reform let him be flagellated with the utmost severity." The following against theft occurs in another collection—"As to the monk convicted of theft, if we may still call him a monk, he shall be flagellated as for a second offence of adultery, and with great severity: since lewdness has induced him to commit theft." Among other offences punishable by flagellation was that of indecencies of any kind with boys or other monks, and in this case the whipping was inflicted in public. Very severe flagellation was ordained against those who, through pride, denied or tried to extenuate their faults, and refused to make satisfaction to their Superior. Attempts to escape from monasteries were to be punished by the rod, and a public whipping was the prescribed correction for wanton conversation or encouraging a brother monk to wickedness. Their intercourse with the other sex was of course very much restricted and fenced round with severe penalties. We find such as the following:- "Let him who has been alone and conversed familiarly with a woman either be kept on bread and water for two days or receive two hundred stripes." This article, in which the founder of a religious order rates the hardship of living on bread and water for one day as equal to a hundred lashes, affords a proof of that love of good living which is commonly said to prevail among monks.

The following story from an old monkish book illustrates their *penchant* for the pleasures of the table:- A certain Benedictine friar had procured a quantity of good wine and some nicely seasoned dishes, and, in order to enjoy these viands in security, he and his fellows repaired to the cellar, and ensconced themselves in a large tun. The Abbot, missing so many of the monks, began to search for them, and at last astonished the guilty ones by popping his head over the side of the tun. The monks, as may be supposed, were very much alarmed, but were soon reassured by the Abbot offering to share their good cheer; and he immediately took his seat among them. After an hour or two spent in an agreeable and convivial manner, the Abbot withdrew. The rest of the party soon broke up, some admiring the condescension of the Abbot, though others were not without misgivings as to the result. The fears of the latter were well founded, for next day the Abbot requested the prior to fill his place, while he himself stepped into the middle of the assembly, and, confessing the sin of which he had been guilty the previous day, requested that discipline might be inflicted on him. The monks had to follow suit, and the Abbot, by means of a proper person selected for the purpose, inflicted a hearty whipping on each of his late fellow banqueters.

The expedition and punctuality with which monks sit down to dinner have given rise to a common saying, *On l'attend comme les moines font l'abbé*, "they wait for him as monks do for their Abbot" —that is, he is not waited for at all, the monks sitting down to their dinner as soon as the bell strikes, without caring whether the Abbot is come or not.

The crime of seeking the company of women was to be corrected by repeated lashings; and it was directed that such as were guilty of looking on women to lust after them, and failed to amend after under going the "discipline of the whip," might be expelled from the society, lest their bad example should corrupt their brethren. In point of fact, the founders of monasteries had such faith in the Rod, that flagellation was the punishment appointed for every imaginable offence, and for several offences the statutes enjoined the Superior to continue the flagellation *ad libitum*. It is scarcely to be wondered at that this arbitrary power should sometimes be abused, so that it was necessary for their bishop occasionally to remind them that they were guilty of homicide if they lashed offenders so severely that they died. The statutes did not neglect the novices, or those who were candidates for ecclesiastical life, but ordered flagellations for the improvement of their morals.

In nunneries the power of flagellation was likewise vested in the Superior, and prescribed for offences against morality and neglect or carelessness in the performance of religious duties. The discipline was ordered to be inflicted in the presence of all the inmates, in accordance with the injunction of the Apostle "Confute sinners in the presence of all."

Opinions differed in those days with respect to the manner of inflicting flagellation. In 817, at an assembly of ecclesiastics held at Aix-la-Chapelle, it was forbidden to lash monks naked in the presence of their brethren. The ordinance was obeyed in a few of the monasteries; but in many of these establishments the Superiors preferred to inflict the correction on the naked penitent, and further were of opinion that the merit of the performance was thereby enhanced.

About the doctrine of nakedness, some have carried their views very far—so far, indeed, as to assert that the mere freedom from clothes had in itself something holy and meritorious. The Cynic philosophers in Greece frequently made their appearance in public without a rag to cover their nakedness; and the Indian philosophers, Gymnosophists (meaning literally *naked sages*), often did the same. In our own part of the world there were the Adamites, mentioned by St. Austin: these Adamites, thinking they would effectually assimilate themselves to our first parents before the fall if they appeared in the same habit, would put themselves in a complete state of nature during certain solemnities of their own, and in that condition ventured to appear both in the streets and in private meetings. About the year 1300, a sect of the same kind, called the Turlupins, which seems to have been a nickname, appeared in France, and proclaimed the doctrine of nakedness. A similar sect arose in Germany, about a century afterwards, and were called Picards. They carried the doctrine to its full extent, and made their appearance always in a nude state. A section of Anabaptists tried to form a procession in the streets of Amsterdam in February 1535, in this hallowed state, but the municipal authorities would not allow it, and treated the processionists rather severely. In the "De Conformitatibus" of the Franciscan monks is an account of brother Juniperus, who made his processions alone in the above-mentioned state, regardless of the contempt and ill treatment of the public and even his own brethren.

These processions and appearances of stark-naked people, whether Cynics, Gymnosophists, Adamites, Turlupins, or Picards, do not seem to have found great or continued favour with the public; and as whippings, without nakedness mere bastinadoes have been generally thought but dull acts of penance, so nakedness without beatings has been indifferently esteemed. A combination of the two has been very differently regarded: then penitents, conscious of merit continued to practise their exercises with perseverance, and the world thought the affair worthy of public ceremonies and solemnities.

Cardinal Damian, a great authority on the subject of whipping, expressed his opinion very clearly in favour of nakedness as the proper plight to receive a correction, and supported it by the argument that the penitent ought not to be ashamed to follow the example of our

Saviour—certainly a very strong argument. The founder of the Abbey of Cluny must have been a man after the Cardinal's own heart, for in the statutes of that establishment it is enacted that delinquents are "to be stripped naked in the middle of the next street or public place, so that every person who chooses may see them, and there be tied up and lashed."

Long before self-flagellation was adopted in a systematic manner by the Church, we find instances of it among saints. Peter the Hermit used it on one memorable occasion at least. Having rescued a young woman from the hands of a military officer who wished to seduce her, his own inclinations became so strong, that he was obliged to lock himself up and subdue them by means of a severe flagellation.—the mother of the young woman being present at the infliction. St Pardulph, who lived about the year 737, during Lent used to strip himself, and order one of his disciples to lash him. His example was followed by St William, Duke of Aquitain. St Rodolph seems to have exercised the discipline with great severity. It is related that he often imposed upon himself the penance of a hundred years, and performed it in twenty days by the assiduous application of a broom. Armed with a besom in each hand, he locked himself in his cell, and lashed himself during the time that he recited the whole Psalter. Three thousand strokes, and the chanting of thirty penitential psalms, were sufficient to cancel the sins of one year, and the hundred years' penance might be accomplished by a flagellation lasting the whole time that the Psalter was sung twenty times!

This was a favourite penance with St. Dominic Loricatus. His constant practice, we are informed, was, after stripping himself naked, to fill both his hands with rods, and then vigorously flagellate himself in times of relaxation; during Lent he frequently undertook the hundred years' penance. The duration of flagellations was thus early regulated by the singing or recitation of psalms, but surely they have sadly degenerated in these later days, since modern disciplines last only during the singing of the *Miserere De Profoundis*, and the *Salve Regina*, in slow time, the *Miserere* being the 51st and *De Profundis* the 130th Psalm. Of St. Dominic Loricatus it is further related that he always carried his scourge with him, and flogged himself regularly at bedtime wherever he happened to spend the night.

Cardinal Damian, Bishop of Ostia, who lived about the year 1056, has the honour of having assisted greatly in promoting the custom of flagellation in the Church. He zealously inculcated it both by precept and example, and in his time the practice made a vast advance in public estimation: pious men of every rank and condition in life were seen armed with whips, rods, thongs, and besoms, lacerating their own bodies in order to merit a share of divine favour. Kings did not consider that their earthly dignity exempted them from such penance, and nobles willingly submitted themselves to it.

At first view it may seem surprising that priests were able to introduce, and induce compliance with so painful a practice as flagellation among those who regarded them as spiritual advisers: but we cease to wonder when we remember that the power of the confessor was practically unlimited in the matter of penance. Penance was a sacrament of the Church and, satisfaction being a necessary part of it, the confessor could withhold absolution until the penitent had performed the prayers, mortifications, or disciplines enjoined. History shews that, at the call of priests, kings undertook wars and crusades to the Holy Land and queens performed long and perilous pilgrimages to distant shrines; it is not very wonderful then that the Church has been able to inculcate successfully the painful exercises of the upper and lower disciplines.

Since its introduction, many able writers among the Jesuit fathers have recommended flagellation as a means of mortifying the flesh, and above all, the pictures of the Church have assisted to perpetuate the practice. Horace, in his "*Arts Poötica*," says:-

"Pictoribus atque Poës
Quidlibet audendi semper fuit æqua potestas."

"Painters and poets have always equally enjoyed the power of daring everything," and especially in religious pictures have painters made a free use of this license. We find that they have never represented any of the ancient anchorites or saints without leaving some spare corner of the canvas whereon to place whips or rods, suggesting that these men often used such instruments; and, if pictures be, as Pope Gregory the Great calls them, "the libraries of ignorant Christians," the lash must inevitably be associated in their minds with a holy life.

From flagellating themselves, priests and confessors soon began to appoint the penance of flagellation to their penitents, and in process of time assumed the power of inflicting the discipline with their own hands. Such a prerogative, we can well believe, led to many abuses, especially when exercised on female penitents, and under cover of it some confessors found opportunity to indulge their own passions.

Confessors being exposed to many dangers of a peculiar kind, it is not surprising that they sometimes contract sentiments not altogether of a Platonic nature towards their female penitents. In virtue of their office, they have to hear long confessions from women of every age of the sins they have either committed or wished to commit; and, under these circumstances, priests must frequently be agitated by thoughts not very conformable to their vows. Further, female penitents sometimes, under the seeming artlessness of their confessions, shroud their designs of creating sentiments of love in their confessors. Miss Cadière's declaration, it is thought, shews that she herself designed the conquest of Father Girard—although he was over fifty years of age—attracted by his fame as a preacher and a man of parts.

In the books intended for the direction and instruction of confessors in their duties, they are warned against the dangers arising from frequent confidential intercourse with the sex, who are much more exact in their confessions than men. In one of these books, they are directed to have all the doors wide open when they hear the confession of a woman, and they are supplied with a set of passages from the Psalms, to be pasted on some conspicuous place in their sight, and which were to serve as exclamations to keep down the wicked thoughts with which they might feel themselves agitated; a sort of *Retro Satanas*—"Get thee behind me, Satan" —in fact, to be used whenever they were likely to yield to temptation.

Many instances are on record, however, which prove that these

rules were forgotten, or ineffectual to prevent confessors from forming serious designs against their penitents; and many curious devices
were resorted to in order to conceal their plans from penitents and
their doings from the public. A Spanish monk, Menus, persuaded
young women to live with him in a kind of holy conjugal union, which
he pictured to them, but which did not end in that intellectual manner which the father had promised. Others have persuaded women
that works of matrimony were no less liable to pay tithes than the
fruits of the earth. La Fontaine has founded one of his tales—"The
Cordeliers of Catalonia" —on this idea. Other confessors have had
recourse to flagellation, to prevent suspicion and successfully carry out
their love schemes. To remove scruples of delicacy, they represented
that our first parents were naked in the garden of Eden, that people
must be naked when christened, and that they shall all be so at the res-
urrection. Others supported the state of nakedness in the penitent by
quoting the text, "Go and shew thyself to the priest," There are
numerous anecdotes extant of the strange doings and practices of the
monks at the time alluded to, but most of them are quite unfit for publication.

We cannot resist giving, in this place, a rather laughable story of
flagellation related by Scott in his *Mensa Philosophica*. A woman having
confessed, the priest took her behind the altar, and prepared her for
the administration of a lower discipline. Her husband, who had secretly followed her through jealousy, was moved to pity by the pain which
he expected would ensue, and offered himself in her place. The wife,
admitting that her husband was better able to bear the punishment,
consented, and cried to her confessor as he was operating, "Now then,
holy father, lay on lustily: I am a great sinner."

Flagellation was regarded as a necessary act of submission to the
Church, as well as part of the *satisfaction* due for sin, and a sentence of
excommunication could not, therefore, be repealed unless the penitent submitted to a public discipline. History affords two
well-authenticated examples of this in the case of Henry II of England
and Henry IV of France. Through some hasty words ("What sluggard
wretches, what cowards, have I brought up in my court, who care

nothing for their allegiance to their master: not one will deliver me from the low-born priest!") uttered by King Henry II, several persons were led to believe that he desired the death of Thomas à Becket, Archbishop of Canterbury. The Archbishop was soon after assassinated, and, although the King expressed great sorrow on that account, the Church would not grant him absolution until he submitted his bare back to the rod. The penance was accomplished at the Cathedral of Canterbury. The King knelt at the tomb of Thomas à Becket, removed the rough cape or cloak which had been thrown over his shoulders, but still retained the woollen shirt, to hide the haircloth which was visible to near observation next his skin, placed his head and shoulders in the tomb, and there received five strokes from each bishop and abbot who was present—beginning with Faliot, who stood by with the "balai," or monastic rod, in his hand—and three from each of the eighty monks. Henry IV of France had to receive a correction from the Church before he was absolved from a sentence of excommunication and heresy that had been passed against him; but this prince took care to receive the discipline by proxy. These proxies were Messrs. D'Ossat and Du Perron, who, as compensation, we suppose, were afterwards created cardinals. The beating was administered by the hands of his holiness the Pope, during the singing of the *Miserere*, and appears from various accounts to have been of a very mild character, bearing but a faint resemblance to the castigations bestowed on less exalted personages.

Heretics were not excluded from the benefits posed to be conferred by flagellation, for it was frequently resorted to in order to reform and convert them to the doctrines of the true Church; and the saints, who have in all times been profuse in their counsels to the benighted mass of mankind, not seldom enforced and strengthened their arguments in favour of godliness by a vigorous application of the Rod, and thus "whipped the offending Adam" out of them.

The fair sex have at various times come in for a goodly share of these emphatic admonitions, if we are to believe the biographers of the saints. According to the lives of the saints, those holy men were assailed by woman's wanton wiles, and in every case the saint was the victor, and seldom dismissed the fair sinner without giving her a sound flagellation. Such was the way in which St. Edmund, afterwards Bishop of Canterbury, acted. While studying at Paris, he was tormented by a very beautiful young woman: summoning her to his study, and there first stripping her, he administered such a flagellation that her body was covered with weals. Brother Matthew of Avignon, a Capuchin friar, gave a similar reply to a young lady who entered his bedroom while he was asleep. Bernardin of Sienna, while out on an errand one day, was called into a house by the wife of a citizen of Sienna. As soon as he entered, she made violent love to him, which he professed to return; but ultimately he laid hold of her, and whipped her severely with his scourge, which fortunately he had with him. The biographer concludes the story by remarking that "she loved the holy man the better afterwards; and so did her husband when he knew how things had been transacted"

The advocates of flagellation did not confine themselves strictly to precept and example in their recommendations; besides flagellating themselves and others on all possible occasions, and writing long and learned arguments in support of whipping, they invented many extraordinary stories in their accounts of it. They may in their enthusiasm have actually believed such stories, or they may have thought that the more extravagant they were—the greater demand made upon the credulity—the more likely they were to be believed by vulgar people. Some holy men maintained that whipping had the power to rescue souls from hell, a feat which masses were not thought to be able to achieve.

One Vincent, who lived about 1256, says that in the monastery of St. Sylvester, in the Duchy of Urbino, Italy, a certain monk died: the brethren as usual sang psalms beside the body, and when they came to the *Agnus Dei* the dead man arose. The brothers, of course, crowded around to hear what he might say, when he began to curse and abuse God, the cross, and the Virgin Mary, stating that he had been tormented in hell, and that there was no use in their singing psalms for him. They exhorted him to repent, but his only reply was curses. The monks then betook themselves to prayer on his behalf, and, as a last

Plate VII.   RELIGIOUS DISCIPLINE

"DEVILS WOULD OFTEN LAY HOLD OF MEN AND FLOG THEM."

—*Abbé Boileau*

In the first monastic institutions the chief kind of flagellation alluded to by the writers of those times is that bestowed on the ancient saints by the "Father of Lies" himself, who was doubtless moved to anger by the exceeding sanctity of those holy men. The devil paid St. Anthony many personal visits, and frequently set upon and lashed him.

resource, stripped off their clothes, and flagellated themselves; when, lo! the desperate man recovered his reason, renounced his errors, and prayed for forgiveness. He continued to live, praising and blessing God, till next day, when he again gave up the ghost.

We have stories not only to shew the merit and efficacy of whipping like the above, but others to terrify those who declined adopting, or argued against the practice. Cardinal Stephen, an early and vigorous opponent of flagellation, was commonly reported to have died suddenly, because he despised this exercise. Thomas de Chantpré relates in his book how a certain canon of St. Victor suffered after death for having neglected during his life to exercise the usual discipline. This learned canon belonged to the monastery of St. Victor in Paris. During his life he refused to flagellate himself, either in private or in the chapter. When near death he promised a brother canon that he would if possible, visit him from the other world. He shortly after died. He was soon able to pay his friend the expected visit. The latter asked "How is it with you, my dear friend?" "It is well with me," replied the deceased canon, " but because I refused while alive to receive discipline, there has hardly been a single spirit in the whole infernal empire who did not give me a smart lash in my way to purgatory." We are told that the devil has prescribed flagellations for sins on certain occasions. It is related in the life of St. Virgil, that a man possessed by the devil was beaten with four rods, by direction of his satanic majesty, for the theft of four wax candles from the saint's altar. The reverend fathers have not failed to inform us that the devil himself got his due in the matter of whipping, and from a female saint. Cornelia Juliana has the distinguished honour of having performed this praiseworthy deed, as Father Fisen relates in his "Ancient Origin of the Festival of the Body of Christ." He says, "the sister nuns sometimes heard a prodigious noise in the bedroom of Cornelia Juliana, being the strife which she had with the fiend, whom seizing, she thrashed with all her might: then having thrown him to the ground, trampled him under foot, bitterly reviling him." The saints who inhabit Paradise have been supposed to descend to this earth again at the request of suppliants, and discipline their persecutors. This misfortune overtook a servant of the Emperor Nicephorus. The servant, after oppressing the common citizens by heavy taxation, proceeded to exact tribute from the inmates of the monastery of St. Nicon. The monks in vain remonstrated, and pleaded poverty—some of them were imprisoned—the others then applied to their patron saint, and besought his assistance. That night the saint appeared and administered a severe beating to the king's servant, after which he interfered no more with the monks. Lastly, we are told the Virgin Mary has applied such a correction to avenge those under her protection: for instance, she caused a certain bishop to be flagellated in her presence because he deposed a canon, who, although illiterate, and possessing no spiritual gifts, was very constant in his devotions at the altar of the Holy Mother. The Blessed Virgin appeared to the bishop by night, accompanied by a man bearing a discipline, and after ordering the bishop to be chastised, commanded him to restore the prebend.

Bernardinus de Bustis, in a sermon written by him in honour of the Virgin, gives another instance in support of the opinion that the flagellation of sinners was especially pleasing to the Virgin Mary, by relating that a Franciscan monk, under the pontificate of Sextus IV, did, in the public market-place, administer a lower discipline to a professor of divinity, in the sight of a crowd of delighted spectators, because he had preached against the immaculate conception of the Blessed Mary. The narrator thus graphically describes the operation— "Seizing hold of him, he threw him upon his knees, for he was very strong; then, taking up his gown, he began to lash him with the palm of his hand upon the lower part of his person, which was bare, for, to the great diversion of the bystanders, the professor of divinity wore neither drawers nor breeches. Then a female devotee who was looking on cried out, 'Give him four more slaps for my sake;' another said, 'Give him also four more for me.' And so did a number of others: so that if he had granted all their requests he would have had nothing else to do the whole day."

Bernardinus adds that the monk acted in this case under the direct inspiration of the Virgin herself, so suitable did the correction appear to be.

CHAPTER VI

FLAGELLATION AMONG THE CARMELITIES.

THE original rules of the Carmelite order were of a mild character, and contained few injunctions with regard to flagellation and other devout torments. St Theresa, who was the founder of the bare-footed male and female Carmelites, was the first to set an example of severe flagellation. Her life affords a perfect study of religious fanaticism. In her case, a naturally vivid imagination and a proud adventurous disposition were utterly perverted by an education without method, so that what was at first enthusiasm soon became madness. When seven years of age, her favourite books were the lives of saints, whose flagellations and sufferings captivated her mind, as the story of Robinson Crusoe does a modern schoolboy. Her elder brother being her chief companion at this time, they resolved to go among the Moors, that they might be flagellated and tortured for the sake of Christ. They were, however, found out, and each had to undergo a good birching from their parents. This was not sufficient to prevent Theresa from leading a hermit's life on her father's estate, after the manner of the ancient hermits of Syria and Egypt. Her next course of reading was tales of chivalry, where love and war took the place of tortures. These romances so excited her warm southern nature that her father deemed it prudent to place her out of temptation within the walls of a convent. Here she resolved to renounce the world and lead a life of devotion; and thenceforth the birch, the scourge, and the haircloth, became her dearest friends. She entered into mysticism with even more enthusiasm than she had shewn for chivalry. Her chief delight was in flagellation. She would have given her life to scourge the whole world, or that the whole world might scourge her, for she delighted alike in the infliction and the reception of the birch. Her example had a powerful influence on her fellows, and monks and nuns tried to emulate her efforts, and consequently the laws of the order became more stringent. She was regarded with veneration and devotedness, and her mode of flagellation became in time the leading penance of the order.

The ordinary penance was performed by the monks every Monday, Wednesday, and Friday, and by the nuns on all the holy days. The singing of the *Miserere* after service regulated the duration of the flagellation, which was inflicted with so much vigour as to bring the blood from the back or whatever part of the body was struck. Special permission was asked of the Superior for any extraordinary flagellation. Some would flagellate themselves during the night, others twice daily, and some three or four times during Lent. On certain days it was the duty of the Superior to give the discipline to all inmates, and it was their duty to receive it with humility and thankfulness. There was a cell set apart as a birch-store, and every novice was at liberty to select an instrument to his or her taste. The mortification called *Ecce Homo* was one of the greatest penances. In this case the penitent stripped himself to the waist, covered his face with ashes, put a crown of thorns on his head, placed a cross under his left arm, and taking a scourge in his right hand, walked up and down the refectory whipping and praying. The novices of this order were severely dealt with. They were punished for the most trivial offences. Paper was frequently burned on their backs, and they were scourged from time to time. Sometimes they were threatened with expulsion, and had to beg for sharper punishment. Blows, torture, and ridicule, were daily heaped upon them. The statutes of the order gave full directions how to receive the discipline. The penitent had to kneel, bare his back, and, after receiving the birch, thank the operator and kiss the hem of his garment.

Among the nuns there were three degrees of penance, according to the offence. Some were scourged in particular places, others before the whole assembly and the Superior, or one of her delegates. The former was the punishment for going into the kitchen, or spending too much time over their toilette. They were carefully watched in the visiting-room. No nun was allowed to go there without being accompanied by another to watch her words and actions. If she committed the fault of speaking about worldly matters, nine days in a cell, with the refreshment of a scourging in the refectory every third day, was the regular punishment. If the duenna failed to inform of a fault, she was liable to the same chastisement. The crime of going into the speaking-room without permission was punished by three flagellations before the assembled sisters, and three days' confinement on bread and water. If in addition to going into the room she also spoke, the punishment was still more severe. She had then to prostrate herself on the ground and beg forgiveness. After that she bared her shoulders, and the Superior gave her such a whipping as she thought proper. On being told to rise, she went to her cell and forfeited all her privileges, until her pardon had been pronounced. During meals she had to lie down in the middle of the refectory very scantily clad, and receive her bread and water: during service she prostrated herself at the door of the choir, and the sisters stepped over or trod on her. Too much work, curiosity, or a serene smile, was punished by an immediate discipline.

The graduated Carmelites who wore shoes had not such hard times of it; but even among them the Rod was in frequent use. The gowns and shirts of the monks were made with a wide opening, so that the shoulders could readily be laid bare for the application of the birch. Reading forbidden books, laziness in the service, getting up too soon in the horœ, &c., were immediately punished by flagellation. There were five degrees or classes of guilt which had their proportionate penance. The first, for very trifling faults, the penitent kissed the feet and gown of the Prior, however dirty they might be. The next was a simple discipline. The third, a few days of fasting, and the flagellation in pleno. The next was a heavy birching—the penitent had to undress in the refectory before the Superior, and after having received the punishment, sit on the ground and partake of bread and water served on a wooden platter. For sins of the deepest die, the imprisonment and torture was increased, and the criminal, after being cruelly flogged, was often exposed, hungry and thirsty, to the cold, entirely divested of clothing, and fettered to a wooden block.

As might be expected in such a severe order, there are many bright examples of flagellation among the Carmelites besides the illustrious reformer St. Theresa. A certain Sister Mary, not satisfied with the common discipline, castigated herself with a pot hook! Father Alexander, when tired of the exercise, would get a novice to inflict it, and when one was not at hand would put himself in position and receive it in spirit.

The nun, Caterina of Cardona, was very severe. She wore a hair-cloth and iron chains which actually cut into the flesh. She flogged herself with chains and hooks as often as possible. Then she became a hermit, and lived in a cave, sleeping on the bare ground, with a stone for a pillow, and a single garment for cover. Flagellation was her favourite pastime, and she was amply supplied with every instrument for whipping and torture. She would flagellate herself for two or three hours continuously, her discipline being furnished with pins, thorns, and other irritating substances. Even in the night she allowed herself little rest. Eventually she became quite mad, and, Nebuchadnezzar-like, crawled into the fields and ate grass like an ox! We have read of a priest who had such reverence for these saints that he shed tears when ever their names were mentioned, and always mixed his wine with water, because these blessed saints had recommended the mixture as a shield against the temptations of the flesh.

The worthy Father Alexander, already mentioned, imposed a humiliating penance on a certain Father Seraphim. He caused him to attend all the exercises of the monastery (Charenton) with a rope round his waist, the accounts of the monastery bound on his back, and otherwise ridiculously attired. He was then flagellated on the most sensitive parts of his body. Flagellation was henceforth his daily bread, and he had to go into the vestry and humbly beg for a little of that refreshment. Stationed on the floor, in front of the altar, each novice gave him three strokes of the scourge and then spat in his face.

Maria Magdalena of Pazzi was a distinguished ornament of the Carmelites. She was born at Florence in the year 1566, and from her youth upwards she shewed a great fondness for penance. Even as early as her tenth year she took discipline. She slept on a bed made of old sacks, and whipped herself several times every day. Another means of self-mortification which she adopted was to lie down with a crown of thorns about her head, and also a belt of thorns round her waist. She became a Carmelite nun in the Convent of the Holy Angel of St Frians in her seventeenth year, and quickly rose to distinction as a miracle of humility and penance. One of her greatest enjoyments was when the Superior ordered her hands to be tied behind her back and, in the presence of the other nuns, administered a discipline with rods on her naked loins. She once begged to be tied with a rope to the altar and to be blindfolded, in order that people might think her mad. She went very scantily clad both during summer and winter, slept on the bare ground, and took the discipline every night, either by herself or by the hands of a sister. She thus attained a high degree of sanctity, and was subject to ecstasies, and saw visions of a heavenly nature.

The Order of Fontevrault may be here noticed; it was founded by Robert of Aubrissel, who, interpreting after his own fashion the passage, John chap. xx., vers. 26 and 27, "When Jesus therefore saw his mother and the disciple standing by, whom he loved, he saith unto his mother, 'Behold thy son.' Then saith he to the disciple, 'Behold thy mother.' And from that hour that disciple took her to his own home," held that Christ had enjoined community between the sexes, and the superiority of the female over the male. An Abbess ruled both monks and nuns, the latter having privileges which they took special care to preserve. Good Saint Robert ordained that the two sexes should live together, and the result of such license may more easily be imagined than described. At any rate, a separation speedily became necessary, as well as a supervision of the founder's rules.

This order existed as early as the year 1100, and at one time numbered as many as fifty establishments. Although the nuns flagellated each other, they greatly preferred, as we read, to apply the birch to the monks and novices. If a nun took a fancy to castigate a novice, he had forthwith to receive his birching with humility and gratitude. If he complained, very probably the Abbess, instead of giving him consolation, gave him another whipping! Promiscuous flagellation was also allowed, and in such administrations both the Father Confessor and the Lady Superior performed. To monks who complained of the zeal of the nuns, and felt shame at being flagellated by them, it was hinted that it was more agreeable to be birched by the soft hand of a woman than by the hard hand of a man.

CHAPTER VII

FLAGELLATION AMONG THE CISTERCIANS, TRAPPISTS, AND OTHER ORDERS OF MONKS AND NUNS.

THE order of the Cistercians, founded by Robert Alberic and Stephen, was moderately addicted to the use of the scourge. The male and female Feuillants were more strict in the matter; the nuns being under the monks, received the discipline from them. Several reforms took place, but none of great importance. Port Royal was founded, and promised at first to set a good example in the way of flagellation, but it did not come up to expectation. In that establishment there was also a spiritual union between the sexes, and they chastised themselves in company, but the union did not last; gradually succumbing to the persecution of the Jesuits, it was dissolved in 1709. The next reforms in the Cistercian order—viz., those of La Trappe and Septfons—were much more important. Rancé of La Trappe flourished in the middle of the 17th century and manifested during his youth a fondness for the fair sex. The death of the Duchess of Montblazan with whom he was in love, caused him to change his life, and begin a reform of the monastery of which he was Superior. He introduced flagellation, condemnatory labour, and the imposition of silence. His contemporaries styled him an executioner of the brethren. The improvements in discipline introduced by Septfons were also carried on about the same time by Beaufort, a co-reformer, but neither of them was so extravagant as La Rancé. In the exercises of repentance enjoined by the reformers, Rancé and Beaufort, the scourge bore a

prominent part. When a lady entered the order she was presented
with a fresh sound instrument, and exhorted to use it actively. On the
death of a nun, the sisters scourged themselves many weeks for the salvation of her soul. In the Trappist schools which were afterwards
established the discipline was excessive: a word, a look, a wink, turning the head, or a smile, were punished by a birching on the bare body,
and solitary confinement was frequently resorted to. The innocent
were made to share the punishment of the guilty, in order to teach
them obedience, and these whippings were continued till their nineteenth or twentieth year. In schools under the charge of nuns, the
same practice was carried on. The nuns at Paderborn, as we are told
in an old volume, felt a positive pleasure in birching their pupils—
indeed, the abuse of the Rod became so notorious that the order was
forbidden to keep schools, and a certain Don Augustine, who had
achieved fame by his style of discipline, was ultimately forced to flee
to Switzerland, where he obtained considerable support for his system.

The order of the Trappists, driven from France at the Revolution,
returned at the Restoration. Some of their practices were perfectly
horrible: hair-cloths, and girdles of iron wire, with points for entering
the flesh, were frequently worn by the monks of La Trappe for
months. Their scourge was made of a bunch of hard and knotted
strings, which cut the skin. Occasionally the delinquent's head was fastened in a hole called by them *Le trou patri*, so that he could not see
who was flagellating him. In the scourging room novices were treated
as if they were pupils in school. The order again flourished under
royal patronage, and enlarged its borders in France. From 1814 to
1827 there were about six hundred nuns in the several establishments.
Mdlle. Adelaide de Bourbon and Madame de Genlis were members of
the order; and the latter displayed in her advanced years a greater
delight for the purifying birch than she ever did in her gay youth. The
former devoutly chastised herself. In Spain the most celebrated
monasteries were the Royal Abbey of Las Huelgas and the hospital of
Bourgos, both rich foundations. They sent inmates to the
Universities; and if any of the student monks acted in a manner that
was thought to be too gallant, they received the scourge in the con-

vent of the town, in presence, we are told, of the fair inmates!

The history of the holy Hildegard of Cologne relates that, disguised in male attire, she acted the part of a brother in the monastery of Citeaux for a long time, and we are gravely assured by a monkish historian that she was an eye-witness when young monks received the birch, on account of various offences.

Mother Passidea of Sienna was a notable flagellator, of the order of the Cistercians. In her early years she would scourge herself with iron disciplines until she was bathed in her own blood. In winter she would lie among the snow, and in the summer time among nettles or thorns. After an energetic whipping she had vinegar or salt dripped on her wounds. She liked exceedingly a flogging with thorns. Broom was more lovely in her eyes than any other flowers, and instead of a bed of roses she preferred a couch strewed with peas or small leaden balls—in fact, it was for her the height of enjoyment to roll about naked on sharp prickly substances. A common whipping was too insignificant for her taste. On one occasion she got herself suspended by her feet in the chimney, and was then smoked with damp straw. After she entered a convent she redoubled her penances and disciplines, begging for a flagellation as for the greatest favour, for which she gratefully thanked the donor. Her confessor was obliged to order her to reduce the number of her disciplines. Mother Passidea attained, we are told, to the sanctified state of seeing Jesus Christ bodily before her.

Elizabeth of Genton was a kindred spirit, and still more mystical, having constant dreams and visions of a strange and remarkable character. It was by means of constant flagellation she brought herself into this mystical condition: her chief delight, so we have read, was to be flogged in a state of entire nudity!

CHAPTER VIII

FLAGELLATION AMONG THE FRANCISCANS AND SIMILAR RELIGIOUS ORDERS

THE order of the Franciscans was founded in the thirteenth century by Francis of Assisi, a man of much talent and great enthusiasm. After sowing an abundance of wild oats he was at length converted, and resolved to renounce the world, and became as energetic in his religious career as he had formerly been in profligacy, excelling in every kind of mortification—spiritual and bodily. He ran naked through the streets, ate hay like a horse, and thistles like an ass, allowing the street boys to cudgel him. During his early years his father tried in vain to beat common sense into him. One day his father thrashed him so severely that he lost all patience, and throwing of his garments, even to his shirt, reproached his parent in an eloquent speech for his unchristian cruelty.

When the renown of his sanctity had spread abroad he began to form the order called after his name. At first he did not include the fair sex in this order, and it was not until he made the acquaintance of Miss Clara Seiffo, who was possessed of a kindred spirit, that he did so. This young lady had given her father quite as much trouble as Francis had given his, and she was in consequence very early in life initiated into the mysteries of the birch; but flagellation only increased her mystic inspiration, and she was thus admirably fitted to be the companion of Saint Francis. Their intercourse mostly consisted of praying together, scourging each other, and such like spiritual exercises. On a separation becoming necessary, Clara resolved to found a community of women similar to the male order, and governed by the same rules as the order of Francis. He was sorry that he could not introduce his spiritual bride into his monastery, but, as the next best thing, he gave her over to the care of the Benedictines. She was taken away from this retreat by force, and having then ran away from her friends, was again seized. Her father and uncle were about to bestow an exemplary punishment upon her for this behaviour, when, lo! all vigour suddenly left their arms, and she escaped chastisement. That same year she carried off her younger sister and founded a convent. The order founded by her soon became popular; numerous branches sprang up, and various cardinals took the nuns under their patronage. Cardinal Hugolinius found great pleasure in their manner of penitence and chastisement, and increased it; but Francis, more merciful, drew up a less stringent code of rules. Clara herself, however, was inclined to severity, and frequently flogged herself. After the decease of Clara and Francis numerous divisions took place in the various orders, and these were not always friendly to each other.

Many remarkable things are related of the Urban nuns, a branch of the Franciscans, founded by Isabella daughter of Louis XIII This young lady, in opposition to the wishes of her friends, had determined to pass her days in a convent. She preferred fasting and chastisement to courtly gaiety, and her palace was like a convent where little else but penance went on. She scourged herself, and received such scourging from others as to cause the blood to flow freely. She then bought an hospital, and turned it into a convent, with the name of "Humility of our Dear Lady." The inmates, principally noble young ladies, became so tired of the severe rules, which included heavy scourging, grave silence, and long fasting, that the Superior was at length obliged to apply to the Pope for a mitigation of the penances.

The founder of the Capuchins, another branch, was also a notable example of sanctity. Maria Laurentia Longa, after the death of her husband, a minister of state, at Naples, founded an hospital for incurables, in which she officiated as a common servant. If she committed the least mistake, she insisted on receiving a severe whipping from the Superior. Stretched on the hard ground, naked to the shoulders, she had herself scourged on the loins with an immense rod made from a stable broom, and it was impossible to lay on too hard for her pleasure.

Her zeal cooled a little with age; but a duchess followed in her foot-steps, and proved a worthy successor—scourging and birching being her prime enjoyments. From the hospital Laurentia went to be Superior in a Capuchin convent, and here she at last succumbed to repeated fasting, watching, and scourging. The community continued to flourish after her death, and Cardinal Baronius founded an orphan-age as a kind of training school for the order. The poor girls had a hard time of it: praying and scourging were the order of the day.

The Capuchin nuns were introduced into France by Louisa of Lorraine. At the convent founded at Marseilles, three monks were appointed as teachers of observances to the young ladies; and they behaved with humanity: but the Lady Superior birched the pupils so severely for every trifle that the monks were forced to interfere, and the Superior was so disgusted at this interference that, quitting the establishment, she went to Paris, where she attended the hospitals as a nurse, preferring those where the severest forms of certain loathsome diseases were treated.

Another branch of the Franciscans was the order of Penitents, and the most distinguished ornament of this order was an Italian Countess, Angelina of Korbain. At the age of twelve she made a vow of perpetu-al chastity, and some years after, having refused to marry according to her parents' wish, her father punished her so severely that she at last assented. Her bridal night was spent in prayer. She permitted her hus-band to witness her devout exercises, and see the scourging which she bestowed on her naked body. Although this was no doubt some satis-faction, he was not devout enough to suffer it for any length of time, and a separation took place. She then became a decided opponent of matrimony, and having persuaded a number of young women to agree with her, retired to Foligny, and established a convent. Other convents on the same principle arose, the most interesting of which was that of Madrid, established by Cifuentis, where a number of young ladies (not nuns) were under the care of the order. The birch was actively used there; ladies of noble descent allowing themselves to be scourged by the Franciscan monks as often as the holy men thought necessary.

Romuald, the founder of the order of the Camalduenses and

Celestines, was a celebrated flagellator, and had a great opinion of himself for the number of whippings that he had received from his master. To this order belonged Cardinal Damian, whom we have mentioned elsewhere as a strenuous advocate of flagellation. Romuald founded convents in which scourging was the most predominant feature. The Celestines took their origin from Celestine V In this order the breaking of fasts and silence, and incontinence, were severely punished. Whilst penance was being performed, the Superiors looked on through a grating in order to convince themselves that everything was done *en règle*. Flagellation sometimes took place before the whole chapter, and occasionally a brother was castigated without any apparent cause—perhaps on the principle of the old schoolmaster, who said a whipping was never thrown away: because if a lad did not deserve it when he got it, he was sure to earn it before long!

CHAPTER IX

DISCIPLINE AMONG THE CARTHUSIANS
AND OTHER ORDERS.

THE Carthusians, founded in the 11th century, were proverbial for
their strictness in the matter of discipline. Their rules were most
minute and particular on this point. Delinquents had to strip, and go
before their Superiors to receive severe punishment. Novices were visited with slighter disciplines. For criminals and apostates fourteen
days' fasting and four teen days' scourging before the whole inmates
was the usual punishment. Even when travelling, the rules of the order
with regard to the birch were strictly enforced. The Superiors were
exemplary in asserting their prerogative of birching the Novices. The
laymen of the order received a double share of the scourging, and on
festival days were well whipped on the back down to the knees.
Sometimes the usual birch was not considered enough, and stronger
instruments were procured. In the convents of this order the discipline
was equally strict. The three principal rules were the punishing, the
regulating, and the voluntary discipline

The Trinitarians were quite as strict in their discipline as the male
and female Carthusians, and regarded the birch and the scourge as
most important means of inspiration.

The order of St. Benedict, for many years a rich and influential
establishment, cultivated the discipline to a moderate degree. The
birch and scourge were provided for the novices and maidens. Among
the most illustrious of its members was Queen Anna of Austria, who
submitted to a heavy penance for sins committed with Cardinal
Richelieu. She sometimes inflicted the discipline herself, and at other
times his Eminence undertook the employment. The penances of
Benedictine nuns were made the subject of some ribald songs.

The Fathers of Death, the Cœnobites, and the Eremites, as might be expected, did not forget the scourge. In these orders it was the duty of the Prior to inflict the discipline, and then to receive it himself. Absence from the *hovæ* was punished by a public scourging.

The order of the Premonstratenses, a branch of the Benedictines founded by Norbert of Cologne, in the 11th century, had minute details as to penance A daily chapter was held, at which every one, without exception, had to appear, and such as had committed faults made a public confession, and prostrated themselves on the ground, to await their punishment at the hands of the Abbot. If the fault was a heavy one, the delinquent had to strip in order to receive the penance. The scourge was given to all the monks by the Superior alone, and the Novices received it every Friday. The allowance was left to the discretion of the Superior, and consequently varied according to the temper of the individual. The monk who had charge of the novices was answerable for all the faults of his pupils, and a sort of court was held regularly, where offenders were tried and sentenced, and the execution of the sentence was carried out on the spot.

It may prove interesting to examine the laws of penance a little more in detail. Offences were divided into four classes. The first class comprehended dilatoriness in beginning the exercises, in coming to table, or in going to the barber to be shaved, forgetfulness or carelessness, making a noise in the monastery, and beginning to read at dinner before asking a blessing. These faults were atoned by a very slight penance, such as repeating a few prayers or kissing the feet of some of the brothers.

The second class comprised, 1st. To have arrived too late on Christmas day in the chapter; 2nd. To be careless in the choir; 3rd. To laugh or make others laugh there; 4th. To be absent without leave in the choir, the chapter, or at table; 5th. To be too late at the early mass; 6th. To eat or drink without asking a blessing; 7th. To go in or out without crossing themselves; 8th. To address a brother of the order without saying Father or Brother; 9th. Breaking silence. The penances for these faults were as follows:- To kiss the feet of all their brothers, to say several paternosters with outstretched crossed arms, or to eat on the floor. Breaking silence was punished by correction in the chapter, and bread and water for one day.

The third class included the following:- To vex by unbecoming behaviour or words, lying, excusing one's own faults or those of another, and speaking to relations without permission of the Superior. If the offender in any of these points acknowledged his faults, and begged for pardon, he was only punished by two days' bread and water, and three public scourgings. If, on the other hand, the offender pled not guilty, and had to be formally accused and convicted, his punishment was three days' fast and four public scourgings.

The fourth class comprehended the heavy sins of cursing and swearing, striking, thieving, gambling, opposition to the Superior, and accusing the latter before a judicial tribunal. The penance for these crimes was very severe. The guilty one appeared in the chapter, confessed his crime, and prayed for forgiveness. He was then scourged either by the Superior himself or another, and the culprit was forthwith sentenced to fast for a period ranging from six to thirty days. During this period he was degraded from his rank, and treated as one excommunicated. His only fare was bread and water.

There were various other offences not included in either of these classes, which were punished by lengthened fasts. Any one who revealed the secrets of the order, or appealed to another order, suffered so many days, and was then imprisoned for three years, or longer, according to circumstances. Breaches of chastity were punished in a similar way, and some other sins, of a nameless kind, brought imprisonment for life. The most heinous of all crimes was apostasy, whether of the monastery or of the faith. If the criminal repented within forty days he had to appear before the brothers with rods in his hand, fall on his knees and make a confession. He was then scourged, and afterwards sentenced according to the fourth class. Determined obstinacy and disobedience was punished by imprisonment and fasting, and, as a last resource, expulsion. The prisons were of various degrees to suit the different crimes. There were two in every monastery, one not quite dark, and the other harder, narrower, and darker. In these last the prisoner was excluded from the sacrament except during his last moments, when his chains were taken off that he might receive the communion, and afterwards replaced. His fare was at all times bread and water. A mistake in partaking of the sacrament was visited by a public confession, two or three days' fasting, and as many self-flagellations. In the letters of the holy Bernard, such a case is mentioned: a certain father had forgotten to pour wine in the cup, and for this mistake the saint advised the whole community to do penance by a public flagellation.

The rules concerning flagellation in the orders of the Augustines and Ursuline nuns were much the same as in the preceding orders. Apostates desiring re-admittance were treated with great severity. The penitent was required to appear at the church door, strip to the shirt, then advance to the assembled brotherhood with a rod or switch in his hand, beg forgiveness, and request a discipline. After receiving a castigation from the Prior he was sentenced to a daily whipping, and to forfeit his rank in the community.

Among the monks of St Anthony the birching was very mild. Except in rare cases they never scourged to bleeding, and other mortifications might sometimes be substituted for corporal chastisement. In the communities regulated by St. Géneviève, although not very strict in other respects, the birch was applied to the younger nuns for laziness or carelessness. Every Friday a regular scourging took place, the Abbess taking her share for the sake of example. Apostasy, or a breach of chastity, brought the penalty of fourteen days' imprisonment, and a heavy flagellation.

In the regular order of St. Augustine there were four degrees of penance. The laymen of this order were summoned to the monastery to receive the discipline when they transgressed the rules. If an individual was obstinate, and refused to undress he was subjected to imprisonment and a heavier punishment. Lying, swearing, and speaking to women, were visited by a discipline on the naked body. Profanation and drunkenness entailed so severe a flagellation that it was almost beyond endurance. A story is told of a doctor having to appear in a miserable gown, being made to undress to the waist, and run the gauntlet of the scourging brotherhood.

The barefooted monks were a division of the Augustines, originating in Spain, and thence spreading through France and Italy. In this order novices were scourged three times a week until they had been three years in the monastery, after which they only received the birch every Friday. A penitent was dressed in a gown, having a slit behind, and received the discipline on his bare back: from the Prior first, and afterwards from the Fathers and Brothers in succession. Criminals in the prisons of the order were scourged every day. One brother Casarius died from the effects of a flagellation inflicted on him for some offence against the rules. The Spanish division of the order excelled all others in the severity of the discipline.

In the convents of this order the novices were scourged by the Mother Superior, but the nuns did not suffer so severely. Maria Vittoria Fornari, founder of the order of Annonciades, was a remarkable character. This lady was subject to visits from the devil, who beat her and dragged her about the house with so much noise as to awaken the other inmates. In order to, counteract his influence she fasted, wore a hair shirt, and scourged herself until she fainted. She chose for her companion a ragged beggar, and walked about with him. Dressed as a medicant, she consorted with beggars in the street, and partook of their punishment when they came under the notice of the police. Her father confessor, a Jesuit, persuaded her to undergo these mortifications, and, in order that she might be still further accustomed to implicit obedience, she was placed under the care of a peasant girl, whom he directed to inflict a nursery chastisement upon her whenever she disobeyed in the smallest point. This teacher heard her repeat a number of paternosters, and administered a box on the ear for every mistake she made. Thus trained, with the assistance of the Jesuit she organised first the smaller and then the larger convent of the Annunciation, the members of which were called the heavenly ones— the blue and the sky-blue.

The Visitantines were formed by Françoise Fremoit de Chantal, a young widow, under the direction of the holy Francis of Sales, and were distinguished more for inward humiliation than outward severity. Humiliating punishments were preferred to chastisements with birches and scourges, and novices were obliged to wear a fool's cap, immense spectacles, or to tie heavy pieces of wood on themselves, or be laden with stones and blocks like an ass. If a novice lay too long in bed, she had, as a punishment, to carry a pillow into the refectory; and if a similar fault was committed a second time, she was obliged to extend herself on the ground, and say to the nuns, "Dear Sisters, have pity on me, that I am so lazy." On a third offence, the delinquent was treated like a little child, wrapped in swaddling clothes, and fed with pap, and only as a last resource would the Mother Superior give her a good birching. Some of the nuns thought the rules too mild, and left the community for more rigid order. One declared that she would far rather have the scourge and hair-shirt of the holy Francis of Assisi than the honey and sugar of Francis of Sales.

The Ursulines, an order of nuns under the Jesuits, were very numerous throughout Germany, and contrasted favourably with similar sisterhoods in flagellating practices. Severe scourging was almost unknown among them, being only rarely applied to apostates and runaways. They devoted themselves to the education of children, and the training of servants. Delinquents were only whipped mildly on the hand.

The orders of the Brothers of the Hospitalities and the Theatines were somewhat similar in flagellating practices to the orders already described. In the first the discipline was severe and combined with strange humiliation. Their prisons were well furnished with blocks, bells, and chains. Common faults were expiated by a flagellation on the bare back, and apostates had to appear naked before the inmates, carrying rods wherewith they were at once scourged. The Theatines seldom applied the discipline, and in this respect differed very much from the order founded by Casar de Bus, where the monks were lashed till the blood flowed about the room. Vincenz de Paula founded the order of the Lazaristes, and instituted a number of severe penances. The Countess Beatrice de Partalegre, who was imprisoned and punished by the jealous Queen Elizabeth of Castile, after her liberation founded the order of Unstained Virginity, under the tuition of Cardinal Ximenes. Johanna de Valois, daughter of Louis XI, instituted the order of the Annunciation of Mary under the Franciscans. She persuaded ten young ladies to submit themselves to her, praying and fasting with them. She directed their devotions, and gave them maternal discipline over her knees every evening after confession if they deserved it. She also wished to unite in one the peculiar mortifications of the other orders—the hair-shirt, the three-fold scourge with five pointed silver nails under it, the Friday scourge, solitude, tears, and repentance. The order of Repentance had for its chief object the reclamation of fallen women, and was distinguished for severity. Flagellation in that order seemed absolutely indispensable—quite as necessary, indeed, as daily bread: even Superiors were not exempt from it.

Although the rules of the female Hospitalites were not so severe, the birch and the scourge were by no means neglected among them.

The reader, after a perusal of the manners and customs of the nuns and monks of old, will probably say to himself, that at the present day, in convents and nunneries, the scourge and all other cruelties have been long abolished. Let him not be too sure. It is not very long since we had certain convent revelations, in the case of "Saurin v. Starr;" and certainly the recent tale of convent horrors in Poland throws the so called revelations of "Maria Monk" quite into the shade.

The story of Barbara Ubryk was so forcibly told by the newspapers, that, beyond a slight abridgement, it requires no further literary art to set it before the public. It is as follows:- One day an anonymous letter reached the Criminal Court at Cracow, to the effect that, in the convent of Carmelite barefooted nuns, Sister Barbara had been forcibly kept in close confinement in a dark cell for twenty-one years. The vice-president of the Criminal Court, Ritter von Antoniewicz, immediately laid this information before a judge of inquiry, who, in company with the public prosecutor, repaired to the Bishop von Galecki, with the request to permit them to enter the convent. Having overcome the obstacles that were offered against their search, the representatives of the law discovered the particular part of the building where the unhappy woman was confined. The place was a cell situated at the extreme end of the corridor, between the pantry, close to the dung-hole, and had a walled-up window and a double wooden door, in which there was a movable grating, through which, very probably, food was handed in. Some rays of light could now and then penetrate into this dismal dungeon by means of a small window. The cell, seven paces long by six paces wide, was opened, but it is almost impossible to describe the view this piece of inquisition of the nineteenth century presented. In a dark, infected hole adjoining the sewer, sat, or rather cowered, on a heap of straw, an entirely naked, totally neglected, half insane woman, who, at the unaccustomed view of light, the outer world, and human beings, folded her hands, and pitifully implored: "I am hungry, have pity on me; give me meat, and I shall be obedient." This hole, for it could hardly be called a chamber, besides containing all kinds of dirt and filth, and a dish with rotten potatoes, was deficient of the slightest personal accommodation. There was nothing—no stove, no bed, no table, no chair—it was neither warmed by fire nor by the rays of the sun. This den, then, the inhuman Carmelite sisters who call themselves women, spiritual wives, the brides of heaven, had selected as a habitation for one of their own sex, and kept her therein in close confinement for twenty-one years—since 1848. For twenty-one years the grey sisters daily passed this cell, and not one of them ever thought of taking compassion on this poor outcast prisoner. With her deeply sunk eyes staring on one spot knelt this wretched victim in her cell in the convent of the Carmelites. Half human, half animal, with a filthy body, with thin knock-kneed legs, hollow cheeks, closely shorn dirty head, unwashed for years, there came forth a horrible-looking being, such as Dante in his wildest imagination was unable to picture. The judge instantly ordered the woman to be clothed, and went himself for Bishop Galecki, who was deeply moved at the awful spectacle. When the unhappy nun was led away she asked anxiously whether she would be brought back to her grave, and when asked why she had been imprisoned, she answered, "I have broken my vow of chastity, but," pointing with a fearfully wild gesture, and in great excitement, to the sisters, "they are not angels." Upon a search being made in the convent, a heavy whip or scourge, like a knout, and several other instruments of torture, were discovered.

CHAPTER X

FLAGELLATION AMONG THE DOMINICANS, AND IN CONNECTION WITH THE INQUISITION.

THIS order, in its own peculiar statutes, and in its regulations for the Inquisition, was notorious for the severity of its discipline. The founder, Dominicus de Guzman, a native of Spain, was a famous flagellator. His mother, before she conceived him, is said to have dreamed that she was with child of a whelp, carrying in his mouth a lighted torch, and that after he was born he put the world in an uproar by his fierce barkings, and set it on fire by the torch which he carried in his mouth. His followers held that this torch presaged the light that his doctrine was to shed on the world; while there were not wanting those who affirmed that it merely foretold an emblem of fire and fagot, by which an infinite multitude of men would be burned to ashes.

Dominicus, when he grew up, often scourged himself till he became insensible, and had to be recalled to consciousness by the cares and caresses of the Holy Mother and three beautiful sisters. His penance was said to be so effectual, that evil spirits filled the air with howlings in consequence of the many thousand souls that he rescued from their grasp. He was no less severe to others than he was to himself, and, under the appearance of mercy and forgiveness, he executed the greatest cruelties. Excommunication was at that time the most dreadful of evils, and, on pretence of removing that ban, and restoring penitents to the communion of the Church, excruciating punishments were inflicted, veiled only by the gentle name of penance.

We give the following order in his own words, as illustrative of the mercy and tenderness shewn by this celebrated saint:- "Brother

Dominic, the least of preachers, to all Christ's faithful people to whom these presents shall come: greeting in the Lord. By the authority of the Cistercian Abbot, who hath appointed us this office, we have reconciled the bearer of these presents, Pontius Rogerius, converted by God's blessing from his heretical sect, charging and requiring him by the oath which he hath taken, that three Sundays, or three festival days, he be led by a priest, naked from his shoulders down to his drawers, from the coming into the town unto the church doors, being whipt all the way. We also enjoin him, that he abstain at all time from meat, eggs, cheese, and all things that proceed from flesh, except on the days of Easter, Whitsuntide, and Christmas: on which days we command him to eat flesh for a denial of his former errors. We will that he keep three Lents in one year abstaining even from fish; and that he fast three days every week, always refraining from fish, oil, and wine, except bodily infirmity, or hard labour in harvest time, require a dispensation. We will have him to wear friars' coats, with two small crosses sewn on his two breasts. Let him every day hear mass, if opportunity may serve, and on holy days let him go to church to vespers. He shall observe all other canonical hours by day and night, wherever he be, and shall then say his orisons—that is, seven times a day he shall say ten paternosters together, and twenty at midnight. Let him altogether abstain from married life; and every first day of the month let him shew these our letters to the curate of the town of Cererim, whom we command to observe diligently what kind of life this bearer leads: Whom, if he should neglect to observe these our injunctions, we declare to be perjured, and excommunicated, and will have him taken for such," &c.

Johann Tauler was another distinguished ornament of this order. His biographer relates that he began his spiritual exercises like a schoolboy, but with a golden A B C, and received a whipping for every fault he committed. He afterwards undertook the task of performing the flagellation himself, at the command of his master, and, it is said, laid on harder than his preceptor had done. As might be expected, with such prominent examples before them, the rules of the order are full of the *disciplina flagelli*. Birchings were frequently applied to the body, particularly and wholly naked, and the novices were early initiated into the mysteries of the scourge. The usual discipline was scourging the body, naked to the girdle; but in many convents of this order the ladies were obliged to receive it like children, and sometimes they were compelled to scourge each other. Occasionally they were obliged to lie on their backs and receive discipline on the opposite part of their bodies. A number of trivial faults were punished by very severe birchings—indeed, they were frequently lashed till the blood came. A very effectual plan for ensuring due severity in the application of the Rod was an arrangement whereby the ladies punished each other alternately, when of course the sister who had experienced no forbearance from the preceding one did not spare the other when her turn came to administer the lash.

The Dominicans, under the authority of the Pope, established the Inquisition, and the severity which characterised the order was displayed in their treatment of heretics. It may interest our readers to know the part which flagellation bore in the punishments inflicted by the Inquisition, and we propose, therefore, to give a short account of some of the more remarkable cases.

One of the first to fall under the displeasure of the holy office was Raymond, Earl of Toulouse. The Pope excommunicated him, as a defender of heresies, and absolved his subjects from their allegiance. Thoroughly frightened at this, the Earl promised obedience to the church, and desired to be reconciled to it. In order to obtain this favour he had to deliver up to the Pope's Legate seven castles, by way of security for his future behaviour, and submit to be scourged in the Church of St Agde. This sentence was executed with very great severity, his body being torn and swelled to such a degree that it was impossible to put on his clothes: he was obliged, therefore, to return home naked. He was also served in the same manner at the sepulchre of St. Peter the Martyr at New Castres, which saint he had caused to be slain.

Each prison in the Inquisition was under the charge of a keeper, who had necessarily great influence on the treatment of the prisoners; but any indulgence shewn by the attendants towards the unfortunate victims of the holy office was visited by severe punishment. There was in the service of a very covetous and cruel keeper, named Gaspard Bennavidius, an old servant maid, who, moved to pity by the distress of the prisoners under her master, took every opportunity of comforting them, and even assisting them with food according to her ability. Being discovered in this charitable act, she was thrown into prison for a year, was condemned to walk in the public procession with a yellow garment on, and to receive two hundred stripes which sentence was executed as she went through the streets of the city. Gonsalvius Montanus mentions another instance of this kind of punishment. Peter ab Herera, keeper of the Tower of Triana, which was a prison of the Inquisition, had, among other prisoners committed to his care, a certain good matron with her two daughters, who were put in different cells. Their urgent prayers to be allowed to see and comfort each other, even for a quarter of an hour only, moved the keeper to compassion, and he allowed them to be together for half-an-hour and then placed them in their separate cells. A few days after they were put to the torture, and the keeper being afraid that through the severity of their torments they might confess what he had done, went himself to the Holy Tribunal and begged pardon for his fault. Being immediately thrown into prison, he was treated so cruelly there that he became mad. After remaining in prison for a year, he was brought out in a public procession, clothed in a yellow garment, with a halter round his neck, in order to be lashed through the streets, and be then sent to the galleys for six years. When he was being taken to be whipped, his madness came upon him, and he attacked the executioner in a fierce manner: he was soon overpowered, however, and the sentence of two hundred lashes duly carried out. For his attack on the alguazil, four years were added to the six for which he was first condemned to the galleys.

Among the crimes and offences punished by the Inquisition was polygamy. After abjuration, the polygamists were enjoined various salutary penances, such as fastings, prayers, and the like, and then were banished to the galleys for six or seven years. If the offender belonged to the lower or middle class, he was whipped, and half his goods confiscated; and in some cases an infamous mitre was put on his head, before he was beatèn. In the year 1612, the Pope Paul V issued a bull against priests who, in the confessional, solicited or provoked women to dishonourable actions; and the Inquisition was appointed to receive complaints and punish the offenders. The sequel revealed an alarming state of affairs. When the edict was published in the churches of Seville, accompanied with heavy penalties against those who, within thirty days, neglected or refused to inform against monks or clergy-men who had abused the confessional, so many women went to the palace of the Inquisition in Seville to inform against their confessors, that twenty secretaries, with as many inquisitors, were not sufficient to take the depositions of the witnesses! The period was then extended to other thirty days, and when this was again found to be insufficient, the same number of days was appointed a third and even a fourth time. At length the Inquisition, finding it impossible to punish so many, revoked the order, and quashed the whole proceedings. In ordinary cases when a confessor was convicted of an offence of such a nature— and these offences were difficult to bring home, because a woman could not be admitted to give evidence unless she was of approved life, and the confessor was known to be given to the sins of the flesh he was, besides the penance of fasting and prayer, condemned to the gal-leys, or perpetual imprisonment.

The punishment for heretical blasphemy varied according to the rank of the offender. If the blasphemer was a mean person, he was made to wear a mitre, his tongue was tied, and pinched with an iron or wooden gag, he was carried through the streets, whipped with scourges, and banished. If he was a noble, he was confined in a monastery for a time and fined. When the blasphemy was not consid-ered very heinous, the criminal had to stand during divine service without hat, cloak, or shoes, with a rope round his waist, and a burn-ing taper in his hands.

Diviners, fortune-tellers, and astrologers were punished with excommunication, suspension of dignities, whipping, banishment, or imprisonment, according to their rank. Jews were especially obnox-ious to the Inquisition, and were on every pretext punished with fines, whipping, and imprisonment.

False witnesses were sometimes condemned to perpetual imprisonment, during which they had to eat "the bread of grief, and drink the water of affliction." If their testimony had done little mischief a smaller penalty was inflicted—the criminal, wearing the usual mitre, had to assist at the public procession, was then bastinadoed or whipped, and finally banished.

When the Inquisition sentenced a monk to be scourged, the discipline was inflicted in the monastery to which he belonged, in the presence of the Notary of the Holy Office. Paramus records such an instance in the case of Laurentius Valla at Naples. He was condemned for heresy, but through the King's favour his punishment was mitigated to a public recantation and whipping; and accordingly, in the convent of the Predicants, being led round the cloisters with his hands tied, he was whipped upon his shoulders and back by the inmates of the house.

The monotony of perpetual imprisonment was varied by causing the criminal to stand at the church door on certain days, as the following instance will shew:- In a decree of the Council of Biterre, where, after commanding that penitents should be present at divine service on Sundays and festivals, this is added: that on the mass of every Sunday and festival, between the epistle and the gospel, heretics shall publicly present themselves with rods in their hands, stripped of their outward garment, and with their veil or hat off, to the priest celebrating mass in the presence of the people, and thereafter, having received discipline, the priest shall declare that they suffer this discipline for heretical depravity.

The decrees of the Inquisition were generally carried into effect en mass at an *Auto-da-fè* or Act of Faith. The general acts of the Inquisition, which in other countries were considered mere executions of criminals, were in Spain, and such Catholic countries, looked upon as religious ceremonies, and manifestations of holy zeal. These generally were exhibited on such public occasions as the accession of a monarch to the throne. After the chief heretics and other sinners had been burned, the victims sentenced to whipping were next day mounted upon asses, and scourged through all the chief streets and places of public resort.

Among all the monastic orders none enjoyed a higher degree of power than the Dominicans, but still they had their enemies, and when their influence began to decline they were not scrupulous as to the measures they adopted to support and extend their authority; indeed, to keep up their power, they practised the most infamous frauds. We give one of the most remarkable, because it is not only extraordinary in itself, but also involves the discipline of the whip, and is therefore pertinent to our subject.

About the year 1509 there was a controversy between the Franciscans and the Dominicans concerning the Immaculate Conception of the Virgin Mary. The opinion held by the latter body, that she was not born without original sin, was unpopular, and to support the credit of the order it was resolved to "get up" some visions and dreams, which were much believed in at the time. A lay brother, named Jetzer, living at Bern, a man simple as a child, and much given to penance, was chosen as the instrument of the delusions. Four Dominicans undertook to manage the plot; and one of these, hiding himself in Jetzer's cell, appeared to him about midnight in the guise of a horrid figure, blowing fire from his nostrils, and surrounded by howling dogs. He informed the affrighted brother that he was the ghost of a Dominican, condemned to purgatory for laying aside the monastic habit, and that he (Jetzer) was the person by whose instrumentality he might be rescued from his purgatorial torments. Jetzer, wild with terror, promised to do what he could to save him from the flames. His visitor told him that nothing but the most extraordinary mortifications, such as the discipline of the whip performed for a period of eight days by the whole monastery, while Jetzer lay prostrate in the form of one crucified in the chapel during mass, could contribute to his deliverance. Before vanishing, the ghost promised to return with other spirits like unto himself. When morning came, Jetzer hastened to relate his vision, and the monks unanimously advised him at once to undergo the discipline that was enjoined him; and every one was willing to do his share of the task—i.e., lay on the stripes. Poor Jetzer obeyed, and was hailed as a saint by the multitude outside the convent. He continued to receive frequent visits from the ghost, who strove to convince him that the Virgin Mary was born in original sin; and one night they gave him a strong opiate, during the power of which they marked the five wounds of Christ on his body; but the visions and frauds were at length overdone, and Jetzer, simple minded as he was, discovered the imposture, and almost killed the Prior, who one night performed the rôle of the Virgin with a crown on her head. The Dominicans were afraid that Jetzer would discover the cheat to the world outside, and resolved to quietly get rid of him. But the vigour of his constitution, which so well supported him in his flagellations and austerities, stood him in good stead in this matter. Five times they gave him poison, and he was not destroyed: they then poisoned the host or consecrated wafer, but he escaped by vomiting it. Having at length found an opportunity of escaping from the convent, he immediately went and discovered the plot to the magistrates. The whole imposture was afterwards fully proved, and the four Dominicans who carried out the plot, after being degraded from the priesthood, were burnt alive. Jetzer died some time after at Constance. This elaborate conspiracy would no doubt have been handed down to posterity as a most surprising miracle, if Brother Jetzer had not had the good fortune to slip through the fingers of his Dominican brethren.

CHAPTER XI

FLAGELLATION AMONG THE JESUITS

THE order of the Jesuits was at one time very wide spread, having branches in Spain, Portugal, Italy, France—in fact, throughout the known world. They occupied the front rank among Flagellants, and although they tried to disprove as slanderous much that was said against them, there is good ground to believe that they had a taste for flagellation and for using the Rod to secure the gratification of base passions.

The founder of the society, Ignatius Loyola, began his education when he was thirty years of age; and it is said that he requested his teacher at Salamanca to inflict the usual schoolboy chastisement on him that he might be properly instructed. Others deny that he did so, but affirm that at Paris, when his preceptors were about to punish him with the Rod, they were suddenly enlightened by heaven as to the future high destiny of their pupil, and, instead of whipping him, humbly begged his pardon. Although it is not very clear to what extent he personally carried the discipline in the order which he founded, there is no doubt his successors had a decided taste for the Rod, and that they inflicted it on many of the beautiful ladies who were entrusted to their care. Even at an early period of their history, scandalous stories were circulated concerning the penitential arrangements of the Jesuits and their abuse of their trust. In the Netherlands they established a sisterhood of distinguished ladies who submitted to a discipline every week. They improved on the ordinary method of inflicting chastisements on the bare back of the person by whipping the penitent on the front. We are informed that the ladies of Holland and Belgium took so much pleasure in this novel Spanish method, that when the ecclesiastical authorities forbade it, they begged their confessors to continue the fatherly discipline. In the Latin versified account of the Jesuit order, it is related that the Jesuit Johannes Ackerbom was convicted of scourging a maiden who had confessed to him. Another brother, Peter Wills, an intimate friend of the former, indulged in the same practice. One of their imitators, Peter Gerson, was so fond of using the Rod that he fell upon country girls at their work in the fields and flagellated them. In the Netherlands the Jesuits punished the boys at school after the Spanish fashion. In Portugal the penitent, after repeating a number of prayers, had then to submit to the Spanish mode of discipline, and the Jesuits even carried the practice into the palace of Queen Louisa

During the next reign, under Queen Donna Maria, Father Malgrida carried out the practice to a far greater extent, by introducing it among the young ladies of the court. In the ante-rooms the beautiful sinners were to be seen on their knees at prayers, and upon a signal being given they removed such portions of their dress as were necessary, and received the discipline. In all probability the Queen herself anticipated in the operations. The penitents, as we have read, felt great pleasure in these disciplines, and, it is said, eagerly longed for the Rod! Foreign princesses were specially invited to come and partake of the discipline after this refined method. In Spain, where it was usual to absolve members of the female sex of their sin after their confession by administering bodily penances, the Inquisition undertook to reform the abuse of discipline by issuing a proclamation against it. It was forbidden in future to strip young women, or to apply the hand or the whip to them. But the Inquisition still retained the right, and did not hesitate to apply the whip to refractory heretics—without remorse stripping and scourging the unfortunate persons of either sex who fell under their displeasure.

With priestly craft, the Jesuits made themselves indispensable friends of the family in every distinguished house, and practised the discipline among the ladies. Such young ladies as were confined in convents for being in love, or for obstinacy or worldliness, were under their charge, and it is recorded that when they were especially pretty the Jesuit fathers never failed personally to take charge of the pre-scribed chastisement. They kept in the good graces of those nuns who fell victims to their arts, and prevented them from betraying the secret of their humiliation. The Jesuits also ingratiated themselves into female societies, as also into boarding and other schools, and were always forward in prescribing the Rod. Nor did Charles Borromeus forget to include the scourge in the statutes which he drew up for the use of the convent of St. Ursula. The Jesuits likewise advised parents who had refractory daughters to send them to their order, and their soul's welfare would be taken care of; indeed, the followers of Loyola were always willing to undertake the education and restraint of young ladies. Pious parents would thank God with tears of joy for the pains which these holy men took upon themselves; but the *Chronique Scandaleuse* tells a different story of the result of their labours.

The Jesuits did not confine their flagellatory practices to Europe, but in their missions to heathen lands also employed the Rod in the work of conversion. In Paraguay they chastised the native parents as if they had been little children; but in Mexico they did not act so inhu-manely as their predecessors who accompanied the conquerors of the New World. A band of missionaries, chiefly Jesuits, were sent to Africa about the year 1634 by the King of Portugal and the Pope, at the request of the Queen of Matamba; and one day, when a missionary met the Queen and a numerous train of attendants giving an airing to an idol, he enforced his arguments against idolatry by the application of a whip to the body of her sable majesty! It is astonishing, he says, how the process of flagellation gradually opened her understanding, till she at length confessed herself wholly unable to resist such sensi-ble proofs of the excellence of his doctrine. Although the King was afraid to resent this usage, the ladies of the court determined to avenge the cause of their sex. For this purpose they selected as their place of bathing the opposite bank of a rivulet which flowed before the garden and dwelling of the missionaries, and here they delighted to exhibit themselves daily in a state of the most primitive simplicity, and in attitudes not at all decorous. The holy men were terribly shocked, but the only remedy available to them was to build a high wall in front of their garden. In Abyssinia it was then a common proceeding with these good fathers to whip the native women out of what they called their idolatry and superstition.

Among modern Jesuits the Rod still holds a place, although not nearly to the extent it did in olden times. Steinmetz, who passed a noviciate of one year at Stoneyhurst, wrote an account of the curriculum there, and gives some details with regard to modern discipline and penance. He says the usual mode of correction is the Rod, but never severely administered, expulsion being reserved for flagrant misdemeanours. But confession obviates, in a great measure, the necessity for the lash. The dormitories are divided into compartments, giving each novice about as much space as a passenger has in a packet ship for his berth. Each compartment contains a small desk (without a lock, of course) and a chair. A crucifix is suspended over the desk, and there is a pot containing "holy water." In the desk are the books, paper, discipline or whip, chain, &c. The discipline and the chain are regarded as the preservatives of chastity among the novices: the former is made of whip-cord, and is a kind of cat-o'-nine-tails, with knots at the ends of each tail. The chain is made of steel-wire about the thickness of whip-cord. The wire is bent into horse-shoe shaped links, and at every link the superfluous wire projects half-an-inch, not rounded off or pointed, but just as it has been cut or filed.

These "helps to holy living" are not in constant operation among the novices, but only at stated times, such as during Lent. Any ascetic-minded youth may obtain permission to use them at other times. Steinmetz says the discipline was very mild, and was just sufficient to keep the novices alive: to kill monotony, to flatter their minds with the idea that they were doing something in the "labour of perfection." During Lent twice a week the porter goes round the cells and gives the order for "mortification." At this the novices—each sitting in his bed—uncover their shoulders and seize the whip. As soon as they are ready, the porter rings a small bell, and the twenty whips descend on the bare backs. They are restricted to twelve strokes given as rapidly as possible, and all ended almost about the same instant. "In the excitement (says Steinmetz), very similar to a shower-bath, we could not help tossing the whip into the desk; and then, diving into the sheets, felt very comfortable indeed!" The chain was worn on the morning following. It was tied by two strings attached to the extremities round the middle of the thigh, next to the skin, drawn tight enough to hinder it from slipping down. It was worn about six hours, and gave some pain, but more annoyance.

CHAPTER XII

THE SECT OF THE FLAGELLANTS.

W^E have seen the customs of flagellation connected with religion taking their rise among heathen nations, and afterwards being adopted in the Christian Church, to form part of its penitential service. From being practised here and there by hermits, who led a life of solitude and self-mortification, it spread through the Church, and took a deeper hold on the minds of the people, until it reached a climax about the middle of the thirteenth century, and led to the formation of fraternities for the regular and public practice of flagellation. This sect first made its appearance in Italy in the year 1210, and the following account of it is given in the "Chronicon Ursitius Basiliensis" of the monk St. Justin of Padua:-

"When all Italy was sullied with crimes of every kind, a certain sudden superstition, hitherto unknown to the world, first seized the inhabitants of Perusa afterwards the Romans, and then almost all the nations of Italy. To such a degree were they affected with the fear of God, that noble as well as ignoble persons, young and old, even children five years of age, would go naked about the streets without any sense of shame, walking in public, two and two, in the manner of a solemn procession. Every one of them held in his hand a scourge, made of leather thongs, and with tears and groans they lashed themselves on their backs till the blood ran: all the while weeping and giving tokens of the same bitter affliction, as if they had really been spectators of the passion of our Saviour, imploring the forgiveness of God and His Mother, and praying that; He, who had been appeased by the repentance of so many sinners, would not disdain theirs. And not only in the day time, but likewise during the nights, hundreds, thousands, and ten thousands of these penitents ran, notwithstanding the rigour of winter, about the streets, and in churches, with lighted wax candles in their hands, and preceded by priests, who carried crosses and banners along with them, and with humility prostrated themselves before the altars: the same scenes were to be seen in small

Plate VIII   RELIGIOUS DISCIPLINE

THE SECT OF THE FLAGELLANTS
Showing the various Instruments selected for Self-punishment

towns and villages; so that the mountains and the fields seemed to
resound alike the voice of men who were crying to God. All musical
instruments and love songs ceased to be heard. The only music that
prevailed both in town and country was that of the lugubrious voice of
the penitent, whose mournful accents might have moved hearts of
flint: and even the eyes of the obdurate sinner could not refrain from
tears. Nor were women exempt from the general spirit of devotion we
mention: for not only those among the common people, but also
matrons and young ladies of noble families, would perform the same
mortifications with modesty in their own rooms. Then those who
were at enmity with one another became again friends. Usurers and
robbers hastened to restore their ill-gotten riches to their right owners. Others, who were contaminated with different crimes, confessed
them with humility, and renounced their vanities. Gaols were opened;
prisoners were delivered; and banished persons permitted to return to
their native habitations. So many and so great works of sanctity and
Christian charity, in short, were then performed by both men and
women, that it seemed as if an universal apprehension had seized
mankind, that the divine power was preparing either to consume them
by fire, or destroy them by shaking the earth, or some other of those
means which divine justice knows how to employ for avenging crimes.
Such a sudden repentance, which had thus diffused itself all over Italy,
and had even reached other countries, not only the unlearned, but
wise persons also admired. They wondered whence such a vehement
fervour of piety could have proceeded: especially since such public
penances and ceremonies had been unheard of in former times, had
not been approved by the sovereign pontiff, nor recommended by any
preacher or person of eminence; but had taken their origin among
simple persons, whose example both learned and unlearned had alike
followed."

The author of the solemn processions of the Flagellants is said to
have been St. Anthony. The sect was re-organised in the year 1260 in
Italy by Rainer, a hermit of Perugia, who speedily found followers in
all parts of Italy; indeed, their number soon amounted to 10, 000, who
went about, led by priests, bearing banners and crosses. In 1261 they

extended over the Alps into Germany, shewed themselves in Alsatia, Bavaria, Bohemia, and Poland, and found there many imitators.

Notwithstanding the opposition of different governments, the tenets of the flagellants spread through Europe, and in the year 1349, while the plague was raging in Germany, they made their appearance in that country. According to the chronicle of Albert of Strasburg, two hundred came from Schwaben to Spira, under one principal and two subordinate rulers, whose commands they implicitly obeyed. They were met by crowds of people. Placing themselves within a circle drawn on the ground, they stripped, leaving on their bodies only a breech-cloth. They then walked with arms outstretched like a cross round and round the circle for a time, finally prostrating themselves on the ground. They soon after rose, each striking his neighbour with a scourge, armed with knots and four iron points, regulating their blows by the singing of psalms. At a certain signal the discipline ceased, and they threw themselves first on their knees, then flat on the ground, groaning and sobbing. On rising, the leader gave a short address, exhorting them to implore the mercy of God upon their benefactors and enemies, and also on the souls in purgatory. This was followed by another prostration, and then another discipline. Those who had taken charge of the clothes now came forward, and went through the same ceremonies.

Another writer graphically describes their mode of operation:- Penance was performed twice a-day: in the morning and evening they went abroad in pairs, singing psalms amid the ringing of bells, and when they arrived at the place of flagellation they stripped the upper part of their bodies, and put off their shoes, wearing only a linen dress reaching from the waist to the ankles. They then lay down in a large circle in different positions, according to the nature of their crime: the adulterer with his face to the ground; the perjurer on one side, holding up three of his fingers, &c., and were then castigated, some more and some less, by the master, who ordered them to rise in the words of a prescribed form—

"Stant uf durch der reinen Martel ere;
Und hüte dich vor der Sünden mere."

Upon this they scourged themselves, amid the singing of psalms and loud supplications for the averting of the plague, with genuflexions and other ceremonies, of which contemporary writers give various accounts. Their ranks contained peasants as well as priests, and both learned and unlearned. They affirmed that they derived their authority from a letter brought by an angel to St. Peter's Church in Jerusalem: this letter declared that Jesus Christ was offended at the prevailing sins of the day—in particular, Sabbath-breaking, blasphemy, usury, adultery, and the non-observance of the appointed fasts. Having implored the forgiveness of Jesus Christ through the Holy Virgin and the angels, they were directed to live exiled from their country for thirty-four days, in order to obtain mercy, disciplining themselves during that time. The inhabitants of Spira treated the sect with great hospitality; but they would only accept donations for the purpose of supplying themselves with candles and banners. These latter were of purple silk, and were carried during the procession. They were joined by about a hundred persons at Spira, and at Strasburg nearly a thousand swelled their ranks. These agreed to the rules; each was required to be able to spend at least fourpence a-day, and to declare that he had confessed his sins, forgiven his enemies, and obtained the consent of his wife. The Brothers of the Cross were not permitted to seek for free quarters, or even to enter a house, without having been invited; they were forbidden to converse with females; and if they transgressed these rules, or acted without discretion, they were obliged to confess to the Superior, who sentenced them to several lashes of the scourge by way of penance.

Hecker, who does not seem to be aware that the sect had previously existed, gives the following account of this their second appearance, in his "Epidemics of the Middle Ages." He says, "While all countries were filled with lamentations and woe, there first arose in Hungary, and afterwards in Germany, the Brotherhood of the Flagellants, called also the Brotherhood of the Cross, or Cross Bearers, who took upon themselves the repentance of the people for the sins they had committed, and offered prayers and supplications for the averting of this plague. This order consisted chiefly of the lowest class, who were either actuated by sincere contrition, or who joyfully availed themselves of this pretext for idleness, and were hurried along with the tide of distracting frenzy. But as these brotherhoods gained in repute, and were welcomed by the people with veneration and enthusiasm, many nobles and ecclesiastics ranged themselves under their standard, and their bands were not unfrequently augmented by children, honourable women, and nuns, so powerfully were minds of the most opposite temperaments enslaved by this infatuation. They marched through the cities in well-organised processions, with leaders and singers; their heads covered as far as their eyes, their looks fixed on the ground, accompanied by every token of the deepest contrition and mourning. They were robed in sombre garments with red crosses on the breast, back, and cap, and bore triple scourges tied in three or four knots, in which points of iron were fixed. Tapers and magnificent banners of velvet and cloth of gold were carried before them; wherever they made their appearance they were welcomed by the ringing of bells, and crowds of people came from great distances to listen to their hymns and to witness their penance with devotion and tears. In the year 1349, two hundred Flagellants first entered Strasburg, where they were received with great joy and hospitality, and lodged by the citizens. Above a thousand joined the brotherhood, which now assumed the appearance of a wandering tribe, and separated into two bodies for the purpose of journeying to the north and to the south."

So great was the enthusiasm in their favour, that the Church seemed threatened and in danger, for the two parties were so much opposed that they excommunicated each other. The Flagellants took possession of the churches; and their new songs, which soon be came well known, operated strongly on the minds of the people. Their chief- psalm, sung at that time in different dialects all over Germany, is full of pious sentiment, and well calculated to promote the prevailing fanaticism. They sometimes undertook to make trial of their power of working miracles—as in Strasburg, where they attempted, in their own circle, to resuscitate a dead child. They, however, failed; and their unskilfulness did them much harm, though they succeeded here and there in maintaining some confidence in their holy calling by pre-tending to have the power of casting out evil spirits. The more enlightened party in the Church opposed these public flagellations. Pope Clement VI (elected to the papal throne in 1332, deceased in 1352) issued a bull against them; and the bishops of Germany con-firmed the apostolic brief, and forbade the Flagellants to form associations in their sees. About this time the sermon of Venturinus, a Dominican friar of Bergamo, induced above 10, 000 persons to under-take a new pilgrimage. They scourged themselves in the churches, and were entertained in the market-place at the public expense.

At Rome, Venturinus was derided, and banished by the Pope to the mountains of Ricondona. Thus opposed, the sect died out for a time; but it was revived in 1414, under the leadership of a man named Conrad, who, as the former leaders had done, claimed a divine revela-tion and mission for the practice of public flagellation. Conrad pretended that the prophet Enoch and himself were one and the same person; that the Flagellants being established, God had been pleased to abrogate the Papacy; and that there was no salvation except by means of the new baptism of blood, through the instrumentality of scourging. On this occasion the Inquisition took action against the sect, and after a grand inquiry into the charges brought against them, caused ninety-one Flagellants to be burned at Sangerhusen, and a great number in other places. How deeply this mania had taken root is proved by the deposition of a citizen of Nordhausen (1446): that his wife, in the belief of performing a Christian act, wanted to scourge her children as soon as they were baptised. Persecutions weakened but did not destroy the sect of the Flagellants, and although disappearing in Germany, we find them practising their rites, but no longer claiming a special mission, in France, Spain, and Portugal.

In the 16th century there arose in France a great number of penance and flagellating companies, distinguished by the names of White, Black, and Grey Penitents. They were most numerous in the southern parts of the kingdom; but even the capital was not exempt from the mania. At Avignon, in the year 1574, the queen-mother placed herself at the head of the Black Penitents, and took part in the usual ceremonies at Lyons and Toulouse. Paris was not behind the age in the use of the Rod; in that city King Henry III took the matter under his patronage, and not only inscribed himself as an honorary member, but afterwards took a very active part in the processions. The first assemblage was at the great jubilee of 1575, when the whole court was invited; but no women were allowed to appear—the King loved them not. Catharine de Medici accordingly whipped her court dames within closed doors. The Parisians thought the whole affair very amusing, and made many jokes about it; the King did not, of course, escape their satire, but got the jesting title of a *"Père conscrit des Blancs battus."* Early in 1585, he established a new White penance brotherhood of the Annunciation Day, which numbered among its ranks many distinguished courtiers and citizens. The order was inaugurated by an exceedingly gorgeous procession, which took place on the 25th of March, the festival day of the protecting saint of the brotherhood. The rules of the order were in conformity with those of other sects of the Flagellants, and were ratified by the Pope. The procession marched from the convent of the Augustines to the church of Notre Dame; the King, without any marks of his dignity, the Keeper of the Great Seal, and other illustrious persons, being present. The Cardinal of Guise carried the cross; the Duke of Mayenne performed the duties of master of the ceremonies; and Auger and Du Peynat were lieutenants. The weather was far from propitious, as the rain fell in torrents during the ceremony. The procession was repeated more than once, and on one occasion the devotees went to the church by torchlight, when the favourites, we are told, whipped themselves so violently that one of them died, but whether from the effect of the whipping or the exposure is not known—probably from the effects of both. The Parisians continued to jest; while the strictest of the clergy preached from the pulpit against the shameless profanation of what was noble and holy, and hinted that the White Penitents deserved to be whipped in another way. The Jesuits, however, encouraged the sect, and made themselves active in framing rules for the brotherhoods; and they likewise, as was their wont, encouraged women to follow the example of the other sex, so that at one time there were numerous whipping companies in the provinces of France. That the women might be spared some shame, they were allowed to wear masks when taking part in the processions. After solemn evening service, and, after supper, the fair sex chastised themselves in an exemplary way; the women appeared barefooted in the procession, which often lasted for six hours. Ladies who could not be induced to appear in public were encouraged by the Jesuits to flagellate themselves in the dark: according to them, the mere carrying of a whip was highly meritorious. Henry III afterwards resumed this penance practice with increased vigour; but his enemies made political capital of the affair, and he therefore lost much of his faith in the supreme virtue of the whipping institution. Crillon, the commander of the guards, caused the favourite of the King, Joyeuse, to be whipped in the most violent manner, while engaged in the procession; and the King was obliged to soothe his minion as he best could, without venturing to punish the pseudo-flagellant. After the death of the Guises, this fanatical mania for fleshly mortification revived. The penance processions were renewed, and this time women and maidens, naked to the shift, ran about with whips. Noble ladies shewed themselves to the populace in a semi-nude state, and gave themselves the discipline, in order to encourage others by their example.

The evil at one time became so rampant, and the cause of religion and morality seemed so much in danger, that many divines preached against it, and Gerson, a famous theologian of that day, and Chancellor of the University of Paris, wrote a severe treatise against the Flagellants. He denounced their practices as contrary to the gospel, and offensive alike to decency and morality. Speaking of the cruelty of these practices, Gerson says, "It is equally unlawful for a man to draw so much blood from his own body, unless it be for medical reasons, as it would be for him to castrate or otherwise mutilate himself. Else it might upon the same principle be advanced that a man may brand himself with red-hot irons; a thing which nobody hath as yet either pretended to say or granted, unless it be false Christians and idolaters, such as are to be found in India, who think it a matter of duty for one to be baptised through fire."

At length, in the year 1601, the Parliament of Paris passed an act to abolish a fraternity of Flagellants, called the Blue Penitents, in the town of Bourges—indeed, the Parliament soon proceeded against all whipping brotherhoods without distinction, declaring the members not only to be heretics, traitors, and regicides, but unchaste. After that time the brotherhood declined, and finally disappeared from France, In the 17th century occasional processions on certain festivals are stated to have taken place in Italy and Spain and Portugal. Father Mabillion relates that in 1689 he saw a scourging procession of the Flagellants at Turin on a Good Friday; and in the year 1710 processions of the cross-bearers were still seen in Italy. Colmenar, in his "Annales d'Espagne et de Portugal," mentions a similar procession taking place at Madrid; and from his narrative we find new elements introduced into the ceremony, which rendered it as much an exercise of gallantry as an act of devotion. Colmenar says, "At this procession are seen all the penitents or disciplinists of the city, who flock to it from every quarter. They wear a high cap, covered with linen cloth, of the height of three feet, and of a sugar-loaf form, from which hangs a stripe of cloth which falls in front and covers their faces. There are some who take this exercise (of the discipline) from a true motive of piety, but there are others who practise it only to please mistresses, and the gallantry of it is of a new kind, one unknown to other nations. These good disciplinarians wear gloves and white shoes, a shirt of which the sleeves are tied with ribbons, and they have a ribbon attached to their cap or to their scourge, of the colour which most pleases their mistresses. They scourge themselves by rule, and on a fixed and settled plan, with a whip of cords, to which are attached at the end little balls of wax with pieces of pointed glass stuck in it. He who flogs himself with most vigour and address is considered the most courageous."

Processions of Flagellants took place at Lisbon, and continued down to a period so late as 1820. Dr. Madden mentions that he saw processions—without the scourging, however—at Lisbon as recent as 1847.

CHAPTER XIII

THE FLAGELLANTS (*continued*).

THE flagellating practices and ceremonies of which we have given a historical sketch in the preceding chapter were certainly very astonishing. Although some writers have assumed the origin of public flagellation to be the moral result of a great plague that broke out in Germany, we think that it was rather the result of a long course of slow innovations on former modes of public worship, introduced by different persons, at different times, and in places remote from one another. There seems to be an innate inclination among mankind towards severe modes of worship of all kinds. In morality, men, whatever may be their private conduct, appear most pleased with the strictest maxims, and in religious matters they seem also to adhere to such as are most laborious and painful. Among all the nations of antiquity, whether worshipping one God or many, physical pain or discomfort, inflicted with religious intentions, has been common; and this is especially true of self-scourging, which, the reader will have observed, existed in one form or another almost universally from a very early period. With Christians it was still further recommended by the circumstance that it formed part of the suffering to which Christ was subjected while on earth; and the thoughts of pious persons were naturally directed towards a style of mortification so frequently mentioned in religious books, hymns, sermons, and conversation. In the practice of flagellation there was, however, a considerable difference between eastern and western Christians. In the east, Christians were always a minority in numbers and influence, and never went to such extravagance, either in theory or practice, as their brethren in the west. For instance, they considered a certain deep sense of past offences—a state of unbounded contrition for the same—as the competent means of atonement for sin, holding tears to be the last stage of such contrition, and a necessary token of it. Weeping was therefore what they aimed at in their devotional acts: and as self-scourging was thought by them to be an excellent expedient for obtaining tears, they had frequent recourse to it for the purpose of bringing them into this saving state. Western Christians, on the other hand, went a great deal farther than this point: self-flagellation with them atoned for past sins, and was resorted to as a direct and immediate method of compensation.

We find many proofs that eastern Christians regarded flagellation in the light just mentioned: the following are a few instances related in their books. Gabriel, Archbishop of Philadelphia, gives this story in his work, entitled "A Collection of the Actions of Fathers or Saints:" —A certain saint had resolved to renounce the world, and fixed his abode on the celebrated mountain of Nitria in Thebaid; and next to the cell to which he had retired was that of another saint, whom he heard bitterly weeping for his sins. Finding himself unable to weep in the same manner, and heartily envying the happiness of the other saint, he one day addressed himself in the following terms:- "You do not cry, you wretch: you do not weep for your sins. I will make you cry; I will make you weep by force, since you will not do it of your own accord: I will make you grieve for your sins as you ought," saying which, he in his passion seized a large scourge that lay by him, and lashed himself so vigorously that he soon brought himself to that happy state which was the object of his ambition. Another author, Saint John Climax, in a passage which has given rise to much controversy, refers to the manner of the devotions of the eastern Christians. He says, "Some among the monks watered the pavement with their tears, while others who could not shed any beat themselves." Although some writers hold that this means religious disciplines performed in the same manner, and having the same end in view, as they now are in monasteries, the obvious meaning of the passage is, that the self flagellation mentioned was similar to that of the saint of the mountain of Nitria, and was inflicted to enable those who could not weep to weep plenteously. But western Christians, enjoying a wider field and greater opportunity for innovations, went much farther in their ideas of the usefulness of flagellation. They did indeed employ mortifications of this kind from the same idea as the eastern Christians—namely, with a view to sanctify themselves by their repentance, and assist their compunction—but they were also actuated by a sense of love for Jesus Christ and a desire of uniting themselves to him in his sufferings. This motive is urged in the statutes of different religious orders, where they are recommended, "when they inflict discipline upon themselves, to call to mind Jesus Christ, their most estimable Lord, fastened to the column, and to endeavour to experience a few of those excessive pains he was made to endure."

The main idea, however, of the Flagellants was to atone for past sins. It is no wonder that so convenient a practice, which enabled every one—by means of an operation of the duration and severity of which he was the sole judge—to pay an adequate price for every offence he might have committed, and silence a troublesome conscience, gained ground and favour, not only with the vulgar but also with the more enlightened part of the community. These notions of the expediency of self-flagellation were carried to a most extravagant pitch by the sect of the Flagellants. They looked upon the cruel disciplines inflicted on their bodies as being of far greater merit than the practice of any Christian virtue. Besides giving out that their whippings were specially commanded by Heaven, that one of their leaders was Elias, and another Enoch, they held such heretical doctrines as the following:- That the blood they shed during the flagellations was mixed with that of Jesus Christ; that self flagellation made confession useless; that they were more meritorious than martyrdom, for they were voluntary, which martyrdom was not; that baptism by water was of no use, as every true Christian must be baptised in his own blood; that flagellation could atone for all past and future offences, and supplied the want of all other good works. Against heretical tenets like these the true Church launched her anathemas, and on several occasions the

Flagellants were forced to seal their testimonies at the stake. "The modern brotherhoods of Flagellants (some of those alluded to) do not hold these extreme views, but dutifully subscribe to all the orthodox principles of the Church, and make it their chief business to discipline themselves in times of great solemnities; such as the Sundays in the Advent, the Sundays before Palm Sunday, Maundy Thursday, and certain days during the Carnival. They have their articles of association, like a freemason's lodge, possessing such property as banners, crucifixes, ornaments for altars, &c., and make a small annual payment to defray expenses. They march through the towns on high days, clothed in a peculiar dress, and wearing masks, and visit various churches. In the church from which they start, and in the others that they visit, they hear a short sermon from a priest on the passion of our Saviour; and as soon as the priest has said the words, "Let us mend and grow better" (*emendemus in melius*), the disciplines begin with the singing of the *Miserere*, and are continued as they walk along the streets. The fraternity is under the jurisdiction of the bishop, who examines and certifies the rules of the order."

When public opinion would no longer tolerate the appearance of the Flagellants on the streets and in the churches, the mania took the form of private whipping companies, and in cells and rooms with locked doors they belaboured the sinful flesh with infinite satisfaction. This was especially the case in Bavaria, which may be termed the classic land of the scourge. Scenes of the most outrageous and scandalous nature took place. We shall mention only one instance, and even here it is impossible to give more than the merest outline of the story, which made an extraordinary sensation, and terminated in a lawsuit.

A Capuchin in the convent of Duren, Father Achazius by name, through his sermons and confessional talk, exercised a great influence on the minds of the people. Forbidding in appearance, but gifted with eloquence of the most persuasive kind, his power over the female portion of his flock was unbounded. Widows and women of mature years were in particular devoted to him. Beginning with these, he soon inoculated others of younger years, for it was part of his instructions that they were to try and win over the young ladies of their acquaintance to elect him their spiritual adviser. His creed was: "Man, considered in and for himself, is incapable fully to tame the desires of the heart; but the spirit can continue virtuous, whilst the body, according to its usual desires, sins. The spirit belongs to God, the body to the world, yet the last itself represents both in its two parts: God speaks from the body to the superior part, the world to the inferior part: that which belongs to each must fall to it; therefore, to keep the soul pure, one must allow the body to continue to sin." It is easy to see where such a doctrine leads to. The father organised a regular Adamite Whipping Club, wherein many strange things were enacted: it is said that he performed the discipline himself, with rods steeped in vinegar and salt. After some years the proceedings of this society came to light, in consequence of the confession which a young nun—carried out of the convent—felt herself compelled to make, upon her marriage to a French officer. An examination was instituted, which continued for a long time, when it was found that the members of many respectable families were involved. One woman who was examined told an acquaintance, who expressed astonishment at her strange taste for such a hateful man as Achazius, that he had so entirely bewitched her that she was bound to him with infinite inclination, and submitted to everything like a child without will. With the consecrated rods he had beaten her so much that she was sometimes compelled, under one pretext or another, to keep her bed for three weeks. There were so many of these details, and others of an unmentionable nature, that the procurator-general was ordered to quash the whole proceedings. The only punishment that was inflicted on Father Achazius was close confinement in a convent. Afterwards the acts came before a court of justice at Liege, but the records have been destroyed or mutilated, through the influence of some families who wished to extirpate such memorials of their shame.

In Spain, as we noted in the preceding chapter, the ceremonies of the Flagellants were distinguished as being scenes of gallantry, as well as acts of devotion. An old writer thus describes the mania: "Lovers will often go at the head of a procession of friends, and discipline themselves under the windows of their mistresses; or, when passing the windows in a procession to which they belong, they redouble the smartness of their flagellation. All disciplinists shew attentions of the same kind to such ladies as they meet, especially if they are good-looking, and they try if possible to sprinkle them with a little blood in passing. The lady is expected to reward the devotee for this delicate and agreeable courtesy by raising her veil. It is somewhat difficult to imagine how the Spanish ladies can be pleased with this feat, unless it may be with ladies that the bare intention of showing them courtesy is enough to procure their good will; or we may suppose that the extreme gracefulness with which the disciplines we mention are performed has the power of rendering them pleasing to the ladies. There ought to be no doubt of the gracefulness of the performance, since in most towns the teaching of the art forms a separate branch of the fine arts, and the whole art and science of the operation may be acquired under a professional master, much the same as we have professors of the noble science of self-defence. Persons of all ranks and conditions in life became members of these brotherhoods."

CHAPTER XIV

CORNELIUS HADRIEN AND THE DISCIPLINA GYNOPYGICA

THE story of Hadrien and his whipping institution forms a remarkable episode in the history of flagellation, and sheds a flood of light over its mysteries, as an abuse of the original doctrine of penance. The main facts of his history and heresies, which are scattered through the records of the Netherlands Church, are well authenticated, and we give them, for the most part, according to the original.

Cornelius Hadrien was born at Dortrecht, in South Holland, about the year 1520, and, after the usual noviciate, was admitted into the Franciscan order. He was settled as Professor of Theology in a convent of that order at Bruges towards the year 1548. He was possessed of great eloquence, and soon became famous, especially among the fair and pious ladies of that city. Cornelius being no stranger to the sense of beauty, had cast his eyes with pleasure upon the many devout visitors of his confessional. As a writer, who was his contemporary, expresses, "he determined, in order to enjoy them and himself, to establish an entirely unique devotional order among them." The objects and character of this peculiar institution will appear from the sequel. In his sermons, Brother Cornelius touched freely on the sin of worldly lusts and their dire consequences, and by his insinuations awakened fears and scruples in the breasts of his fair hearers, till they naturally resorted to the confessional for counsel and instruction. Brother Cornelius was prepared with the necessary medicine. To those who were neither young nor particularly handsome, he prescribed that they should diligently confess their temptations to their former clergymen, in order to obtain from them absolution; but to those whom he wished to admit into his order he said, "In consideration that you cannot withstand such inward sins and desires, these must be chastened with an outward punishment and penance." They vowed to do all that he should impose upon them. After binding them by an oath to keep secret the penance to be suffered, because mere men of the world could not understand or appreciate such matters, and would assuredly try to bring disgrace and contempt upon the order, he appointed them a rule, in conformity with which they were required to appear before him in the confessional every month. Here they were to be particular in confessing to him all their unchaste thoughts, words, and actions, and these, he explained, could only be expiated by a course of private discipline and secret penance, applied and superintended by himself.

Hadrien cunningly arranged that these disciplines should take place in a house adjoining the convent, kept by a seamstress who possessed his confidence. When the devotees came for the first time to this house, the mistress gave them a rod, with the injunction to carry it into the discipline room; but at the same time to remember to bring one for themselves on the next occasion. When his penitents were assembled, Cornelius made his appearance, and, with serious countenance, announced that in order to receive the discipline properly, it was necessary for them to divest themselves of a portion of their clothes. This done, they humbly handed to him the rod, with which to chastise their sinful bodies. He accordingly did so, very slowly and very gently, enlarging at the same time on the efficacy of whipping, and the great benefit of receiving it in a primitive condition. The order embraced maidens, married women, and widows, and this secret gynopygic sect, as the Dutch writers named it, lasted for ten years without any of the devotees ever entertaining the least suspicion of its impropriety. They remained quite tranquil and happy, firmly believing in the piety of Cornelius, until a circumstance brought his peculiar style of discipline before the public, and led to the dissolution of the order.

Towards the year 1553, among the many hearers of Brother Cornelius was a virtuous and much esteemed widow, who took with her from time to time her handsome and amiable daughter, Caleken Peters, who was not more than sixteen years of age. Caleken soon became intimate with a number of young women who were under the authority of Brother Cornelius, and naturally enough, she heard much from them about obedience, submission, and private discipline. Curiosity led her to ask her companions what these things meant. They replied that Brother Cornelius was the only one who could give her the necessary information, and he would certainly be willing to inform her whenever she went to confess to him. In due time she went to confession, and at the first interview Brother Cornelius impressed upon her the necessity of being obedient to him, and teachable, if she desired to preserve her maiden purity, and desired her, if she obtained the consent of her mother, to visit him weekly, in order to receive the necessary instruction in holy obedience. Her mother gladly consented, and at the next interview Caleken promised, at his request, to confess faithfully even her most secret thoughts and wishes. After six or seven weeks' instruction, Brother Cornelius said that she must take an oath not to confess to any other priest, and that then she would be fit to come into the discipline chamber and undergo penance like the other maidens. The first visit to this sanctum was very unsatisfactory to Brother Cornelius. She either could not, or would not, make those revelations which the confessor desired, and he therefore dismissed her, with an admonition to be better prepared next time.

At a subsequent interview, in exhorting her to imitate the example of his other penitents, he asked her if it was in perfect seriousness that she confided to him her soul's health. She affirmed strongly that it was.

"Well, then," he continued, "if you trust your soul's welfare to me, you can with still less danger entrust your earthly perishable body to me; for if I am able to make your soul holy, I must, before everything else, make your body pure and capable of all virtue, devotedness, and penance. Is it not so, my child?"

"It is so, worthy father," she answered.

"Well, now," he replied, "it is necessary that you be submissive to me in holy obedience in the way shall tell you."

He then commanded her, in order to conquer that modesty which was a hindrance to holy discipline and penance to undress herself completely, and explained that it was impossible for her ever to become a perfect devotee without such self-humiliation, and it was the first means to accommodate herself to that holy and private discipline. Caleken proceeded to do so, but before her task was accomplished she fainted. The worthy father was prepared, however, for this contretemps and quickly recovered her with smelling essences. He then dismissed her, with the observation that it was enough for this time, and promised that on her next visit he would have some other young ladies there to shew her a good example. Accordingly, when she came again, two young women were with him, and they without hesitation complied with the father's requisition as to dress, and, kneeling over a cushion, very humbly received their discipline.

So matters went on for some months, during which period the initiated members of the order sedulously cultivated the friendship of Caleken, and exhorted her to entire obedience to Cornelius. Thus was her mind gradually corrupted until she had really something to confess, and the priest, delighted at the change, informed her that she was now in a fit and proper state to receive private discipline, and requested her to bring a rod with her when she came again, which she accordingly did, and with which she was flogged in the same retroussé fashion as the other young ladies.

In 1558 an incident occurred which awakened some doubt in Caleken's mind as to the worthy father's motives in this discipline. The older members of the chastising order held an anniversary meeting, at which Brother Cornelius was present. There was no lack of good cheer, of which Cornelius partook very freely, afterwards insisting on dancing with one of the young ladies, and otherwise conducting himself in a manner hardly becoming his profession. Caleken heard of it, and talked to some of her companions on the subject. She put the case to one: "Suppose that the father should give way to any human weakness while in the discipline-room, how am I to conduct myself?" The other replied that she herself would submit with all humility. Caleken

said, "As to myself, I am not so sure that my oath of obedience reach-
es so far." This came to the ears of the monk, who was very indignant.
When Caleken appeared before him, he demanded what she thought
of him. The maiden replied that she had no bad opinion of him, and,
completely disconcerted by his firmness, expressed herself thoroughly
convinced of the utility and necessity of the holy discipline. At last she
begged pardon for thinking evil of him, and before being absolved,
had to submit to the discipline and protest her confidence in him. In
order to guard against anything that she might say of him in future,
Cornelius induced her to sign a declaration stating that she knew
nothing of a private discipline. Caleken remained two years after that
observing her vow of obedience to Hadrien, and conducting herself as
a modest and virtuous maiden. Then her scruples returned, and she
asked the father one day for what particular reason this private discipline was so essential to salvation, and why, since so many other men
also upon earth sought salvation, they were not also disciplined in this
way?

Cornelius—"One cannot publish the holy discipline before the
world on account of the scandal and indignation which would arise
from it. The want of understanding of carnally minded men would
never comprehend the virtuous and the holy in it, but would rather
ridicule and make sport of it, like fools. It is the same with all the holy
mysteries that one sees daily. It is not wise to cast pearls before swine."

Caleken—"I see that well; but all scandal, anger, misunderstanding,
abuse, jesting, and ridicule of worldly men should not be taken into
account in opposition to the importance of the duty of making holy so
many human beings who sought salvation. One ought directly to
endeavour that these might be of no account also with these children
of the flesh."

Cornelius—"God is Almighty. He often predestines many men to
salvation through other means. In any case, however, private discipline
cannot become known to the world."

Caleken—"Worthy Father, I pray you, from the bottom of my
heart, do not take it ill, or scold me, if I trouble you further with questions."

Cornelius—"Continue to ask, my child, that I may set your mind at rest regarding everything."

Caleken—"If it be then possible that men can come to heaven also through other means than private discipline, then the latter is not so absolutely necessary to salvation as I, till this hour, have believed it to be."

Upon this the Franciscan became uncommonly perplexed; he looked strangely at the maiden, uncertain whether to become indignant or not. At last he again found words—

Cornelius—"Ah! That is a question! I call that wonderfully asked. It appears to me that you rather seek to begin strife with me than to receive counsel. However, I see, I must come to your help with a similitude. Suppose the city of Rome is the kingdom of heaven. A great multitude of people would like to journey to it, a considerable portion of whom take their way through a frightful wilderness where a thousand dangers from wild beasts threaten them: another part take a peculiar path, dangerous in its turn from highwaymen and bandits. A third part, to escape these dangers, choose a passage over a very high mountain, where they run the risk of falling down precipices or sinking in the snow. A fourth company take their way by the sea, and have to contend with its storms and dangers. At last they all alike come to Rome, not without great mutual surprise at the many calamities they have undergone. But now there is a little company who have discovered a secret path, and who have come to Rome without undergoing any toil or danger. Which way of all these would you, my daughter, now have rather trod?"

Caleken—"Certainly the last mentioned—the one without danger and without trouble."

Cornelius—"Aha! Do you now discover the application of my parable?"

Caleken—"Yes, Father."

Cornelius—"I thought that I could put your head right in this matter."

With this conversation the visit ended.

Yet, despite this assertion, Caleken was far from satisfied with the explanations of the monk. She searched the scriptures for some account of this concealed pathway to heaven. On her next visit to Cornelius she demanded his authority for the private discipline. He at first accused her of being a follower of Erasmus, and warned her against apostasy. He asked if it was not written in the 31st Psalm, Many whips or rods are for sinners; and does it not stand in the Holy Gospel, A servant who knows the Lord's will and does it not, shall receive many stripes? Caleken asked why he never mentioned the holy discipline in his public discourses. Cornelius replied, "Oh, when I stand in my pulpit I preach not for you, but for the men of the world, who merely follow the promptings of nature, and submit to the flesh, which, therefore, will be punished in purgatory with a multitude of blows, torments, and penalties, and so be cleansed and purified. But you, even in this life, by means of the holy private discipline, become so cleansed from your natural desires, that your purity remains internally preserved even whilst the external body sins. I therefore advise you, my child, to let all the sermons which I preach to the world in at one ear and out at the other. Torment not, therefore, yourself with cares, but fasten them to the ring of the church door when you leave the temple."

Caleken's doubts were by no means cleared away; and the monk then produced a number of Latin books on the subject of discipline, and read extracts from them. These only shocked and disgusted the maiden. Cornelius, now almost at his wit's end, resolved in this instance to chastise her in good earnest for her obstinacy; he commanded her by her oath to prepare to receive the discipline in the usual manner. She refused, and the father was at length obliged to dismiss her, giving her three weeks to consider the matter.

At the end of that time Caleken visited the Franciscan convent, and, not finding Cornelius there, resolved to ask counsel from the Governor himself. The Governor at first refused to have anything to do with Caleken, because he knew that Cornelius was her confessor; but after much hesitation he entered upon the subject and the result of the interview was that Caleken determined not to go near Father Cornelius again. Cornelius, finding that she did not come to him at the end of the three weeks, sent for her. She returned him her thanks, and said she would in future "chastise, punish, and impose penance" on herself without his assistance. He continued his importunities, so that Caleken was forced to pay him a final visit. After upbraiding her for her apostasy, he excommunicated her. Caleken, in no ways alarmed, denounced him as a deceiver and a hypocrite, and in fact gave him such a sermon, that in a transport of fury he seized her by the arm and pushed her to the door, crying out at the same time, "Away, away from this: I give you over to the devil!" Caleken went quietly home, lived a peaceful God-fearing life, and some time after was married. She did not publish the secret of Hadrien's manner of penance, as much out of consideration for the Franciscan convent as for her own honour and peace.

The secret was, however, made public in 1563 through another victim, and Caleken was brought before the magistrate to bear testimony in favour of her penance sister. In the society of Brother Cornelius was a woman named Betken Maes, who devoted herself to the care of the sick, and was famed for her virtue and piety. She made the acquaintance of an Augustine monk, who warned her against Cornelius, which warning coming to the ears of the latter, he immediately denounced Betken as a follower of Paul and Erasmus, and warned his flock to have no intercourse with her. Betken suffered in silence; but happening to attend a lady who was thought to be dying, this lady caused her attendant Betken to fetch a monk's hood, which she kept concealed, that she might breathe her last sigh in it. Betken inquiring the grounds of this strange request, discovered that the hood was a valuable present of Brother Cornelius, who informed the woman that, if she put on the same in the hour of death, she would have absolution of all her sins, and be spared the pains of purgatory. Betken sought to reason her out of this folly, but in vain; indeed, she rather irritated the sick one, who recovered instead of dying, and took the earliest opportunity of going to the Franciscan convent to see Cornelius. The father was very indignant at Betken's interference, and denounced her everywhere—in the confessional, in the pulpit, and in private—as a heretic. In the convent of the Carmelites, where Cornelius had a niece whom he visited, as well as the other nuns, he slandered her; and her friends refused to see her, and would no longer accept her service as a nurse. In this extremity she went to the provincial of the Augustines, and revealed the true cause of Hadrien's hatred to her, and also the secrets of the private discipline. The Augustine sent for Cornelius, and set before him the dangers to which he exposed himself if he did not make peace with Betken. He demanded a formal recantation of what had been said by him in the pulpit, the convent, and in private houses. In the pulpit Cornelius put the matter so obscurely that no one understood him, and in private houses things remained as before. After this he continued his opposition to Betken, who, as a last resource, took the following course: she related in several dwellings the deceptions of the monk, and the peculiarities of his penance plan. This soon spread, and the magistrates at length took up the matter, and summoned Betken Maes to give a full deposition of the secrets. The public were highly entertained with the private discipline, but even at this time it was still possible for Cornelius to have saved himself if he had gone properly to work, as the examination would have been completely suppressed— so many noble families being involved in it. Cornelius, however, continued to thunder against his accusers, and the examination went on. All women who were pointed out as members of the discipline company were obliged to appear before the magistrates in person for examination, and many distinguished ladies, young and old, were found concerned in it. Great was the shame in many families at the discovery of the disgrace of long years. Every one acknowledged their innocence, and the gross deceit of the monk, but that did not remove the blot of ridicule from those concerned, and the holy discipline was the subject of many squibs and pasquinades. Brother Cornelius was removed to an other convent at Ypres, where he remained a few years, and then returned again to Bruges. He explained to the simple Flemish that the story of his discipline was a slander of his enemies; he preached vigorously against the doctrines of the Reformation; and at last, in 1581, he breathed his last, in all the odour of sanctity.

CHAPTER XV

THE CELEBRATED CASE OF FATHER GIRARD AND MISS CADIÈRE.

THIS case, in addition to being one of the most famous in the annals of flagellation, affords at the same time an admirable exposé of that wonderfully lax morality and persevering cunning which was at one time held to be characteristic of the Jesuit order. The details of the case have been most minutely chronicled in more than one European language, but the particulars of the disciplines and other spiritual transactions that occurred between Father Girard and his pupil are much too gross for publication; we dare only venture, therefore, to lay one or two of the chief points of the case before our readers.

The biography of Miss Cadière during her earlier years presents nothing eventful, and may be summed up in a few words. Catherine Cadière, daughter of Joseph Cadière and Elizabeth Pomet, was born at Toulon on the 12th November, 1702. Her father died while she was a minor, leaving, besides Catherine, three sons. The widow was left in comfortable circumstances, and brought up her children in the fear of God. The eldest son married, the second entered the order of the Dominicans, and the third became a lay priest. The daughter was reared with great care, and as she advanced in years fully repaid the pains that had been taken with her education. Catherine became distinguished among her companions for her affectionate disposition, the

HENRY II SCOURGED AT THE ALTAR OF THOMAS À BECKETT.

St. EDMUND, Bishop of Canterbury, while studying at Paris, was tormented by a very beautiful young woman: summoning her to his study he administered such a flagellation that her body was covered with weals

purity and innocence of her spirit, and the beauty of her person. Several offers of marriage were made to her, which she refused, because her mind was wholly taken up with heavenly things. She was twenty-five years of age when, in April 1728, the Father Jesuit John Baptist Girard, received an appointment at Toulon. He had previously resided at Aix-la-Chapelle, from whence the fame of his eloquent preaching and his stern moral life had preceded him.

Girard at once became highly popular in Toulon, and crowds went to hear him preach, and to confess to him. Ladies of all ages unanimously adopted him as their confessor and spiritual adviser, a confidence which was in the highest degree pleasing to the holy father; but the young ladies of Toulon formed themselves into a kind of order for devotional exercises, of which Father Girard was appointed superintendent, and held forth the system of Molini to his pupils with a subtlety and impudence that did credit to his training. He set to work with great caution, and for a long time employed only ambiguous and mystical discourse, but gradually and imperceptibly, although surely, he led his fair penitents from the ordinary penance which he was accustomed to impose to the use of the discipline in the old established form. Before his persuasive eloquence, all doubts as to its propriety and usefulness soon gave way. A number of young ladies are mentioned as having entered fully into Father Girard's ideas on the matter of discipline; but the leader of the band appears to have been Miss Guiol, who, naturally clever and artful, seemed from the first to have had an intuitive perception of the holy father's designs. Father Girard found in her a kindred spirit; and thorough confidence being soon established between them, she was of great assistance in leading the younger and more inexperienced women into the trap. Girard administered the Rod personally to several of his lady disciples, holding a kind of whipping *soirée* at which many of them attended. The disciplines were at first administered in a most refined and modest way, but by-and-by the desires of Father Girard led him to impose the greatest chastisement for the most frivolous acts, while so infatuated were the fair penitents that the process of correction only increased their love and veneration for their confessor. Miss Cadière was among his pupils,

and being beautiful, interesting, and spirituelle, she very soon attracted the father's notice. He became completely fascinated with her
mental and bodily qualities, and resolved, if possible, to make her a
proselyte to his system of penance. Communicating his design to
Guiol, that lady, moved by his passionate pleadings, promised him her
support. His plan of operations was to manifest an extraordinary interest in the welfare of his novice: after inquiring in the most anxious
manner for her parents, and the health and well-being of her soul,
Girard then expatiated on the wonderful disposition she possessed,
and the great purposes which God designed to fulfil through her
instrumentality, and demanded that, in order to accomplish these
ends, she should resign herself entirely to his will. Miss Cadière
accepted the flattery, but still would not absolutely resign herself to
him. This system of "polite seduction," as it has been called, was carried on for a year, when one day Father Girard reproached her because
she had not sent for him during her illness. A tender kiss from the holy
father concluded the gentle chiding, and during the confession which
followed he inquired minutely into her inclinations, disposition, and
ideas. He recommended her to visit the different churches in the
town, to take the communion daily, and predicted that she would soon
see visions, of which he entreated to have full reports. This had the
desired effect: Catherine Cadière fell into a hysterical and mystical
condition, the image of Father Girard being ever in her mind. She
even declared her passion for him, bemoaning at the same time her
weakness. Father Girard calmed her by the following words: "Prayer
is only a means for God to accomplish. If man has once attained that
end, and is united to him, he no longer needs the same. The love
which so draws you to me should cause you no grief. By love, God
wills that we both should be united with each other. I carry you in my
bosom and in my heart. Henceforth you are nothing more than a soul
in me—yea, the soul of my soul. So let us therefore love each other
right ardently in the holy heart of Jesus." From this time all Girard's
letters to Miss Cadière closed with the words:- "I am united with you
in the holy heart of Jesus." Miss Cadière at length accepted the formula of submission which the holy father proposed: "I surrender

myself, I deliver myself up, I am prepared to say, to do, and to suffer, all that you may desire of me."

Father Girard not only ministered to the spiritual wants of his penitents, but provided for their bodily wants as well. He kept good servants and a well supplied table, besides contriving pleasure parties and other devices, in order to please his disciples. He amused himself with his older companion Guiol while awaiting the effects of his operations on the young Miss Cadière, who, in the meantime, suffered much in spirit. She was troubled with peculiar dreams, of which Father Girard was the chief hero, and at times she appeared to be possessed with an evil spirit, and uttered curses against the religion of Christ and the saints. Towards the end of 1730 these attacks became more frequent. Her brothers witnessed them, but on praying that she might recover, were continually cursed by her. It seemed to be suggested in her dreams that a peculiar spiritual union had been made between Father Girard and herself.

The friends of Miss Cadière, becoming alarmed about her health, consulted Girard, and the priest then obtained his long wished for opportunity: being allowed the *entrée* to the house of Cadière, he had frequent opportunities of being alone with the maiden. In order to avert any suspicion that might arise, he was accompanied to and from the door by the younger brother of Miss Cadière, who was then a student at the College of the Jesuits. The father improved his interviews by administering Cornelian disciplines on the naked person of his patient whenever she fell into one of these convulsions. Miss Cadière complained to Guiol, and even to the other sisters, that Father Girard had used such liberties with her, but they only laughed, and related how he conducted himself in a similar manner with them. He gave his pupil the discipline frequently. Miss Cadière had one of her remarkable visions during Lent of 1729: it was followed by a severe illness which confined her to a bedroom. Girard was of course frequent in his visits, and was particularly careful in examining certain stains of blood which, after this manifestation, appeared on her left side, as also on her hands and feet. One biographer remarks, that he was never tired of looking at these marks, especially those on the left side. The visions continued, and crucifixes were found as if they had dropped from heaven.

One day, Girard prophesied to his penitent that she would have a new and remarkable vision, and would be drawn up into the air. He alone was to witness this spiritual performance. At the appointed time Miss Cadière was in a refractory mood, and, in spite of the father's entreaties and commands, refused to quit hold of the chair on which she sat, and allow herself to be drawn up. The holy man threatened her with the fearful consequences of resisting spiritual influences, and finally left the room in a rage. Guiol was then sent to rebuke the penitent, and under her management she came into a calmer mood, asked pardon, and promised implicit obedience in future. This high handed behaviour was of course to be expiated only by a heavy penance. The next morning Father Girard came into her room, and pulling out a discipline, said, The justice of God demands that, because you have refused to allow yourself to be invested with his gifts, you should now undress yourself and be chastised; certainly you have deserved that the whole earth should be witnesses there of, yet the gracious God has permitted that only I and this wall, which cannot speak, remain as witnesses. However, beforehand, swear to me the oath of fidelity, that you will not betray the secret, for the discovery would plunge both me and you in ruin." Miss Cadière, as has been stated by more than one writer, submitted to the discipline as desired, and what followed must be left to the imagination of the reader. "*Concipe animo.*"

All this time the mother of Cadière was without the least suspicion of the holiness of Father Girard, and was even angry with her son when he hinted that there might be something wrong. It is impossible to give all the details of the intercourse that took place between Father Girard and Miss Cadière; the continual examination of the wounds, the bestowal of frequent kisses, and the infliction of the discipline, with or without ostensible cause, were only a part of the priest's system, and his other acts were, if possible, still more coarse and revolting. In order to provide against the consequences of this spiritual mystical union, Girard, under various pretexts, induced Miss Cadière to drink a potion which he had prepared, and although she became very weak, dissuaded her from submitting to a medical examination. He now determined that change was necessary, both for security and comfort, and with consummate address he arranged that Miss Cadière should become a nun in the convent at Ollioules, with acceptance to the Abbess, and full consent of her own relatives. She was, under these circumstances, favourably received at the convent, and for a fortnight thereafter Father Girard did not visit her. At the end of that time he had an interview with the Abbess, whom he persuaded to permit him to see, and to correspond with, Miss Cadière. Most of the letters written to her by him were afterwards destroyed, but those that have been preserved disclose the whole system of the most refined Molinism which this Jesuit had turned to the seduction of the unhappy creature. He also wrote during this period other letters of quite a different stamp, and these fell into the hands of the Abbess, and, as they were intended to do, convinced her of the purity of the worthy father's intention. Suspicions were however, awakened by his behaviour. He had the self assurance to inquire in the presence of the other nuns as to the physical condition of Miss Cadière, asking if she had lost much blood lately. One of his letters, threatening his pupil with the rod, administered by himself, "her dear father," fell into the hands of another man, and his visits were for a time prohibited, but through the mediation of a Capuchin father his privilege of visiting was restored. His infatuation increased. He again resorted to the examination of the wounds, administered the discipline after the old style, and would remain for hours at a time with his penitent. Miss Cadière herself sometimes boasted to the other nuns of her superior spiritual enjoyments. At one time she was confined in a cell, and the father only allowed to converse with her through an opening in the wall; but the priest's ingenuity overcame this difficulty: he persuaded his devotee to stretch her body out of the opening, and so receive the discipline! He would cause his food to be brought there, and the lay sisters frequently surprised the pair lovingly sharing the same.

The father, in time becoming tired of his spiritual daughter, determined to consign her to the Carthusian nunnery at Premole. The Bishop of Toulon, however, would not suffer this, and forbidding any further intercourse between the pair, he caused Miss Cadière to be conveyed to the country house of M. Pauque, near Toulon. Convinced that affairs were coming to a crisis, Girard sought, and through the intervention of Sister Gravier, an old pupil, obtained possession of all the letters written by him to Cadière, with the exception of one, which was not kept in the same box. The bishop having appointed the new Prior of the convent of the Carmelites at Toulon to be confessor to Miss Cadière, the secret of the coarse treachery, and wickedness of Father Girard was disclosed gradually, by means of the confessional, to the Prior. He immediately informed the Bishop, who, after hearing the whole series of abominable events, swore he would rid the country of the devouring wolf. Miss Cadière, on her knees, and with tears, entreated him not to make the matter public, and the Bishop at last promised to conceal the scandal. As he considered Miss Cadière to be still at times "possessed," he undertook to exorcise the evil spirit, and the maiden slowly recovered.

The Bishop soon repented of his resolution to hush up the scandal, and, acting on the advice of the Jesuit Father Sabatier, he suspended Father Girard, and appointed an ecclesiastical commission to investigate the whole matter. This commission was, from the first, prejudiced against Miss Cadière, and the inquiry was prosecuted with the design of exonerating Girard. The lady, conscious of her innocence, confessed everything, but, as was natural under the circumstances, in a very confused manner, and her adversary took every advantage of inaccuracies as to dates and other minute points. The spiritual court made out a strong case against Miss Cadière. The only letters produced were three to the Abbess at Ollioules, and two to Miss Cadière, and these did not in any way implicate Girard. Eight Jesuits were examined, and gave evidence favourable to their brother, and the nuns also shewed their devotion to the persecuted father. Miss Cadière was set down as a liar, a slanderer, and a traitor, and as one who had been bribed to injure the Jesuits. The matter next came before the High Court of Justiciary at Aix, and the Jesuits spared neither pains nor money to gain the case. More than one million of francs were spent by them for the defence. Girard now gave up certain letters which involved the Carmelite Prior and Miss Cadière's brother, and rendered them suspected of conspiracy. Miss Cadière at this time was treated as a condemned criminal, and confined in a noisome filthy room which had shortly before been tenanted by a madwoman. She was threatened, tortured, and annoyed in every possible way, till she at last retracted the accusation which she had made against Girard. Soldiers were placed in her room, and she was watched day and night. The court gave judgement against her, and she was consigned to a convent in the town. Appealing to a higher court, she pleaded that her original confession was true, and that the recantation she had signed was extorted from her through fear. The court could not agree as to their decision. Twelve voted that Father Girard had been guilty of great spiritual weakness, which had made him an object of scorn to the order, and that the complaint be dismissed. The other twelve voted that he should be condemned to death for incest, and an attempt to procure abortion, and for dishonouring his spiritual functions through shameful passions and crimes. The president declined to give a casting vote, ruling that both parties should be dismissed. One member having suggested that at least Miss Cadière should undergo some slight chastisement, another cried out, "We have but now acquitted probably one of the greatest criminals, and must we inflict even the slightest punishment on this maiden? Sooner ought we to set this palace in flames."

The trial had been productive of great excitement, and the popular feeling was strong in favour of Miss Cadière. Those who voted against Girard were received by the crowd with cheers and blessings, and Girard himself was assaulted with stones, and was with great difficulty rescued from the fury of the mob. He died about a year after, and many regarded his premature death as a special judgement for his crimes. The Jesuits proposed to canonise him, but we do not know that the proposal was carried out. Miss Cadière was treated with great kindness by numerous sympathising friends. She, however, soon after vanished from the scene of her suffering, and it remains unknown whether she went into exile, or ended her days in a convent. The popular opinion was that the Jesuits quietly and secretly removed her out of the way. Her beauty has been highly extolled by her contemporaries, and there is no reason to doubt that she possessed extraordinary personal attractions. Voltaire, in his usual profane manner, says—

"Cette belle voit Dieu; Girard voit cette belle;
 Ah! Girard est plus heureux qu'elle."

Another tragic story of this nature occurred shortly before the downfall of the Jesuits in France. A maiden of high rank was entrusted to the care of a Jesuit, a friend of her family, and she was shamefully abused after Father Girard's style. In this case the superiors of the holy father bribed a surgeon by costly presents to mutilate him, in order to shew that it was impossible for him to have committed the alleged acts. The exposure, however, hastened the ruin of the order.

A third affair, of a nature similar to the infamous Cadière case, full of shocking and disgraceful details is recorded in Gavin's "Passe-partout" as having occurred at Salamanca.

Plate X.   RELIGIOUS DISCIPLINE

1. CASTIGATION OF A PENTIENT. 2. DISCIPLINE PRACTISED BY THE JEWS

CHAPTER XVI

PENAL FLAGELLATION

FLAGELLATION, under the various names of whipping, scourging, and flogging, was, as has been shewn, a common punishment in ancient times, and it can easily be traced down through the annals of the Middle Ages till a comparatively recent period.

In our day the tide of public opinion has turned against the use of the Rod, and many hold that this mode of punishment ought not to be practised even in the interests of justice, as its tendency, they affirm, is to harden and debase the criminal. Besides its injurious moral effect, there are also physiological reasons why it should not be applied to women; the tissues of the body of the female are more vascular than those of the male, and consequently more liable to be permanently injured by application of the lash or rod. On the other hand, the supporters of flogging assert that the lash is the most appropriate and only efficient punishment for certain crimes; and with some natures, undoubtedly, the fear of receiving the lash is likely to have a more powerful influence than any other punishment. Although indiscriminate and injudicious flogging is bad, both in schools and prisons, the lessons of past ages and all experience shew that a judicious administration of the Rod is calculated to further the interests of virtue and good behaviour. For example, the birch might, with propriety, be introduced into many public establishments, and some aggravated offences in our workhouses might be punished and checked by whipping. We would not, however, advocate a return to the process of whipping the criminal through the streets at the cart tail; yet the sentences for robbery with violence and similar crimes are, as we know, usefully strengthened by the addition of a flogging to the usual imprisonment with hard labour. At present, however, there is a tendency to sacrifice justice to mercy, and to deal very gently with criminals, and it is a question whether this excessive tenderness towards that class may not in the course of time be followed by disastrous results. But, leaving argument, let us follow the course of flogging.

The Egyptians have immortalised the custom on their monuments and in their hieroglyphics. The Jews, as has been already mentioned, dealt out their constitutional number of stripes with a liberal hand, as appears from many passages of the Old Testament, such as Rehoboam's well-known answer to the deputation of the people, "My father hath chastised you with rods, but I will chastise you with scorpions." Without mentioning at present the whipping practices of Oriental nations, we proceed at once to observe that the system of flogging and whipping as a judicial punishment, so far as European nations are concerned, has been derived from the Roman law, Although the scourge was at times slightly in abeyance, it held a prominent place in the Roman courts; and later nations have signified approval by introducing it in their legislative enactments. While the mania for flagellation flourished in the monasteries (with what vigour our readers have already seen), running the gauntlet, and whipping with rods and ropes in prisons, or *sous la custode*, were everywhere of daily occurrence. The better classes were at times exempted from this punishment, but there are passages in the ordinances of Henry IV and Louis XIV where even noblemen were condemned to be publicly whipped. As an example, we may mention that Boniface, Marquis of Tuscany, father of the Countess Matilda, and by far the greatest prince in Italy, was flogged before the altar by an abbot for selling benefices, about the middle of the 11th century. Hallam says the offence was much more common than the punishment, but the two combined furnish a good specimen of the customs of the period. Other nations differ little in this respect. Throughout Europe soldiers ran the gauntlet, immoral women were whipped at the corners of streets, women and girls of less bad character were whipped in houses of correction or prisons, mostly on the lower part of the body; while in the galleys the culprits, naked to the loins, were frightfully flagellated with rods. In Holland culprits were put in the pillory, and scourged in the open market place with rods made of long broom, receiving thirty or sixty, and sometimes seventy, stripes on the bare back. It is only recently that the Dutch abolished the public whipping of women.

In Italy each district, province, and town, had at one time its own peculiar method of bodily chastisement. The Tuscan criminal code, published by the Duke of Tuscany in 1786, shews that, even at that date, whipping was much resorted to for the maintenance of law and order. The preamble of the edict sets forth that the legislator does not publish without due experience; but that, having by his sovereign authority mitigated all punishments for the twenty years he has reigned, he has found that crimes, instead of increasing, have remarkably diminished—the less very rarely happening, and the greater being totally unheard of. The edict then proceeds to abolish all capital punishments, branding, *strappado*, and all chastisements that mutilate; torture; confiscation of goods and forfeiture of estates; and finally, treasons of every kind, equalling them to crimes against individuals. It then proportions the following punishments to the nature of the crimes:- Trifling fines, in no case exceeding 300 crowns; private whipping; imprisonment, never to exceed a twelvemonth; banishment to a less or greater distance; pillory, without banishment; pillory, with banishment: public whipping; public whipping on an ass; for the women, confinement in the house of correction for one year and upwards; if for life, the substitute for death, the criminal to have a different dress, on which are to be sewed the words *ultimo supplizio*; for the men, condemnation to the public works of the mines of the Isle of Elba, the scoop boats of Leghorn, &c., from three years upwards; if for life, a different dress, like that for women, and, besides a ring to the leg, a double chain, naked feet, and employment of the most fatiguing kind.

The scourge, beating with sticks, and whipping with brooms, are the varieties of flagellation which the student finds in the older law books and the archives of judicial proceedings in Germany. Many abuses of the power of whipping took place in the houses of correction. In Germany and Switzerland the magistrates and judges had almost unlimited power in this matter; and, for the smallest offence, ordered unfortunate persons to be whipped or punished with a cane. There were towns in which they placed female offenders in an ingenious kind of machine, where they could not make the slightest movement, in order that the blows might fall all the more conveniently. One of these instruments may still be seen in the old prison at the Hague. In some instances female culprits were allowed to retain one garment, and the flagellation was performed by a woman; but in general the idea of making any such sacrifice to decency was scouted. Women were flogged by the dozen in the police courts of Holland, and the sight was considered so interesting that persons paid the officials to be allowed to witness it. In England whipping prevailed to a great extent. When servants were all serfs or slaves, as during the Anglo-Saxon period, flagellation was the common punishment for every offence; indeed, it was no unusual thing, as we can read in history, for servants to be scourged to death by order of their masters or mistresses.

The ecclesiastical canons, and the collections of local miracles, relate numerous instances of the cruel treatment to which female slaves were subjected, and early illuminated manuscripts give illustrations of the Saxon method of administering the Rod. In one we see the culprit being vigorously thrashed by two executioners. The patient, entirely naked, is tied by the feet, and each executioner is using a very small bundle of twigs or rods, apparently not more than three. In a picture in Alfric's version of Genesis, the man scourged, instead of being tied by the feet, is fixed by the body in a cloven post in a very singular manner. The Saxon ladies had no hesitation in occasionally applying the Rod to their women with their own hands. This aptness is well illustrated in a story which was told by William of Malmesbury. He says, when King Ethelred was a child he once so irritated his mother, that, not having a whip at hand, she beat him with some candles, which were the first thing that came to her hand, until he was almost insensible. In the "spacious times of great Elizabeth," the whipping-post was an established institution in every town and village. Taylor says:-

"In London, and within a mile, I ween,
There are of gaols or prisons full eighteen;
And sixty whipping-posts, and stocks and cages."

An old writer thus sums up the benefits of the whipping-post:- "If to put in execution the laws of the land be any service to the nation, which few I think will deny, the benefit of the whipping-post must be very apparent, as being a necessary instrument of such an execution. Indeed, the service it does to a country is inconceivable. I myself know a man, who had proceeded so far as to lay his hand upon a silver spoon with a design to make it his own, but upon looking round and seeing a whipping post in his way he desisted from the theft. Whether he suspected that the post would impeach him or not, I will not pretend to determine; some folks were of opinion that he was afraid of a *habeas corpus*. It is likewise an infallible remedy for all lewd and disorderly behaviour, which the chairman at sessions generally employs it to restrain; nor is it less beneficial to the honest part of mankind than the dishonest, for though it lies immediately in the high road to the gallows, it has stopped many an adventurous young man in his progress thither."

The municipal records of the time inform us that the executioner's remuneration for inflicting a whipping was fourpence a-head. In the corporation records of a town in Huntingdonshire there is an entry of eight shillings and six pence, being the charge for taking up a distracted woman, watching, and then whipping her the next day; and there is a further charge of two shillings to pay a nurse for her. The authorities of this town thought the lash a sort of universal specific, for they paid eightpence "to Thomas Hawkins for whipping two people that had the smallpox." We find one village paying fourpence "to a woman for whipping the said Ellen Shaw," and then, to prevent any disastrous consequences, expending threepence "for beare for her after she was whipped." By Statute 39 Elizabeth, chap. 4., it was enacted that every vagabond, &c., should be publicly whipped, and sent from parish to parish, by the officers thereof, to the parish where he or she was born; or if that was not known, then the parish where he or she dwelt by the space of one whole year before the punishment; and if that was not known, then to the parish through which he or she passed last without punishment. After which whipping, the same person was granted a testimonial, subscribed with the hand, and sealed with the seal of the said justice, &c., testifying that the said person had been punished according to the act. The act was confirmed and enlarged in the first year of James I's reign, but repealed in the reign of Queen Anne.

In the time of Charles I, flogging was a common sentence for such offences as came under the cognisance of the Star Chamber. A few extracts from the reports contained in Rushworth's "Historical Collection" may be of interest to the reader. In the third year of Charles' reign (commenced in 1625), Susan Boyes and Grace Tubby brought a complaint against the justices of the peace, because they had sent them to the House of Correction for light behaviour to be whipped there: by reason of which whipping they fell dangerously sick, and one of them was near death. Witnesses were offered to prove the too great severity of the whipping. One of the justices replied, that so far from appearing to suffer from the whipping, they drank a health to him, and craved a bell to be tolled in derision of the justices, and afterwards continued in their bold courses.

Joan Faulk, at the instigation of Tolwyn, brought a false accusation against Taylor, was convicted, and the sentence of the Star Chamber was that Tolwyn be fined £200, and be disqualified from sitting on a jury; that both parties be bound to good behaviour for life, and apologise to the plaintiff at the assizes; and that Joan be whipped.

Dorothy Blackburn, out of malice against Monk, who had arrested her husband for debt, intercepted two letters from Monk's attorney, and inserted some treasonable words in them, for which Monk was imprisoned and tortured in the Tower. She was convicted, and sentenced to be imprisoned during his Majesty's pleasure; to be disabled from being a witness; to be well whipped in the Palace-yard at

Westminster, standing on a high place, with a paper on her head, declaring her offence; to be branded on the face with the letters F. A. (false accuser); and to stand in like sort and be whipped at Leicester.

Richard Beck and Eleanor Beck were convicted of false accusation against Dalton and were sent to the House of Correction for three months, with hard labour, to be well whipped, and fined £40 each.

Travers, Frost, and Katherine Bampton, accused Dr. Peterson, Deacon of Exeter, of misconduct; and the Star Chamber found the charge false and malicious, and fined Travers £1000, and ordered him to ask forgiveness. Frost was fined £500, and set in the pillory at Exeter, with a paper on his head, declaring his offence. Katherine Bampton was committed to the Fleet: she was thence to be conveyed to the country to be well whipped at Colampton, and through the city of Exeter, and then to be committed to the House of Correction for a year, and to find security for good behaviour.

We could multiply these examples by numerous other quotations, but as they have all a family likeness, it is quite unnecessary to extend this chapter to greater length.

CHAPTER XVII

THE FLAGELLATION OF QUAKERS AND POLITICAL PERSONS.

THE punishment of flogging was not only awarded to vagrants and rogues, male and female, as the municipal accounts shew, but in the time of the persecutions directed against heretics it was sometimes applied to convert, or at any rate to punish, the obstinate. Owen Hopton, a lieutenant of the Tower of London, caused one of his prisoners, a young lady of respectable family, to be severely scourged, because he could not prevail on her to attend the public service of a church which she deemed heretical.

The tenets of the Quakers, when they first made their appearance, were particularly obnoxious to the church party, and "the Friends" in consequence suffered much in body. Sewell, in his history of the Quakers, relates many examples of the violent whippings to which the leaders and preachers of that sect were subjected. In 1654, one Barbara Blangdon was an advocate of the principles of the Society. She was taken before the mayor at Great Torrington, and the priest was very anxious that she should be whipped for a vagabond; the mayor, yielding to his entreaties, sent her to prison at Exeter, twenty miles distant, where she remained till the assizes were held. There she was tried, and sentenced to a whipping, which sentence was carried into effect imme-

THE SCOURGING OF TITUS OATES FROM NEWGATE TO TYBURN
—*From a Dutch print 1685*

A PUBLIC WHIPPING IN THE LONDON SESSIONS HOUSE YARD
—*From the Malefactor's Register, 1745*

diately in the presence of the sheriff, the executioner being a Beadle, who performed his duty so faithfully that the blood ran down the poor victim's back in perfect streams. She suffered the punishment very cheerfully, the spectators being much more affected than herself; and Barbara afterwards declared that she would not have been either terrified or dismayed although she had been whipt to death.

The same year two male preachers, named W. Caton and J. Stubs, were made to suffer in the flesh. In the course of their itinerant preaching they arrived at Maidstone, in Kent, where they were both arrested, and sent to the House of Correction, in which their money, ink horns, Bibles, &c., were taken from them. Afterwards they were stripped, and being made fast in the stocks, were desperately whipped. The historian adds, "A hard encounter, indeed, especially for such a young man as Caton was, but they were supported by an invisible Hand." In 1656 the mayor of Southampton, Peter Seal, took summary vengeance on a Quaker, named Rigg, who came to visit some of his friends in the prison at Southampton. The mayor dispensed with the formality of either examination or trial, had Rigg fastened to the whipping-post in the market place, and severely lashed by the executioner; then he was placed in a cart, and sent out of the town, being forbid to return under the penalty of being whipt again and branded on the shoulder with the letter R as a rogue. He did return, and the mayor would have punished him, but his brother magistrates would not consent; "and," says Sewell, "not long after the mayor died of a bloody flux." The Quakers likewise endured much persecution in New England, but their sufferings will be noticed when we come to describe whipping in America.

Whipping for political offences was very rife during the end of the 17th century. Judge Jeffreys flourished about this time, and was notorious for awarding cruel sentences. King Charles II said of him, "That man has no learning, no sense, no manners, and more impudence than ten carted street-walkers."

Jeffreys was educated at St. Paul's school, where he was occasionally flogged for idleness and insolence, and afterwards at Westminster school, under the celebrated Busby, who would no doubt have made

him well acquainted with the Rod. He took extreme delight in out-
raging the feelings of all who came before him, and gloated over the
sufferings which they were forced to endure. Thus, when he had a
chance of sentencing a woman to be whipped at the cart's tail, he
would say, "Hangman, I charge you to pay particular attention to this
lady! Scourge her soundly, man. Scourge her till her blood runs down!
It is Christmas, a cold time for madam to strip in! See that you warm
her shoulders thoroughly." When passing judgement on Lodowick
Muggleton, the drunken tailor who fancied himself a prophet,
"Impudent rogue," roared Jeffreys, "thou shall have an easy, easy, easy
punishment." One part of this "easy punishment" was the pillory, in
which the wretched fanatic was almost killed with brickbats.

In the year 1685, when Jeffreys was Lord Chief Justice, Titus Oates
underwent a whipping almost unprecedentedly severe. Titus Oates
was the son of an Anabaptist teacher; and, assuming holy orders, be
came chaplain on board a man of war, whence he was dismissed on
complaint of his having committed some horribly unnatural practices.
His after career was simply a course of villainy and perjury. It was
proved beyond all possibility of doubt that he had, by false testimony,
deliberately murdered several guiltless persons; but his time at length
came, and he was tried for perjury. The pictures of the period shew
him as a bull-necked, bandy-legged figure, with "forehead villainous
low," and purple bloated face. He stood his trial with great effrontery,
although bullied and reviled by the judges and witnesses. He was
found guilty on both indictments, and here is the sentence:- "To pay
on each indictment a fine of 1000 marks; to be stript of all his canonical habits; to be imprisoned for life; to stand in the pillory on the
following Monday with a paper on his head, declaring his crime; next
day to stand in the pillory at the Royal Exchange with the same
inscription; on the Wednesday to be whipped from Aldgate to
Newgate; on the Friday to be whipped from Newgate to Tyburn; upon
the 24h of April in every year during life to stand in the pillory at
Tyburn opposite the gallows; on the 9th of August in every year to
stand in the pillory opposite Westminster Hall gate; on the 10th of
August in every year to stand in the pillory at Charing Cross; and the

like on the following day at Temple Bar; to be continued on the 2nd
of September every year at the Royal Exchange;" the court expressing
deep regret that they could not do more, as they would "not have been
unwilling to have given judgement of death upon him."

There was no thought whatever of sparing the smallest detail of this
frightful sentence. King James, when appealed to, said, "He shall go
through with it if he has breath in his body," and the Queen would not
say a word in the criminal's favour. While standing in the pillory at
Westminster, Oates was mercilessly pelted, and nearly pulled to
pieces. On the morning of his first flogging, an immense crowd almost
blocked up the line of march from Aldgate to the Old Bailey; and the
hangman—according, no doubt, to instructions—laid on the lash with
such special vigour that the blood streamed down his body. The poor
wretch bore the infliction for a time without a murmur, but at last the
pain became too much for his endurance, and his cries became frightful. Swooning several times, and apparently half dead, the end of the
journey was at length reached. Forty-eight hours after he was again
brought out, but in a stupefied condition, and quite unable either to
stand or walk. He was dragged on a sledge the whole way from
Newgate to Tyburn, and, it is said, received seventeen hundred stripes
in the course of the journey. In Partridge's Almanack for 1692 it is stated that Oates was whipt with a whip of six thongs, and received 2, 256
lashes, amounting to 13, 536 stripes.

Contrary to all expectation, Oates survived the severe punishment,
and being set at liberty early in the next reign, he crept again into
some degree of favour.

Another "miscreant," as he was called, suffered a severe punishment
about this time, which terminated fatally, for being, like Oates, concerned in a popish plot. Dangerfield, we are told by Burnet, had gone
through all "shapes and practices of roguery," and in particular, that he
was a false coiner, who had undertaken to coin a plot to serve the ends
of the Papists. While in prison for debt, his mistress, one Cellier, a
Catholic midwife, procured his release, and introduced him to the
Countess of Powis, in concert with whom he tried to organise a plot
which came afterwards to be called the Meal-tub Plot. Causing

rumours of a revolution to be circulated, he fabricated, at the same time, a number of seditious letters, in order to implicate Colonel Mansel. The letters were discovered, but there being suspicions of their genuineness, Dangerfield's own papers were searched, and so the fraud was brought to light. Dangerfield, who was imprisoned, afterwards confessed his guilt, mixing up, however, much of his own invention with the truth. Five years afterwards, upon being tried for libel against the king, he was convicted and sentenced to be whipped from Aldgate to Newgate, and from Newgate to Tyburn. The wretched man, convinced that this whipping would be his death, made his last arrangements—among the rest, choosing a text for his funeral sermon. The first whipping having been inflicted, he was conveyed in a hackney coach back to the prison. On their way to Newgate, the officials stopped at Gray's Inn Coffee-house to give him a drink, at which place a Tory gentleman of the Inn, named Francis, said to him, "Well, friend, have you had your heat this morning?" Dangerfield's answer was a shower of curses, both loud and deep, at which Francis raised his cane, and struck him in the face, knocking out one of his eyes. This blow, and the whipping which he had endured, speedily put a period to Dangerfield's life; and Mr. Francis, who was so ready with his cane, being apprehended, was tried for murder, convicted, and shortly after hanged.

Whipping went on busily during Jeffreys' memorable and bloody campaign in the westcountry counties of England. When he could not convict prisoners of high treason, he sentenced them to be scourged for misdemeanours and indiscreet words. One woman was sentenced by him to be whipped through all the market towns in the county of Dorset, and suffered part of the punishment before Jeffreys returned to London. After Jeffreys had departed, the magistrates, being moved to mercy, remitted the remainder of the poor woman's sentence.

A mere lad, named Sutchin, was happily rescued from suffering still more severely for seditious words. The judge, as usual, interrupted the accused in his defence with much abuse, and finally sentenced him to be imprisoned for seven years, and during that time to be annually flogged through every market town is Dorsetshire. The audience were

horrified at the severity of the sentence. The clerk of the court ventured to remark to his lordship that the prisoner was very young, and
that as there were many market towns in the county, the sentence was
equal to a whipping once a fortnight for seven years. Jeffreys emphatically declared that the punishment was not half enough, and that he
would not alter it; whereupon the prisoner begged with great earnestness that he might rather be hanged. However, the boy fortunately
became ill of smallpox in the prison, and as he was not expected to
recover, the Chief Justice was induced by a heavy bribe to remit the
sentence. Sutchin recovered, however, and lived to be a most bitter
enemy of the house of Stuart.

Samuel Johnson, or, as he was sometimes called from a tract which
he wrote, "Julian" Johnson, became another victim to the merciless
flogging which was then an ordinary punishment for all political misdemeanours. Johnson was a priest of the Church of England, and had
been chaplain to Lord Russell. He was of a strictly moral and religious
character, but held, at the same time, extreme, republican opinions,
and during the previous reign had published a book called "Julian the
Apostate," controverting the doctrine of non-resistance. This work
provoked a controversy, and Johnson replied to his opponents by
drawing a parallel between Julian and James, then Duke of York. For
doing this he was prosecuted for libel but, not being able to pay the
fine imposed, was thrown into prison, and while there came in contact
with a man named Hugh Speke, who was also confined for a similar
offence. Speke, being of a base and depraved nature, whose very pastime was plotting and intrigue, soon perceived that Johnson would be
a capital tool for his machinations; and Johnson falling into the snare,
at Speke's instigation wrote a succession of violent treatises, which
Speke readily contrived to get printed and circulated. Finally, when
the camp was formed at Hounslow, Johnson wrote an address exciting
the troops to mutiny, which was widely disseminated among the soldiers. A subordinate agent, in order to protect himself, incriminated
Johnson, who, very honourably, did not think of betraying Speke. A
conviction being easily obtained, Johnson was sentenced to stand in
the pillory, and to be whipped from Newgate to Tyburn. When told

that he ought to thank the Attorney-General for this leniency, Johnson replied, "I owe him no thanks: am I, whose only crime is that I have defended the Church and the laws, to be grateful for being scourged like a dog, while popish scribblers are suffered daily to insult and to violate the laws with impunity?" To prove what he said he produced some Roman Catholic books and trinkets, which were at that time for sale under the royal patronage, and challenged the Court to do its duty by them. In addition to putting Johnson in the pillory, it was also resolved to degrade him from the priesthood, and the ceremony was duly performed before the Ecclesiastical Commission in the chapter house of St. Paul's Cathedral; at this Johnson, we are told, was much affected, especially when the Bible was taken out of his hands. An endeavour being vainly made to obtain a remission of the sentence of flogging, James is reported to have said, "Mr. Johnson has the spirit of a martyr; and it is fit that he should be one." Johnson endured the flogging with great fortitude, no less than three hundred and seventeen stripes being laid on with a whip of nine lashes. That he had indeed the spirit of a martyr was manifested in remarks which he afterwards made. He said the pain was cruel, but that, as he was dragged at the tail of the cart, he remembered how patiently the cross had been borne up Mount Calvary, and was so much supported by the thought that, but for the fear of incurring the suspicion of vain-glory, he would have sung psalms with as firm and cheerful a voice as if he had been worshipping God in a congregation.

A curious scene which occurred in the House of Commons in 1621, may be mentioned before going farther. Floyd, a Roman Catholic barrister, then lying in the Fleet prison by order of the Council, was accused of having rejoiced at the news of the battle of Prague. He denied the charge, but witnesses were called who proved to the House that the charge was correct. So heinous was this offence in the eyes of members of the House of Commons, that there was great difference of opinion as to what punishment ought to be awarded, each member proposing a more barbarous expedient than another. It was objected that the Lords might resent any interference with their prisoner, but that objection was laughed at. One proposed that Floyd should ride with his face to a horse's tail from Westminster to the Tower, bearing on his hat a paper with the inscription, "A popish wretch, that hath maliciously scandalised his Majesty's children," and that then he should be lodged in the cell called, appropriately enough, "Little Ease," as long as he was able to stand it. The majority, how ever, were in favour of making whipping an essential part of the punishment. "Let him be flogged to the place from whence he came, and then let him be left to the Lords," said one. "Let his beads be hung about his neck, and let him have as many lashes as he has beads," said another. A whipping in the pillory at Westminster was a third suggestion. But these proposals were not severe enough for some. Let him be twice pilloried, and twice whipped; cut out his tongue, chop off his ears, and slit his nose; make him then swallow his beads, and afterwards brand him in the forehead; whip him twice as far as those who offended against the ambassador. These were among the chief proposals. Only one or two members were on the side of mercy. The future keeper of Charles I held that the evidence was not sufficient, and another member said the real cause of Floyd's offence was the difference of religion. If his religion was touched he would be regarded as a martyr, and, besides, it was not proper to whip a gentleman. They finally sentenced Floyd to be pilloried three times, to ride from station to station on a bare-backed horse, with his face to the tail, and an inscription on his hat explaining the nature of his offence. Lastly, he was to pay a fine of £1000. The King was asked to confirm the sentence, but he declined to interfere, and left the matter to the Lords. This did not mend the unfortunate gentleman's position, for they, after discussing the question of jurisdiction, whether the House of Commons had a right to proceed, shewed their good will to the Papists by raising Floyd's fine from.£1000 to £5000. They further declared him an infamous person, whose testimony was never to be received in any court of justice, ordered him to be imprisoned for life, and to be whipped at the cart's tail from London Bridge to Westminster Hall; but the King, at the urgent request of the Prince of Wales, remitted the whipping.

Cowper, in a letter to his friend, John Newton, relates a droll incident which he witnessed at Olney. A young fellow, having been caught thieving, was ordered to be flogged through the town. As he performed this penal pilgrimage at the cart's tail, the ruddy stripes upon his back stirred the compassion, while the fortitude with which he bore them excited the admiration, of the spectators. But it turned out that it was all an imposition on the public. The Beadle, who was the executioner, wielded his whip with the utmost tenderness, and before every stroke drew the lash through his left hand, which was filled with red ochre, so that when he applied it to the culprit's skin it left an imprint like a bleeding gash. A constable detecting the deceit, applied his cane in an earnest manner to the shoulders of the Beadle, by way of exhorting him to do his duty. A country lass, pitying the pitiful Beadle, assailed the pitiless constable. "Thus the Beadle thrashed the thief, the constable the Beadle, and the lady the constable, and the thief was the only person concerned who suffered nothing."

Another very curious fact in connection with flogging at the cart's tail is related in an old magazine. A young man sentenced, for some slight misdemeanour, to be whipped through the streets of Glasgow, proved on being stripped to be a female! She was identified at the time, by a mark on her shoulder, to be the daughter of a highly respectable merchant, who had ran away from her home at an early age, and been lost sight of for a great many years. After leaving home, she made her way to Port Glasgow, and became cabin boy in a West Indian sugar vessel. As her uncle was a town councillor at the time, she was pardoned the public exposure by the Lord Provost of the period, on condition of submitting to be whipt by the matron of the gaol.

The last whipping through the streets of Glasgow by the hangman took place on the 8th of May, 1822. On that day, at twelve o'clock, a strong detachment of the 4th Dragoon Guards paraded in front of the gaol, and at the same time a large party of police and civil officers attended under the direction of the superintendent of police. Soon afterwards the culprit, a man sentenced to be flogged at the cart's tail for assisting and encouraging a riot, was brought out of the gaol by the north door, and bound to the cart which was in waiting. Parties of the dragoons were placed in front and rear to keep off the crowd; and when all was ready, the cavalcade moved round to the area on the south side of the gaol, where the culprit's back was laid bare by the hangman, who then gave him his first twenty lashes with a formidable cat-o'-nine-tails. The like punishment was repeated at the foot of the Stockwell, and also at the head of the Stockwell; but the last twenty lashes—making eighty in all—were given by Thomas Young, the hangman, at the crowded Cross of Glasgow: the prisoner all the time groaning and lamenting his fate. "This example," says a commentator, "had the most salutary effect: it taught the mob that there was a power over them after all; and there was an end of rioting."

CHASTISING A QUAKER AT ST. PAUL'S CROSS CHEAPSIDE, IN THE
TIME OF CROMWELL

CHAPTER XVIII

THE WHIPPING OF THIEVES AND GARROTTERS.

WHIPPING was at one time the penalty for thieving as well as "vagabondism and sedition."

We gather from a calendar of prisoners tried at the Old Bailey in December 1689, that Mary Lamb, indicted for stealing a silver spoon, value nine shillings, from William Story of St. Martins-in-the-Fields, with whom she was a servant, was found guilty of theft to the value of 10d.; and that Jane Peel, servant, indicted for stealing money and jewellery to the value of between £30 and £40, was also found guilty of theft to the value of 10d., along with Hannah Basset, who was indicted for stealing some cloth of the value of £4, and likewise found guilty of theft to the value of 10d., were all sentenced to be flogged. The first mentioned was ordered to be whipped from Newgate to Holborn Bars, and the other two from Newgate to Aldgate. In the calendar for the next year, 1690, at the same court, we find one Jane Symson, alias Bibbey, sentenced to be whipped from Newgate to Holborn Bars for stealing various articles from the house of Mr. Todd, her master. Part of the goods were found upon her, and she was at once found guilty to the value of 10d. This restriction of value to the small sum of 10d. saved thieves from being convicted of a capital offence

Here is a curious whipping, or rather no whipping anecdote,

extracted from Vol. 86 of the Gentleman's Magazine:- The Lord Mayor having lately committed to the House of Correction a working sugar baker, for leaving his employment, in consequence of a dispute respecting wages, and the man not having during his confinement received any personal correction, conforming to the statute, in consequence of no order to that effect being specified in the warrant of committal, he actually brought an action against the Lord Mayor in the Court of Common Pleas for nonconformity to the law, as he had received no whipping during his confinement. The jury were obliged to give a farthing damages, but the point of law was reserved.

The law for the whipping of women continued in force till the present century. The public infliction of the punishment was abolished by Statute 57 Geo.III, c. 75, in 1817; and three years afterwards they were exempted from private whipping by the Statute 1 Geo.IV, c. 57, in 1820. The recent Acts under which the punishment of whipping is to be inflicted are the Garrotters' Act and the Juvenile Offenders' Act.

A few years ago, in order to try and put a check on crimes of violence, an Act was passed whereby the judge might at discretion, add flogging to a sentence of imprisonment or penal servitude, but, so far as we are aware, this discretionary power has been very sparingly used. The first instance of such punishment occurred at Leeds, where two garrotters, named Thomas Beaumont, 47 years of age, and Michael Ginty, 26 years of age, before entering on their respective five and ten years' terms of penal servitude, were compelled to receive each twenty-five lashes with a cat-o'-nine-tails.

Modern flogging is no longer an ambulant punishment performed at the cart's tail from street to street, but takes place within the walls of the gaol, and before a very limited audience. In this case, the spectators were the gaol officials, the visiting justices, the reporters of the public press, and the refractory prisoners, on whom it was hoped the spectacle would have a beneficial influence. The performers were two strong warders, and the instrument was a new "cat," direct from the Home Office, specially made for the castigation of garrotters. It consisted of a long handle with nine cords about a yard long, decorated with knots, and twisted hard as wire at the ends - an instrument, in fact, which was sure to make the stoutest ruffian quail. Beaumont was first fastened up to a sort of triangle erected in the middle of the prison. He was firmly bound by the arms and legs, and his neck was protected from the blows of the "cat" by a leathern strap, the whole of his back being of course, bared. Each warder administered a dozen stripes, and we were told in the newspapers that the culprit, after the first blow, groaned and writhed as if in great agony, and was taken down very much exhausted. His skin was of a bright purple colour, and covered over with long weals, although no blood was drawn, at the end of the first dozen. His companion was then fixed up in a similar manner. After the first stroke he yelled fearfully and struggled so violently that he required to be held. The first flogging lasted one minute and a half, and the second two minutes. In due time several other sentences of flogging were carried out at the same gaol. John Edwards, aged 36, Solomon Robinson, 19, and Joseph Robinson, were Convicted of garrotting; and, in addition to the sentence of penal servitude which was passed upon them, they were each ordered to receive twenty-five lashes. The exhibition came off under similar circumstances to those already mentioned. Edwards was first brought to the post. He howled and struggled fearfully, trying to pull down the triangle to which he was fastened. Joseph Robinson also cried out and appealed for mercy in a piteous manner, but he was made to endure the full number of stripes. Solomon Robinson took his punishment "like a man," almost without a murmur. The cries of the flagellated convicts continued after they had been conveyed to their cells, and seemed to indicate that they experienced but little relief from the surgical applications which the doctor applied to their wounded backs.

Newcastle Gaol was the scene of a flogging inflicted on three miners who had been convicted of robbery and violence. The details of this performance are not so complete, because the gentlemen of the press were not allowed to "assist," the Governor of the gaol informing them that the visiting justices, having considered the Act of Parliament, were of opinion that the only persons entitled to witness the execution were the prison officials and the medical men appointed as judges. We learn, however, that the criminals were in succession fastened to a pillar, and received eighteen lashes on the naked back with an ordinary "cat" borrowed for the occasion, and were then handed over to the doctor. Two men, named Hart and Cooke, tried at Chester assizes for robbery, were sentenced to penal servitude and flogging—fifteen lashes for Hart, and twenty for Cooke. Hart was in such terror that he cried while being fastened up, and continued to yell and shout until the due number of stripes had been laid on. His companion in crime, after witnessing the flogging in a very uneasy way, had then to take his own twenty. He cried out at the first stroke of the cat. Both were taken to their cells pale and exhausted, more, perhaps, from fear than actual pain.

By powers contained in an Act known as "The Juvenile Male Offenders' Act," passed in 1862, magistrates are empowered to inflict a summary whipping on boys under the age of fourteen. Little can be said as yet concerning the working of this Act, but we can give at least one instance where it appears to have been somewhat harshly put in force. From a return presented to the House of Commons, we learn that a child, only six years of age, received twelve lashes from a birch rod, with seven days' hard labour, for taking a pocket-knife. The Act is exceedingly precise: it gives full instructions concerning the instrument to be used, and prescribes the number of strokes to be given. For offenders under fourteen years of age the stripes are to be applied on the breech, to the number of twelve, with a birch rod: above fourteen years, the instrument may be either a leather taws or a birch rod, and the number of stripes must not exceed three dozen, applied to the aforesaid very fleshy and exceedingly sensitive part of the body. The rods and taws must be made subject to the approval of the sheriff of the county, and that functionary must also approve of the person who inflicts the punishment. The whipping, which is required to be sufficiently severe to cause a repetition of it to be greatly dreaded, is to be witnessed by the Governor of the prison and the surgeon. It is the duty of the surgeon to examine the prisoner before the punishment, and if he considers that the criminal is unfit to suffer the prescribed number of stripes, without detriment to his health, he may restrict the number, and if he thinks the prisoner cannot stand half the punishment, then the whole must be remitted. During punishment the surgeon has a discretionary power to stop it whenever he sees fit. When the offender is sentenced to a whipping without imprisonment, the same must be inflicted not later than the day after the prisoner is taken to the prison, unless the surgeon thinks it necessary to delay it. If the whipping is not inflicted within ten days, the offender is entitled to his discharge without being flogged. When the criminal has to undergo imprisonment, he can get his whipping at any convenient time during his incarceration in the prison. It is further recommended that, in order to provide against the contingency of the offender being deemed unfit for corporal punishment, the sentence should contain an alternative of some other punishment, depending on that contingency.

STROUD, THE NOTORIOUS CHEAT, WHIPPED AT THE CART'S-TAIL FROM
CHARING CROSS TO WHITEHALL.
—From a Rare Print of the Reign of Queen Anne

CHAPTER XIX

PENAL AND CHURCH FLAGELLATION IN SCOTLAND.

SCOTLAND—although the historical records of that country cannot boast of such distinguished political offenders as Oates and Dangerfield—was by no means behind England in the use of whipping as a punishment during the 17th and 18th centuries. At one time, indeed, the scourge was not only employed to punish offenders, but was also used for the far more questionable purpose of extracting evidence against persons who were accused of offences.

We have discovered more than one instance of whipping witnesses, as the following notable case of legal procedure will shew:- In 1596, John, Master of Orkney, was tried for the alleged crime of attempting to destroy the life of his brother, the Earl of Orkney, first by witchcraft, and secondly by more direct means. The witchcraft was established by a confession drawn from a woman named Alison Balfour, who had been executed for that supposed crime in 1594 The counsel for the Master detailed the process of extorting this confession. When the poor woman confessed, she had been already forty eight hours in the *cushielaws*, an instrument of torture, consisting of an iron case for the leg, to which fire was gradually applied till it became insupportable. Her husband, an old man of ninety-one, her eldest son and daughter, were kept in torture in the mean time, that the sight of their sufferings might aggravate her own. The old man was in the *lang irons*, the son in the *boots*, and the daughter in the *pilniewinks*, all instruments designed to give the most excruciating torture. Another confession was extorted from Thomas Palpla. This unfortunate person, after "being kept in the *cushielaws* eleven days and eleven nights, twice in the day, by the space of fourteen days callit (driven) in the boots, he being naked in the meantime, and scourgit with tows (ropes) in sic sort that they left neither hide nor flesh upon him," confessed that he had conspired with the Master to poison his brother.

Traces of this mode of refreshing the memory are to be found in various annals of a much later date. At the trial of Archibald Stewart and Charles Gordon for housebreaking, at the High Court of Justiciary in Edinburgh in 1785, some sheriff-officers were examined as witnesses with reference to the depositions of the accused. One man, named Middleton, said "*some admonition* had been given to Stewart to extort the truth." Being pressed to explain what this "admonition" was, he said that, when persons accused of crimes not capital were brought before his court to be examined, in case they refused to confess their guilt, the practice was to order the culprits to be carried into a separate apartment, where they were scourged by the common hangman at the sight of an officer of court till they became willing to confess the truth; that Fraser, an accomplice in this robbery, was flogged in the presence of Stewart till he confessed; and the witness and the hangman were proceeding to admonish Stewart for the same purpose, when he saved them the trouble by making confession, just as the whip was going to be applied.

The Solicitor-General declared that he never suspected the existence of such a practice, and pledged himself that it should not exist a day longer. Sheriff Cockburn, who was absent from Edinburgh at the time of the trial, denied that it was a general practice in the investigation of crimes for all persons under accusations, not capital, to be flogged into confession, and afterwards condemned upon such confession. The real circumstances of the case, according to the Sheriff, were these:- From the great number of boys in the city who committed crimes, but who from their youth were not amenable to public trial and punishment, it was the practice, after repeated transgressions, sometimes to order them a private chastisement, and dismiss them. Stewart and Fraser had been repeatedly taken up as thieves and pick-pockets, and were both banished in 1784. They were again taken up for housebreaking, and Fraser was on that occasion ordered a private chastisement, and then dismissed. Stewart was let off without a whipping; he did not see Fraser get his beating; and there was no deposition taken from them at the time.

The criminal annals of Scotland during the 17th and 18th centuries present some exceedingly curious examples of whipping. In 1630 the Town Council of Edinburgh issued an order forbidding the wearing of plaids by women on the streets, under pain of corporal punishment. The Scottish plaid being used to cover the face, it was supposed by the magistrates to afford protection to immodest conduct. The order seems to have been ineffectual, for in 1636 the use of this disguise was found to have increased rather than diminished, and it was then resolved to try the effect of heavy fines. About that period the influence of the clergy was very great. The minister of a parish and his kirk session formed a legislative body, acted as public censors of morality, and passed laws, to which the people were bound to submit with humility and repentance. Whoever fell under their ban was liable to be imprisoned, to be fined or to be whipped, to be branded with a hot iron, or to do penance before the whole congregation, humbling themselves bare footed, and with their hair cut on one side, while the minister stood by and lectured severely on the unfortunate individual's offence.

We have culled from various authors examples of these punishments. Wodrow, date 1635, makes mention of a correction-house, to which the session ordains persons to be taken, both men and women, and appoints them to be whipped every day during the session's will. On the 22nd of October 1648, the kirk session of Dunfermline ordered that a certain Janet Robertson "Shall be cartit and scourged through the town, and markit with a hot iron." In "Presbytery Displayed" occurs the following:- "As they punish by pecuniary fines, so corporally too, by imprisoning the persons of the delinquents; using them disgracefully; carting them through cities; making them stand in jouges, as they call pillories (an iron collar put around an offender's neck and attached to a wall or post, which in the country churches are fixed to the two sides of the main door of the parish church); cutting the halfe of their hair; shaving their beards, &c.; and it is more than ordinary by their original and proper power to banish them out of the bounds and limits of the parish or presbytery, as they list to order it."

For scandal-exciting persons there was likewise the "cutty stool" or the stool of repentance, where the culprit had to sit in full view of the congregation, for three successive Sundays, during the time of public worship. The Rev. Mr. Dysart, parish minister of Coldingham, was a stern upholder of church discipline. One of his first acts on being placed was to set up a seat for scandalous persons to sit on when they appeared before the congregation; and where every lapse of virtue had to be duly expiated by exposure and rebuke. In the course of sixteen years, he and his session held 1169 meetings, being at the rate of about one and a-half every week, at which the private affairs of members' of the congregation were reviewed and investigated by the session, which made periodical visitations among the people. As a sample of their vigilance, here is one report.—"In William Spur's house there were Gavin Dale, in this parish, and John Dale, in the parish of Ayton, his brother, in time of divine service, at drink: and being reproved by the elders for misspending the Lord's day, Gavin answered that their kirk (meaning the meeting-house set up and kept up in contempt of the Government) was but just "scaled" (dismissed), and that they were but refreshing themselves. Elizabeth Cockburn, wife to William Spur, expressed her concernedness to the elders that such a thing had fallen out in her house, and promised to the elders never again to do the like. The session, considering the wickedness of the persons, and the disadvantage they (the session) are under by the said meeting-house, by which they fortify themselves against censure, concluded to pass this, and to accept of the promise aforesaid from the woman, who seemed to be grieved for the offence. "Sitting on the stool of repentance was no joke, and the operation was seldom relieved by any display of humour; but on one occasion a preacher is said to have ventured a pun. A woman named Ann Cantly being made to do penance, "Here," said the minister, "here is one upon the stool of repentance. They call her *Cantly:* she saith herself she is an honest woman, but I trow scantly."

In the time of James VI there was an act passed against perturbers of the kirk; and by it, tumults in kirk-yards were punished by confiscation of the offenders' movables. In the case of children and minors, the offenders were "only" to be scourged. The attempt to establish

Episcopacy in Scotland became a signal for many acts of cruelty and oppression. After the appointment of Sharpe to the archbishopric of St. Andrews, a Court of Ecclesiastical Commission was established, which filled the prisons, and when they would hold no more, the victims were transported to the West Indies. A case in point is narrated by Crookshanks in his "History of the Church of Scotland." He says: "The treatment of some of the parishioners of Ancrum is not to be omitted. When their excellent minister, Mr. Livingstone, was taken from them, one Mr. James Scot, who was under a sentence of excommunication, was presented to that charge. On the day fixed for his settlement, several people did meet to oppose it; and particularly, a country woman, desiring to speak with him, in order to dissuade him from intruding himself upon a reclaiming people, pulled him by the cloak, entreating him to hear her a little: whereupon he turned and beat her with his staff. This provoked two or three boys to throw a few stones, which neither touched him nor any of his company. However, it was presently looked upon as treasonable tumult; and therefore the sheriff and justices of the peace in that bounds fined and imprisoned some of these people, which, one would think, might atone for a crime of this nature. But the High Commission, not thinking that sufficient, ordered those criminals to be brought before them. Accordingly, four boys and this woman, with two brothers of hers, of the name of Turnbull, were brought prisoners to Edinburgh. The four boys confessed that upon Scot's beating the woman, they had each thrown a stone. The Commissioner told them that hanging was too good for them. However, the sentence of this merciless court was, that they should be scourged through the city of Edinburgh, burnt in the face with a hot iron, and then be sold as slaves to Barbadoes. The boys endured their punishment like men and Christians, to the admiration of multitudes. The two brothers were banished to Virginia; and the woman was ordered to be whipped through the town of Jedburgh. Burnet, Bishop of Glasgow, when applied to that she might be spared, lest she should be with child, mildly answered, "That he would make them claw the itch out of her shoulders."

The two following notes are from the kirk session records of

Dunfermline:-"22nd October 1648.—That day compeirit Jonet Robertson; she wellowing in her former filthiness and prophanitie;—it is ordanit that she shall be cartit and scourgit throw the toun, and markit with ane hote yron, and so banished furth of the Paroch." "27th December, 1653.—This day compeirit (before the session) Margaret Robertson, spous to William Scotland, and Catherine Westwood, spous to James——, who being fund guiltie of cursing and scolding and oftymes before censured by the Kirk are now recomendit to the magistrates to be corporalie punished as they shall think fitt and as their faultes deserve."

Crimes arising from irregularities of the affections were severely dealt with. Mackenzie states that the punishment of adultery was arbitrary: it might be either banishment, whipping, fine, or imprisonment—and discusses the question whether, by the same laws, the magistrate might not inflict the punishment of death. In 1642 one Redpath, a tinker, was scourged; in 1666 there was a case where the punishment was a fine; and in 1668 an Englishwoman was banished for this crime. We are told that in the case of Redpath, the tinker, he was only scourged, banished, and burnt upon the cheek, although the case was an aggravated one, because tinkers, as a class, are rather loose in their habits, and are seldom lawfully married, and even when they are married, have an absurd custom of living promiscuously, and considering wives to be "a sort of common property." At a later date, a tailor in Currie was condemned to be beheaded for wedding his first wife's half-brother' s daughter.

About 1692 a woman of bad fame, named Margaret Paterson, was found guilty of debauching two very young men, the sons of a minister of Trinity College Church, and was sentenced to stand an hour in the jougs then to be scourged from the Castle Hill to the Nether Bow, and thereafter to be sent to the plantations for life. The two men, however, forfeited their bail of five thousand marks, rather than stand trial with their associate in guilt. Their uncle petitioned for a modification of the penalty, as it was a very hard case, their entire patrimony being involved, and the Court of Justiciary recommended the Lords of the Treasury to mitigate the penalty if they saw fit.

The laws of Scotland were equally severe in other respects. Blasphemy was punishable by death. The punishment for perjury was banishment, and fustigation or scourging. Vagabonds, and those who fled from their master's service, were appointed to be burnt in the ear and scourged for the first fault, and to suffer death for the second: a thief might of course be hanged. If a thief was taken with bread worth a farthing upon him—from one farthing to four, he might be scourged; for four farthings, he might be put in the jougs and banished; from four to eight farthings, he might lose an ear, and if the same thief was afterwards taken with eight pennies he should be hanged; and a thief taken with thirty-two pennies and a farthing, as a first offence, might be hanged. The punishment for "fire raising" by the civil law was various, and suitable to the several degrees of that crime: raisers of fire within a town were burnt alive; those who set fire to corn, as well as houses, were bound and beaten, and then burnt "but not burnt quick."

CHAPTER XX

FLAGELLATION IN SCOTLAND (*continued*).

A FEW additional examples of flagellation will bring us down to the time when whipping at the cart's tail was abolished, and will place before the mind more clearly the nature of the offences for which whipping was deemed a suitable and sufficient punishment.

In 1692 a great number of recruits were collected to be sent out to Flanders; but a considerable delay took place in finding transport vessels for them. So many deserted during this time, that a proclamation was issued on the subject in 1694, setting forth certain pains and penalties for the crime of desertion, and those who aided and abetted it. A Glasgow schoolmaster, John M'Lachlan, who was charged before the Privy Council with having induced a number of the soldiers to desert, was tried, found guilty, and sentenced to be whipped through the city of Edinburgh, and banished to the American plantations. The sentence was subsequently commuted to an hour in the pillories of Glasgow and Edinburgh, under the care of the hangman, with a paper on his brow setting forth, "John M'Lachlan, schoolmaster at Glasgow, appointed to be set on the pillory at Edinburgh and Glasgow, and sent to the plantations, for seducing and debauching soldiers to run away from their colours and desert their majesties' service." A further prosecution was recommended on account of "disloyal and impertinent speeches uttered by him when he stood in the pillory at Edinburgh." This was not carried out, however, in consequence of his being liberated because of bad health and the destitution of his family.

A singular case came before the Court of Justiciary in the beginning
of the year 1700. Some months previously a boy named John Douglas,
son of Douglas of Dornock, attending the school of Moffat, was beat-
en to death by the master, Mr. Robert Carmichael, who thereupon
fled, and kept out of the way for some weeks, "but," as the narrative
piously puts it, "by the providence of God, Carmichael was discovered
and seized." The indictment charged him with beating and dragging
the boy, and giving him three lashings without intermission, so that he
never spoke afterwards and was carried dying, if not dead, out of the
school. The punishment awarded to the schoolmaster was, appropriately enough, a severe scourging. The judges decreed that Mr. Robert
Carmichael "be taken from the Tolbooth of Edinburgh by the hangman, under a sure guard, to the middle of the Lawnmarket, and there
lashed by seven severe stripes; then to be carried down to the cross,
and there severely lashed by six sharp stripes; and then to be carried to
the Fountain Well to be severely lashed by five stripes; and then to be
carried back by the hangman to the Tolbooth: Like as the Lords banish the said Mr. Robert Carmichael furth of this kingdom, never to
return thereto under all the highest pains." The penalty for returning
from banishment was usually a whipping.

In 1747 the Lords of Session sentenced William Stevenson,
younger of Dykes, a forger, to stand in the pillory and then to be transported to America for life. He duly did penance in the pillory, and was
sent to the plantations, but taking the liberty of revisiting his native
land a few years after, he was discovered, and condemned to twelve
months' imprisonment, during which he got fresh air and a whipping
at the cart's tail through the streets of Edinburgh on the first
Wednesday of every month, and at the end of the year was sent back
to America. At the spring circuit in 1752 David Goodwillie was tried
for theft and forgery, and sentenced to be whipped through Cupar of
Fife, and thereafter to be sent to America for life. The circuit court
held at Aberdeen in 1749 sentenced the servant of a travelling show-
man to a whipping through the streets of that city, for the crime of
rape. At Stirling, in the summer of 1746, occurred a whipping not

exactly in terms of the statutes. Lieutenant Stoyt of the Regiment of Old Buffs, then stationed in the garrison, employed William Pollock, a barber in Stirling, to make a wig for him. The lieutenant refused to take the wig because it did not suit him, and the man who brought it muttered some insolent words as he went away. The lieutenant, rushing after the barber, and catching him at his master's shop, gave him a good beating, and other officers coming to assist, treated Pollock himself in the same way. Not satisfied with this, they carried off the man and informed Lieutenant-Colonel Howard of the matter, who *sans cérémonie* ordered the unfortunate barber's man to be stripped, tied to the halberts, and whipped by a drummer of the regiment. The magistrates being informed of the affair, desired that the man should be handed over to them, and they would see justice done; but the lieutenant colonel said he had taken the matter into his own hands, and would have his own way. Ultimately the barber's man gained his liberty, but not till his back was severely cut by the stripes. Information was then given to the Court of Justiciary at the instance of the barber, Mr. Pollock, his man Maiben, and the magistrates of Stirling, charging Lieutenant Stoyt as guilty of hame-sucken against Pollock and Maiben, and Lieutenant-Colonel Howard and Lieutenant Neilson of a barbarous and cruel abuse of Maiben's person, in a most ignominious manner, and of a manifest invasion of the office of the magistracy, and of the rights and liberties of the subject: and therefore craving a warrant for apprehending their persons and imprisoning them till they should underlie the law. The Lords remitted to the Sheriff of Stirling to investigate the matter; but, as the regiment left Stirling shortly after, nothing more was heard of the affair.

James Forbes, Chaplain and Schoolmaster to the charity workhouse of Dalkeith, was committed to prison in Edinburgh, and put on trial at the High Court, in 1758, for debauching some of the young girls under his care. The libel detailed the most wicked lewdness, and the prisoner on his apprehension partly admitted his guilt. The court sentenced him to be whipped through Dalkeith, and then through Edinburgh, and afterwards to be transported to the plantations for life. William Brown, at one time a servant, and afterwards a soldier in the

49th Regiment, was tried at Aberdeen, in 1771, for fraud and imposition, in obtaining money by means of forged letters. The jury
unanimously found him guilty, and he was sentenced to be whipped to
the number of fifty lashes, at the cross of Aberdeen, and then to be
banished for life. Next year at Ayr, James Cassie, a soldier, and two
women were tried for theft and receipt of theft, and found guilty. The
sentence was that Cassie should be whipped through the streets of Ayr,
and the two women should attend at the ceremony with their heads
bare and their hair tied behind; and that they all be banished for life,
with the addition of three years' servitude in the plantations.

A very imposing whipping took place the same year at Edinburgh.
On the 23rd of August 1772, at the High Court of Justiciary, William
Anderson, James Paul, and William Welsh, were tried for encouraging and calling together the mob which, on the 7th of June, attacked
the Canonmills Distillery. The first two were found guilty: and they
were sentenced to be publicly whipped through the streets of
Edinburgh by the common hangman, on the 8th of September, and
thereafter to be banished to one or other of His Majesty's plantations
for fourteen years, and their service adjudged for seven years, with cer-
tification if they shall be found in Scotland during that period they
should be whipped, imprisoned, and again banished. The whipping
accordingly came off in terms of the sentence on the 8th of September,
when more ceremony was used than is generally observed on such
occasions. Fifty of the military of the Castle led the way, followed by
the Lord Provost and magistrates, with white rods in their hands.
Then came the officers of the trained bands, constables, fire masters,
&c. The prisoners, attended by the city guard and town officers, followed; and fifty soldiers closed the procession. In 1807 Archibald
Begg, joiner—who was tried in 1803, and sentenced to be banished
from Scotland for fourteen years, for lifting dead bodies from church-
yards—was whipped through the streets of Edinburgh for returning
from banishment. Begg was very roughly handled by the populace on
returning to prison. On Friday, 21st October 1808, a woman was
placed in the pillory at Haddington in pursuance of a sentence of the
sheriff-depute, for stealing money from her master: and the next week,

three carters belonging to Edinburgh were publicly whipped through the streets of Haddington for a cruel and unprovoked assault on the toll-keeper at Drem, and a further attack on a millmaster. Haddington has been the scene of many floggings. We witnessed the flogging of a man at the cart's tail there in the year 1832. In the ancient records of the burgh such entries as the following are quite common:—"23 Jan 1536.—The Asy. hes fild Jok Greg and Howme of Pikre, and ordains thaim to be banist the towne and scourgit, and evir thai cum in it to be hangit; of the quhilk the bailzes tuk an act." "10 Dec. 1538.—The Assyss ordains Howm to be bundyn at the erss of ane cart, and to gang trow all the streittis of the town, and the lockman to stryik him with ane vand, and that the servands se that he execut his office on him, and to haif ane freshe vand at ylk streit end, and to forsweir the towne, and obliss him to be hangit by the sheriff and ever he cum in the towne again."

Many curious instances of flagellation might be selected from the public records of Edinburgh and other large towns in Scotland; but some of these we have already given. Sentences of flagellation by the Scottish magistrates have all a family likeness, as a few instances will shew. In Edinburgh, on the 30th of April 1736, Elizabeth Hodge, found guilty of theft, was sentenced "to be carried to the House of Correction, there to remain till the 16th day of June next; thence to be carried to the Weigh-house, and from that place to be whipt through the town by the common hangman, and to receive at each of the usual places three stripes upon her naked shoulders." Henry Henderson, a vagrant, was sentenced to be whipped on the 18th of May 1737, for rambling the streets at untimeous hours; he was ordained to be taken out of the Tolbooth, between the hours of ten and twelve, and carried to the Weigh-house, and there to be stripped naked, and, by the hands of the common hangman, to receive on his naked shoulders five stripes at each of the ordinary places. The flogging of "common whores" was an almost every-day occurrence; and we also find that some of them were drummed through the town at the sight of the common hangman. Common prostitutes and thieves were at one time marked in Edinburgh by a piece being taken out of their nose. Colin Rhind, mason, was found guilty by the magistrates of Edinburgh, and whipt on the 20th of April 1739, for opening a grave in the West Kirkyard, and taking out Mary Stewart's corpse; he was sentenced "to be carried to the Cross, there and at the Cowhead Well, West Port, and at the end of Portburgh, to receive on his naked shoulders three stripes." Besides these public flagellations, there was a great deal of private whipping in Edinburgh. On a demand being made by some of the city officials for a perquisite of five shillings for each private whipping, it was resolved by the magistrates to inquire into that matter, as the demand amounted to "a pretty considerable sum."

In Edinburgh the whipping course lay down the High Street, stopping at various points according to the circumstances of the crime. The last whipping that took place in the streets of Edinburgh is worthy of being detailed at some length. Edinburgh was at that time infested with a gang of housebreakers, who had with impunity carried on their depredations for a considerable time. One night a most daring burglary was committed in the house of a member of the town council. The master and mistress were awakened by the noise, but the robbers gagged and bound them, and carried off all the money and valuables they could find. The lady of the house had, however, recognised one of the band as a young man who was engaged to be married to her daughter in a few days; and as soon as the morning dawned, she hastened to the authorities and denounced him, notwithstanding his intended relation to her family. The officers of justice proceeded to his mother's house in the Lawnmarket, and apprehended the young man, who was immediately thereafter brought to trial for housebreaking. The lady, of course, swore that he was one of the robbers, and her testimony was strengthened by the evidence of an old servant, who stated that she had often to rise and let him into his mother's house at all hours of the morning.

The young man was sentenced to be flogged at the cart's tail by the common hangman, and the very day that had been appointed for his marriage witnessed his whipping. At an early hour the crowd began to block up the street; twelve o'clock was the hour appointed for the culprit to endure his flogging, but long before that time, from the city

Weigh-house to John Knox's corner, there was not an inch of standing room to be had, so great was the crowd which turned out to witness the spectacle. Jock Heich, the hangman, who officiated on the occasion, had got a new whip, which the cripple wretch cracked in the Tolbooth with savage joy, as he stood impatiently waiting for the coming of his victim. Jock Heich was the very stuff that hangmen are made of: he seemed to have been born for the trade, and to glory in being on the gallows or in officiating at the cart tail, and a fiendish smile of satisfaction, it is said, lurked about his mouth as he operated, in the name of the law, upon his fellow mortals.

The criminal alluded to was a tall young man, apparently about twenty years of age, with fair hair, and no appearance of a beard upon his smooth face. The cart to which he was tied was a common one, bired by order of the authorities for the nonce, from among a number that were standing in the Lawn market. The moment the young man was placed in the hands of Jock Heich, the active functionary lost no time in making him strip and fastening him to the back of the cart, and when the pure white skin of his naked back was exhibited to the gaze of the crowd, on which a brilliant sun was shining, many were the expressions of sympathy that were heard in the vast multitude. The magistrates took their places, and a number of the town guard, armed with their long Lochaber axes, closed around. The rat-tat of the town drum was soon heard. It was beat to drown the yells of the sufferer, as Jock Heich with hearty will and strong arm began his work. Blood followed at the second stroke, and the offender, uttering a piercing shriek, cast a long and wistful glance away down towards the Nether Bow, where he was to receive the last instalment of his punishment, while groans and screams from women and children testified to the emotion of the crowd. The Lord Provost and magistrates were apprehensive of a riot, for opinion was very much divided as to the justice of the sentence. Such seemed likely to be the case when the slow plodding procession reached the cross. Here a lighted squib, that was thrown from a window, fell at the horse's feet, and hissed and cracked as the fiery sparks flew from it. The frightened animal started and reared, and then in its terror fell on the street on its side with the shafts of the cart above it. When the shafts thus fell forward and downward, the criminal, from the manner in which he was fastened to the cart, was lifted off his feet, and suspended in the air by the cords that bound him, the red blood all the time streaming down his back. A man, who was apparently a leader among the people, called on the hangman to loose the prisoner, and when the executioner shewed no signs of doing so, he cut the ropes himself, and set the criminal on his feet. The mob cheered the act, but the huzzahs were soon changed into groans and hisses, when they saw the hangman seize the prisoner, lest the crowd should carry him off before the full complement of lashes had been laid on his lacerated back. They indeed seemed quite in the mood for doing so, and a disturbance was imminent. A few words from the captain, however, allayed the tumult; and the cart being put to rights, the criminal was again tied up to endure the remainder of his punishment, the last stroke of which was given at the Nether Bow.

The story has a still more tragic side. The prisoner's home was, as we have said, in the Lawnmarket, and the yells of his frantic mother were heard by the people in the street, as her neighbours fought with her to keep her back from the window when the cart was passing; but ere it had reached the end of the weary journey, the poor woman's senses had fled: the sound of that whip made her a hopeless maniac for the rest of her days.

In the "Life of Colonel Jack," Defoe has a most unique description of a flogging in Edinburgh. Premising that the colonel and his friend the captain have come to that city to follow their profession of thieving, we shall allow the colonel to tell his own story:- "We went out for a walk, and coming through a gate that they call the Nether Bow, into the great High Street, which went up to the Cross, we were surprised to see it thronged with an infinite number of people. Then we came to the Market Cross, and there, besides the great number of people who passed and re-passed, we saw a great parade or kind of meeting, like an exchange of gentlemen, of all ranks and qualities. It was while we were looking and wondering at what we saw there that we were surprised with a sight which we little expected; we observed the people running on a sudden as to see some strange thing just coming along, and strange it was indeed: for we saw two men, naked from the waist upwards, run by us as swift as the wind, and we imagined nothing but that it was two men running a race for some mighty wager; of a sudden we found two long small ropes or lines, which hung down at first pulled straight, and the two racers stopped, and stood still one close by the other; we could not imagine what this meant, but the reader may judge at our surprise when we found a man follow after, who had the ends of both those lines in his hands, and who, when he came up to them, gave each of them two frightful lashes with a wire whip or lash which he held in the other hand; and then the two poor naked wretches ran on again so the length of their line or tether, where they waited for the like salutation; and in this manner they danced the length of the whole street, which is about half-a-mile. This was a dark prospect to my captain, and put him in mind, not only of what he was to expect if he made a slip in the way of his profession in this place, but also of what he had suffered when he was but a boy, at the famous place called Bridewell. But this was not all, for, as we saw the execution, so we were curious to examine into the crime too; and we asked a young fellow who stood near us what the two men had done for which they suffered that punishment. The fellow, an unhappy ill-natured Scotchman, perceiving by our speech that we were Englishmen, and by our question that we were strangers, told us, with a malicious wit, that they were two Englishmen, and that they were whipped so for picking pockets and other petty thieveries, and that they were afterwards to be sent away over the border into England. Now, this was every word of it false, and was only formed by his nimble invention to insult us as Englishmen; for when we inquired further they were both Scotchmen, and were thus scourged for the usual offences for which we give the like punishment in England; and the man who held the line and scourged them was the city hangman, who (by the way) is there an officer of note, has a constant salary, and is a man of substance; and not only so, but a most dexterous fellow in his office, and makes a great deal of money by his employment."

One of the last public whippings of a female offender took place at

Inverness in 1817—the year that public whipping was abolished. The *Scots Magazine* of the period gave the following notice of it:- "A woman of the name of Grant was flogged through the streets of Inverness, we understand, for the third time (once the previous week), for intoxication and bad behaviour in the streets. No doubt example is necessary, and was here made with the best intention: yet public flagellation on the naked body of a woman is revolting to all our ideas of decency and humanity; and we doubt whether such a disgraceful exhibition is calculated to amend our morals; on the unfortunate object in question (a young and handsome woman), the hardened indifference and audacity with which she bore and ridiculed the punishment shewed that it failed of that effect."

CHAPTER XXI

WHIPPING IN BRIDEWELL AND OTHER PRISONS

TAYLOR says —

"I think a gaol a school of virtue is,
A house of study and of contemplation:
A place of discipline and reformation."

But this was scarcely Smollett's opinion of the ancient Bridewell. He makes one of his female characters say that it, of all the scenes on earth, approached nearest to her notion of the infernal regions. In the midst of scenes of rage, anguish, and impiety, and sounds of groans and curses, the prisoner was set to perform impossible tasks, and was whipped for her incapacity. She was often whipped into a swoon, and then lashed out of it, to find that her fellow prisoners had robbed her of her clothing. Rendered desperate by the misery of her condition, the poor wretch delineated by Smollett attempted one night to commit suicide, and being detected, the attempt was punished next morning with thirty stripes.

The City Bridewell, London, from which Houses of Correction in general acquired the name of "Bridewells," was originally a palace, and was chartered to the City of London by Edward VI as a place of penal confinement for unruly apprentices, sturdy beggars, and other disorderly persons. It formerly contained a portrait of the donor with these lines—

"This Edward of fair memory, the Sixt,
In whom with greatness goodness was commixt,
Gave this Bridewell, a palace in olden times.
For a chastening house of vagrant crimes."

The gift was made in the year 1553, at the request of Bishop Ridley, who begged it as a workhouse for the poor, and a house of correction "for the strumpet and idle person, for the rioter that consumeth all, and for the vagabond that will abide in no place."

The regular whippings in Bridewell were for offences committed outwith the prison, although the prisoners were also caned or scourged by the warders if their appointed task of beating hemp was not duly performed to the satisfaction of the overseer. Unchaste women (at least those of that class who had made themselves conspicuous by rioting and brawling, or were found in the company of thieves and highwaymen) and dishonest knaves of either sex were taken before the magistrates and committed to Bridewell for so many days or weeks. They were kept till noon on board day, when the court of governors held their usual sitting. On the appointed day the culprit was brought by the blue-coated Beadles into the large room where sat the governors. The accusation being stated, the board at once gave decision, which was generally to the effect that the prisoner should be corrected on the spot, in presence of the governors. The Beadles seized the unfortunate one, and prepared her at once for flagellation by stripping the clothes off her back. The whip was wielded by the youngest Beadle, and the stripes were laid on until the president thought proper to give a signal to stop, by striking with his hammer on the table before him. When a woman was under the lash in Bridewell the cry, "O good Sir Robert, knock! Pray good Sir Robert, knock!" was loud and frequent; and outside the prison such a cry was quite common among the lower orders as a reproach to women who had been whipped in Bridewell. After her flogging the criminal was handed over to the officials of the prison, to pass her term of imprisonment in beating hemp. The fourth plate of Hogarth's series of pictures, illustrating the Harlot's Progress, as is well known, is a view of the interior of Bridewell. Men and women are beating hemp under the eye of a savage taskmaster, and a lad, too idle to work, is seen standing on tip-toe to reach the stocks, in which his hands are fixed, while over his head is written, "Better to work than stand thus."

A good story, apropos of Bridewell, is related of Madam Creswell, a noted procuress of the time of King Charles II She had been often whipped, and ultimately died a prisoner in Bridewell, and left a will in which she desired to have a sermon preached at her funeal, for which the preacher was to have £10; but upon this express condition that he was to say nothing but what was well of her. After a sermon on the general subject of mortality, the preacher concluded by saying, "By the will of the deceased it is expected that I should mention her, and say nothing but what is well of her. All that I shall say of her therefore is this: She was born well, she lived well, and she died well; for she was born with the name of Creswell, she lived in Clerkenwell, and she died in Bridewell."

The whipping of prostitutes in Bridewell was at one time considered an interesting and entertaining sight. It was quite the fashion, indeed, to make up parties to go and see the flagellating spectacle on the Wednesdays, the day when the inmates of that abode were "had up" before the court of Governors. A "tip" in the proper quarter would no doubt admit distinguished visitors to the instructive scene. But many such shows, although the culprits were not so often of the softer sex, were to be witnessed on the streets without fee or favour—now a pickpocket yelling under a pump, and now a half-naked wretch dancing along at the tail of a slow plodding cart, and howling dolorously under the lash of the hangman's whip.

Defoe, in his "Life of Colonel Jack," gives a minute and circumstantial account of correction in Bridewell. One of the personages of his story, when a mere lad, belonged to a horrid gang who kidnapped children and sent them to America. The gang being captured and imprisoned in Newgate, the hero of the story says: "What punishment was inflicted upon the rogues of that gang I cannot tell now, but the captain, being but a lad, was ordered to be three times soundly whipt

at Bridewell, my lord mayor or the recorder telling him it was done
out of pity to him to keep him from the gallows, not forgetting to tell
him that he had a hanging look, and bid him have a care on that very
account: so remarkable was the captain's countenance even so young,
and which he heard of afterwards on many occasions. When he was in
Bridewell I heard of his misfortune, and the major and I went to see
him, for this was the first news we heard of what became of him. The
very day that we went he was called out to be corrected, as they call it,
according to his sentence; and as it was ordered to be done soundly,
so, indeed, they were true to the sentence: for the alderman, who was
the president of Bridewell, and who, I think, they called Sir William
Turner, held preaching to him about how young he was, and what a
pity it was such a youth should come to be hanged, and a great deal
more, how he should take warning by it, and how wicked a thing it was
that they should steal away innocent children, and the like; and all this
while the man with a blue badge on lashed him most unmercifully, for
he was not to leave off his thrashing untill after Sir William knocked
with a little hammer on the table. The poor captain stamped and
danced, and roared out like a mad boy; and I must confess I was fright-
ed almost to death: for though I could not come near enough, being
but a poor boy, to see how he was handled, yet I saw him afterwards
with his back all wealed with the lashes, and in several places bloody,
and I thought I should have died with the sight of it; but I grew better
acquainted with those things afterwards. I did what I could to comfort
the poor captain when I got leave to come to him. But the worst was
not over with him, for he was to have two more such prolonged whippings before they had done with him; and, indeed they scourged him
so severely that they made him sick of the kidnapping trade for a great
while."

     While such flagellation went on within the walls of Bridewell, pub-
lic whipping was also being constantly performed at the cart's tail. The
common and mildest pilgrimages in London were from Newgate to
Ludgate and from Charing Cross to Westminster; but extraordinary
criminals bent beneath the lash all the way from Newgate to Charing
Cross. There were plenty of posts and kennels on the sides of the

street along the route, and the hangman gave the poor wretch a lash at every kennel the rear wheel of the cart grated against.

Flogging with the birch and the cane are among the punishments meted out to delinquents in modern reformatories—the cane was used for correction of minor offences, and the birch for runaways, or such boys as are caught making preparations for running away. Mr. Blanchard Jerrold has described one or two punishments which he witnessed at the Feltham Reformatory for Boys. He says: "The corporal punishments are administered by a tall muscular drill-master, who has, I believe, been in the army. The frequency of entries in the punishment book shews that his muscle is not seldom brought into requisition. Strokes on the hand, or a dozen with the birch, meet many offences, as ' very gross insubordination, ' and altering blouses with a view to absconding. I witnessed three canings and two birchings. For the birching the boy was stripped, stretched out upon a table, and forcibly held down by two or three men, while the drill-master gave him the allotted number of strokes with a long birch, and with great severity. When a delinquent was given a caning, the big drill-master made the cane whistle through the air as it descended onto the boy's hand, and the boy in his agony ' writhed like a cut worm.'"

From the want of statistics we have not the means of knowing how far these public and private prison scourgings proved effective in diminishing crime, but we are in possession of a well authenticated instance of a person who was publicly flogged rising to eminence. James Macrae entered on public life by being whipt through the streets of Ayr. Macrae was a lad of spirit, and was always in some scrape or another, but why he was flogged is not now known; probably it was for orchard breaking or some such boyish offence. He was so ashamed of his punishment, however, that he disappeared from his native land, and was not heard of for many a long year, until he came back to his native land as governor of Madras! Having enlisted as a private soldier, he had risen by his own bravery to be a field officer, and returned home to Scotland with a very large fortune.

Flogging went on about the dates mentioned in all the prisons of the United Kingdom, and so did whipping at the cart's tail.

Magistrates of burghs and county justices took a good deal upon them
when sitting in judgement. A worthy Scottish magistrate of whom we
have read prescribed flogging with the taws for all juvenile offences,
and without any very formal trial or leading of evidence, ordered disorderly lads and lasses to be summarily corrected after the domestic
fashion of the time. This gentleman was not particular as to the age of
the culprits. On one occasion a young woman whom he had ordered
to be flogged tried to get off on the plea of being married.

"Married! Are ye married?" exclaimed the Bailie.

"Yes, Sir, I am." said the woman.

"Then it's the mair a shame that ye're here this day. Skelp her weel;
be sure to skelp her weel," added his honour to the gaoler.

On the continent of Europe whipping was common at the same
periods, both sexes being whipped in the prisons of Germany and
Italy. Indeed, it is only of recent date that whipping in prison was abolished throughout Fatherland. At one time every inmate person was
flogged both on entering and leaving prison! In some of the gaols the
whipping instruments, and other paraphernalia of punishment, are
exhibited to visitors.

An anecdote of the flogging of a servant in Holland derives some
point from the innocence of the victim. She had been accused and
found guilty of robbing her mistress, proofs of the theft, placed there
by her mistress, being found in her trunk. She was flogged, brand
marked, and confined to hard labour in the rasp house. Whilst she was
suffering her sentence, the guilt of her mistress was discovered. The
mistress was prosecuted, condemned to the severest scourging, a double branding, and hard labour for life. A heavy fine was inflicted on the
tribunal, and given to the innocent sufferer as an indemnification. So
lately as 1807, ten young ladies of very respectable, and some of them
of very high, families were confined in the workhouse at Amsterdam,
sent there by their parents or friends for undutiful deportment. They
were made to wear a particular dress as a mark of degradation, and
occasionally had to suffer a domestic whipping. Drunken wives were
also sent to the same place, and had to submit, for a period of years, to
the discipline of the workhouse.

In the prisons of Rome there might have been seen quite recently an instrument of punishment of a severity worthy of the Middle Ages. It was called the "Cavaletto," and was in use for those accused of common crimes, and particularly of a refusal to receive proper discipline. It consisted of a large piece of marble or other stone, before which the patient or prisoner was obliged to kneel, putting his stomach over the stone; he was then fastened by the ankles to the rings in the ground, and his hands or wrists were in like manner fastened in front. Thus it was impossible to move. After he was tied down his proper torture began. On his naked back or shoulders he was beaten with a thong, about two feet long, twenty-five times or more, according to the gravity of his crime.

In the prisons of Hungary there is a similar plan of flogging, for in that country flagellation is still a legal punishment. Formerly the law allowed the seigneur, on his own authority or that of his bailiff, to order twenty-five blows as a summary punishment to the peasant; and, indeed, the peasant held it a point of honour to bear a flogging without flinching, and nothing was more likely to render him irresistible to his mistress than a heroic endurance of the five and twenty. Flogging is now employed only in a strictly judicial sense, and the flogging-board is a necessary adjunct of the prison. This board is simply a low table, upon which the sufferer is stretched and fastened. When the prisoner is laid down and secured, the liveried haiduk stands over him with a long hazel stick about the thickness of a finger, with which he gives a forcible blow, waiting a minute between each stroke. Considerable skill is required to flog well, the object being to inflict the maximum of pain, and, at the same time, the minimum of bodily injury; and therefore no one is allowed to perform who has not perfected himself in the art by practising on a stuffed sack. Many of the old castles of Hungary are used for prisons, and the gateways are usually adorned with handcuffs, leg irons, whips, and other instruments of punishment and torture.

CHAPTER XXII

THE REPUTED CURATIVE AND MEDICINAL POWERS
OF THE ROD.

MANY curious anecdotes have been from time to time related of the medicinal powers of the Rod. Flagellation as a remedy, was supposed by some physicians to re-animate the torpid condition of the capillary or cutaneous vessels, to increase muscular energy, promote absorption, and favour the necessary secretions of our nature. But an eccentric writer goes much further than this, and regards the Rod much in the same light as Dr. Sangrado looked upon cold water and blood letting: according to him there is nothing like the Rod; it is a universal specific—it stirs up the stagnating juices, it dissolves the precipitating salts, it purifies the coagulating humours of the body, it clears the brain, purges the belly, circulates the blood, braces the nerves; in short, there is nothing which the Rod will not accomplish when judiciously applied!

The medicinal use of flogging was well known and appreciated by the ancients. Asclepiades, Cœlius Aurelianus, and others, strongly recommended it in the treatment of madness. Cœlius speaks of ordering "them to be disciplined with rods, that their under standing, being, as it were, quite banished, they may come again to their senses." In the case of mania, however, it is more a moral influence that is exercised on the patient—he is supposed to be forced by the fear of pain to keep within the bounds of reason. Even up to a recent day, such treatment prevailed to a considerable extent in the management of the insane, and enlightened and humane physicians found it exceedingly difficult to convince the insanes' keepers of the cruelty or inutility of the practice. Dr. Millingen, a modern authority on this point, says, "I had charge of a military lunatic asylum for a considerable time, and, with one exception, never found myself warranted in causing corporal punishment to be inflicted, notwithstanding the association of ideas of discipline which such a chastisement must have produced amongst men, then exposed to the capricious infliction of the lash. The case I allude to was one of Sergeant N— who had twice attempted my life, and who fully remembered every circumstance in the remissions of his malady; so much so, indeed, that doubts were entertained in the minds of casual visitors as to the real condition of his mental faculties."

Cases may and do occur where bodily punishment becomes indispensable, in order that the body may feel what the judgement cannot comprehend. For instance, take the case of the hypochondriac who swore that his legs were made of straw; and it was not till an officious servant-maid, who was sweeping the room, struck him across the shins with her broom stick, that he was brought to a sense of his erroneous impression.

The Rod, properly applied, is an infallible cure, we have been told, for those who feign diseases, and it has often happened that persons shamming an epileptic fit have grown well and been thoroughly cured by the sharp and wholesome remedy of a birch. The Rod is highly valuable in cases of constitutional laziness, and servants afflicted with this malady, and pretending to be ill with some strange distemper, have been known to be able to go about their work after an application of the discipline. In Iceland a native doctor employed corporal punishment in a somewhat modified form in such a case; an artisan suffering from indolence, the Icelandic Galen gave him the following prescription:- "Let the patient allow himself to be sewn up in a sack stuffed with wool, and then be dragged about, rolled down hill, thumped, kicked, and jumped upon by his friends and acquaintances: when he has emerged from the sack, let him take a draught to open his pores, and then go to bed." The remedy was tried and succeeded. A nobleman cured his fool both of a dullness of wit and a propensity for stealing fowls in a similar manner. He ordered him to be sewn up in a hop-bag and well thrashed, then rolled down hill, and thrashed again. The cure was quite effectual—the fool never stole again, and from that day he became as much famed for his wit and humour as he had formerly been notorious for deficiency in these qualities.

Ubi stimulus, ibi affluxus, has been a physiologic axiom since the days of Hippocrates; and flagellation thus used is only a modification of blistering or exciting the skin by any other irritating method; it has the effect of drawing the circulation from the centre of our system to its periphery. It has been known to dispel the cold stage in a fit of ague. We are recommended, on high authority, to use the Rod for the purpose of giving *embonpoint* to the lean: so Galen prescribes, and he founded his opinion from observing that horse dealers were in the habit of bringing their horses into high condition by giving them an occasional moderate flagellation. It is said that a dealer in slaves by this method, in a short time, fattened a boy who was almost consumed with hunger, giving him daily, or at least every other day, a moderate flagellation on that part of his person which is said to have been made to be kicked. Antonius Musa successfully treated a sciatica, or rheumatism of the hip, of Octavius Augustus by this process. Elidœus Paduanus recommends whipping with nettles, or urtication, as it is called in medical parlance, as being good for assisting the development of the eruption in exanthematic diseases. In a medical point of view, urtication, or stinging with nettles, is a practice not sufficiently appreciated. In many instances, especially in cases of paralysis, it is more efficacious than blistering or stimulating frictions. Its effects, although perhaps less permanent, are, it is said, more general and better diffused over the limb. This process has also been found effectual in restoring heat to the lower extremities; and a case of obstinate lethargy was cured by Corvis art by repeated urtication of the whole body. During the action of the stimulus, the patient, who was a young man, would open his eyes and laugh, but sink again into profound sleep. However, in three weeks, a perfect cure was obtained. Thomas Campanella mentions the employment of flagellation as a remedy for the obstruction of the bowels, in the case of a prince of Italy who could not be relieved unless when beaten by a servant whom he kept for that purpose.

Flogging was in ancient times frequently prescribed for the cure of love. Cœlius Aurelianus remarks that is was no uncommon thing to order persons grown melancholy or mad for love to be beaten and corrected and that the method very often succeeded and brought the patients to a right use of their reason. Rhases, another medical author. advocates the same treatment, and Valescus de Taranta says: "If the patient be young let him be flogged with rods like a child, and if the madness (that is of love) is not so cured, let him be put into a dark hole and dieted with bread and water, till he returns to his senses, and let this discipline be continued."

Lockjaw and choking are also to be cured by blows! When the passage of the throat is obstructed by a bone or any other substance, we slap the patient vigorously on the back to force up the obstructing matter. If the lower jaw becomes dislocated by immoderate laughter or yawning, it may be reduced by a smart slap on the face. A story illustrative of this cure may be here quoted:- Nicolas Vorburg, an oriental traveller, in the course of his wanderings, visited Agra, the capital of the Great Cham—to which illustrious personage he was introduced at dinner. The Great Cham, in filling his mouth with rice, unfortunately over-estimated the capabilities of his mouth, and dislocated his jaw. Of course the servants and nobles were paralysed with fear, and their imperial master sat on his throne, purple in the face, his eyes protruding, his mouth gaping and full of rice. Suffocation was imminent, when Nicolas Vorburg, regardless of courtly etiquette, ran up the steps of the throne, and hit the Great Cham a violent slap with the palm of his hand on the cheek. The rice at once fell out of the royal mouth, while another slap set the royal jaws in working order. The servants and courtiers, horrified at the flagrant breach of the proprieties committed by Vorburg, would have taken summary vengeance on the offender, if the Emperor had not fortunately recovered his breath in time to reprove them for their over-zeal. It is satisfactory to know that he rewarded the ready witted Vorburg by a present of a thousand rupees.

Seneca tells us that some quartan fevers have been cured by blows, and a learned commentator conjectures that this arises from the viscid bilious humour being warmed by the strokes, and dissipated by motion! Another author holds that the Rod is a capital specific for tertian fever. A lawyer once suffered from this complaint, which left him at times unable to pursue his vocation. In the course of one of his pleadings he ridiculed a certain gentleman, who determined to have his revenge at some convenient opportunity The lawyer was one day riding home past the house of the gentleman, when the latter sent him a message, requesting a few minutes' conversation. Dreaming only of fees, the lawyer unwittingly complied, and soon found himself a prisoner within the gates. The gentleman soon explained his business, and offered him the choice of two modes of suffering. "You shall either sit on an ant hill in the clothing provided you by nature, till you have learned by heart the seven penitential psalms; or you shall run the gauntlet in the same *dégagé* costume round my court-yard, where will be ranged all my servants armed with rods wherewith to belabour you." The lawyer pleaded for mercy to himself as he had never yet done for a client, and begged his tormentor to think of his wife and family, his illness, his fever; but the gentleman was inexorably deaf to the cry of pity, and his bowels of compassion would not be moved. The unfortunate lawyer reluctantly chose the gauntlet, as he could not bear to think of the ants, coupled with the penitential psalms. So he ran the course, and was dismissed black and blue, bruised and bleeding, to return to his family, a sadder and a wiser man; but he was so fortunate as to derive one advantage from the flagellation bestowed on him—he was cured for ever of his tertian fever!

In old times flogging was supposed to have the effect of subduing the passions; and the saints adopted it for the purpose of restraining carnal desires both in themselves and their followers. There were not wanting, however, those who held quite an opposite opinion, and it is well known that during the festival of the Lupercal the Roman ladies threw themselves in the way of the Luperci, that they might receive stripes from them, in order to ensure a happy delivery. Instances might be quoted of persons who had recourse to whipping their bodies in order to stimulate them—"an effect of flagellation which may easily be referred to the powerful sympathy that exists between the nerves of the lower part of the spinal marrow and other parts of the body."

A medical journal (*The Lancet*), while commenting on the flogging of garrotters at Leeds, which we have noted elsewhere, made some observations on the results of flogging considered from a medical point of view, which we have abridged for the benefit of our readers. There is first, we are told, the direct injury to the skin—the laceration and bruising of its structure; but that appears to be of no great importance. The reparative process is active, and satisfactorily sets to work (except where the system is thoroughly out of order). There is, in the second place, the shock to the system, which is easily recovered from where the flogging is moderate in quantity. In the third place, there is the feeling of pain, which is really most acute at the early stage of a flagellation; in fact, the pain is much lessened in severity when the punishment is heavy, say a hundred or more lashes because the surface of the body becomes deadened or benumbed. This fact is well known to schoolboys, and, if it were not so, the criminal would undoubtedly succumb from the tremendous shock produced by the gradual intensification of his sufferings. The reaction is, of course, much more severe in proportion to the duration of the punishment. Fourthly, there is spasm of the whole of the muscles of the back, especially the deep ones. When a man is about to receive a blow he braces himself up—puts himself and his muscles on guard, as it were—the foot is firmly planted, the teeth set, and the whole muscular system contracted. In operations before the blessings of chloroform were known, the patient about to be operated on grasped, with a death-like grip, the table on which he was placed; and the same condition of the body was intended to be produced by placing a bullet in the mouth of the soldier for him to bite when about to be flogged. In all these cases, the muscles are placed on their guard, and owing to their elasticity a great deal of injury might be inflicted without apparent harm. The man under the lash being in this state, the cat descends, and by-and-bye the muscles are irritated as the number of lashes increases, and contract spasmodically in the agony of writhing. This involuntary contraction becomes, in instances of prolonged and excessive flogging, so violent as to tear asunder the fibres of the muscles. After a time, subsequent to the punishment, this may be repaired; but inflammation is likely to follow, and the muscle becomes soft, pulpy, and disorganised. Our authority, however, is of opinion that serious results are only to be apprehended in the abuse of flogging. A couple of dozen lashes produce no ill effects of the kind. More than this, the working powers of the criminal, which ought to render his incarceration remunerative, are only crippled for a few days. When, therefore, a severe flogging appears absolutely necessary, it might be well to dole it out in small batches of lashes, and spread them over a greater or lesser period. With regard to the safest portion of the body on which to bestow flagellation, modern opinion endorses the old monastic view of the lower discipline—namely, that it is safer to flog the miscreant's buttocks rather than the back or loins, because the important organs that underlie the latter are liable to be injured. For many reasons also, the "rattan" (cane) is to be preferred to the "cat" as the instrument of flagellation.

CHAPTER XXIII

CELESTIAL CASTIGATION

THERE was formerly considerable doubt as to the real or practical machinery by which the Chinese Government was enabled to keep together, in one bond of union, the multitudinous population of that extensive empire. It was thought, and the early Jesuit missionaries encouraged the opinion, that "this learned and virtuous people," as Voltaire called the Chinese, had attained the secret of governing men by means of certain refined maxims of morality. The researches of travellers have, however, settled that point, and it has been ascertained beyond a doubt that the Chinese are governed entirely by the whip and the bamboo.

The bamboo is the great moral panacea of China; and offences of every description are punished in all ranks of society by means of fla-gellation. Corporal punishment is indeed the most remarkable feature of the Chinese penal code; and the highest officer of the state is as liable to be whipped as the common pickpocket. There are at least fifty clauses in the penal code of China by which, for particular offences, a general officer in the Celestial army may be ordered to receive fifty lashes; and, strange to say, he may still continue in the command of the army after receipt of the punishment. It is indeed to us the strangest thing about it—that in China there is no feeling of degradation attached to castigation. No doubt it is accompanied in a certain sense with that general abasement of character which, according to our notions, must exist in some degree before it can be endured. The fact, however, probably is, that the degradation which attaches to a blow in modern Europe is some thing more than natural, and that we are indebted to the peculiar institution of "chivalry" for the refined system of manners that makes it worse than death for a gentleman to receive a blow, or be convicted of telling a falsehood. In China they have no such delicacy: a blow is thought a bad thing in so far as it is painful, but no further; and in a country where there seems to be absolutely no sense of honour, there is no punishment so equal and manageable. In some particular cases the law of China allows the corporal punishment to be redeemed by a fine, at the rate of about thirty shillings for each blow. Another peculiarity of the Chinese penal code is that persons are not only punished for committing crimes, but that others have to suffer if they do not detect them. For example, in cases of theft and robbery, the soldiery and magistrates of the district are exposed to repeated floggings if they do not discover and convict the offenders. In the case of trivial breaches of the Chinese laws, such as drunkenness, cheating, squabbling, fighting, pilfering, insolence, or inattention to a superior, or the like, any magistrate is empowered to administer punishment in a summary manner, and the trials for such offences are conducted after much the same fashion as at our own police courts. It is the custom for a mandarin of justice to hold a court for the administration of the law daily morning and evening, in his own house, where he is attended by his secretary or clerk, and by various other inferior officers, some of them bearing iron shackles, and others *pan-trees* or bamboos. Upon the mandarin's right hand stands the prosecutor or informer, and before him (the judge) is a table covered with silk, and the implements of writing, for a secretary to take down the depositions and defence, which have to be written in black ink, as the magistrate signs them with red ink, and seals them with wax of the same colour. On the table a number of small sticks tipped with red are placed, and these are used in the following manner:- If a culprit is convicted of a petty offence, the magistrate causes him to be immediately chastised, and released. The usual punishment upon such occasions is the pan-tree or bastinade, and the mandarin signifies the number of blows to be inflicted by casting so many of the above-mentioned sticks on the floor, each stick denoting five blows. The culprit, who during his trial and examination has awaited the decree of the magistrate on his hands and knees, is then seized by the attendants and punished. The offender is thrown flat on his face, and is held in that position by one or more, if necessary, of the magistrate's attendants kneeling upon his back, whilst another applies the pan-tree. This instrument is a thick piece of split bamboo cane, the lower end of which is about four inches in width, but the upper end is small and smooth to render the instrument more convenient for the hand. Mandarins of power have usually some persons in their train who attend them with these pan-trees whenever they travel or go any where in public, and who are ready, at the nod of their master, to exercise their office in the manner described.

After being beaten, it is customary for the delinquent to return thanks to the mandarin for the good care he takes of his education. The position of witnesses is sometimes almost as bad as that of the accused, as, if their depositions do not please the judge (who is also in a sense the public prosecutor and the jury), they are liable to be cuffed or whipped by the executioner, who is always in attendance.

Not only does the magistrate see the bastinade inflicted, but very often the tribunal is used for a prison, the condemned cells being placed in the first court, where may be seen a crowd of unfortunate criminals crouching in the sunshine, with livid faces and wasted limbs, scarcely covered by a few rags, some having on their shoulders an enormous *cangue;* others may be observed loaded with chains, as also some with fetters on their hands and feet. Wearing the *cangue* is a very common punishment—that instrument is, in fact, a moveable pillory, formed of a large block of wood, with a hole in the middle, through which the head of the criminal is passed. It presses with all its weight upon his shoulders, and gives the appearance of a huge table walking about on two legs.

The Chinese code of law, which has been translated into English by Sir George Staunton, and from which the following information has been derived, is called Ta-tsing Lu li - that is, Laws and Statutes of the Grand Dynasty of the Tsing. It is divided into seven portions on the following subjects:—1. General Law; 2. Civil Laws; 3. Fiscal Laws; 4. Ritual Laws; 5. Military Laws; 6. Criminal Laws; and 7. Laws Concerning Public Works; and the title of Penal Code given by the translator, though not literal, is by no means inapplicable. Its penal

character is a peculiarity of the legislation of the Chinese empire—
every ordinance of the law, every regulation, is made under penal
sanction, not only in criminal, but in purely civil affairs. All irregularities, faults, negligence, and errors, that in European legislation would
entail only forfeitures, incapacities, or some slight civil reparation, are
punished in China by a certain number of strokes of the bamboo.

There is a lavishness and minuteness of punishment in the code of
China which indicate the thorough viciousness of the social system.
Utilitarianism, and not morality, is the prevailing principle: punishments are not graduated according to the moral gravity of the crime
considered in itself, but merely on the amount of damage that may be
occasioned by it. The punishment of each theft, for instance, is proportioned to the value of the object stolen, according to a scale drawn
up expressly to that effect. It must be admitted, however, that the system is well adapted to keep together the nation in its present state.
The immense population of China, depraved by the absence of faith
and moral education, and wholly absorbed in material interests, would
not subsist long as a nation, but would be speedily dismembered, were
a system of legislation, founded on the principles of absolute justice
and right, to be suddenly substituted for the strange one that now governs that country. Among a nation of speculators and sceptics like the
Chinese, the social bond is found in the penal, not in the moral law,
while the rattan and the bamboo form the sole guarantees for the ful-
filment of duty. Again, there is a vagueness of definition in some of the
articles of the code which seems expressly contrived to favour the
oppressive shuffling and dishonest propensities of the executive mandarins, so that the law in their hands becomes elastic, and their power
unlimited. What tradesmen could escape if the mandarin chose to put
in force the following:- "When a trader, after having observed the
nature of his neighbour's business, stocks his shop, and puts prices on
his goods, in such a manner that his neighbours cannot sell theirs, and
thus obtains more than the customary advantage, he shall be punished
with forty strokes of the bamboo." Another specimen of obscurity and
elasticity may be also quoted:- "Whoever shall observe a line of conduct that offends propriety, and that is contrary to the spirit of the

laws, *even without any special infraction of their enactments*, shall be punished by forty blows, or eighty, if the impropriety be very great."

The system of responsibility, by which every subject of the Emperor becomes in some measure responsible for the good conduct of his neighbour, his relative, his superior, or his inferior, is a notable feature of the Chinese code of laws. Public functionaries are principally subject to this responsibility, and the laws relating to their conduct are very stringent. Whenever a tribunal or body of official persons have incurred guilt by wrong decisions, or such decisions as, being either too mild or too severe, are contrary to the laws, or have become chargeable with negligence, the registrar must suffer most, as he is considered the principal author of the crime, and all the other participators are punished with less severity up to the president, whose punishment is the slightest. The lower the officer, the higher the responsibility; for it is said no crime would be committed if he refused his assistance. Thus the subordinate is liable to punishment if he concurs an illegal act, and he incurs the resentment of his superior if he refuses. It seems to European ideas very curious that a judge should be whipped for giving an erroneous decision; but in China not only is a tribunal punishable for a wrong decision on a cause, the facts of which it may be presumed to be well acquainted with, but even when a superior tribunal confirms the erroneous sentence of an inferior tribunal or the reverse, as when a cause has been sent from the superior to the inferior court. A little carelessness may involve great consequences, for there are cases in which an inferior officer would be put to death for having sealed a letter badly. If the imperial seal is awkwardly placed or turned upside down on any document, all the officers responsible for affixing it are to receive eighty strokes; and if the person to whom the document is sent should on this account feel any doubts of its authenticity, and hesitate to execute the orders it contains, and any military operation should thus have failed, the clerk in the office is to be put to death.

The civil capacity of public functionaries is restrained within certain limits—certainly a very wise arrangement. No government officer in towns of the first, second, or third order may take a wife within the limits of their jurisdiction, under pain of eighty strokes of the bamboo, or a hundred if her father or mother have a suit before the courts; and he is to undergo the same punishment if he marry such a woman to his son, grandson, brother, or nephew. The Chinese system of responsibility affects private persons as well as government officials: thus, in each territorial division, composed of a hundred families, there is a head chosen by his fellow-citizens, along with six others, to watch over the payment of the taxes and the performance of other duties, and this head is responsible for a multitude of offences that may be committed within his district. When the lands are badly cultivated, the punishment he may incur varies from twenty to eighty strokes of the bamboo, according to the extent of the land in question. There are various regulations to promote a perfect knowledge of the laws, both among the officials and the general public, all officers and persons in the employment of government being ordered to make them a particular study; and a special enactment of the code ordains that at the end of every year, and in all localities, the officers shall be examined upon their knowledge of the laws, and if their answers are not satisfactory they are fined a month's pay if they hold a high office, or receive forty strokes of the bamboo if they are of inferior rank. All individuals, artisans, and others, who on occasion of their first offence (if committed by accident or through the fault of others) shall be able to explain the nature and object of the law affecting them, shall be pardoned and released.

There is a very bitter ingredient in the sweets of high office. The number of officers for each tribunal and for every department is fixed by law; and whoever shall be appointed unnecessarily over and above this number, or shall cause another to be so appointed, shall receive a hundred strokes of the bamboo, and an in crease of punishment for every supernumerary officer whose nomination he shall have procured! The treatment of culprits in prison, and the mode in which they are to undergo their punishment, is subject to minute regulation, and when a magistrate commits prisoners to the gaol and neglects to take with respect to them the measures of rigour prescribed by the law he is punished with a number of strokes of the bamboo, proportioned to the crime which the said offenders have committed. This accounts for the severity with which offences are usually punished; for it is natural that the magistrate should err on the safe side, and not expose himself to the bamboo by any deficiency in rigour.

The organisation of the family in China is a political as well as social institution. Very much has been made of the filial piety exhibited among the Chinese; but we suspect the fear of the *cangue* and the rattan has quite as much to do with it as natural affection. The marriage laws are careful and minute. It is easy to conclude a marriage without at all consulting the parties most interested, but this is only the case with the first marriage. The father of a family cannot compel a son who has become a widower to marry a second time, under a penalty of eighty strokes of the bamboo. If between the betrothal and the marriage the relations of the bride promise her hand to another, the head of the family receives seventy strokes, or eighty if she had been already presented and approved.

Any person who accepts a promise of marriage, knowing that negotiations were begun with another, also receives eighty blows. Marriage is forbidden under certain circumstances. It is illegal to marry during the time fixed by law as the time of mourning for a father, or mother, or husband, and the marriage is declared void, and the parties punished by a hundred strokes of the bamboo. A marriage contracted during the time of mourning for a grandfather or grandmother, an uncle or aunt, an elder brother or sister, remains valid, but is punished by eighty blows. A widow who has received any distinction of rank from the Emperor during her husband's life may not marry again under penalty of a hundred blows and separation from her new husband. The penalty for marriage between parties bearing the same name, with any one concealing himself on account of crime, or with an actor or musician, is so much bamboo, and the marriage to be declared null and void. Days of mourning on the death of a member of the family are fixed by law, and any neglect of their observance is punished by sixty blows and a year of banishment. Adulterers of both sexes are punished with the stick. Women who have previously lived honest and virtuous lives are beaten in public, and are further disgraced by having their clothing removed; but this ceremony is considered unnecessary with women of bad fame.

The ritual laws of China contain some curious provisions. It is the duty of the Astronomical Council of Peking to take accurate observations, and any error as to time or appearance is punished by sixty blows of the bamboo. It is forbidden to musicians, sorcerers, and fortune tellers to frequent the houses of civil and military officers, under pretext of announcing calamities that menace the nation, or fortunate events that may be in store for it; they are decreed five hundred strokes for every one of their predictions. Although the Chinese are supremely indifferent to matters of religion, they have very precise and severe laws relating to official worship in their temples, and all negligence, imperfection, or irregularity in the observance of the rights is repressed by the bamboo, applied equally to the delinquent and to the master of the ceremonies. Even the sacred pigs, which are fattened in the pagodas for solemn sacrifices, are under the shelter of the law, If they are not legally and properly fed, or from official neglect become thin or indisposed, the official in charge receives fifty strokes of the bamboo, and so many more for every pig that does not thrive. The welfare of the pigs is therefore an important matter: any symptom of porcine illness is enough to throw a whole pagoda into consternation.

The penal scale is of the simplest. The ordinary punishments are the *cangue* and the bamboo—so many days of the former and so many strokes of the latter. Punishment of death is effected by strangulation or decapitation. There is also for great crimes the *peine forte et dure*, the "slow and painful death," or torture by the knife, which is inflicted in this manner: the executioner puts his hand into a covered basket, in which are a number of knives marked with the names of various limbs and parts of the body, and drawing out one at random, he cuts off the part indicated from the body of the victim, and so on until the poor wretch is dead. There is in China a peculiar mode of chastisement for boatmen. If a boatman is convicted of misbehaviour, he is compelled to kneel, and one of the officers of justice prevents him from flinching, whilst another grasps his hair and bestows a certain number of blows upon each side of his face with a sort of double battledore, made of leather. The severity with which punishment is frequently inflicted is something fearful. A recent traveller gives an instance which came under his observation. The prisoner was one of a gang of robbers who had been committing dreadful atrocities, such as cutting out the tongues and tearing out the eyes of men, women, and children, besides perpetrating other cruelties too horrible to mention. During his trial he was suspended in the middle of the hall like one of the large lanterns common in pagodas. Ropes attached to the great beam in the roof held him tied by the wrists and feet, so as to throw his body into the form of a bow. Beneath him stood five or six executioners, armed with rattan rods and leather lashes, in ferocious attitudes, their clothes and faces spotted with blood—the blood of the unfortunate creature, who was uttering stifled groans, while his flesh was torn almost in tatters. After his sentence, which was fifteen blows, but interpreted to mean an indefinite number, the executioners took their places, and soon the body of the criminal was swinging and turning about under a shower of blows, while he uttered terrible shrieks, and his blood spurted on all sides, and ran down the rattans, reddening the naked arms of the executioners.

Pictures of Chinese punishments have been more than once published. A graphic series, illustrative of the penal code of China, and designed as a satire on Celestial civilisation and refinement, was published some years ago by Mr. Percy Cruickshank. The drawings are rough and quaint, but effective. The processes of penal starvation, of flaying alive, of tearing a woman's arms from her body, of flogging with a scourge, dipped in boiling oil, of garrotting, disembowelling, and tearing out the ears, are depicted. The executioner is represented cutting a man in two, disjointing him, tearing him asunder; but the most horrible picture of the series is "sawing a female in two" between boards.

The Chinese are remarkable for their firmness of purpose. Generally they suffer the bamboo without making any great noise. But the Chinese character when under suffering is, we are told, best seen at executions. The victims, as we have frequently read, are carried, bound hand and foot, in baskets, and tumbled out into the blood of the last sufferers, hustled up on their knees in long lines, and in five minutes a hundred headless bodies lie weltering in their gore, and not a murmur or a groan will be heard, though none are gagged. Meadow's "Notes on China" contains an account of the execution of an innocent man, and states that as he was being carried to the execution ground the people heard him proclaiming his innocence, and warning them from interfering with him, as the mandarin would only ruin them too. "This was the only instance of speaking," says a British resident, "I have heard of. Out of a large number I saw beheaded, more than one half of whom were stated to be perfectly innocent, not one uttered a cry. They may have been drugged. A striking case is related to a man that was being flayed alive, railing at his tormentors to the last; and one of the rebels at Shanghai, who was being cut to pieces, got his death-blow sooner than was intended, owing to his being saucy before the executioners. He was a Canton man, and his countrymen at Shanghai spoke of his behaviour with pride."

It is said that Chinese marriages are seldom happy, and that peace and harmony do not often reign in the interior of the family. The husband beats the wife, and the wife beats the husband when she can, but the woman is almost always the sufferer. In some parts of the country it is so much the fashion to fustigate a wife, that a man would hardly like not to do so, as to show himself negligent on this point would be to forfeit his marital dignity, and proclaim himself a simpleton, who understood nothing of his prerogatives. We have heard of such a case. A young husband almost thrashed his wife to death. Being asked what crime she had committed to deserve such treatment, he replied, "None: she never deserved any punishment; we have only been married two years, and you know we have always lived in peace. But for some days I have had something on my mind. I thought people were laughing at me, because I had never beaten my wife; and this morning I gave way to a bad thought." The bad thought ultimately cost his wife her life.

Mr. Ellis, in his account of the embassy to China, published in 1817, mentions a rather ludicrous use of the whip, that came under his observation. On one occasion a crowd of princes and mandarins had impeded the way to the ambassador's carriage, upon which Ho, the Duke, seized a large whip, with which he laid about him indiscriminately, without regard to yellow vests, red, blue, or white buttons, or peacock's tails; and it is observed by Mr. Ellis, that "however indecorous, according to our notions, the employment might be for a man of his rank, the whip could not have been placed in better hands."

In Cochin China flogging is quite as frequent and as severe as it is in China proper. An old traveller describes the *modus operandi* of Cochin-Chinese flagellation in the *Scots Magazine*. Those to be flogged are pegged down in a row, men and women indiscriminately, their faces, of course, being to the ground. The requisite portion of their dress being removed, the soldier whose duty it is to inflict the punishment, on a signal being given, brings down the tip of his rattan very sharply on the naked person of each of the prisoners in turn. The prisoners when they are tied down are quite ignorant of the number of blows they will receive. The judge stops the flagellation when he thinks proper. Accused persons are often flogged in order to make them confess, which they seldom do, because the blows received do not count in the after punishment which is sure to follow. When the flagellation is completed, the punished one has to perform the kowtow to the presiding mandarin. The punishment of the rattan is exceedingly severe: each stroke raises a large pustule, and as these are broken by subsequent blows a mass of bloody wounds speedily accrues on the body of the sufferer which is not easily healed. Indeed, some of those who are severely punished never recover, but wander about crippled for life.

CHAPTER XXIV

FLAGELLATION AMONG EASTERN NATIONS.

CHINA is not the only nation that is governed by means of the bamboo: there are other peoples in Asia who have had to bow low before the stick since the earliest period of their history; but none of them, so far as we know, possess such an elaborate penal code as that by which the Chinese are taught to revere the sacred majesty of the law.

In the neighbouring kingdom of Corea, a division of Chinese Tartary, the industrious student may discover many curious circumstances connected with the administration of justice, a few of which may be cited:- If a woman kills her husband she is buried alive up to the shoulders, near a highway or other well frequented road, and an axe being laid beside her, every person passing that way, who is not a nobleman, is obliged to give a stroke on her head until she is dead. It is lawful, in the kingdom of Corea, for a man to kill his wife for adultery or any other heinous offence, on his giving full proof of the fact; and if the woman so killed was a slave, the penalty is to pay three times her value to her owner. Masters possess full power over the life of their slaves, and it is reckoned no crime whatever to kill one, even for a trifling fault; but slaves who kill their masters, it is ordained, are to be tormented to death. The Corea mode of capital punishment for murder is a fearful one: after they have trampled on the criminal, they pour vinegar (in which the putrefied carcass of the person murdered has been washed) through a funnel down his throat, and when his stomach is sufficiently distended they beat him on that part of the body with sticks till he bursts. Thieves are trampled to death! In a case of adultery, if the parties have been caught *in flagrante delicto*, the man is stripped, his face daubed with lime, and an arrow run through each ear; a small drum is then fastened on his back, and he is led through the town, the drum being beat upon at all the cross streets. He is then discharged after receiving forty or fifty strokes on his bare body. The offending woman, clothed only with one very fine garment, is then soundly beaten *à la mode* with the bamboo.

The people of Corea have an effectual remedy for bad debts— either taxes due to the government or debts owing to private persons. If the debtor does not pay the amount due at the appointed time, he is beaten twice or thrice a month on his shin bones, and this treatment continues until he can find the means of discharging his debt: if he die before he has satisfied his creditor, it is the law that his nearest relative must pay or suffer the same punishment. The bastinade is the chastisement applicable to all minor offences, and considerable ingenuity is displayed in the different ways of inflicting it. It is applied to the hips, to the calves of the legs, and to the shin bones, as well as to the soles of the feet. When the culprit is to undergo the *shin plaster*, his feet are tied together on a little bench, and he is bound to another by his hams, when an oaken lath about three feet long, two inches broad, and an inch thick, flat on one side and rounded on the other, is employed to strike the shins. The number of blows is restricted by the law to thirty at one time; and if the culprit has to receive more, then, according to the code, two or three hours must elapse before the dose is repeated, and so on until the sentence be fulfilled. When the offender is sentenced to be drubbed on the soles of his feet, he is made to sit down on the ground, when the executioner, tying his feet together, by the great toes, takes them between his own legs, and beats them with a stick, as thick as a man's arm and about three or four feet long, for the number of times ordered by the judge. For the bastinade *à la mode* a long bamboo is employed, and the culprit being bound to a bench with his face downwards, the strokes are laid on; if the criminal is a woman, she is compelled to wear a pair of wet drawers while being punished. This is the most severe style of bastinade: a hundred strokes are considered equivalent to a sentence of death, and many criminals die even before they have got fifty.

The usual punishment for women and apprentices is an administration of the bastinade on the calf of the leg, which is accomplished with rods as thick as a man's thumb. Europeans find the bastinade a very severe punishment, as was related by some Dutchmen who were shipwrecked on the peninsula of Corea, and retained as prisoners. A party of them attempting to make their escape, were seized and brought back and being carried before the governor; he caused them to be laid flat on the ground, and their hands to be chained to a great log. The other prisoners were then brought up, and examined as to whether they knew of the attempt of their companions to escape. They all denied knowledge of it, and those who had made the attempt being interrogated as to their design, replied that they intended to go to Japan, and that they would rather brave the dangers of the passage without provisions than remain prisoners any longer. Upon this confession they were immediately subjected to the bastinade *à posteriori*, receiving each twenty-five strokes, and it was fully a month before they recovered from their punishment.

An old traveller, writing of the administration of justice in Tartary, says that for light theft, such as stealing a ram, the criminal, although not caught in the act, but convicted on circumstantial evidence, is cruelly beaten; the executioner being in the court ready to put the sentence into execution as soon as it is delivered. Fraud, sacrilege, heinous theft, or murder, are punished by death. Marco Polo tells us how they punish malefactors. He says: "If any steal a thing of small value, and is not to be deprived of life, he is seven times beaten with a cudgel, or seventeen, or seven-and-twenty, or thirty-seven, or forty-seven, giving the strokes according to the measure and quality of the offence, and that unto a hundred: some die through these strokes." In the Imperial city, persons found by the royal guards walking in the streets at a late hour are taken up and beaten with cudgels, and on the occasion of a court festival there are placed at all the doors two gigantic fellows with cudgels to see that none touch the threshold, and whoever is unlucky enough to do so is deprived of his garments by the sentinels, and he must either redeem them by accepting a certain number of blows or lose them altogether.

It seems strange that the bamboo is so little used in Japan, a nation having so much resemblance to China in its manners and customs, but it is nevertheless true that flagellation is scarcely known among the Japanese. Even in domestic life the Rod is seldom used either to punish children or wives; the former are, indeed, educated and brought up with much tenderness and indulgence.

We have not read, either, of the use of the Rod in Japanese schools. A person who passed some years in that country says that the schools there are a great contrast to our own. The finishing schools of Japan are conducted as follows:- "A Japanese female finishing establishment has the following amongst other peculiarities—viz., all the masters pay for the privilege of teaching, instead of (as is the case in our country) being paid for their lessons. This makes the instruction a labour of love. Then, again, to a certain extent, a Japanese young lady is allowed considerable freedom as to the selection of her instructors: she generally prefers the best looking. A lady-principal of one of our English finishing establishments for young ladies would not be a little surprised if she could be suddenly transported to Japan, there to study the peculiarities of Japanese customs. She would find herself, not in a close pent-up room, filled with girls bolt upright, each perched upon an educational stool, but in a delightful garden, fragrant with the odour of tea and flowers. She would see a number of little summer houses, embowered in the midst of those charming vegetable products for which Japan is so justly celebrated, brought to perfection by the most exquisite horticulture. She would see bright-eyed damsels, with cheeks pink as the roses, moving about with graceful step, each bearing a small lacquer tray with tea and cakes. She would see those damsels with joyous smile and modest mien, wending each her way to a summer-house. In each of the summer-houses she would see a master or professor, either waiting the return of one of the refreshment-bearing damsels or else sitting by the side of one who had already come back. It is impossible for a stranger new to Japan not to be struck with the peculiarities of an educational discipline so different from our own."

The Japanese criminal code is, however, a very sanguinary one, death punishments being inflicted for the slightest crimes, and particularly for theft: whoever has stolen, even to the value of one penny, has no pardon to expect. Gambling is also punishable by death. Homicide, and all crimes punished by death in Great Britain, are also punished by death in Japan. Everyone must suffer the punishment of his own crime; and when an offence is committed against the state, punishment falls upon the whole race of the offender! There are various modes of punishment, all of which are shockingly cruel: among these are—burning alive, crucifixion with the legs in the air and the head down wards, tearing into four quarters by infuriated bulls, and some criminals are cast alive into boiling water or oil. The nobles and the military enjoy the privilege of exercising the happy dispatch upon themselves; they slash open their bodies when they are condemned to death with much *sang froid*. The privilege is indeed gladly taken advantage of: the doomed gentleman bidding his friends farewell, quietly rips himself up.

Among the Kirghese Tartars, flogging plays a principal part in the punishment awarded for horse stealing. Dr. Eversman, in his "Journal of a Tour to Bokhara," relates the following instance of which he was an eye-witness:- The criminal was originally condemned to death, but his punishment was mitigated. First of all, the delinquent, having been stripped almost naked, with his hands tied behind him, and his face blackened with coal, was hunted up and down through the group of tents forming the encampment, and if his legs did not carry him fast enough he was soundly belaboured with stripes by those who rode after him. After an interval he was driven a second time through the village with a cord in his mouth, being fastened to the tail of a horse, on which a man rode, whilst another rider goaded him onwards from behind: in this manner he was again hunted and flogged between the tents. After this the throat of the culprit's horse was cut instead of his own, and every individual in the crowd of Kirghese who witnessed the scene cut off a piece of the animal's flesh, while it was yet warm and quivering, as a dainty morsel for his evening meal; in fact, there was not a remnant of the animal left. Among the same nation minor offences, such as wrangling, tumult, assault and battery, &c., are punished by flogging with whips, instead of bamboo, as is perhaps natural to a nation of horsemen.

In India corporal punishment is one of the established institutions of the country. Masters use it as a matter of course to their servants, parents to their children, and all superiors to their inferiors; while servants of all kinds give each other "the slipper" on the softest part of their person. Whipping excites no surprise in that country, and hardly seems to provoke the indignation of the sufferer himself, much less of the onlooker. The late Hyder Ali applied the same "cat" to all transgressors alike—gentlemen and horse-keepers, tax-gatherers and his own sons. The flogging of collectors was of daily occurrence: any day one or two of these men might be seen tied up and being flogged by two men with whips, their flesh torn with nails, and then scourged again.

Flogging and torture were and are still, we believe, extensively employed in the collection of the revenue. The system—a very old one—has been handed down through the various native governments, and been continued in a covert manner under British rule. The natives imbibed long ago the notion, and tradition has only strengthened it, that a certain degree of compulsion is absolutely necessary in the collection of the public revenue. In the report of the commissioners for the investigation of alleged cases of torture in the Madras Presidency in India, submitted to Parliament in 1855, it was shewn, upon indisputable evidence, that tortures of various kinds and different degrees of severity were employed upon the natives in the collection of the revenue. One of the ordinary instruments used to expedite the collection of revenue was the scourge. In most cases the defaulter was hung up by the arms to a tree or the beam of a house, in which position he was made to suffer the lash, the instrument employed being either a scourge of leather thongs (called *cornechewar*, and sometimes *jerbund*) or the tough fibres of the tamarind tree, and sometimes a whip of coir rope. The commissioners give a capital illustration of the popular feeling in the matter by noticing the fact that in the rude dramas of the populace, a favourite scene, and one which never fails to be received with shouts of laughter and applause, is "the exhibition of revenue squeezed out of a defaulter coin by coin, through the appliance of familiar 'provocatives' under the superintendence of a caricatured *tahsildar*."

Besides flogging, the two most common forms of torture appear to be the *kittee* and the *anundal*, both of which are noticeable for their ingenuity. The *kittee* corresponds to the thumbscrew of the European torture. It is a wooden instrument something like a lemon squeezer, between the plates of which the hands, the thighs (in women also the breasts), the ears, and other more sensitive parts of the body, are squeezed to the last point of endurance, often to fainting, and frequently to permanent disablement. In many places the *kittee* has been superseded by the more simple plan of violently compressing the hands under a flat board, on which a heavy pressure is laid, sometimes even by the assistants standing on it. The *anundal* is a purely Eastern torture. It consists in tying the victim in a stooping or otherwise painful and unnatural position, generally with the head forcibly bent down to the feet, by a rope or cloth passed round the neck and under the toes. Sometimes a poor wretch is made to stand on one leg, the other being forcibly tied up to his neck. Sometimes the arms and legs are curiously interlaced, and the frame, thus violently distorted, is kept bound up for hours in a condition little short of dislocation. It is not uncommon to apply to the most sensitive parts of the body (enclosed in a cloth, or cocoa-nut shell, or other similar receptacle) a biting insect or reptile, such as the *poolah* or carpenter-beetle, and to leave it to gnaw the flesh of the miserable sufferer. It is an ordinary practice to put pepper or powder, also *chillies*, into the eyes or the nostrils, and to apply these, and similar irritating drugs, in ways which are too revolting to be even hinted at.

A case which came before the Supreme Court of India shews that flogging was sometimes resorted to in other matters besides the collection of the revenue. It was an action brought by a native of the Brahmin caste against the superintendents of police for assault and imprisonment. The plaintiff being brought before them charged with assault, was refused a day's time to send for witnesses, his offer to find bail was rejected, and he was at once placed in confinement. An application by letter was then made to the defenders by an attorney to release him, which, however, was unavailing—indeed, on receipt of the letter, the Brahmin was flogged with twenty stripes, as some of the witnesses said, for having employed an attorney. The defendants endeavoured to justify their right to apprehend persons charged with such crimes, under appointment by the Governor General and Council. The court took a different view of the question, and awarded damages to the amount of 2000 rupees with costs. One of the judges observed that he thought the refusal of bail, and the non-hearing the plaintiff's witnesses, highly improper, and also that the punishment was severe, and the plaintiff entitled to serious damages. He observed that as punishment by beating, after summary examination, had been constantly used in Bengal under the Mogul government, he could not help thinking it was highly expedient it should be still used, though he owned that the defendants had not even this power since the bye-law was disallowed. But by beating he did not mean that severity should be used. He thought the plaintiff was entitled to a proper compensation, but could not imagine that a poor Brahmin, who had consented to become a servant and to accept of wages, should make his fortune by receiving a beating.

The following account of the Buffalo or Flagellating Waren of the Hindoos is from the *Dublin University Magazine* of 1849: it is a scene which takes place in the worship of the goddess Devee:—A great crowd of the Mhars or Purwarees (low castes) having collected round the temple of Kalika-Devee (i.e., Devee in her black or bloody character) with flags, drums, horns, and all the varieties of shrill and stridulous music usually employed in native processions, an immense black female buffalo was brought to the spot, its horns gilt, its forehead streaked with vermilion, and its neck hung with garlands of flowers. The animal having been there secured by a chain, a man advanced from the crowd naked from the waist, with his head bare, and his long black hair cast loose over his shoulders, back, and breast; in his right hand was a naked sword. On his left stood an older man, who held a long thick scourge of twisted and knotted hemp, and who appeared to act as a director of the ceremonies. Coming up to where the buffalo stood, the sword-bearer uttered some words, which were taken up and repeated by the crowd around him; then eyeing the neck steadily, and waving the weapon gently three times over his head, he brought it down suddenly, with the speed of a sunbeam, on the neck of the victim, and at one stroke severed the head from the body. The black quivering mass fell forward: the image of Kalee was bathed in the spouting blood, in which the whole arena soon swam; the multitude shouted with savage exultation, and the diabolical native music set up its infernal din. Stooping down amidst the pool of blood, the sacrificer lost not a moment in skinning the slaughtered victim, and then, clothing himself in the yet reeking hide, and seizing in his right hand the chain by which the animal had been bound, he rose from the ground and commenced dancing about and shaking his head in front of the idol, amidst a deafening din of shouts, drums, horns, and hautboys. As he danced, the man with the hempen scourge wound this formidable lash three or four times round his waist and legs. It elicited no expression of pain, but merely increased his motion. His excitement soon rose to a tremendous pitch; his eyes grew blood shot, his mouth foamed, and at last he began to bellow out and scourge himself with the iron chain, till the blood ran down his back and legs. He was now in Waren. The afflatus of Devee herself had entered and possessed him. The whole multitude acknowledged and worshipped their bloody divinity present in his person, and went forward rejoicing towards the river, with him in the midst, still continuing his convulsive dance and flagellation. After advancing a few paces, he suddenly struck one of the surrounding crowd with the chain. The man thus smitten staggered and shivered for a moment as if he had received a shock from an electric battery; then, apparently convulsed, he tore the chain from the hands of the man-buffalo, and began dancing, shaking his head, bellowing, and flogging his own body, precisely as the first had done. The man-buffalo, mean while, though deprived of the chain, maintained his high excitement and spasmodic dance. The bearer of the hempen scourge lashed them both from time to time without any perceptible effect, and seemed to triumph in this proof of their genuine possession.

After a time, the second demoniac struck a third individual, who seized the chain in his turn, and began the same round of convulsive action. From the third the rabies was communicated to a fourth, from him to a fifth, and so on till the Waren of Devee was propagated through the whole multitude; and before the procession had proceeded half-a-mile there was a crowd of some fifty or sixty individuals, their long hair dishevelled, their backs streaming with blood—all bellowing out, all shaking their heads and limbs with a simultaneous convulsive motion, all dancing forward in a sort of rhythmical movement, amidst the bounding clatter of tom-toms, the mellow booming of drums and cow's-horns, the blare of the great brazen trumpets six feet long, and the wild and exciting dissonance produced by the intermingled screaming, wailing, and prolonged too-tooing of multitudinous flageolets, hautboys, and bagpipes.

Flagellation in the form of the bastinade is in daily use among the Turks and Persians. Their mode of administering it is considerably different from the Chinese method, but there can be no doubt the effect is very much the same. It is as follows:- Two men support between them a strong pole, which is kept in a horizontal position: about the middle of the pole are placed some cords with two running knots or nooses; through these the naked feet of the sufferer are forced, and then made tight in such a manner that the soles of the culprit are fairly exposed; the sufferer is then thrown on his back, or left to rest on his neck and shoulders, with his feet inverted which are forthwith beaten by a third man with a tough heavy stick. When the presiding officer or magistrate gives the word, the heavy blows cease, the maimed feet are cast loose from the cords and pole, and the victim is left to crawl away, and cure himself as he best can. According to the letter of the penal code of the Ottoman Empire, this punishment can only be inflicted on the men of the fourth and last class of society, which comprises the slaves and the rayhas of tributary subjects of the empire, such as Jews, Armenians, Greeks, &c. The other three classes—viz., the Emirs, or issue of the race of the prophet Mohammed, and the Oulemas or men of the law, public functionaries, civil and military, and free citizens, and private individuals who live on their rents or the proceeds of their industry—were all exempted by law from this cruel and degrading punishment. By the original code the number of blows to be given was from three to thirty nine: but a later clause permitted them in certain cases to be carried to seventy-five; and in practice this is often exceeded, nor are privileges always respected.

The bastinade was a punishment used among the ancient Greeks and Romans. The latter called it *fustigatio, fustium admonitio, fustibus cædi*, which differed from the *flagellatio* in being done with a stick, instead of a rod or scourge. Fustigation was a lighter punishment, and inflicted only on freemen, flagellation being reserved for the slaves. It was also called *tympanum*, because the sufferer was beat with sticks like a drum.

CHAPTER XXV

THE ROD IN RUSSIA.

Russia, despotic and semi-barbaric, is, *par exellence* the land of the Whip and the Rod, the Russians from time immemorial having been governed by the lash. Corporal punishment, in various forms, by rod and stick or whip, is freely and indiscriminately applied to offenders of every description. A rod is still the chief instrument in the hands of the municipal and police authorities, and even the officials themselves are not exempt from such discipline. Neither age nor sex is a safeguard against being beaten like a dog, and the poor peasant may be sent to the next police station, although it may be twenty or thirty miles away, with a note to the superintendent requesting that functionary to supply the bearer with so many lashes at sight; and such a note is always certain to be duly honoured, the number of stripes being frequently given with liberal interest. The police take full advantage of the arbitrary power vested in their hands, and even subordinate officials, who have no proper legal authority to beat, kick, and cuff the poorer classes without mercy, often do so; and a beating, whether administered by the properly authorised official or not, is, as a Russian proverb says, always a beating.

Blows, however, do not count for much in Russia, the highest as well as the lowest personages of the empire are liable to suffer them. No lady, at least no Russian lady, considers it *infra dig.* to box the ears of her maid; but when the maid happens not to be a Russian, there may be, according to the following anecdote, considerable danger in the practice:- A princess, whose hair was being dressed by a French waiting-maid, having received some accidental scratch, at once turned round and slapped the face of her attendant. The Frenchwoman, it seems, had the lady's back hair in her hands at the time, and being indignant at the insult, she grasped it firmly, and holding her head fast, she administered a sound correction, with the back of the hair brush, on the cheeks and ears of her highness. Of course a lady of her highness' blood could not allow it to be said that she had been struck by a servant: thus she was unable to resent the insult publicly, and had therefore to pocket the affront, and bribe the Frenchwoman, by money and kind treatment, to hold her tongue.

In Russia the stick is the *ultima ratio* of man towards his fellow: every noble or official has the right to beat any one he pleases—male or female, for being of the weaker sex is no defence against this punishment. The education of serfs and soldiers is accomplished by the stick. Has a peasant not enough intelligence or a fine enough ear to learn music?—the stick. Does a soldier not turn on his heels quick enough, is he foolish or stupid.?—the stick. For the disobedience of the slave, for the thousand and one little faults that servants daily commit, for the merchant that fails to show due respect to his noble customer, everywhere and always—the stick. A tailor of Bordeaux, established at St. Petersburg, having refused credit to a nobleman, who already owed him a pretty considerable sum, the nobleman, being enraged at the refusal, struck the plebeian who had the audacity to object to be duped by a lord. The tailor retaliated, and the nobleman then went and denounced him for striking a superior. The unfortunate Bontoux was arrested, received the bastinade, and was obliged to dispose of his establishment and quit the country immediately.

The stick is so much in use among Russian nobles that they cannot conceive any other means for the repression or punishment of ordinary faults and offences, or for the indulgence of vengeance. We give an instance. Count Panin, an old minister of Paul I, lived at his country house, in company with his physician, his housekeeper, and a Frenchman who conducted the education of two young lads. "The attentions of the tutor towards Madame Panin, all innocent as they were, displeased the count, and filled him with such jealousy that he resolved to expel the young man, and send him away with a mark of his disapprobation. One day the count called his medical adviser into his cabinet, and said to him, 'Doctor, I wish to consult you on an important matter: I flatter myself you will agree with me. Dubois (the tutor) is a rogue whom I wish to dismiss; but dismissal is not enough: I wish to punish him effectually. I shall order some of my servants to lie in wait for him on the road, to stop him, and then to give him a sound beating. He deserves it, does he not? What do you think?' Stupefied and indignant, the doctor replied that in France such an action would be called criminal and cowardly; and he hurried to M. Dubois, and revealed to him the project of the noble count. The young man departed, and, thanks to the pistols with which the doctor had furnished him, he left the territory of M. de Panin without opposition. From that moment the doctor perceived that the count treated him with marked coldness, and he was not long in quitting a place that was disagreeable. Count Panin was nevertheless an enlightened, witty, philosophic, liberal minded man; but he was a Russian, and in the opinion of a Russian noble the stick is the most natural argument that can be used to an inferior

The police are adepts in the use of the same argument. The celebrated Russian poet Pouchkin, a few days before being killed in a duel, was whipped in the rooms of the Prefect of Police, by command of the Czar, in order, he was told, to soften down the ardour of his caustic humour. Not a week, not a day, passes (says a recent writer) without some officers, some students, or some officials suffering from the same kind of punishment: with their trousers unbraced, or their shoulders bare, they are whipt for the least intemperance of language. A poor peasant, in the employment of a hairdresser at St. Petersburg being unable longer to endure the bad treatment of his master, resolved to put an end to his days by committing suicide, but he succeeded only in wounding himself, and a short time in the hospital was sufficient to cure him. As soon as he was able to bear punishment he was ordered to be whipped, to teach him how to live, and the wounds of the whip were quite as difficult to heal as the hole he had made in his throat.

It is satisfactory to know that in the way of whipping the engineer was sometimes hoist with his own petard. A certain gentleman, who was rich in "blood and ore," employed his faculties in the invention of what may be designated a truly "infernal machine" for the castigation of his slaves. It was constructed in such a manner that when an unfortunate delinquent was placed in it so that he could not move, a piece of mechanism, ingeniously contrived, was put in motion, and inflicted severe blows on his back. The slaves, driven to desperation at being made victims for the amusement of their owner, one day placed him in the machine, in order that he might feel the pain he had so often, out of mere wanton cruelty, caused them to endure.

A curious instance of the penchant for the Rod is found in the Russian social circle. The married women, we are told by various writers, take it as a token of love from their husbands to be well beaten. They consider it as a real contempt, and as evidence of a waning tenderness, if they are not chastised from time to time; and such a custom is not peculiar to persons of the lower classes, but is common to them with the higher classes of society. More than one traveller records this trait. Barclay says of the Russian wives, that they estimate the kindness of their husbands from the number of strokes they receive from them; and are never more happy, in their opinion, than when they have met with a man of a barbarous temper. A capital and *apropos* story is related of a Frenchman who married a handsome Russian lady; the new wife, after fourteen days of supreme enjoyment, became very sad and melancholy, shewing signs of the most profound grief. The young husband being very anxious to know the cause of her grief questioned her, she explained the matter, after much questioning on his part, by saying, "How can I believe that you love me? We have already been united four weeks, and you have not yet beaten me once!" The husband was delighted to learn that her grief could so easily be assuaged and lost no time in procuring a tender and elegant rod, with which he, on suitable occasions, bestowed on her the necessary tokens of his love! Other travellers relate that the whip is considered as necessary a part of the lady's "providing" as any other domestic article.

Whether the same idea has given rise to the use of the birch in Russian baths it would be difficult to determine, but it is well known that this instrument is employed in the bathing houses. The Russian bath is a thing *per se*. It consists of a room, not lofty, furnished with a large oven, several rows of benches at different stages of elevation, and a large tub of water. When the oven is glowing hot, water is thrown on it from time to time, that a vapour may be produced to fill the room. Among the most essential requisites of the bath, we are told, are bunches of birch twigs with the leaves on. In the spring season, whole roods of young verdant birch twigs are cut and tied together at one end for bathing whisks. Previous to being used, they are dipt in water to make them soft and pliant. With this bunch of twigs the body of the bather is well flogged all over. A Russian bath in full operation is a scene almost beyond description. A crowd of both sexes, old and young, in a state of nudity, enjoy the luxury of the bath at the same time, and laughing, talking, and jostling, pour almost scalding water upon their bodies, and then rub and flagellate each other with the birches. This done, they rush out, in the same costume, and complete the operation by rolling themselves in the snow, or plunging into cold water. One traveller says, "On opening one of the doors to see the interior, I could see nothing for the density of the vapour, and I could hear nothing but the confused murmuring of human voices, accompanied with the sound of the scourgings with the leafy bundles of birch."

Mr. Stephens, in "Incidents of Travel in Greece, Russia, Turkey, and Poland," narrates his own personal experience of the Russian bath:- "At Moscow, riding out to the suburbs, the drosky boy stopped at a large wooden building, pouring forth steam at every chink and crevice. At the entrance stood several half-naked men, one of whom led me to an apartment to undress, and then conducted me to another, in one end of which were a furnace and an apparatus for generating steam. I was then familiar with the Turkish bath, but the worst I had known was like the breath of the gentle south wind compared with the heat of this apartment. The operator placed me in the middle of the floor, opened the upper door of the stove, and dashed into it a bucketful of water, which sent forth volumes of steam, like a thick fog, into every part of the room, and then laid me down on a platform about three feet high, and rubbed my body with a mop dipped in soap and hot water from my head to my heels, long enough, if the thing were possible, to make a blackamoor white, then gave me another sousing with hot water, and another scrubbing with pure water, and then conducted me up a flight of steps to a high platform, stretched me out on a bench within a few feet of the ceiling, and commenced whipping me with twigs of birch with the leaves on them, dipped in hot water. It was as hot as an oven when he laid me down on the bench; the vapour, which almost suffocated me below, ascended to the ceiling, and finding no avenue of escape, gathered round my devoted body, fairly blistering and scalding me; and when I removed my hands from my face, I felt as if I had carried away my whole profile. I tried to hold out to the end, but I was burning, scorching, and consuming. In agony I cried out to my tormentor to let me up, but he did not understand me, or was loath to let me go, and kept thrashing me with the bunch of twigs until, perfectly desperate, I sprang off the bench, tumbled him over and descended to the floor. But my tormentor had not done with me, and as I was hurrying to the door he dashed over me a tub of cold water. I was so hot that it seemed to hiss as it touched me; he came at me with another, and at that moment I could imagine—what had always seemed a traveller's story—the high satisfaction and perfect safety with which the Russian in mid-winter rushes from his hot bath and rolls himself in the snow. The grim features of my tormentor relaxed as he saw the change that came over me. I withdrew to my dressing-room, dozed an hour on the settee, and went out a new man."

Many of the Russian monarchs were adepts at using the whip, and were particularly ingenious in tormenting those around them. It is well known that, during the reign of Peter I, it was the custom of that monarch to punish those nobles who offended him by an imperial order that they should become fools. From that moment the unfortunate victim, however endowed with intellect, instantly became the laughing-stock of the whole court: he had the privilege of saying anything he pleased; but it was a questionable advantage, since it was exercised at the peril of the fool being kicked or horse-whipped without daring to offer any kind of resistance. Everything he did was ridiculed; his complaints treated as jests, and his sarcasms sneered at and commented on as marvellous proofs of understanding in a fool. The Empress Anne excelled in this practice, and sometimes mingled with it so much oddity, that it was impossible not to be amused. One of her most bizarre inventions in this line was an order for a certain prince to become a hen, to punish him for some trifling misdemeanour. For this purpose the Empress ordered a large basket stuffed with straw, and hollowed into a nest with a quantity of eggs inside, to be placed conspicuously in one of the principal rooms at court. The prince was condemned, on pain of death, to sit upon this nest, and render himself to the last degree ridiculous by imitating the cackling of a hen.

Catherine II was an adept in the use of the Rod, and once had one of her maids of honour punished with the birch for telling a secret. This maid of honour had been her mistress' confidante in one of those numerous love intrigues with which Catherine amused her royal fancy. The maid was at the time engaged to be married, and could not keep a certain secret from her lover. Accordingly she communicated to him the particulars of her royal mistress' affaire du cœur, but unfortunately neglected to caution him not to tell it; and, as a matter of course, it was a secret no longer—indeed, it very soon came to the ears of the Empress. Catherine knew very well that the scandal could only have one source, and affecting to take no notice of it, helped on most zealously the marriage of the lady. On the day the young couple were united, and after they had retired to the nuptial chamber, the Empress sent six women (or rather, as is said, six men dressed as women) to the room, and having demanded admittance in the name of the Queen, "hoisted" the bride, and inflicted upon her a very severe flagellation with rods, the husband being compelled to witness the ceremony on his knees. At the conclusion of the chastisement, the culprit was politely informed that a repetition of the offence would send her to Siberia.

This royal lady did not disdain personally to handle the Rod—in fact, whipping was a pastime, or rather a passion, with her. She whipped her housemaids, dressers, and footmen, when she was *ennuyée* with the greatest possible gusto: the maids being horsed on the backs of the footmen, and the footmen in their turn being hoisted on the backs of the maids. The Empress used also, by way of pastime, to bestow elegant flagellation on her ladies of honour. She compelled some of them, it is said, to dress themselves as children, and to act as if they were children; and then, pretending to be their mamma, she chastised them in truly maternal fashion! At times she acted as governess, and ordering her maids of honour to learn impossible lessons, she whipt them for not being perfect. It is related that she carried this craze so far, that the ladies had to come to school in one of the grand saloons of the Winter Palace ready for the Rod—that is with their dresses so adjusted that the Empress could whip them at once. Her Majesty would some times personate a Roman lady surrounded with slaves, whom she either whipt herself or caused to whip each other— indeed, there was no end to her eccentricities. She would visit incognito certain noble families, and insist upon the grown up young ladies being severely birched for some real or fancied misdemeanour, and would not disdain at times to administer a chastisement with her own royal hand. The Empress Catherine was equally peculiar in her other amusements. At Oranienbaum she went hunting and shooting dressed as a man; and when on horseback, she preferred to ride like a man whenever it was practicable. Her "lady's saddle" was provided with a second stirrup, which could be let down or raised at pleasure.

We get an amusing glimpse of Russian manners in the time of the Empress Catherine from the following order issued by her for the regulation of polite society:- "No lady shall get drunk under any pretext, and the gentlemen not before nine o'clock. Ladies who play at forfeits and games of that sort must behave themselves respectably. No gentleman may steal a kiss, and no one is permitted to beat a lady in the assembly under the penalty of being excluded for the future." Much might be said upon this subject of "getting drunk," either before or after nine o'clock. The Grand Duke in Catherine's time also amused him self with the whip, and often exercised himself by whipping everybody about the room with an immense coachman's whip, making the valets jump from one corner to another, and skip through the room to escape the lash. He would hold nocturnal orgies with the servants. They got drunk, and were apt to forget that they were with their master, and that that master was the Grand Duke; then his Imperial Highness would have recourse to the whip, or stick, or any other weapon that he could get, to reduce them to a proper sense of their duty.

Golovin says of the Emperor Nicholas I that history will be puzzled which title to give him, "a crowned Don Quixote," a "drill sergeant spoiled," or a "woman whipped." This author relates several anecdotes of his ferocious disposition, one of which we transcribe. At a training school for governesses at the Female Orphan Institution, St. Petersburg, a young lady, who had loved not wisely but too well, found herself one day in an interesting condition, and became a mother, without the superintendent, curiously enough, being able to indicate precisely what lady it was. The Emperor proceeded to the place in person, and harangued the whole school, declaring that unless the guilty lady named herself he would cause them all to be visited by the doctor, or else have them all flogged. After confession, the lady, he announced, would be pardoned; but as no one presented herself, the Czar left in a towering rage. While he was passing through the corridor, one of the students threw herself at his feet, and declared that, to save her companions from an affront, she would confess herself the guilty one; but Nicholas kicked her away with his foot, saying "It is too late."

Here is another story: The Emperor was visiting the hospitals at Moscow. At one of them an old man raised himself in bed and said, "Your majesty at last must know how they treat us. The dying generally speak the truth, but Czars do not like to listen to it." "Speak, you rascal," exclaimed Nicholas, "but if you are unlucky enough to utter a word that does not prove to be true, I'll have you flogged to death." The old man became pale, fell back, and never rose again.

The people at this time groaned and writhed under the imperial rod. The Emperor abused his courtiers, and they revenged themselves on their subordinates, who, not being able to find words sufficiently energetic, raised their hands against those who in their turn had found the hand too light, and had armed themselves with a stick, which was ultimately displaced by the whip. "The peasant in Russia is beaten by everybody; by his master when he condescends so far to demean himself by the steward and the starosta, by the public authorities, by the first passer by if he be not a peasant. The poor fellow, on his part, has no means to indemnify himself except on his wife or his horse, and these he thrashes energetically." Such is Golovin's picture of a phase of Russian manners, and he ought to know something of that empire and how it is governed, as he is himself a Russian subject. "What a happy lot," says this author, "is that of the Russian nobles! They live like kings or demigods! A noble, retired to his estate with a handsome wife, at the head of some thousands of peasants, with large revenues, passes days of delight, and enjoys an existence which has not its parallel in the whole world! You are absolute sovereign on your own estates: all cringe and tremble at the sound of your voice. If you order a hundred or two *coups-de-baton* to be inflicted on Peter or John, your order will be executed, and his back will immediately become as black as a coal. You have merely to throw your handkerchief to any woman who pleases you: you are not a sultan for nothing."

In the state prisons a great deal of whipping goes on, and flogging cases occur in the police cells with which the public are totally unacquainted. This we learn in part from M. Pernet, a Frenchman residing in Russia, who having had the misfortune to awaken the jealous suspicions of the Russian police by some incautious expressions, was thrown into prison. He was liberated through the interference of the French ambassador, without a word of explanation, and ordered to quit Russia without delay. During his incarceration, as he tells us, he was only separated by a slight partition from the chamber in which unhappy serfs were tortured at the request of their masters, and thus had an opportunity of acquiring the secrets of the prison house, and witnessing the unmitigated exercise of the Rod. Among others whom he saw whipped were two unfortunate young girls who worked under a fashionable milliner at Moscow, and who were flogged before their mistress, because they had transgressed the rule of her establishment, "no followers allowed," and had had the audacity to introduce their lovers into the house. The mistress, standing by, exhorted the executioner to strike harder, and the girls received no less than a hundred and eighty lashes. It was quite common for servants and serfs to be brought to the prison by stewards of estates, or sent by their masters, with the request that they might be punished. But whippings were by no means confined to the above class, as the following narrative will shew:- A lady of rank, supposed to have committed some treasonable action, was summoned to the bureau of the secret police: having arrived, and the door being shut, she was politely requested to walk forward, but as she did so a trap-door suddenly gave way under her, and she slipped down till she was supported only by her clothes, which had gathered up all around her arms; in this helpless condition she hung through the ceiling of a room below, where an executioner had been previously stationed to ply the whip upon her unprotected body.

A beautiful serf-girl was betrothed to one in her own station. Her lord, however, wished the young woman to become his mistress, and because she refused this degradation in the most decided manner he resolved to have her flogged: a charge of some kind was therefore trumped up against her, and on this false charge she was sent for to the prison, and the door of the room locked. Being then stripped quite naked, she was laid face down on a broad bench, having two holes near one end, through which her arms were put: then a couple of men held her by the head and feet, while another lashed her until she was covered with blood, and so severely that she did not recover from the effects of the whipping for three months.

The "Englishwoman in Russia" mentions that a lady of the highest rank, having used a lady's privilege, at a masked ball, of chattering in the ear of the Emperor, let fall some rather indiscreet suggestion. Followed home by a spy, she was summoned the next day to Count Orloff's office; where, upon arriving, she was pointed to a chair, and quietly interrogated. Presently she was gently let down to a lower chamber, where she was vigorously birched, just as if she had been a little child, by some unseen person. The "Englishwoman" vouches for the correctness of this anecdote. She knew the lady, and had the story from an intimate friend of the family. We will mention, on excellent authority, a similar one. Soon after the outbreak of the Crimean war, an order was issued by the Russian Government for supplies of lint, rags, &c., for the use of the wounded—these supplies to be furnished by the wealthier classes. Among others who came to Moscow on the appointed day was the Governor's lady, and, alluding to a report which prevailed among the common people of the allied troops being so formidable that they would destroy the Russians, she remarked in jest that these supplies would not be needed. Her unfortunate speech was at once reported to the authorities, and she was summoned to appear before the police. She could not, of course, deny her own words, and was thereupon told that they were treasonable, as calculated to discourage the troops in the prosecution of a war set on foot by the state. She was summarily sentenced there and then to be whipped; and although the court was crowded with people, a space was at once cleared in the centre, where the culprit was laid down, her clothes turned up over her head, and being held by four men, the whip was lustily applied to her bare body. After about a dozen strokes, drops of the lady's blood and bits of her flesh were flying about in all directions, yet the whole number of blows to which she was sentenced was duly administered.

Many noble ladies have been flogged in Russia—indeed, anecdotes of such flagellations could be multiplied to almost any extent. It was stated a few years ago in a German newspaper that three of the most beautiful women of St. Petersburg were driven direct from one of the Imperial balls in their own carriages, in all their finery of satin and lace, to the police station, and after being mounted on a man's shoulders, with their dresses tucked up, were smartly whipped with a birch rod. No explanation was given; but they were dismissed with the significant caution to hold their tongues in future. At another Imperial party, some young ladies, who had been chatting too freely, were politely escorted by a *maître d'hôtel* to a distant apartment, where, being made to kneel over an ottoman, they were severely smacked by a female housekeeper with their satin slippers, and then sent home!

Female domestics of all grades used to be whipped in Russia for misbehaviour, generally by the steward personally, in a very rough and ready way, one culprit being made to horse the other in schoolboy fashion! Mr. Sala has hinted in one of his works (whether in jest or earnest we know not) that disobedient ballet girls are also made to endure the birch; and we once read in an old number of the *Weekly Despatch* newspaper of a Russian landowner who birched his grown up daughters and their governess as well, and who used to parade his female serfs once a week for the purpose of flogging a few of them with his own hand.

A noble Russian lady, who had no less than seven "own maids" to dress and wait upon her, used to birch them for the most trifling faults. They were dressed and lodged in excellent style, and had to undergo their punishments with many humiliating ceremonies, such as undressing themselves, kissing the rod on bended knees, thanking her highness, &c. These young women were, of course, the serfs of their lady, and had no redress; but the punishments inflicted were not cruel, as the rod used was a large one, which was more noisy than painful. We have seen an account of the ceremonies observed on these occasions in an old periodical called *The Whim*, published in Edinburgh about thirty-five years ago. The same lady, as we read in the periodical in question, also delighted to whip her pages after a similar fashion: they were boys of twelve and thirteen years of age.

Verily, the Rod in Russia is no joke.

CHAPTER XXVI

THE KNOUT

THERE is a great variety of instruments of torture and flagellation in active use in Russia other than those we have indicated. There is, for instance, the *plit*, which is a piece of iron made hot and put into a heated iron box to be taken up and held by the victim. There is also a tourniquet or thumbscrew, made out of the twigs of trees, twisted till the parts are compressed; and for flagellation the Russians have the stick, the plêt, and the knout. The plêt is a whip made of strips of raw hide, and having three lashes tipped with small leaden balls; but the principal instrument of punishment is the knout, a Tartar invention, as the name denotes, and the most formidable *punisher* ever invented by the ingenuity of man.

Descriptions of the knout vary. In its ordinary form it appears to be a heavy leather thong about eight feet in length, attached to a handle two feet long, the lash being about the breadth of a broad tape, and curved so as to give two sharp edges along its entire length; it is sometimes bound with wire thread, the end terminating in a little hook. At each blow of this formidable instrument of torture, the sharp edges of the curved lash fall on the criminal's back, so as to cut him like a flexible double-edged sword, and the executioner does not roughly draw back the lash, but deftly pulls it towards him, so that the cunningly devised hook at the end brings off at each blow a long thin strip of flesh. According to M. de la Motraye, the knout is a whip, the lash of which is made of the skin of an old ass, boiled in vinegar and mare's milk, and about an inch broad. Count de Lagny says the knout "consists of thong of thick leather, cut in a triangular form, from four to five yards long, and an inch wide, tapering off to one end, and broad at the other. The small end is fastened to a little wooden handle two feet long." Peter the Great fixed the maximum number of blows to be given by the knout at one hundred and one, but as no criminal was ever able to support that amount of punishment, the number has been gradually reduced; indeed, Baron Haxthausen in his "Notes on Russia," published in 1852, says the use of the knout in Russia was entirely abolished several years ago, and that for some time before it had been reduced within narrow limits and strict control—any one punished unjustly having a right to recover 200 silver roubles a stroke from the court which sentenced him.

In order to receive this punishment properly, the criminal was dressed in a pair of drawers only, and was fastened flat on his belly on an inclined frame, the hands and feet being extended at full length, and firmly bound to iron rings at the extremities of the frame. The head of the sufferer was sometimes so closely fixed that he was quite unable to cry out, which adds greatly to the pain. The proper handling of the knout demanded, we are told, a long apprenticeship, besides considerable natural fitness of nerve and muscle. The chief execution-er—who was always a criminal condemned to the punishment which he inflicted (the only capital punishment in Russia)—received a free pardon, and was sent home at the expiration of twelve years, during which period he was kept in close confinement except when he was led out to operate. In his prison abode he had to give instructions to his pupils. They practised daily on a sort of lay figure; and he shewed them the art of dealing their blows so as to inflict more or less injury on the criminal, according to the nature of his crime, or the bribe which the executioner might have received—how to cut into the loins when it was merely a civil criminal, or murderer, or felon: how to inflict immediate death by making the victim dislocate his own neck: or how to ensure death in a day or two after the infliction, by making the lash wind round the body, cutting into the chest or tearing the intestines. According to the instructions he had received, the execu-tioner could make every blow fall within a space of the size of a crown piece. He could, it is said, smash a brickbat into dust with a single blow of the formidable weapon of which he was master.

One lady who suffered the discipline of the knout and survived the ordeal was Madame Lapuchin. Her story has been often told. Madame Lapuchin was one of the most charming ladies of the court of Elizabeth of Russia, but having been compromised by some treasonable practices, carried on in the name of a foreign ambassador with whom she had a liaison, she was condemned to suffer the knout. The conspirators were at first sentenced to have their tongues cut out, and to be broken on the wheel; but her imperial majesty was graciously pleased to order a very doubtful mitigation of the sentence, and to substitute knouting and banishment for the latter punishment. Madame Lapuchin appeared on the scaffold dressed in a negligé costume that heightened the charms of her person. Well known during a long period at court for her wit and beauty, she hoped some at least of her old friends would countenance her in this trying moment, but her suppliant glance over the surrounding multitude only revealed a crowd of ignorant people eager to see the blood of a woman. The executioner, advancing, began to remove her clothing, at which necessary preparation she grew pale, shed tears of shame, and struggled modestly under the horrid grasp of the wretches employed to torture her. But she struggled in vain. In a few minutes the clothes that covered the upper part of her body had disappeared, and it is related that at the sight of the unfortunate young woman, naked to the waist and half dead with despair, the relentless crowd shewed some slight signs of pity. Suddenly one of the executioners took hold of her hands, and turning quickly round, placed her on his back with her feet some inches from the ground. Another of the executioners then seized her limbs and arranged her in the most convenient attitude for receiving the appointed punishment. The chief executioner then took up the knout, and holding it in both hands and advancing till within a few paces of the unfortunate lady, brought it suddenly down on her back. The first stroke of the weapon took off a strip of skin from the neck to the reins, and a stream of blood testified to the skill of the executioner. Retracing his steps, and advancing again, that functionary struck another blow which descended with great force on the fainting victim. In a few minutes the shoulders of the poor woman were completely frayed, while torrents of blood flowed from the wounds. At last, when not a particle of skin was left, the sufferer was relieved, bruised and dying. This was not enough, however. Her tongue was cut out, and her mutilated body immediately sent to Siberia, to end in exile a punishment which began with the knout. She survived these horrors, and actually lived to be recalled from banishment in the next reign, thus offering the very rare example of a feeble woman escaping death after a punishment that often kills men of the strongest constitution.

"The Englishwoman in Russia" tells of a student being knouted for striking a professor. A poor student, of more than ordinary talents, had by great perseverance twice merited a prize, but he was regarded with jealous hostility by a certain professor whom he was too poor to bribe. Twice cheated, the poor fellow made a third effort, though barely able to sustain himself in his humble lodgings until the period of examination came. His future hung on the result, for upon his passing the ordeal with credit depended his access to employment that would give him a living. He strained every nerve, and succeeded well. All the professors testified their approbation except one, whose voice was necessary to complete the votes. He rose and withheld his suffrage on false grounds, that cast dishonour on the young man's character. It was his old enemy: and the young man—a widow's son—with starvation before him, and his hopes all cast to the wind, rushed forward by a sudden impulse of despair, and struck his persecutor. He was arrested, tried and condemned by the Emperor himself to receive the punishment of the knout. All the students and professors were ordered to be present at the execution of the sentence; and many of those who witnessed the scene fainted. Long before it was complete the youth was dead: but the full number was inflicted.

In 1823, seven Tartars, who had been found guilty of various acts of robbery and murder in the southern parts of Russia, were sentenced to receive the punishment of the knout in the several towns where lay the scene of their operations. They suffered the first flogging at Akmetchet, and were then conveyed, heavily ironed, to Theodosia. Here they were taken to the market place, where hundreds of spectators were assembled to witness the dreadful spectacle. Each culprit was in turn fastened to an inclined post, having a ring at the top, to which the head was so tightly fixed by means of a rope as to prevent the sufferer from crying out. The hands were closely tied on either side, and at the bottom were two rings for the feet, which were in like manner secured. The back was then bared, and the plaster or rag which had been applied after the previous flogging was torn off. The Tartar Sacerdotal, attended by a Tartar priest, next advanced and read aloud the crimes for which the offenders were punished, together with the sentence of the law, a ceremony which occupied nearly half-an hour. The thong of the knout was very heavy, and as thick as a man's wrist. With this weapon the executioner approached, gave one cut, and walked back to the distance of about forty yards, then returning, and flourishing his whip, he struck again, till the appointed number of strokes was given. At every blow the blood spurted from the wound, but the previous preparation prevented the possibility of exclamation. Each one, when his flogging was finished, was unbound, and, having the rag replaced on his back, was removed to a cart, till all had been thus disposed of: having witnessed the sufferings of their comrades, and endured their own. Before they left Theodosia one of them died; and not one of the seven lived to undergo the whole punishment.

A British merchant, resident in Russia, witnessed a knouting in 1836. The father of the culprit was a respectable shopkeeper, remarkable for his industry and sobriety; but his son was the very reverse, being an idle, dissipated, and worthless character. In a paroxysm of rage at a well-merited rebuke from his father, he plunged a knife into the body of the old man; for which offence he was tried and condemned to the knout. The blows adjudged for infliction amounted to 101, a number considered equivalent to a sentence of death. The place of execution was a field used as a market place for horses, about a mile from the Admiralty; but early on the appointed morning the place exhibited few signs of the approaching event: a stake planted in the middle of the field, a battalion of soldiers drawn up, and some scores of people sauntering about were the only appearances indicative of the tragedy about to be enacted. The whipping-post was a stake driven firmly into the ground, about five feet high, four inches in thickness, about two feet broad at the top, and tapering to a breadth of eight inches where it entered the ground, and sloping eight or ten inches off the perpendicular. On the top it was hollowed out into three semicircles, the central one being for the criminal's neck, and the two others for his arms. Near the ground there was a hole in the stake, some two or three inches in diameter, for the reception of a cord to bind the prisoner's ankles. Some mats were spread on the ground around, to afford a firm footing for the executioner. On the arrival of the prisoner, accompanied by a guard and two executioners, each carrying a bundle of knout thongs under his arm, the battalion was formed in a hollow square, the principal actors in the scene being of course in the centre. After the warrant signed by the Emperor had been read, the criminal was handed over to the executioners. The chief executioner, on this occasion, was a man named Kozloff, who had originally belonged to the higher classes, but had been degraded and sentenced to the knout on account of cruelties to his serfs; he had escaped the knout, however, by accepting the office of executioner. He was a tall, strong man, apparently about fifty years of age, with a countenance in which it was impossible to say whether ferocity or stupidity most predominated. His assistant was a young man, about two-and-twenty years of age, formerly a postilion in the service of the Grand Duke Michael, and had been sentenced to the knout for robbery, but had escaped that doom by becoming an executioner. The culprit, a young man of twenty five, of low stature but firm build, was stripped to his trousers and boots, and fastened to the stake. The knout consisted of a handle a foot long, with a piece of twisted hide of the same length. To this hide was attached by a loop, a piece of thong prepared to almost metallic hardness, about four or five feet long, perfectly flat, and an inch broad. It was changed after every six or eight blows, because it is considered unfit for use when it becomes soft. Kozloff, having placed himself five or six feet from the prisoner, with the thong of the knout on the ground, rather behind him, then drew it steadily forward, raising it slowly till it had attained the proper elevation, then he brought it down, with tremendous force, upon the middle of the criminal's back, leaving a deep crimson mark of nearly an inch in breadth, extending from the neck to the waist-band of the trousers. Upon receiving the blow the wretch uttered a scream, or rather a yell, of agony, and every fibre of his body seemed in a state of violent and instantaneous contortion. With scarcely any interval the blow was repeated, followed by the same result—the same frightful yell and shudder. The second mark appeared about an inch from and parallel to the first; a third, fourth, and fifth blow followed in quick succession, when the operator stepped aside and resigned his place to his assistant. The blows from the latter were light compared with those inflicted by the elder executioner. After giving eight blows the assistant retired in his turn, when his principal, who had in the meantime fitted on a fresh thong, resumed the task. He was again succeeded by the young man, who, in like manner, had renewed his lash. In this manner they continued to relieve each other, and at each pause to put on a new thong, until the destined number of blows was inflicted on the back of the parricide. About the fiftieth stroke, his struggles having partially loosened the fastenings, it was found necessary to stop and fix them more firmly. From the first till the twentieth blow, each was followed by the same scream and convulsions, and these gradually became weaker till the fiftieth, after which the criminal's head fell on one side, and he seemed perfectly unconscious of pain. After the knouting was finished, the executioner branded the criminal on the forehead, cheeks, and chin. The criminal's back now exhibited a horrid spectacle: it was one mangled, bloated mass of deep crimson hue; yet still, mangled as it was, no blood ran from it. The prisoner was removed in a cart, quite insensible, and most likely died from the fever and mortification certain to follow such punishment. The whole affair did not last more than twenty minutes.

Another variety of flagellation in Russia is called running the gauntlet. It is chiefly employed in the army; but has also been used towards unfortunate Poles. After the judgement of the court has been read in the presence of the assembled regiment, the executioner seizes the criminal, and ties him firmly by the two hands to the muzzle of his musket. Another assistant holds the butt end before him at the height of the waist, so that the bayonet is horizontally directed against the criminal's stomach. Two assistants hold the soldier by the arms to prevent him from falling backward or to the side. A roll of the drum gives the signal for the punishment. The criminal, who has previously had his head half shaved from back to front, steps out, and advances to two

Plate XIV

RUNNING THE GAUNTLET
A punishment employed in the Russian Army

lines of soldiers, drawn up to form a long lane. Each soldier is armed with a very pliant hazel wand or switch, with which he strikes his unfortunate comrade the moment he comes before him. If the culprit wishes to quicken his pace to avoid the blows or to hasten his deliverance the bayonet of the gun held by his own hands, and pushed back by the assistant in front, who holds the butt end, pierces his belly. If he tries to fall down, he is upheld by the two side assistants. He is seldom able to pass from end to end of the file, and if he faints or swoons, so as to be insensible to the blows, he is conveyed to the hospital, and as soon as he is somewhat recovered he is taken out to get the remainder of his punishment. Peter the Great limited the number of blows to twelve thousand: but unless it is intended to kill the man they seldom inflict more than two thousand at a time.

In 1841, a triple military execution of this kind took place at Moscow. Three soldiers, recruits, were condemned for assaulting and robbing their master, and sentenced, the one to receive three thousand, the others two thousand, blows of the rod; one died after his beating; another received his whole three thousand; and the third, having fainted during the operation, was handed over to the doctor, and after being cured, received the balance of his stripes. A special circular was issued by the police authorities, inviting the citizens of Moscow to witness the flagellation of these men.

The progress of dissent in Russia forms a strange and peculiar chapter in the history of religious fanaticism; and it is not at all wonderful to find in it traces of that mania for self-flagellation which prevailed in other parts of Europe during the Middle Ages. There was a sect of dissenters called Stare-vests, or "Men of the Old Faith," who met together, men and women, stripped to the waist and barefoot, on a floor strewed with sharp flints, and confessed and scourged themselves till their backs were torn. The religious services of these Khlisti, or Scourgers, is a wild dance, accompanied by severe castigation. In the middle of the room in which they meet stands a vessel containing water, and to this they go from time to time in order to wet their heads, or to drink out of their hands. Then they resume their stamping and their flogging until they fall down utterly exhausted, or convulsions seize them, during which they utter ravings which they call prophecies. Every Easter night they assemble for a great solemnity—the worship of the mother of God. A virgin, fifteen years of age, whom they have induced to act the part by tempting promises, is bound, and placed in a tub of warm water; some old women come and first make a large incision on the left breast, then cut it off; and staunch the blood in a wonderfully short time; while other barbarities follow, too shocking to be told. During these operations a mystical picture of the Holy Spirit is put into the victim's hand, in order that she may be absorbed in regarding it. Afterwards a wild dance takes place around the tub, kept up by the whole congregation, till their strength is exhausted. The girls who have been thus mutilated are ever afterwards considered sacred. At the age of nineteen or twenty they are said to look like women of fifty or sixty years old, and they generally die before reaching their thirtieth year. Later sects have improved on this leading idea of mortifying the flesh for the sake of saving the soul, and carried out the principle to a much greater extent. The Skoptsi have formed their system on a strict interpretation of the gospel of Matthew ch. xix. v. 12. According to this doctrine, they declare the whole human race as wholly sinful and worthy to die out. They therefore regard matrimony as a deadly sin, the very possibility of which must be guarded against. As long as mankind are unfortunately not exterminated, they ought to live virtuously, become teetotallers in regard to spirituous drinks, tobacco, and meat, and prepare for a better life by practising every other description of abstemiousness. The Skoptsi, more especially, have to set an example to their benighted brethren. They—every one having a passport, signed and sealed by Christ himself, ensuring immediate entrance into paradise—have no other business in life than to inculcate the necessity of devoting the entire race to death. If they live at all, it is to convince others less enlightened than themselves that life is a sin of itself. But for this holy purpose, they would be justified in making away with themselves. As far as compatible with this "dogma," they acknowledge the creed of the orthodox church.

CHAPTER XXVII

THE SAD STORY OF THE NUNS OF MINSK.

TOWARDS the end of the 16th century, a large body of the Greek Church separated itself fromt he orthodox or state establishment, and, under the name of the Uniate or United Greek Church, embraced the Roman Catholic faith. It being of importance to the Government to root out this branch of schism, the usual machinery of persecution was speedily put in motion for that purpose. Laws of various kinds were passed against the Catholics, which in due time produced the desired result. In 1839, the whole body of the Uniate signed an Act of Recantation, and were received into the bosom of the orthodox church. Among those who recanted, Bishop Siemaszko was conspicuous, and as one proof of his zeal he undertook the task of converting the Basilian nuns of Minsk. He first tried preaching, but finding that would not do he selected a far more peremptory method, and went with a troop of soldiers to the convent, offering to the nuns their choice of renouncing their religion or being sent to Siberia, and they chose the latter alternative. The ladies were marched through the town followed by the tears and lamentations of the people, to whom they had shewn much kindness. Once out of the town they were chained in couples, and with irons on their hands and feet were marched seven days until they reached Witebsk, where they were placed in a convent of Czermick, or Black nuns, chiefly widows of Russian soldiers, and appointed servants to the inmates.

They found some other Basilian nuns there who were subjected to like treatment, being made to perform all the dirty menial work of the convent. This continued for two months, when there began a system of flogging. Siemaszko ordered the nuns to be flogged twice a week, fifty lashes each time. These floggings took place in the courtyard, under a kind of shed, in the presence of the deacons, the priests, the children, the nuns: "of everything," says Mother Makrena, "that lived and blasphemed in this dwelling." The flesh of the poor ladies often hung in strips from their bodies, and the way to their daily work was tracked with blood; but they made neither resistance nor complaint, and only wept when they did not pray. It was in the winter, and they were not allowed any fire, so that the cold froze their limbs and poisoned their wounds, making their punishment still more severe. After one of these flagellations a nun, Colomba Gorska, fainted on her way to work. They beat her until she recovered her senses, when, staggering to her wheelbarrow, she fell dead as she attempted to move it. Another nun, Baptista Dounar, was burnt alive in a large stove, the Czermicks having shut her up in it after she had lighted the fire. Another, Nepomucena Grotkowska, was killed, perhaps accidentally, by the Czermick abbess, "who clove open her head by striking it with a log of wood, because she dared to make use of a knife to scrape from a plank a stain of tar which she could not remove in any other way." It was a breach of discipline and disobedience to a rule laid down by the abbess.

Another nun, Susannas Rypinska, died from a flogging; and a fifth, Coletta Sielawa, was also killed accidentally by a Black nun, who broke her ribs by knocking her down violently against a pile of wood. As they still continued steadfast in their faith, fresh tortures were invented. One of these was the manner in which they were made to bring water from the river. To "prevent the Polish spirit from passing into the water," the nuns were obliged to hold the heavy copper jars at arm's length. The river was a considerable distance from the convent, and they were often unable to keep the jars at the required distance. If they drew them nearer, the water was polluted; and the Czermick nuns, who were always with them, armed with whips and sticks, flung the water over them, and obliged them to go back for more.

In 1840, two years after their arrival at Witebsk, they were suddenly marched to Polosk, where more labours and trials were in store for them. They were set to work as labourers on a palace which was being built for Siemaszko. Many died there from the severe labour and harsh treatment they experienced. One morning a Russian verse was found written on the walls;

"Here, instead of a monastery,
Are Siberia and the galleys"

The Basilian nuns were accused of having written this, and were flogged so brutally that two died, one the same evening and the other the next morning.

In the autumn of 1841 Siemaszko came to Polosk, and on this occasion he broke the upper cartilage of the mother's nose, and flogged the sisterhood as he had threatened, "till he had taken off three skins, one that they had received from God, and two from the Emperor—that is to say, those that will come after:" when he affirmed they would be less obstinate and repent. After this scourging, another nun, Basselisse Holynska, died, like so many others before her.

In 1843 they were again flogged twice a week—fifty blows each time; and again, three nuns died from the torture: one during punishment, and the twenty blows that remained of the number were struck on her corpse; one died two hours after; and the third lingered in great agony until night. After they had been thus scourged six times, the Russian general and his wife interfered, and the punishment was stopped for a short time. But Siemaszko returned, and more bitter cruelties were practised towards them. One of the punishments was that they were shut up for six days and fed on salt herrings, without a drop of water.

In 1843 the nuns of Minsk were removed to Miadzioly to a convent of Black nuns. Here they were subjected to the torture of the baths. The nuns, excepting those who were blind, were put into a kind of sack, with both arms thrust into a single sleeve. They were marched to the lake, flung in, and when up to their chests in water, with ropes fastened round their necks, men in boats dragged them along. This punishment lasted three hours. Three nuns were drowned in this ordeal.

In 1845 there were only four of the nuns left who were able to use their limbs or work. The rest were either dead or blind, or crippled. Having heard that they were to be sent to Siberia, these four, among whom was Makrena, the mother of the original sisterhood, made their escape when the guards were all drunk on the occasion of some festival. They reached Posen in August 1845, and there Makrena made her depositions on oath to the authorities of the sufferings that she and her nuns had experienced. Makrena is now an inmate of a house near the Scala Santa at Rome, where she is establishing the order of St. Basil. This brief narrative of the sufferings of the nuns of Minsk has been abridged from *Household Words*.

CHAPTER XXVIII

FLAGELLATION IN AFRICA.

F LAGELLATION, both with whips and rods, prevails to a considerable extent in the various countries of Africa.

We have already noticed its use among the Egyptians in ancient times, but modern Egypt no less believes in the Eastern proverb, "The stick came down from heaven a blessing from God;" and rulers take care that their subjects have full enjoyment of the blessing. It is deemed impossible in that country to collect the taxes without a liberal employment of the bastinado; and an Egyptian feels ashamed if he cannot shew those numerous marks on his body which evince his endeavours to evade the taxes. Mr. Wilkinson records an anecdote illustrative of the Egyptian sentiment on this point. "In the year 1822, a Copt Christian, residing at Cairo, was arrested by the Turkish authorities for the non-payment of his taxes. and taken before the Kehia or deputy of the Pasha. 'Why,' inquired the angry Turk, 'have you not paid your taxes?' 'Because,' replied the Copt, with a pitiable expression, perfectly according with his tattered appearance, 'I have not the means.' He was instantly ordered to be thrown on the floor and bastinadoed. He prayed to be released, but in vain. The stick continued without intermission, and he was scarcely able to bear the increasing pain. Again and again he pleaded his inability to pay, and prayed for mercy. The Turk was inexorable, and the torments he felt at length overcame his resolution: they were no longer to be borne. 'Release me,' he cried, 'and I will pay directly.' 'Ah, you Giaour, go!' He was released and taken home, accompanied by a soldier, and the money being paid, he imparted to his wife the sad tidings. 'You coward! you fool!' she exclaimed. 'What! Give them the money on the first demand? I suppose, after five or six blows you cried, "I will pay, only release me!" Next year your taxes will be doubled through your weakness. Shame!' 'No my dear,' interrupted the suffering man, 'I assure you, I resisted as long as it was possible: look at the state I am in before you upbraid me. I paid the money, but they had trouble enough for it: for I obliged them to give me at least a hundred blows before they could get it.' She was pacified, and the pity and commendation of his wife, added to his own satisfaction in having shewn so much obstinacy and courage, consoled him for the pain, and perhaps, in some measure, for the money thus forced from him.

The tax-payer is not always the first to suffer in this matter. The sheikh of each village is held responsible to the government for the performance of the labour prescribed to the people and their payment of the taxes. It is no uncommon thing to see the sheikh under the stick for some obstinate peasant; but he generally takes ample vengeance in his turn. Other travellers record the fact that the tax-gatherer and the tax-payer are alike subject to the bastinade. Sometimes the instrument of punishment is a whip made of the hide of the rhinoceros. The police regulations of Cairo are of a primitive nature. When any great man is passing through the narrow streets, he is usually preceded by a half-naked Arab, running at full speed, and cracking a long whip to clear the way. The "agent in advance" does not confine himself to mere cracking, but makes the lash descend with vigour on the shoulders of those who do not get out of the way fast enough.

The young Egyptian learns to endure the bastinade at school. A recent traveller was making enquiries as to the punishments employed in educational training, and one day he remarked to a schoolmaster in Cairo that he had often read of the bastinade, but had never seen it applied. "Then you shall see it now," replied the schoolmaster, who immediately seized one of the biggest boys, and inflicted upon him the usual eastern castigation. The traveller, upon inquiring for what offence the boy was punished, was promptly told that it was simply to shew him how the thing was done!

Farther south along the Valley of the Nile the Rod is in active use among the natives, both in their domestic and judicial arrangements. Their idea of beauty is immoderate fatness, and in order to secure this the princesses are fed on milk. Speke relates how he saw a daughter of the king sitting sucking at a milk-pot, while the father kept her at work by holding a rod in his hand. The same traveller remarks that all acts of the king are counted benefits, for which he must be thanked: and so every deed done to his subject is a gift received by them, and must be suitably acknowledged, whether it assume the shape of a flagellation or a fine. Misdemeanours committed by women are punished by flogging, or being sold into slavery. Captain Grant also noticed the process of fattening the princesses by whipping them into drinking great quantities of milk.

The punishments among the Karague are very severe. For adultery, an ear is cut off; and if the case occurs with a slave or a princess the offender is tortured, and his throat cut. If a husband catches the parties *en flagrant délit* he may kill the offender on the spot. For theft they commit the offender to the stocks for a period ranging from two to ten months. Assault is punished by fine, and if the culprit has no property he must do penance in the stocks. In the case of murder, the whole property of the criminal goes to the relatives of the murdered person, and the criminal has his eyes gouged out, or is thrown over a precipice.

The punishments at Muscat and Zanzibar, under Arab government, are still more barbarous. At Zanzibar the hand of the thief is cut off, and sometimes he is buried in the sea-shore up to the neck to allow the tide to reach him. The Arabs are very strict with their servants, and flog them severely. To enforce dispatch, a master will spit on the ground, and say to his servant, "If that dries up before you return with an answer to my message, you'll get flogged." Captain Grant had on one occasion to punish one of his party in this way who was convicted of theft. The offence was a grave one, and the thief was condemned to receive fifty lashes. They were administered with a whip of buffalo hide, and although the culprit's back was well scarred, he ate his dinner after the operation and carried a load the following day.

In Southern Africa, among the Bechuana and Cafire tribes south of the Zambesi, there is a curious whipping ceremony, similar to the flagellation of youths before the temple of Diana among the Lacedæmonians. Dr. Livingstone says these tribes practise circumcision (boguera), but the rites observed are carefully concealed. He was, however, on one occasion, a spectator of the second part of the ceremony of the circumcision, called "Sechu." Early in the day, all the youths of the tribe about fourteen years of age, who are to be initiated, are drawn up in a row—each quite naked, and having a pair of sandals as shields on his hands. Opposite them stand all the men of the town, also in a state of nudity, armed with long thin wands of a tough, strong, supple bush, called *moretloa*. The men engage in a dance called "Koha," in which questions are put to the boys, such as, "Will you guard the chief well?" "Will you herd the cattle well?" While the boys answer in the affirmative, the men rush forward to them, and, each selecting a victim, aims a blow at his back. The boy shields himself with his protected hands above his head, and the rod descends on his back, usually making the blood squirt from a wound twelve or eighteen inches long. At the end of the dance the boys' backs are seamed with wounds and weals, the scars of which remain through life. This process is intended to harden them, and fit them for being soldiers. After passing through this ordeal, and further proving his courage by killing a rhinoceros, the youth ranks as a man, and may marry. In the "Koha" dance much respect is paid to age. A younger man rushing from the ranks to exercise his wand on the backs of the youths may be himself the object of chastisement—a chief may even receive a cut from one of his grey-haired subjects. Livingstone further remarks that the "Sechu" is practised by three tribes only. Boguera is observed by all the Bechunas and Caffires, but not by the Negro tribes beyond twenty degrees south. It is a civil rather than a religious rite.

When the son of a chief has attained the age of fourteen or fifteen, all the other lads of that age are selected to be his companions for life, and to qualify them they have to submit to a certain amount of training. They are taken out to some retired part of the forest, and huts are erected for their accommodation. The old men go out and teach them to dance, initiating them at the same time into all the mysteries of African politics and government. Each one is expected to compose an oration in praise of himself, and to be able to repeat it with considerable fluency. This training is conducted with great rigour, and the Rod is in active operation to bring the lads up to the required excellence in different matters. They are generally able to shew, by the scars on their backs, that the Rod has not been spared. These bands or regiments are thereafter under the chief's son. There is perfect equality in the ranks, and each addresses the other by the title of "comrade." In cases of offence against their rules, such as eating alone when any of their comrades are within call, or in cases of cowardice or dereliction of duty, they may chastise one another, or any member of a younger, but never of an older, band.

In Western Africa there are many flagellating customs, native as well as imported. The early missionaries to Congo, being of the Roman Catholic Church, introduced the system of penance among the natives, who took to it with commendable vigour. A Capuchin, who was a missionary at Congo about 1667, says one evening he heard a noise of singing of a very doleful nature, and on inquiring what it was he was informed that the people were come to discipline themselves in the church, because it was a Friday in March. He immediately went and opened the church doors, lighted the candles, and rang the bell. Before they went into the church, they continued a quarter of an hour singing the *salve regina* in their native language before the building. They then went into the church, where the priest gave them holy water. There were altogether about two hundred men, carrying great logs of wood for the greater penance. After a short sermon from the priest on the benefit of penance, which must be endured either in this world or the next, the candles were extinguished, and the people disciplined themselves for a whole hour with leather thongs and cords made of the bark of trees. There was then more singing, and a few additional words from the priest. The missionaries likewise issued a number of ordinances which were enforced by flogging. It was a custom of the natives to shut up women during the time of their conception. The priests ordered that those women that should be shut up on that account in future should be scourged. Whipping was the usual penalty for robbing or damaging a neighbour's field, and the natives were enjoined to make use of consecrated palm branches, and the sign of the cross, to guard their fields instead of the usual magic guard.

One of them relates how he dealt with a native wizard:- "At my first going out on my mission, I found near a city, called Tubii, a place where the wizards practised their sorceries. No doubt Providence directed me to discover this hellish trade, for whilst I was walking along I saw a large white bird flying before me, such as I had never seen before in these parts. My curiosity led me to have a nearer view of it, and in order thereto I followed it into a thick and shady grove, somewhat dark, at the end of which I observed a large heap of earth, in form like a tomb, with a great number of arches and calabashes at the top and both ends. Being pretty well assured what this was, I presently sent for the Mani who came trembling to me, and protested he knew nothing of the matter. I commanded him to inform himself then, and to get me the wizard speedily seized. He said he would but I, not caring to trust his diligence, returned the next night to the same place, expecting to have found the wizard there; but he, it seems, having been acquainted with my proceedings, took care to disappoint me by running away, as they all do as soon as they hear me make any search after them. Then I ordered the Mani that within ten days he should grub up and level the place, which he nevertheless disobeyed me in, whereupon I caused him to be summoned before the court of our convent, where, after a severe reprimand, I commanded him to discipline (scourge) himself in the middle of our church during the whole time I was celebrating mass, adding withal several other punishments in case he did not level the said grove at his return home."

The priests found the marriage laws very unsatisfactory, and had to resort to flogging to reform them. A man when dying would sometimes hand over his wife to some kinsman, in order that her portion might not have to be returned to her parents, and to prevent this the priests ordered a flogging to be administered to any one receiving a woman in this way. One man was discovered to have taken his cousin to wife after this fashion, and although he was a man of rank the priest determined that he should not go unpunished. He was admonished and lectured; but all in vain—he would not give up his spouse. He was therefore handed over to the people to be dealt with as they thought fit, and they severely scourged both the man and his wife, and, moreover, deprived the man of his living into the bargain.

According to the native code, flagellation was a common enough punishment. For adultery, if a husband caught his wife in the act, he was lawfully entitled to the whole effects of the male offender. The wife he might chastise very heartily with a cudgel, and drive her from his house to seek her fortune. Her only resource in such a case was to retire to another town or village, and try to pass for a widow, "or," as an old traveller has it, "else she strives to subsist herself by a trade not very difficult (for her, at least) to learn." Other crimes are atoneable with money, and where there are "no effects" the body must pay. In a country where a plurality of wives is lawful and common, the stick is almost a necessary part of the domestic economy. When the wives quarrel among themselves—a circumstance which, from the nature of their situation, must frequently happen—the husband decides between them, and sometimes he has to enforce his decision by the application of the Rod. When a wife complains to the chief that her husband has unjustly punished her, and shewn partiality to some other of his wives, the affair is brought to a public trial. The judges being mostly married men, the case is not always decided in the woman's favour; not unfrequently she herself is found to be in the wrong. If she murmurs at the decision of the court, the magic rod of *mumbo jumbo* soon, puts an end to the business.

The people of southern Guinea have secret associations, with rules, fees, and mysteries. One of the most prominent among them is the Ndâ, an association confined to the adult male population. It is headed by a spirit of this name, who dwells in the woods, and appears only when summoned by some unusual event, such as the death of a person connected with the order, the birth of twins, or the inauguration of some one into office. His voice is never heard except at night, and after the people have retired to rest. He enters the village from the wood side, and is so bundled up in dried plantain leaves that no one would suspect him of belonging to the human species. He is always accompanied by a train of young men, and the party dance to a peculiar and somewhat plaintive air on a flute-like instrument, as they parade through the streets. As soon as it is known that he has entered the village, the women and children hurry away to their houses to hide themselves. If they should have the misfortune to see the spirit, or should be discovered peeping at him through the cracks of the houses, they would be thrashed to death. Perhaps no woman has had the temerity to cast eyes upon this mysterious being.

Although the children in Western Africa are not much liable to the Rod, they are, at times, subjected to a much more terrible discipline. It is common to punish disobedient boys by rubbing pepper in their eyes. Their screams and yells under the operation are described as being perfectly frightful, and it is a wonder that their sight is not completely destroyed. Adults are punished by a severer application: they are made fast to the roof of the house, and thoroughly smoked with pepper.

A settlement for liberated slaves was formed at Sierra Leone, in Western Africa, and here the whip was used as an incentive to labour among the Negroes: indeed, it was held that the blacks would not work without this stimulant. The work which these Negroes were set to perform was to carry upon their heads bricks, iron pillars, timbers, &c., for the new barracks, from the shore up to the top of a hill, a distance of about a mile and a-half. The labour was performed from morning till night, and there was a number of drivers armed with whips, which were freely applied to the backs of the Negroes to compel them to work. It is known that a missionary flogged a Negro boy to death, and also that a person in authority flogged a Negro boy so severely that he died. Flagellation was the common punishment for Negroes offending in the place as late as 1827. The offender was tied to a cart's tail and whipped through Freetown, or bound to a whipping-post and flogged with the "cat." Sometimes the liberated Africans who neglected their duty or committed petty thefts were formed into gangs chained two and two together by the neck, and in that situation compelled to labour under the whip. A large church was built in Freetown, with money collected in this country. It stood some time unfinished with only the roof and the bare walls, and in that state was made use of as a common market place and a house of correction, where Negroes guilty of minor offences were tied up and publicly whipped, usually before ten o'clock in the morning.

The latest revelations of the whipping of Negroes on the west coast of Africa were made in a case which was tried at the Liverpool Assizes before Mr. Justice Shee. The plaintiff was a Dr. Evans, and the defendant was an agent for the Liverpool firm of Charles Horsfall & Sons at Benin. In 1864 the plaintiff entered into an engagement with the Horsfall firm to act as medical officer at their Benin station. Matters went on smoothly enough for some time between the doctor and the defendant, but ultimately they disagreed, and Evans gave the defendant three months' notice. Some letters that passed between the parties were read in court, in which it was stated that one of his great objections to residing at the station was the fact that the defendant practised great cruelties upon the natives in the employment of the firm, frequently tying Negroes up to posts and flogging them severely. He also stated that the defendant lived with a black mistress in the same hut where he (the plaintiff) was also obliged to dwell. Finding that he would not consent to his leaving, the doctor went on board a vessel lying in the bay; and it was alleged that the defendant, accompanied by a number of Kroomen, went on board this vessel, forcibly carried the plaintiff off to the shore again, and seized a quantity of his clothes and property, including a collection of dried snakes. For these various acts the plaintiff sought damages. The defence was that the statements of the plaintiff were very much exaggerated, and in some cases untrue. During the trial the defendant admitted that the statements as to his whipping Negroes at times were perfectly true, and held that in an uncivilised country like Africa it was impossible to carry on business without resorting to such measures. The judge, in summing up the case, severely censured the immorality and cruelty of the defendant, though he said that those acts should not influence the jury in the case. The verdict was £50 damages.

Captain Canot, in "Twenty Years of an African Slaver," gives an account of a trader's harem on the Rio Pongo Ormond:- The wives took advantage of the age and carelessness of their lord and master to seek congenial companionship outside the harem. Sometimes the preference of two of these sable belles alighted on the same lover, and then the battle was transferred from a worthless looking-glass to the darling beau. When such a quarrel arose, a meeting between the rivals was arranged, where, throwing off their scanty waist-cloths, the controversy was settled between the female gladiators without much damage, although now and then the matter was not left to the ladies: the sable heroes themselves took up the conflict, and a regular challenge passed between the gay Othellos. At the appointed time the duellists appeared upon "the field of honour," accompanied by friends who were to witness their victory or sympathise in their defeat. Each savage leaped into the ring armed with a cowhide, whose sharp and triple thongs were capable of inflicting the harshest blows. They stripped, and having tossed to settle as to who was to have the first lashing, the unfortunate loser took his stand, and received the allotted number of stripes. Then the whipper had to receive the scourge from the hands of the sufferer. Thus they continued until one gave in, or the bystanders decided in favour of him who suffered most without shrinking. The scarred backs of the heroes were ever afterwards displayed in token of their bravery.

CHAPTER XXIX

FLAGELLATION IN AMERICA.

SO LITTLE is known of the customs of the aboriginal races of America, that it is impossible to say whether flagellation formed a part of their judicial system. But it is a remarkable fact that some of the most subtle and far-fetched notions that have entered into the minds of men were to be found among the Indians. Thus prayer, prophecy, monastic life, the confession of sin to an appointed confessor, the immortality of the soul, and hopes of a state of future bliss, belief in witchcraft, and the propitiation of idols by living sacrifices—the deepest thoughts and the wildest superstitions—it was found, were not unknown in the new world. The system of penance was inculcated in Mexico and some parts of South America. Amongst the Mexicans there suddenly appeared Quetzalcohuatl (green-feathered snake—green feathered means eloquent), a white and bearded man, of broad brow, dressed in strange dress, a legislator, who recommended severe penances, lacerating his own body with the prickles of the agave and the thorns of the cactus, but who dissuaded his followers from human sacrifice. While he remained in Anahuac it was a Saturnine reign; but this great legislator, after moving to the plains of Cholula, and governing the Cholulans with wisdom, passed away to a distant country and was never heard of any more.

It is, however, more particularly in the United States that we propose to follow the course of flagellation in this chapter. The early settlers in the Northern States carried with them a firm belief in the Rod as an efficacious reformer of morality, and likewise a good deal of that intolerance in religious matters from which they sought to escape in the mother country. They established the whipping-post, and it remains a recognised institution of the country to the present day, the

Quakers being the first to receive the benefits of flagellation; and for them, as in the old country, there was abundance of whippings at the post and at the cart's tail. The leaders and preachers of the sect were much persecuted.

At Boston in 1657, Mary Clark, after preaching, was seized, and rewarded with twenty stripes of a whip made of thick cords, with knots at the end, the hangman wielding the lash with both hands. She was then thrown into prison, and kept there for twelve months. The next to suffer were two male preachers, Christopher Holder and John Copeland, who had previously been sent out of the town, but having returned to resume their ministrations, they were taken and gagged, and then whipped. The hangman laid on severely with a knotted whip until their backs were torn, and some of the spectators fainted. They were further punished with nine weeks' close confinement in a cell, without bed or straw or fire, although it was winter. Some persons were punished for shewing sympathy for them—Samuel Shattock, because he tried to prevent the gag from choking Holder, and an aged couple, named Southick, because they had in their possession a paper belonging to Holder and Copeland. Richard Dowdney, who had just come from England, received thirty stripes. Next year, Sarah Gibbons and Dorothy Waugh were taken to the House of Correction, kept three days fasting, then whipped, and again made to fast three days. Not long after a woman named Gardner was taken at Weymouth and carried to Boston, where she and her maid were publicly whipped with a "cat" of three tails.

The following is the law passed at that time against the Quakers:- "That whosoever of the inhabitants should directly, or indirectly, cause any of the Quakers to come into that jurisdiction, he should for- feit an hundred pounds to the country, and be committed to prison, there to remain till the penalty should be satisfied. And whosoever should entertain them, knowing them to be so, should forfeit forty shillings to the country for every hour's entertaining or concealment, and be committed to prison till the forfeiture should be fully paid and satisfied. And further, that all and every of those people that should arise among them there should be dealt withal and suffer the like punishment as the laws provided-for those that came in—viz., that for the first offence, if a male, one of his ears should be cut off, and be kept at work in the House of Correction till he should be sent away on his own charge. For the second, the other ear, and be kept in the House of Correction as aforesaid. If a woman, then to be severely whipt and kept as aforesaid, as the male for the first. And for the third, he or she should have their tongues bored through with an hot iron, and be kept in the House of Correction close at work, till they be sent away on their own charge."

The whippings and fines inflicted under this law were many and heavy, and the sentiments of the orthodox party were expressed in the words of the Governor of Plymouth, who said that in his conscience he thought the Quakers a people that deserved to be destroyed, they, their wives and children, their houses and lands, without pity or mercy. The Dutch settlers followed the example of their Puritan neighbours. One Robert Hodshone was accused of holding a meeting on a Dutch plantation at Hamstead, and was carried before the Dutch Governor, who put him in prison until inquiries were made concerning his conduct. He was then dragged at the tail of a cart, along with two women who had entertained him, to New York, where he was sentenced to work at the wheelbarrow in charge of a Negro, or pay a fine of six hundred guilders. As he was unable to pay the fine, he was set to work, and kept hard at it by the Negro with a rope's end. His body was soon so much bruised and swelled with the beatings he received that he was unable to work. He was again taken before the Governor, and told that he must work, or he should be whipped every day. Early next morning he was taken into a room, stript to the waist, hung up by the hands, with a heavy log of wood tied to his feet, and a Negro was set to whip him with rods, after which he was again thrown into his dungeon. Two days after he suffered the same treatment; but as the Quakers continued to prosper notwithstanding these persecutions, more stringent measures were adopted. One William Robinson was, at Boston, sentenced to be whipped, and then banished on pain of death. The constable being commanded to get an able man to do the whipping, the culprit was brought into the street, tied to the carriage of a gun, and the executioner gave him twenty stripes. In 1662 Josiah Southick, whose parents were among the first that were banished, returned to Boston. He was sentenced to be whipped, and was tied to the cart's tail and flogged by the hangman through the streets. On this occasion the lashes of the whip were not of whipcord, but of dried guts with three knots at the end; and the handle, being long, was held by the hangman with both hands. The same day Southick was whipped at Rocksbury, and next day at Dedham, after which he was set at liberty.

At Dover (New England), three women, named Anne Coleman, Mary Tomkins, and Alice Ambrose, were sentenced to very cruel whippings. The warrant was as follows:- "To the constables of Dover, Hampton, Salisbury, Newberry, Rowley, Ipswich, Wennam, Lynn, Boston, Roxbury, Dedham, and until the vagabond Quakers are carried out of this jurisdiction: You and every of you are required, in the King's Majesty's name, to take these vagabond Quakers, Anne Coleman, Mary Tomkins, and Alice Ambrose, and make them fast to the cart's tail, and, driving the cart through your several towns, to whip them upon their naked backs, not exceeding ten stripes a-piece on each of them in each town; and so to convey them from constable to constable till they are out of this jurisdiction, as you will answer it at your peril; and this shall be your warrant. At Dover, Dec. 22, 1662, per me, Richard Walden."

The whipping began at Dover, where, on a very cold day, the three women were stripped from the middle upwards, tied to a cart, and whipped through the streets. Some of their friends protested against the cruelty, and for doing so two of them were put in the stocks. The constable at the next town, Hampton, shewed some compassion, and offered to allow them to be whipped with their clothes on; but they said he must either free them altogether or whip them according to his warrant, on their naked backs. They were whipped accordingly, and were afterwards discharged without suffering the rest of their sentence; but Anne Coleman, with four of her friends, again falling into the hands of the authorities, she was whipped at Salem. On this occasion the knot of the lash split the nipple of her breast, and she nearly died from the effects of the wound. In 1664 her two friends, Mary

Tomkins and Alice Ambrose, were pilloried and whipped in Virginia. The instrument was this time a cat-of-nine tails, instead of three. A man, Edward Wharton, who visited them in their sufferings was sentenced as follows:-"To the constables of Boston, Charlestown, Malden, and Lynn. You are required to take into your custody respectively Edward Wharton, convicted of being a vagabond, from his own dwelling-place, and the constable of Boston is to whip him severely with thirty stripes on the naked body. And from constable to constable, you are required to convey him till he come to Salem, the place where he saith he dwelleth: and in so doing, this shall be your warrant. At Boston, 30 June 1664. John Endicot."

The warrant was executed with full severity, the constable ordering the hangman to do his work well. The last case which we shall mention—it being unnecessary to enumerate more—is that of Anne Needham, fined at Boston for belonging to the sect; and her husband refusing to pay the fine—asking the authorities, seeing the law for adultery was death, whether, if his wife had committed adultery, he must by that law have suffered death—she was then sentenced to be whipped, and the constable performed the flagellation with great cruelty, because the unfortunate sufferer disdained to cry out.

A newspaper of 1774 gives an account of an amusing whipping which was given to the Boston saints about forty years before, when many of the over-righteous met with a sad mortification. Captain St. Leo, commander of a war-ship, then in Boston harbour, being apprehended for walking on the Lord's-day, was sentenced by a Justice Of The Peace to pay a fine, and on refusing to pay, had to sit in the stocks an hour during the time of change. While in the stocks the good people supplied him with much good advice as to his future conduct on the Sabbath-day. After he was released the captain expressed great regret for his past transgressions, and declared to them that he was in future resolved to lead a new life. The saints were of course delighted at this sudden reformation, and in order that the captain might still further profit by their good counsel, many of them invited him to dinner. The captain proved to be a most zealous and genuine convert. He attended the meeting-house regularly, went to every prayer-meeting, and, in short, shewed every outward mark of grace. At length he was obliged to put to sea; but before the day of his departure he invited a number of the leading men and saints to dine with him on board his ship, which lay all ready in the Nantasket Roads. A capital dinner was provided, and many bottles were drained, to the captain's health. When the after-dinner harmony was at its height a body of sailors burst into the cabin, and, in spite of remonstrances, seized the guests. They were dragged on deck, tied up to a grating, and their breeches let down, while the Boatswain and his assistants administered to them the law of Moses in the most energetic manner; the captain meanwhile assuring them that the mortification of the flesh tended to the saving of the soul. After a proper whipping they were bundled into their boat, immediately after which the ship set sail.

The pillory and whipping-post are still in active use in some parts of America. In the State of Delaware there are three whipping-posts— one at Dover, one at Georgetown, and one at Newcastle. The whipping post is considered the best penal institution in the country for the punishment of minor crimes. A newspaper published in that State thus eulogises the reformatory and restraining influence of the whipping-post:- "We should not, did time and space permit, waste a moment in useless encomiums on the merits of that effectual and invaluable judicial weapon—the whipping-post. Its satisfactory results speak loudly for themselves; and the absence in our courts of the class of criminals known as 'old offenders,' together with the proportionate annual reduction of crime in the community, declares that its terrors are rarely brought into requisition the second time for the benefit of the same convict. We may add, however, while speaking on this subject, that the 'cat' has been lately reinstated in New York as a punishment for petty larceny, and offences of that degree, with the most gratifying results in the speedy suppression of crime and depopulation of penitentiaries and other criminal boarding-houses; and in England, where it was abolished some years ago, it has become actually necessary for statutory enactment, and the effects of its re-introduction are already happily perceived. The pillory and whipping-post need no defence in Delaware from Delawareans."

The pillory at Newcastle consists of a heavy up right post, of about twelve feet in height, with a platform, through which it passes at the distance of six feet or more from the ground. At about four feet above this platform is a cross piece, with three holes on each side of the upright—one hole for the head and neck, the other two for the hands and wrists of the victims. This cross piece is divided so that the upper half may be lifted to admit the necks and hands of persons doomed to the punishment. When this is closed down there is just room enough for these indispensable members of the human frame, and sometimes, in the case of a large man, the circulation of the blood is almost stopped by the pressure. Beneath the platform, and on either side of the upright, are the manacles by which men who are to be whipped are strung up by the hands. The whipping is inflicted by the Sheriff with a cat-of-nine-tails, and is sometimes performed in a perfunctory manner, the magistrate being evidently ashamed of this part of his duties. Thus, at a recent whipping at Newcastle, two Negroes were sentenced to a heavy fine, to stand in the pillory for an hour, and then receive thirty lashes, for theft. The criminals, after doing penance in the pillory, were fastened to the whipping-post, and the Sheriff, accompanied by the gaoler, who has to certify that the appointed number of stripes is laid on, inflicted the whipping so lightly that the culprits appeared to think it quite a farce. This, however, is not always the case. A local newspaper records one of the periodical whippings at the same place, when the majesty of the law was vindicated in a much more vigorous manner on the backs of a number of criminals. After the usual pillory scenes, the whipping commenced about one o'clock. The first victim was a Negro boy of about fifteen, who had been sentenced to thirty lashes for assault. The thirty lashes were well laid on, but beyond the shrinking with each blow he gave no sign of any severe pain. Another Negro boy then got twenty lashes for stealing a pair of boots. The next was a very small boy—he had to stand on a block to allow his hands to reach the manacles on the post—and his twenty lashes were very lightly laid on. Then came two Negroes, convicted of stealing corn, and they received twenty lashes. Another Negro, who had stolen a horse and bridle, received forty stripes. The next victim was a white boy, who had pled guilty to theft, and he received ten lash-es. An Irishman, sentenced to twenty lashes for robbing a boarding-house, came next. The marks of the "cat" shewed very plain-ly on his white skin, and he cried and groaned considerably. Another white man then got his back well marked with twenty lashes, but he made no outcry. The last victim was a young German, convicted of theft. He seemed much affected by the degradation of the punish-ment, and wept bitterly, although he did not cry out when receiving his twenty lashes.

A case, which caused considerable discussion a few years age, brought to light the fact that whipping is still one mode of correction adopted in American schools. A young lady, seventeen years of age, a pupil in a public school in Cambridge, Massachusetts, having been detected in the heinous offence of whispering in school, her teacher decreed that she should receive a whipping. The young lady resisted vigorously, so that it was necessary to call in the assistance of the Principal of the school and two assistants. These three men seized the girl, two of them held her limbs, while the Principal administered fif-teen or twenty blows with a stout leather strap. The punishment was inflicted in the old-fashioned style in the presence of the whole school. The case was brought before a jury, but they acquitted the teachers who had administered the punishment. The public school committee of Cambridge held a meeting, and they decided that they could not interfere in the matter, as punishments of that kind were part of the regular discipline of public schools. The last step was to hold a meet-ing to nominate a new committee. This meeting resolved "that corporal punishment should be abolished in each and every school in the city;" and they appointed a committee favourable to that rule.

Domestic flogging, or what is called "spanking," prevails more or less all over America, so far as the younger branches of families are concerned. Whipping was a common punishment for both sexes in the time of the Puritans. Sons and daughters, we are told, had to endure the Rod till they were of a marriageable age.

CHAPTER XXX

THE FLOGGING OF SLAVES.

THE page for whipping and flogging contains its most shocking features when it gives the history of slavery and the slave trade. This is especially true of slavery in America, where it was held to be an in disputable maxim that the slave system could only be maintained by physical power; and the maxim gained strength from the fact that owners had a legal right to inflict corporal punishment on their slaves. An Act of Legislature, passed in 1740, for the protection of slave-owners, says:- "In case any person shall wilfully cut out the tongue, put out the eye, or cruelly scald, burn, or deprive any slave of any limb or member, or shall inflict any other cruel punishment, other than by whipping, or beating with a horsewhip, cowskin, switch, or small-stick, or by putting irons on, or confining or imprisoning such slave, every such person shall for every such offence, forfeit the sum of one hundred pounds current money."

The civil code of Louisiana contains the following:- "The slave is entirely subject to the will of his master, who may correct and chastise him, though not with unusual rigour, nor so as to maim or mutilate him, or to expose him to the danger of loss of life, or to cause his death."

In fact, the master's power "to wallop his own nigger," to inflict corporal punishment to any extent short of life and limb, was fully sanctioned by law in all slave-holding States; and in at least two States the master was expressly protected in using the horsewhip and cowskin as instruments for beating his slave.

Occasionally a slave was beaten to death. Simon Souther was indicted at the October term (1850) of the Circuit Court in the county of Hanover for the murder of his slave, and, being found guilty, was sentenced to the penitentiary for five years. Judge Field gave the following narrative of the punishment inflicted on the slave:- "The negro was tied to a tree and whipped with switches. When Souther became fatigued with the labour of whipping, he called upon a negro man of his, and made him cob Sam with a shingle. He also made a negro woman of his help to cob him, and after cobbing and whipping he applied fire to the body of the slave. He then caused him to be washed down with hot water, in which pods of red pepper had been steeped. The negro was also tied to a log and to the bed-post with ropes which choked him, and he was kicked and stamped by Souther. This sort of punishment was continued and repeated till the negro died under the infliction." The accused owner moved for a new trial, but the superior court held that he should have been hanged for murder of the first degree. In another case tried at Washington the following year, Colonel James Castleman was indicted because he whipped his slave to death for the crime of stealing. He was acquitted. He afterwards caused his counsel to draw up and publish a statement in vindication of his character. The statement set forth that two of the slaves were caught stealing, and were immediately punished. The first, named Lewis, was whipped with a broad leathern strap. He was punished severely, but only to an extent proportionate to his offence. He confessed his crime. His companion, it was acknowledged, was punished with greater severity. Lewis, after his punishment, was fastened by a chain around his neck to a beam above his head. There was just length of chain to allow him to stand perfectly upright: if he bent or leaned his body, he would be strangled. This was precisely what occurred on the slave being left alone for half-an-hour. A policeman, giving evidence in the "Rescue Trials" at Boston in 1851, said it was his duty, as a policeman, to take up coloured persons who were out after hours in the streets. They were locked up, and in the morning brought into court and sentenced to receive the scriptural number of thirty-nine lashes. The officers were paid extra (fifty cents) for administering the punishment. Men, women, boys, and girls, were all flogged by the police at the request of the masters. Mr. Weld, in his "Slavery as it is" (1839), mentions how they treated runaways. A handsome mulatto woman, about eighteen or twenty years of age, whose independent spirit could not brook the degradation of slavery, was in the habit of running away: for this offence she had been repeatedly sent by her master and mistress to be whipped by the keeper of the Charleston workhouse. This had been done with such inhuman severity as to lacerate her back in a most shocking manner—indeed, a finger could not be laid between the cuts. But the love of liberty was too strong to be annihilated by torture, and, as a last resort, she was kept a close prisoner, and whipped at several different times.

As an illustration of the necessity for corporal punishment among the slaves, Olmsted has the following anecdote:- "A lady of New York, spending a winter in a southern city, had a hired slave servant, who one day refused outright to perform some ordinary light domestic duty required of her. On the lady's gently remonstrating with her, she immediately replied, 'You can't make me do it, and I won't do it; I ain't afeard of you whippin' me.' The servant was right: the lady could not whip her, and was too tender-hearted to call in a man, or send her to the guard-house to be whipped, as is the custom with southern ladies when their patience is exhausted under such circumstances."

In order not to mark the backs of the slaves, and thus deteriorate their value, in Virginia they substituted the pliant strap and the scientific paddle. By the old system the cow-hide cut and lacerated the backs so badly as to almost spoil their sale when brought to the market; but the strap was a vast improvement in the art of whipping negroes. It is said that with this instrument a slave could be punished within an inch of his life, and yet come out with no visible injury, and with his skin as smooth as a pealed onion. The paddle is a large, thin, ferule of wood, in which many small holes are bored: when a blow is struck, these holes, from the rush and partial exhaustion of air in them, act like diminutive cups, and the continued application of the instrument is said to produce precisely similar results to those of the strap.

The enlistment of negroes in the Federal armies during the late American war gave painful evidence of the great amount of whipping to which slaves were subjected. Mr de Pass, surgeon to a Michigan regiment, Tennessee, says that out of 600 negro recruits whom he examined, one in five bore the marks of severe flogging, "scores shewed numerous gashes that you could not cover the scars of with one, and often with two fingers," whilst in one case he found more than a thousand marks of from six to eight inches in length. Another officer stated that not one recruit in fifteen was free from marks of severe lashing, and that more than one-half were rejected because of disability, arising from lashing of whips and biting of dogs on their calves and thighs. Mr. Westley Richards, a surgeon, says that of 700 recruits whom he examined at least one-half bore evidence of having been severely whipped and maltreated in various ways: some stabbed with a knife, others shot through the limbs, some wounded with clubs till their bones were broken.

The whipping of slaves was sometimes performed in this manner: the slave was stretched out on his face, with his arms and legs tied to bolts or rings, and then, a firm resisting position being thus secured, lashed till the flesh was laid open. A more refined mode of torture was to bury the slave in a hole in the ground just large enough to receive his body, put a door on the top, and keep him there for two or three weeks or even for a month—if life, of course, held out so long. Solomon Bradley, a negro, who enlisted into a northern regiment, describes a punishment which he saw inflicted by one Mr. Fanaby, owner of a large plantation on the South Carolina coast, near Port Royal. Attracted by the noise of fearful screams in Mr. Fanaby's own yard, he went up, and saw a slave girl stretched on the ground on her face, her hands and feet tied fast to stakes, her master standing over her beating her with a leather trace from a harness, every blow of which raised the flesh, if it did not gash it, and now and then kicking her in the face with his heavy boots, when she screamed too loud. When he had become exhausted with this exertion, he sent for sealing-wax and a lighted lamp, and dropped the blazing wax into the gashes; after which, his arm being now rested, he switched the wax out again with a riding-whip. Two grown-up daughters were all this while watching this series of operations from the upper windows.

The Rev. William Taylor says: "A dear friend a mine in my native county, in the Shenandoah Valley, Virginia, was passing the house of a neighbour, and saw in the barn-yard, suspended from a beam, a coloured woman hung up by her hands. She was nearly naked, had been whipped till she was unable to moan aloud, and had an ear of Indian corn stuck in her mouth as a gag. In that condition she was left hanging till her master should take his breakfast and have family prayers. My friend went in to see him, and remonstrated in vain to have her taken down till after the family devotions were over." He adds, that his three children were taught authority between the ages of five and ten years, by being set to whip the poor woman at will, and she was beaten and scarred up so as to present a most unnatural and hideous appearance. Another minister mentions several cases of women and children being flogged to death. One gentleman punished his negroes by slitting the soles of their feet with his bowie knife. He put one into a cotton press, and turned the screw till life was extinct. He stated that he only intended to alarm the man, but carried the joke too far. In the case of one slave boy whipped to death, the coroner's jury returned a verdict of death by cruelty, but nothing more was done.

On the southern plantations, at the close of the day's work, the negroes were collected before the overseer. If they had not laboured to suit him, or if their task was unfulfilled, they were immediately chained to a post and severely whipped. A Mrs. Peters and her broth-er-in-law, Mr. John Peters, were fined at St. Louis for flogging a slave girl. A number of ladies were attending a lecture in that city, when their, attention was diverted by the sound of blows. It appeared to them that some one was mercilessly belabouring a horse. The noise went on without intermission for two hours, when some of the audi-ence proceeded to a contiguous building, and peeped through chinks in the fence. They saw a girl about eighteen years of age, naked, with face to the ground, and her hands tied behind her back. Above her stood Mrs. Peters with her foot on the slave's neck, laying on lash after lash with a cow-hide. When she was tired her brother-in-law took the whip, and scourged the victim until her back was one ghastly wound, and the blood flowed away on all sides from her body, after which the girl was suffered to rise.

Many such whipping atrocities were perpetrated in the whipping houses of the south. A traveller tells us he saw "a young lady," almost purely white, handed out of a carriage at the door of a professional whipping house, that her exposure and pain might solace the irritated jealousy of her proprietor. Every variety of instrument and apparatus has been invented to inflict the utmost possible pang of degradation and torture on hapless slaves, male and female. They are put in slings—that is to say, suspended by the arms—while heavy battledores crush the flesh on their persons. They are skewered up into frightful distortions that the distension of their muscles may aggravate the anguish of the lash; they are fastened naked to four stakes in the ground, amid a concourse of spectators, and scourged until they swoon, or, maybe, die. Husbands are made to flagellate their wives in public, and young quadroon girls are forced to stand by while gangs of negroes are stripped for the whipping-post. Happily, these are stories of the past; and there will be no more whipping of slaves in America.

Slavery in the West Indies was accompanied by an equal degree of severe flagellation. Overseers carried out the commands of the slave-owner, dictated some times from harshness, and sometimes from the mere wantonness of cruelty. With the scourging were combined tortures of every description—branding cutting off the ears, slitting the nose, tearing out the eyes, roasting alive, breaking on the wheel, and the like. A tragedy always began with a whipping. A slave-owner would cause negresses to be stripped and whipped in sight of his guests at dinner. Capt. Scott saw a negro, who had been rather tardy in the execution of a commission, hung to a crane by both arms, with heavy weights on both feet. In this position they whipped him with thorny ebony shrubs so fearfully that next day his body was much swollen, and the thorns had to be drawn out of his flesh by another negro. Often a negro, for the fault of late rising, has been bound to a ladder, hands and feet, and lashed with a heavy whip, and afterwards had his wounds washed with a mixture of pepper and salt water to increase the pain. Frequently negro women who were *enceinte* were made to miscarry by being whipped. Many witnesses testify that the majority of slaves whom they saw in the West Indies bore deep furrows on their backs as indelible marks of hard punishment.

An English traveller in Surinam relates his experience there:- "The first object which attracted my compassion during a visit to a neighbouring estate was a beautiful Sambo girl of about eighteen, tied up by both arms to a tree, as naked as she came into the world, and lacerated in such a shocking manner by the whips of two negro drivers that she was, from her neck to her ankles, literally dyed over with blood. It was after she had received two hundred lashes that I perceived her. A remonstrance on my part unhappily produced the effect of doubling the punishment. The only cause for this matchless barbarity was her refusal to submit to the loathsome embraces of her detestable executioner. Prompted by jealousy and revenge, he called this the punishment of disobedience, and she was thus flayed alive."

This same Surinam overseer, Mr. Ebbes, was afterwards fined twelve hundred florins (about one hundred guineas) for flogging a male slave to death. Two slaves had brought a fugitive to Mr. Ebbes, and afterwards had somehow allowed him to escape, at which he was so much enraged that he flogged them both until one of them expired under the lash. Ebbes had therefore to pay the owner compensation. It was the rule in Surinam that a proprietor might kill his own slaves at the rate of £50 per head. Ebbes flogged a boy of fourteen every day for a month. These were exceptional cases with him, for he was proud of his handsome slaves, and, for fear of disfiguring their skins, would let them off with twenty lashes for theft, and the like. His successor in office commenced his reign by flogging every slave on the estate, male and female, for having overslept a quarter of an hour. The Surinam planter, when he lived on his estate, held a levee every morning, at which whipping was the principal part of the entertainment. Rising about six o'clock in the morning, he would make his appearance, under the piazza of his house, and after he had taken coffee, attended by half-a-dozen slave domestics, his overseer would attend, and make his report of the previous day's work—what negroes had deserted, died, fallen sick, recovered, been bought or born, and above all, who had neglected their work, shammed illness, been drunk or absent. The offenders were generally present, and were immediately seized by the negro drivers, and without ceremony tied to the beams of the piazza or to a tree, and there whipped with long whips, which cut round the body at every stroke, and cracked like pistol shot. Meanwhile the planter would walk up and down with his overseer, paying no attention to their cries until they were sufficiently mangled, when they were taken down, and ordered to attend to their work, without so much as a dressing to their wounds. At six o'clock in the evening he was waited on by his overseer, attended, as in the morning, by negro drivers and prisoners, and the flogging scene was repeated under similar circumstances.

It has been remarked as a curious psychological fact that the fair sex has been distinguished *par excellence* through cruelties of this kind. Many ladies made it a point to be present at the whipping of slaves, and stimulated the severity of the overseer both by precept and example. The house negroes were fully worse treated than the field hands. Lieut. Davison saw a servant maid whose nose had been slit with a knife by her mistress, on account of some slight carelessness. Another maid, at the command of her mistress, who was jealous of her, was so severely whipped that she died next day. Dropping boiling sealing-wax into the wounds caused by the lash was a favourite torture. Sometimes a negro was whipped, and being besmeared with honey, was then hung in chains under a blazing sun until he was gradually eaten alive by insects and birds of prey. When a proselytising priest once painted to a negro the punishments of hell, which all those should undergo who did not obey the precepts of the Church; the latter shook his head and said, "No, father, punishments like these are not for negroes, but for the whites who so fearfully ill-treat their black brethren." When the negroes rose in the West Indies, they took a fearful vengeance on their white masters for these cruelties.

What has been said of the West Indies is applicable to other colonies established by European nations. The Portuguese, the Dutch, and the French, practised many cruelties towards their dependants. Everywhere the whip, the scourge, the rod, and the bamboo formed the chief pastime of the European ladies and of the Creoles. In South America the Spaniards treated their slaves in a comparatively

mild manner. But even where the negroes were in some degree protected by the laws, the slave-owners found little difficulty in
exculpating themselves for acts of excessive cruelty, on the plea of
necessity. In the Dutch settlements in the East Indies, flogging was
constantly carried on among the slaves. Here the ladies were exces-
sively jealous of their husbands and their female slaves. If they
discovered the smallest familiarity between them, they set no bounds
to their thirst of revenge against the poor bondswomen, who, in most
cases, did not dare to resist the will of their masters for fear of ill treatment. They were whipped with rods or beaten with rattans until they
sank down exhausted, or the mistress was fatigued. Among other
methods of tormenting them, the mistresses would make the slaves sit
before them in such a position that they could pinch them with their
toes in a sensitive part of their bodies, with such cruel ingenuity that
their victims fainted with the pain.

The latest, and by all accounts the most wholesale flogging to
which the "nigger" has ever been subjected was that which occurred
during the *émeute* in Jamaica towards the end of the year 1865. No
doubt many of the reports that reached this country during the insur-
rection were somewhat high coloured and exaggerated, but the
inquiry of the commission, sent to Jamaica to investigate the matter,
placed the fact beyond doubt, on the evidence of white as well as negro
witnesses, that men and women were flogged for no other apparent
reason than that they had the misfortune to be born black. For three
weeks the country was under martial law; and during that reign of terror, men and women were flogged, hung, or shot, without the slightest
form of trial. Lieutenant Adcock, in one of his dispatches, says, "In the
morning I first flogged four and hung six rebels. At Leithhall, there
were a few prisoners, all of whom I flogged." Mr. Ford, who acted
under Lieutenant Adcock, stated, "This morning we made a raid with
thirty men: back at 4 pm., bringing prisoners. Having flogged nine
men and burned three negro houses, we then held a court martial on
the prisoners, who amounted to about fifty or sixty. Several were
flogged without court-martial on a simple examination. One man,
John Anderson a kind of parson or schoolmaster, got fifty lashes, one

man got one hundred; the other eight were hanged or shot." Again he wrote, "The black troops shot one hundred and sixty people on their march from Port Antonio to Manchioneel."

This man stated to the Commissioners that, under the orders of Lieutenant Adcock, he directed the execution of a man who was shot, merely because he was found eight miles from home, and could give no sufficient reason for being there. During the continuance of his command at Leithhall, he flogged from fifteen to twenty men, and about two women daily; but he thought so little of the matter that he kept no account of the punishments he inflicted. At Morant Bay, Provost-Marshal Ramsay seems to have absolutely revelled in flogging. Men were flogged by the dozen, simply because they violated an order which the Provost-Marshal had issued, that niggers were to be in their houses at a certain hour in the evening. "Flog them first, and try them afterwards," was evidently his motto. It was stated to the Commissioners that "it was a common practice when the constables or maroons brought men in, and said that they had been guilty of murder, for the Provost-Marshal to order them to be catted, and then sent down to the tents for trial. Even a sentence of death was accompanied by a flogging. One unfortunate nigger ground his teeth while being flogged, and for this he was hanged. Running the gauntlet was another of Ramsay's punishments. Prisoners, after being subjected to the cat in the regular way, were made to run between two lines of men—soldiers and sailors—by whom they were pelted with stones or struck with sticks. At a court-martial held on the 1st of November, a number of prisoners, against whom there was no proof that they were ever in arms or present at any murder, &c., were, with some exceptions, catted and sent adrift. On the testimony of some of the negroes themselves, we find that at Long Bay a woman named Collins and her daughter were flogged because another woman was induced, by the threat of similar punishment, to give evidence that Collins had said she wanted to take a hog belonging to a Mr. Codrington, in place of one which she alleged he had poisoned; and at Portland a man was shot and a number of others were flogged. While under the lash these niggers cried out, and the officer who was superintending the punishment ordered them to be gagged, which was accordingly effected by forcing stones into their mouths. It was rather a severe lesson in politeness to give a man thirty-five lashes because he did not make a bow to the satisfaction of a white gentleman. We hear of an overseer who settled accounts in a summary manner with his work-people by having them flogged all round. Soldiers escaped from the control of their officers, and hunted down the unfortunate negroes like so many head of game The case of a black drummer named Phillips, who was under the command of Lieutenant Adcock, is almost grotesque. This worthy held full sway at Leithhall for several days. He fulfilled in his own person the whole duties of accuser, judge, and executioner, and flogged and hanged his black brethren at pleasure. It is said that he even took upon himself to hang one man whom his lieutenant had ordered him to spare. In short, during this reign of terror, no circumstance was wanting to enhance the number and severity of the floggings—iron wire being sometimes twisted into the tails of the "cat" which was used. In the case of the woman Collins above mentioned, the man who performed the flogging said "She was tied hands and feet to a cocoa-nut tree; I gave her more than twenty blows. The cat was made of black fishing lines. The woman's back bled." Another poor woman gave evidence to this effect:- "I was taken by Charles Hunter before Mr. Codrington at Long Bay, and he ordered Daniel Biggerstaff to give me thirty-five lashes. He did not try me or examine me at all. Biggerstaff took off my clothes, and made me naked to the waist, and tied me to a wain wheel, and flogged me on my bare shoulders with a guava stick. My back bled, and Codrington washed it with salt pickle—it burned me. I was in the family way, and I was sick for two months and two weeks after the flogging."

We conclude this chapter with an account of the execution of two slave-owners. During the administration of Spencer Percival, on the 8th May, 1811, the Honourable A. W. Hodge, a member of His Britannic Majesty's Council at Tortola, was executed for the murder of one of his negroes by excessive flogging. For the trivial offence of stealing a mango he had caused a slave to be whipped to death; and this was perhaps the least shocking of the repeated acts of cruelty which he was known to have committed upon the slaves of his estate. This is the only actual execution that took place in the West Indies through the abuse of the power of flogging: there were many instances where the delinquent was acquitted in defiance of the evidence. A similar case occurred in South Africa. Mr. J. V. L. Gebhard, son of the Rev. Mr. Gebhard, was tried at Cape Town on the 21st February, 1822, for the murder of a slave by excessive beating. He was found guilty and sentenced to death. The sentence was carried into effect on the 15th November, amid an immense concourse of spectators.

CHAPTER XXXI

FLAGELLATION IN FRANCE.

LAGELLATION has always occupied a comparatively insignificant place in the penal code of France. In early times the punishments for even trivial crimes were generally death, mutilation, or banishment. In domestic life, however, and in schools, the Rod flourished with the greatest vigour. Monsieur and Madame Croquemitaine, who took charge of naughty children, had plenty of work. In the *Maisons de Correction*, in the lunatic asylums, and in the prison hospitals of Bicêtre and La Salpétrière, girls and women were frequently scourged: in all these places, whipping was more or less practised during the last century, and anecdotes and reminiscences of the Rod are abundant. Madame de Genlis, in her memoirs, records the fact that her mother applied the Rod with great severity, and that she first became concerned for her parent's health when she found that she was unable to wield the birch with her former strength and vigour. In *Maisons de Correction*, or female reformatories, refractory girls were punished by whipping, but not without the consent of the government authorities, and the instrument used was the martinet, a scourge of leather thongs.

As in England, flogging was frequently the portion of such of the insane of France as were confined in madhouses; and apropos of flogging in such asylums, Voltaire relates a good story, which we have translated:- In 1723, Father Fouquet, a Jesuit, returned to France from China, where he had passed twenty-five years. Religious disputes had embroiled him with his brethren: he had carried with him to China a gospel different from theirs, and now brought back to France memorials against them. Two Chinese literati made the voyage along with him; one of them died on the way, the other came with Father Fouquet to Paris. The Jesuit father was to take the Chinese to Rome, secretly, as a witness of the conduct of the good fathers in China, and in the meantime, Fouquet and his companion lodged at the house of

An Illustration from "*Les petites Heures à l'usage de Chartres,*" imprimees par la Veuve de Thielman Kerver, 1596, presenting a school scene of the period. The elder schoolmaster administers "*une vigoreuse fessée*", whilst the younger holds the hand and head of the victim. The picture is curious as showing the homely illustrations which were readily admitted into the books of devotion of that period.

The Professed, Rue St. Antoine. The reverend fathers received advice of their reverend brother's intentions, and Fouquet was no less quickly informed of the designs of the reverend fathers; he lost not a moment, but set off post the same night for Rome. The reverend fathers had interest enough to get him pursued; but the Chinese only was taken. This poor fellow did not understand a word of French. The good fathers went to Cardinal Dubois, who at that time needed their support, and told him that they had amongst them a young man who had gone mad, and whom it became necessary to confine. The cardinal immediately granted a *lettre-de-cachet*, than which there is sometimes nothing that a minister is more ready to grant. The lieutenant of police went to take this madman who was pointed out to him. He found a man making reverences in a way different from the French, speaking in a singing tone, and looking quite astonished. He expressed great pity for his derangement, ordered his hands to be tied behind him, and sent him to Charenton, where like the Abbé Desfontaines, he was flogged twice a day. The Chinese did not at all understand this method of receiving strangers; he had passed only two or three days in Paris, and had found the manners of the French very odd. He lived three years on bread and water, amongst madmen and keepers, and believed that the French nation consisted of these two species—the one half dancing, while the other half flogged them.

Voltaire makes frequent mention of the Rod in his writings, more particularly in ridicule of the Jesuits. In the "Maid of Orleans," in "Candide," in "Cortes," &c., he jests on the subject, or alludes to it in a satiric vein, when it has no connection whatever with the subject he is writing upon; and in this he has found many imitators. In his "Dictionnaire Philosophique," under the article *Verges*, Voltaire has treated of whipping at some length. Fenelon also, in his renowned work on education, has given an expression of his opinions on corporal punishment. What Rousseau has written on the subject will be found detailed elsewhere.

In the memoirs of the famous religious visionary Madame Bourignon, who herself kept a kind of reformatory school, the whipping of children is repeatedly mentioned; and it was generally to

escape an impending whipping that the girls used to denounce themselves as being bewitched or possessed by an evil spirit, and thus they
became objects, not of anger but of sympathy. Flagellation in France
used, in the days of old, to begin at a very early age, by the nurses practising it on the children. The bonnes or "bairnswomen" in great
houses used to delight in slapping the hips of their youthful charges,
affirming that the practice was good for the little ones, and that it
developed the flesh and hardened the skin. The house-governesses of
the youngsters continued the practice—so much so, that it used to be
a common matter for them to say: "*Prenez garde, mademoiselle, ou nous
irons dans le Pays-Bas.*" The flogging of the young people of both sexes
was quite common before the great Revolution, as will presently be
shewn.

In all French schools connected with convents, the custom of whipping girls with a rod was at one time universal, as might be expected
from the fondness for flagellation which prevailed among the nuns.
The holy sisters delighted to correct their pupils after the same fashion as certain holy confessors used at one time to absolve their
penitents. They insisted on the naughty pupil being in the proper
position with *cotillons retroussés*, and also required that after her punishment she should kiss the rod and thank the donor. La Fontaine
illustrates in an amusing manner the readiness of nuns to employ flagellation in his tale, "The Pair of Spectacles," where certain nuns
bestow a flagellation to revenge an affront brought upon their convent. The chief incidents of the story are as follows:- Several of the
nuns were found to have been debauched by a young man dressed like
the sisters who had effected a lodging among them. We need not
detail how the young man was found out, but found out he certainly
was; and the nuns laying hold of him, led him to a neighbouring wood,
and tied him to a tree, that he might be whipped. Having forgotten the
instruments of correction, they returned to the convent, and by some
accident were detained a little time. Meanwhile, a miller happened to
pass, and in reply to his question how he came to be there, the young
man said the nuns had used him so because he declined to kiss them.
The miller offered to put himself in the young man's place, and war-

ranted that he would give the nuns full satisfaction. The exchange was scarcely completed, when the nuns rushed out with all the disciplines and besoms they could find which were at once applied to the miller's back. In vain the unfortunate man remonstrated, and expressed his great ability and willingness to gratify the wishes he supposed they had. The nuns, however, did not cease their whipping until the disciplines were worn out.

In schools for male pupils whipping was also carried on. Among these, the school kept by "the good Fathers of St. Lazare" in Paris bore the palm. In their school "of the good boys" (*des bons enfants*) the fathers not only inflicted flagellations on their pupils, but on any strangers that might be recommended to them for that purpose. A note, such as "M. So-and-so presents compliments to Father —, and begs him to reward the bearer with twenty stripes well laid on," if accompanied with the proper fee, was sure to be promptly honoured. Being situated in the metropolis, a very extensive whipping business was carried on in the seminary. Fathers or mothers who had undutiful sons, tutors who had unruly pupils, uncles who were entrusted with the education of ungovernable nephews, masters who had wickedly inclined apprentices, whom they were themselves unable or afraid to correct, applied to the fathers of St. Lazare, and by properly feeing them had their wishes gratified. Indeed, the fathers found means to increase their trade in flagellation: they were well stocked with the necessary instruments for giving disciplines, and had such a stout crew of *cuistres* to inflict them, that they never failed to execute any job they engaged to perform, and, regardless of age, courage, or strength, they willingly undertook the most difficult flagellations. So regular was the trade carried on by the good fathers in that branch of business that letters of the above kind directed to them were literally notes of hand payable at sight; and provided such notes did but come to hand, whoever the bearer might be, the fathers were sure to have them discharged with punctuality. This kind of business frequently gave rise to accidents or mistakes of a laughable nature. Young men who had letters to carry to the house of St. Lazare, and not knowing the contents of these letters, would often undesignedly charge other persons to deliver them if they chanced to pass that way, and the unfortunate bearer, of course, had no sooner delivered the dangerous note, which he had good naturedly suffered himself to be entrusted with, than he was collared, horsed, and flogged. Ladies, it is said, who had been forsaken or otherwise cruelly used by their admirers, would recur, when other means failed, to the ministry of the fathers of St. Lazare; and if they took care that the fathers received the proper fee, and got the gentleman once within the walls of the school, they were certain to get the satisfaction of knowing that he had been properly whipped

According to a song by Béranger, the whipping of children was practised by the Jesuits of St. Acheul under the Restoration:-

"Hommes noirs, d'où sortez-vous?
Nous sortons de dessous terre,"

and each stanza ending thus —

"Et puis nous fessons et nous refessons
Les jolis petits, les jolis garçons."

That public sentiment has considerably changed on the question of corporal punishment in French schools since the time when the good fathers of St. Lazare held high revel, appears from a case recorded in the *Journal des Débats* in 1832. The Abbé Loison, head of an establishment for education at Boulogne-sur-Mer, appeared before the tribunal of that town, upon the charge of having inflicted blows with a whip on the young Alexis, aged ten years. The tribunal President asked the accused what was the form of the whip which he had used. He replied that it consisted of seven thin strings with small knots. On the President observing that the schoolfellows of Alexis who were called as witnesses had declared that the strings were as thick as a quill, and the knots as large as gooseberries, the accused replied that the witnesses, being at a consider able distance from him, could not see well, and that fear must doubtless have magnified the objects to their eyes. To settle the question, the *Procurer du Roi* required the whip to be produced; but the accused made no reply to this demand. The tribunal, after ten minutes' deliberation, pronounced sentence by which, on the ground that the Abbé Loison had struck the young Alexis without having any right to do so, he was condemned to pay 100 francs, to undergo twenty days' imprisonment, and to pay costs according to Article 311 of the Penal Code.

The last female publicly whipped by judicial decree in France was Jeanne St. Remi de Valois, Countess de la Motte, for her share in the abstraction of that celebrated diamond necklace which has given point to so many stories. The history of the diamond necklace has been often told; we therefore limit ourselves to an outline of Madame de la Motte's share in the transaction:- Jeanne St. Remi de Valois was a descendant of Henry II of Valois, King of France, through an illegitimate channel. She was reared in extreme poverty. Passing over a part of her early life, we find her in Paris, married to De la Motte, a young gendarme. Calling herself a countess, she sent out memorials and petitions to the King and his ministers for the restoration of the estates of her ancestors, and also for money to supply her immediate wants; after which she made the acquaintance of Cardinal de Rohan, the grand almoner, and became a regular recipient of his bounty. The cardinal was at the time consumed by a romantic passion for the Queen, so that by practising on this foible, and by a series of forged letters, Madame de la Motte extracted large sums of money from the cardinal, and finally persuade him to buy a gorgeous diamond necklace, valued at one million eight hundred thousand francs, which had been ordered by Louis XV for the Countess du Barry, but left in the jeweller's hands owing to the unexpected death of that lady. The Cardinal, having arranged the terms of purchase with the jewellers, believed that he had now found a way to the favour of the Queen; but the necklace came into the possession of the countess, who at once proceeded to dispose of the diamonds separately. A few only could be sold in Paris, but despatching her husband to England, he disposed of the remainder, and they received nearly fourteen thousand pounds for three hundred out of the five hundred and forty-one stones of which the necklace was composed. The fraud was at length found out by the jewellers memorialising the Queen with regard to the payment, when her majesty at once indignantly denied all knowledge of the transaction. The Cardinal, Madame de la Motte, and their accomplices, being lodged in the Bastille, were, after the preliminary examination, brought to trial before the Grand Chamber. Madame de la Motte conducted herself with the greatest *sangfroid* during the trial, which resulted in her condemnation, and that of Villette, who had forged the letters in the Queen's name by which the Cardinal was deceived, and in the acquittal of the others. Villette was sentenced to banishment for life. In accordance with this sentence, he was brought from the prison by the hangman, with a halter about his neck, to one of the gates of the city, where his sentence was read; after which, according to an ancient custom, a loaf of bread was presented to him by the executioner, who then pointed out his way to the country, and, with great solemnity, turning the culprit's back upon Paris, gave him a smart kick on the breech, and bade him never return. The countess was sentenced to have a halter slung round her neck, and then to be flogged and beaten naked with rods, and branded with a hot iron on both shoulders with the letter V (*voleuse*); and finally to be confined in the prison of Salpêtrière for the rest of her life. As usual in those days, she did not hear the sentence until it was just about to be executed. She was brought to the scene in an undress, and while the sentence was being read she broke out into curses, and uttered the most calumnious and unheard of imprecations against the Queen, the Parliament, and the Cardinal. The executioner and his assistants seized her and fastened her to a cart, with a halter about her neck; but the whipping is said to have been very slight, and owing to her struggles the executioner had considerable difficulty in performing the operation of branding. This done, she was dressed and hurried away to the Salpêtrière, from which prison she escaped after a year's confinement, and her subsequent career was not very creditable.

The whipping of women in Paris was not always done according to law. In the "tumultuous horror" that filled the time of the great French Revolution, during the Red Terror, when butchers, ruffians, kennel heroes, the grim and savage outlaws of the street, were in the ascendant, and again when the *jeunesse dorée* had the upper hand, flagellation was not forgotten. During the former period the Tricoteuses were accustomed to waylay such nuns as had been driven from or refused to leave their convents, and shamefully whip them. The most noted case of this kind was that of Théroigne de Méricourt, who, having been publicly flogged in a very rude way by a mob of women on the Terrasse des Feuillants, went mad through rage and shame, and was afterwards confined for twenty years in the lunatic asylums of Bicêtre and Charenton. Whenever she could escape from the vigilance of her gaolers, she would strip herself naked, and endeavour to administer to herself the degrading punishment she had suffered at the hands of the populace.

When the reaction came, the atrocities of the *jeunesse dorée* were equally great. The party, composed of the white-handed *élégantes*, delicate libertines, ladies of fashion, and professors of religion, blew men to pieces with grape shot, stabbed disarmed prisoners, and whipped young girls in public. At Montbrison women were tied to a tree of liberty, stripped, and scourged. A girl of fifteen, for kissing her father's corpse, underwent a shameful flagellation in the streets. The anti-terrorist youth of Paris began to surround the hall of the Jacobins during the evening sittings, with the intention of insulting, if they could not silence, the members: they threw stones at the windows and into the hall, and when the members came forth to resist they met with harsh treatment. The women who frequented the galleries—"the furies of the guillotine," as they were called—were particularly the objects of their vengeance. Whenever they were caught in the courts they were flogged, and their cries and lamentations increased the ire and terror of the Jacobins.

CHAPTER XXXII

FLAGELLATION IN FRANCE *(continued)*

THE French literature of the last century abounds in stories illustrative of flagellation, a punishment which seems to have particularly recommended itself to the fair sex. In most cases they were directly or indirectly the cause of many a whipping. This assertion might be supported by several examples. There is, for instance, the custom which prevailed in Italy and France, of ladies flagellating their acquaintances, while yet in bed, on the morning of the day of the Festival of the Innocents—or the fool's day; "innocent," both in Italian and French, signifying fool or simpleton. On that day ladies could exact satisfaction for the offences they might have received from their friends throughout the year. Those ladies who had agreed to go in the same party met in the morning according to pre-arrangement, and having laid their plans, set out, fully supplied with instruments of correction, to visit their acquaintances. Woe to the unlucky one who had forgotten to secure the door of his apartment, for the ladies burst in upon him, and did not leave him until he was well disciplined.

Here is another explanation of Childermas or Innocent's Day. On this day it was the custom to whip up the children in the morning, "that the memorie of Herod's murder of the innocents might stick the closer, and in a moderate proportion to act the crueltie again in kinde." The French extended the practice beyond children; they even coined a word to designate it *Innocenter.* Clement Marot tells his mistress,

> "Si je savais où couche
> Votre personne au jour des Innocens,
> De bon matin j'irais à votre couche," &c.

Early rising did not rescue the poorer classes of females from this infliction, which a princess of France has not hesitated to record; and in *Les Escraignes Dijonnoises* we have the subtle scheme of a poor maiden of that city to escape the ordeal.

In the "Tales of the Queen of Navarre" we find a story of a man who avails himself of the flagellating custom of the Innocent's Day as a ruse to escape the vigilance of his wife. Having a liaison with his servant-maid, he was at a loss to find an opportunity for an interview with her without raising suspicion. However, on the eve of Innocent's Day he commenced to find fault with the maid, observing to his wife that she was so lazy and careless that he proposed the next morning to give her "the Innocents," and his wife was quite delighted with his resolution. He accordingly rose early next morning, and taking a large birch in hand, went up stairs to carry out his threat—his unsuspecting wife being almost sorry to think of the severe correction that, judging from her husband's stern looks, would befall the maid. It may be inferred, however, that the birch was not much used, and that the maid did not get the Innocents, although she was heard to scream, and also to weep, a good deal.

Very richly deserved was the flagellation bestowed on a certain surgeon by a princess of France, on whom he had been called to attend professionally. This lady, afterwards the wife of Henry IV, had a turn for political intrigue. During the civil wars of the League, she tried to obtain possession of the town of Agen, but the attempt failed, and she was forced to make a precipitate flight. In the hurry of departure it was impossible to procure a pillion for her seat on horseback, and consequently she had to ride many miles seated behind a gentleman. The flight was accomplished through great danger, and she at length reached a place of safety in the town of Usson in Auvergne. The effects of the fatigue she had endured brought on a fever, and besides, owing to the want of the proper accommodation of a pillion during flight, that part of her body on which she sat was in a sad condition. A surgeon being called into requisition, he was successful in performing a cure in a very short time. So far so well; but the surgeon, in defiance of all professional etiquette, made a joke of the cure that he had performed, and circulated many merry tales at the expense of her highness. By and bye these reached the ears of the princess, who put a stop to his pleasantry by causing him to receive a hearty flagellation;

in the words of the story, elle lui fit donner les étrivieres, a fate which he very well merited.

In the causes celbres of the French law courts, we find an interesting instance of one lady of rank serving another with a flagellation. The affair took place during the reign of Louis XIV, and made a great stir at the time. The Marchioness of Tresnel and the lady of Liancourt lived near the town of Chaumont, and were rivals, striving on every occasion who should outshine the other. The contest was carried on for some time with much bitterness, until the Marchioness determined upon a stroke of policy that would at once and effectually silence the pretensions of her rival. Accompanied by a number of servants, she waylaid the lady of Liancourt, caused her servants to take the unfortunate lady from her coach, and execute a lower discipline upon her. The whipping was made the subject of a criminal action, in which the lady of Liancourt was the complainant and the Marchioness the defendant. The latter was condemned to ask the plaintiff's pardon in open court upon her knees, to pay two thousand pounds damages, and to be banished from the jurisdiction of the court—rather a heavy price to pay for the satisfaction of flagellating a rival. Nor was that all: the unfortunate servants, who only executed the orders of their mistress, were sent to the galleys.

In the same collection (*causes celebrés*) there is related a case of two ladies of noble family, living near Saumur, being tried for punishing in the same way the daughter of a farmer, for competing with them in beauty. A flagellation was not a bad way of settling the claims of a rival or enemy, when there was no danger of the law. At an opera ball in Paris, two courtesans, named, Rosalie and Sainte Marie, had a quarrel, the termination of which was very curious. Invectives, or rather severe truths, were liberally bestowed by both parties. Rosalie being obliged, in this sort of combat, to give up the field to her adversary, she retired almost stifled with rage and a desire for vengeance. The next morning a young man of genteel appearance presented himself at Sainte Marie's door, and as she had not then risen from bed, her woman refused him admittance; but he insisted, and penetrating into the chamber where the fair one was reposing, he shut the door and window, drawing the curtain with no small bustle: it was Rosalie herself who came in this fashion to demand satisfaction from her adversary! She produced two pistols, and presented them to Sainte Marie, who, hardly awake, sprang from the bed, and falling at the feet of Rosalie, implored forgiveness. Rosalie offered to decide the affair with pistols, but the other tremblingly refused. She then, after reproaching her rival with poltroonery, produced from under her greatcoat an excellent birch rod, and compelling Sainte Marie to take up her night gown and to lay herself in the most convenient posture across the bed, she whipt her till the blood came and then retired, satisfied with the vengeance she had taken.

Many curious records and anecdotes might be given of flagellation in France, for at one time the practice of flogging, either as a punishment or as an amusement, was extensively indulged in. It is recorded, for instance, that the Countess du Barry inflicted a whipping on the Marchioness of Rozen, in revenge for a slight. The Marchioness was at one time a lady in waiting to the Countess of Provence, and was introduced to the Countess du Barry, with whom, in a short time, she became very friendly, being frequently invited to the splendid entertainments given by du Barry. The friendship was not, however, of long duration, for the Countess of Provence, her mistress, having remonstrated with the Marchioness on her intimacy with the king's favourite, and especially for assisting at her entertainments, she broke off her connection with Madame du Barry, or, at least, treated her with marked coldness. Madame du Barry, resenting the change, complained to the King, and Louis replied jestingly that the Marchioness was only a child, for whom a rod was the proper punishment. Madame du Barry, interpreting the reply in her own fashion in its most literal sense, took measures for carrying the hint into effect. One morning the Marchioness paid Madame du Barry a visit, and was received in the most cordial manner. They breakfasted together, after which Madame said she had something very particular to tell her, and invited the Marchioness into her closet. The latter complied, but no sooner had they entered that apartment than the door was shut and four stout chamber-maids seized the unfortunate Marchioness, and having extended her on a bed, whipped her with great severity. The sufferer complained to the King, but when he questioned Du Barry on the matter, she replied that she had only followed his own advice. Indeed, some venture to say that Louis was a hidden but delighted spectator of the whole scene. Be that as it may, the Marchioness, by the advice of her friends, was reconciled to the Countess, and it was agreed to let bygones be bygones.

Another instance of the aptitude of ladies in the use of the Rod may be found in a passage in the life of the poet Clopinel or John of Meun, one of the wits of the court of Charles le Bel, King of France. Clopinel wrote several books, but owed his reputation chiefly to his continuation of the *Roman de la Rose*. The *Roman de la Rose*, a very popular work in those days, was begun by William Loris, who died about the year 1260, and was finished by John of Meun; from it our own Chaucer has drawn many of the materials of his poems. John of Meun gave great offence to the ladies, especially those belonging to the court, by four lines in this poem:-

"Toutes êtes, serez, ou fûtes,
De fait ou de volonté, putes;
Et qui bien vous chercheroit,
Toutes putes vous trouveroit;"

which is just a very coarse way of expressing the well known line of Pope:-

"Every woman is at heart a rake."

The court ladies considered Clopinel's lines a libel on their sex, and unanimously resolved to make him smart for them. One day as the poet was on his way to court, profoundly ignorant of his approaching fate; the ladies seized him, and lost no time in making him ready for correction. No escape seemed possible, but the poet's wit did not desert him. Asking permission to say a few words, and on being allowed to do so, he acknowledged the justice of his sentence, and begged as a favour that the lady who felt most aggrieved by his lines should give the first blow. This completely disconcerted the maids of honour: each was afraid to give the others an advantage over her; the rods fell from their hands, and the poet escaped.

A somewhat similar story is related of Gonnella, the court fool of Ferrara, a personage who was celebrated for his wit and humour at the court of Niccollo III, Marquis of Ferrara. He was allowed to visit Florence for a wife, and on his return he perpetrated a joke at the expense of his mistress, the Marchioness. He first made the Marchioness believe that his wife was deaf, and then told his wife that the Marchioness was afflicted with the same infirmity. On presentation of the jester's wife, few things can be imagined more ludicrous than the scene that followed between these two ladies of high and low degree, each believing the other deaf, and screaming out high strained compliments at the top of their voices, while the rest of the company stood round them in a ring, enjoying, as seriously as they could, a joke that told itself so loudly. When the jest was blown the Marchioness apparently took it in good humour, but privately resolved to have her revenge. Accordingly she sent for the jester one morning into her chamber; and no sooner did he come than the door was locked, and the fool found himself surrounded by a crowd of women, with her highness as their general, all armed with switches of the most cutting description. "Now, thou varlet," said the Marchioness, "thou shalt be chastised. I will teach thee never again to pass a jest on any woman above the condition of thy paltry wife." The fool penitently declared himself deserving of their most feminine and tender anger, merely entreating they would grant him one small request—then they might cut him to pieces. His petition was unadvisedly acceded to; upon which, kneeling down among the enraged Amazons, he thus continued, "Most honourable lady, and ye undoubted maids of honour, I request no more than that she, and she alone, will be the first to lay a switch across my back, who hath at any time or in any way forfeited her aforesaid honour, and all that ye all wot of." Upon this the honourable lady herself, of course, could not strike first; but she commanded three or four of the oldest to commence, a very unfair and preposterous demand, and it was accordingly declined. The young ones were then appealed to, but they laughed outright in defiance of etiquette. In fact, every switch was laid down, and Gonnella got clear out of the scrape.

Brantôme relates in his memoirs a story of Mademoiselle de Limeuil, a maid of honour in the court of King Henry II of France, being whipped. Mademoiselle de Limeuil, a handsome and witty young lady, wrote a *jeu d'esprit* at the expense of the ladies and gentlemen of the court. The queen, who was of a serious turn, and was besides annoyed at the prevailing practice of writing satires and pasquinades, resolved to make a striking example of this offender in her own household. Mademoiselle de Limeuil and the young ladies who assisted her, were therefore rewarded with a flagellation.

Brantôme also gives a story of the princess of the House of Austria ordering the flagellation of a reverend Jesuit father. Philip II of Spain, his first wife being dead, proposed to marry this lady, a daughter of Maximilian II, and his own niece, and who had formerly been married to Charles IX, King of France. The princess rejected his suit, and Philip and his sister, the princess's mother, procured the assistance of a father Jesuit, a man of learning and suavity. The Jesuit exerted all his powers of persuasion in vain: the princess refused to accede to the proposal, and, on the Jesuit continuing his importunities, she first threatened, and finally caused him to be severely whipped.

Another notable instance of flagellation is related by Brantôme as occurring at the court of this same Philip II. His queen was one day conversing with her ladies about two country seats belonging to the King, situated, the one at Madrid, and the other at Valladolid, which she had fancied. She wished that they were so near each other that she might touch one with each foot, making a motion at the same time with her extended legs. The court jester was present, and could not restrain his wit—the occasion being too tempting, he made a coarse remark on the subject, and was immediately hurried out and well whipped.

In regal and other great houses the scene of these flagellations appears to have been the kitchen, that place being not only well supplied with instruments of correction, but also with people able and willing to carry out the orders of the higher powers.

A great personage appears to be referred to in the following paragraph, evidently of French origin, which appeared in a gossiping German journal, stating that a certain illustrious lady who lived in Paris was regularly birched for her sins twice a week, by a holy sister who dwelt with her as a kind of confessor. This great lady, we were told, was seen *en chemise* after a gay ball walking on her naked feet along a passage paved with tiles. She was received in a small oratory at the end of this *via dolorosa* by the sister in question, who, commanding her illustrious visitor to extend herself before an altar upon the floor of cold marble, administered to her a very sharp discipline with a monastic scourge. The lady then had to find her way back to her luxurious apartments on bended knees. This story is almost equal to some of those told of the nuns of the olden time in previous chapters. But is it true will be asked? We cannot say it is, of our own knowledge: we simply abridge it from the columns of a journal in which it appeared about seven or eight years ago.

We might give numerous other anecdotes of flagellation in France, but as many of them would be similar to the foregoing, we conclude this chapter with the following notice of a ladies' whipping club:- An old French novel which we cursorily examined at one of the quays on the Seine in Paris, contained a graphic description of a kind of romantic whipping club which existed in that city a short time previous to "The Terror." The ladies who were members of this gay institution administered the Rod to each other with charming elegance! A trial preceded each correction, and if a lady was found guilty, she was straightway disrobed and birched by her companions. Many women of high rank, if we can believe what was written in the book—the title of which was, we think, "The Chateau at Tours" —belonged to this society, and received from their companions personal chastisement. These noble dames were also described in the book as leaders of fashion and inventors of new modes, some of which, judging by the description given of them in the book, must evidently have been not unlike the dress worn by Mother Eve.

CHAPTER XXXIII

THE ROD IN GERMANY AND HOLLAND.

Having considered Flagellation in Russia and France, we now turn to other parts of Europe, as Holland, Germany, Prussia, Austria, and Poland had also their flogging customs. In all these countries the whipping-post or the House of Correction had a place, and the Rod was very extensively used in the domestic circle, whilst scholastic and judicial whipping was not forgotten. In various towns of Germany the whipping-post stood in the market place, and the culprit being led out, was stripped to the waist, and whipped by an appointed officer with rods composed of long birch. As many as seventy stripes were sometimes inflicted. The crowd of spectators usually included many ladies, old and young, who took extreme delight in witnessing the performance—they were so familiar with the Rod at home that they had no scruples about being present at public whippings. Indeed, parents in Austria, Germany, and Holland neither hesitated to whip their grown-up children at home, nor to send them to the whipping-houses to be corrected when necessary and, as we have read, young ladies belonging to most respectable families were subject to this discipline, and in the case of either male or female the Rod was held to be a capital remedy for the vagaries of a first love, especially when it was not palatable to the parents.

The son of a respectable tradesman of Amsterdam, a youth of twenty years of age, fell violently in love with the mayor's daughter. For weeks he could neither eat, drink, nor sleep, nor yet behave in a rational manner, and at one time seemed to be in a fair way for a lunatic asylum. His father procured the best medical advice that his means would permit, but only to find that the doctor's prescriptions were useless. At length, getting hold of a letter written by his son to his lady love, this epistle was the means of enlightening him as to his son's state of mind, and speedily caused him to alter his mode of treatment. The doctor received his *congé*, and, the young man being sent to the House of Correction, a smart whipping speedily had the effect of completely dispelling "love's young dream," and the young man returned home completely cured.

Children at school were not exempt from the birch, and received it plentifully both on the hands and elsewhere. One school custom, which prevailed up till the end of the last century at Groningen, was of a very whimsical nature. When the children had obtained a holiday, before leaving school they had to jump through a hoop, and while they did so the master so stationed himself as to take advantage of their position and slap their posteriors. Sometimes, too, the master posted himself within the entrance-door, and performed the above ceremony as the children wriggled through between his legs. Occasionally, too, they were treated to a kick in, as well as a kick out, and in commemoration of the practice the children had a rhyme which they sung in anticipation of their holidays:-

"Uitslag, inslag,
Heele wake speuldag!"

"Kick us out, kick us in,
Weeks of holiday begin!"

The birch is in considerable use, even at the present day, in most of the rural districts of Holland, and in many of the houses a rod may be seen hanging in some convenient place, ready for use. A recent traveller, in visiting one of the windmills of the country, made his appearance at rather an awkward moment, just as mamma was dispensing a birchen chastisement to a lubberly lad who was sprawling over her lap. A girl evidently, from her lugubrious countenance, was waiting her turn, and "the worthy frau, not in the least discomposed at my entrance," says the traveller, "finished off the boy by giving him two or three rather hot slaps with her naked palm, after she had thrown down the rod."

The ancient laws of Germany were liberal with the whip: the rooms of justice and the Houses of Correction abounded with flagellation in every shape and form—the whip, the cane, and the birch being all brought into play. The magistrates and officers of justice had complete control and unlimited power in the matter of whipping. In the Houses of Correction where the chief culprits were unfortunate women, not unfrequently innocent females, through the intrigue of distinguished persons, or of unfeeling relatives, were brought under the Rod in the most exposed manner. Sometimes there was a degree of decency in the performance, female culprits being allowed to retain an under garment, and the executioner being a woman. In ordinary cases, however, this regard for appearances was held to be quite unnecessary, and the gaoler officiated on the bare body of the culprit. Vagrants, and unfortunate wanderers who could not give satisfactory account of themselves, were alike treated to this kind of discipline. In some German towns female offenders were stuck into an ingenious kind of machine, in which they could make no resistance, in order that they might be more conveniently whipped. Sometimes the chastisements were inflicted publicly, in the court of the police buildings, and at these, and the semi-private whippings in the Houses of Correction, it was customary, as at one time in London, for the people to make up parties of friends and relations to enjoy the spectacle! German literature abounds with allusions to the good old flogging days. The older law books and the police and municipal records preserve the history of judicial flagellation, and the general literature of the country gives ample evidence that the Rod was in frequent use in household and scholastic management.

In the judgements of the court of love we find plentiful strokes of the Rod prescribed for breaches of the seventh commandment, and in the tapestry of the period the fact is commemorated by figures of women with rods chastising the offending knights who kneel before them. In the old German epic, the *Nibelungenlied*, the noble Chriemhild, sister to King Gunthar, was beaten by her adored husband, the hero Sigfried, because she told a secret that had been confided to her. The Princess Gudrun was bound to a bed-post and beaten with thorny rods, at the command of the wicked queen whose

ugly son she refused to marry. In a play written by Jhan, and acted by
Augsburg, there is prescribed verbally to a young free-thinker after he
had been unmasked in his wickedness, the punishment of the Rod.
The Jesuits, as has been already related in a previous portion of this
work encouraged the use of the Rod, especially as a means of correction for young women. St. Kresenzia of Kaufbeurn deserves special
mention on account of the belief she entertained of the efficacy of the
Rod; and much has been written both in praise and blame of her fondness for it. Whenever she was asked for counsel, she invariably
recommended the Rod. On one occasion her own cousin consulted
her concerning the best means of maintaining her authority over her
daughter, a handsome young lady of seventeen years of age, already
deeply in love. St. Kresenzia said that if the young woman was sent to
her, she should carry an effectual remedy home with her. As soon as
Mariele (so the young woman was called) appeared before her relation
she was met by her with a tremendous rod and violently beaten. She
was then sent back to her mother, with a letter earnestly advising a
repetition of the dose, and to be continued until the maiden had
attained her nineteenth year. Mariele was obliged to submit to the
stronger power, and when either time or strength failed her mother,
she was sent to her relation, who did not fail to make up the deficiency, and the means of correction was indeed continued until Mariele
was of age for wedlock.

In the convent schools plenty of whipping went on. The "Boot
Nuns" of Augsburg had an ingenious method which they practised
with much perseverance. These nuns, so named from the small boots
which they were bound to wear in winter, kept a boys' school, where
pupils of from six to ten years of age were received. The offenders,
when sentenced to punishment, were forced to creep head foremost
into the mouth of a stove, leaving the lower parts of their bodies outside. The mistress then drew down their clothes and administered the
Rod!

We have mentioned elsewhere that in the gymnasia of Germany,
punishment was inflicted by the "blue man," but in the schools taught
by Jesuits, or persons educated by them, the master performed the

ceremony himself. Many of these schools were mixed—that is, attended both by boys and girls—and the latter, like the boys, were openly stripped and beaten with the rod. "The Rod," they wrote in defence of their theory of discipline, "was an indispensable integral part of the whole."

Having such a principle to start with, it is scarcely to be wondered at that abuse of the Rod was frequent. The cases of a Father Marell in Bavaria and a Belgian abbé at Ghent attracted considerable notice. The abbé's fondness for flagellation was made the subject of a lawsuit, and although the priest was acquitted, it was understood that his acquittal was entirely due to political causes. It was proved that he had quite a mania for flagellation. The boys in his school suffered it frequently from his own hand, and even when he was not personally visible, he took pleasure in witnessing the operation through a glass window. The holy fathers made quite merry over the administration of the Rod, and had several standing jokes on the subject. A slap on the hand with the rod was called *positive*, a spanking on the buttocks was named *comparative*, and the whipping in its full purity was *superlative*. The taste for whipping, thus developed and fostered by the Jesuits, was carried into the family circle, and children received whipping in the *superlative* degree as often at home from their parents as at the school.

A tailor in a German town had a half-witted son who was one day left alone in the house. During the absence of his parents he amused himself by drawing some original figures with his fingers, which he had dipped in the ink bottle, on a pair of silk breeches that his father had made to order for a nobleman. The mother was the first to discover the mischief, and, so far from appreciating her son's taste for the fine arts, seized the yard-stick and administered to him a severe castigation in the *superlative* degree. The boy, of course, escaped as soon as possible, and his father, the tailor, tried to efface the ink marks, but without success—at any rate, the customer refused to take the breeches. Towards evening the boy returned home, and no sooner had he entered the house than his father seized him, and completed the flagellation that his mother had begun so energetically in the morning.

We are told that in this instance parental discipline had the desired effect of destroying in the youthful culprit all inclination for the fine arts.

Formerly political prisoners were subject to the lash in different German countries; for instance, in Hesse. A few years ago, a bill was brought into the Prussian Chamber for the restoration of this punishment, but without effect. A gentleman, who was recently an inmate of a German prison, describes the forms of punishment now adopted there, and some of them are so cruel that the moderate infliction of the whip would be merciful in comparison. Little infractions of the rules of the prison are punished by reprimands before a committee of the house officers, or by deprivations of favours and permissions; others by hunger or "darkanest," the deprivation of the bed, the putting on of chains, and applying the "*strafstuhl*," or chair of punishment. This ingenious instrument of torture is a wooden arm chair. The delinquent, sitting upon it, is attached to it by straps, fixed to his neck, breast, belly, arms, and legs. By the straining of these thongs at so many parts of the body, the circulation of the blood is very soon checked, and the result is a most painful sensation, which increases every moment. Sometimes prisoners have been for six hours in this situation, until blood came from the mouth, nose, and ears. The cries from the unfortunate sufferers were described as something horrible.

Though Poland no longer exists as a separate country, the Poles retain many of their national characteristics, and their mode of living is in some respects peculiar. Flagellation occupies a prominent part in the management of their children and servants. At the time that all peasants were serfs or slaves beating was a matter of course, and since serfdom was abolished, the gentry have been loath to give up their ancient prerogative. When the imperial ukase was promulgated, and the serfs, wishing to taste their newly acquired liberty, refused to work, they were severely beaten. One Polish gentleman is reported to have said, "There is no bearing our slaves since they imagine that they are independent. Before I left home, I had a dozen men and as many women beaten, just to shew them that I am still their master. A few days before I found the head cook enlightening the others on their rights; so I had the fellow severely flogged." Those of the Poles who are rich keep a great many servants, and the usual way of preserving order among them is to keep the whip going. If anything goes amiss the delinquent must be whipped. If the dinner is badly prepared the head cook has to suffer for it, and he indemnifies himself by flagellating his subordinates. One day a nobleman had a dinner party, and the dinner not being prepared to his satisfaction, he sent for the cook; the servant who went for him returned, saying the cook could not be found; some one present expressing surprise at this, the host remarked, "He is hiding, afraid of being beaten, as he was the last time that the dinner was not to our taste." It is the custom for the mistress of the house to bestow a flagellation on all her dependants and guests, on a particular morning about Easter. The workwomen and maids are all assembled in a room, when the lady enters with a whip in her hand and lays on quite promiscuously. The young ladies are subject to the same treatment, only they are whipped separately, instead of *en masse* like the servants. A lady residing with a family in Poland was alarmed one morning by hearing most terrific screams resounding through the house, but on making inquiry as to the cause, she was laughingly informed that it was only the mistress of the house bestowing this wholesome correction.

CHAPTER XXXIV

MILITARY FLOGGING.

FLAGELLATION has long held a prominent place among military punishments. The Romans set the example to later nations, as may be proved from passages in Livy, Polybius, and Tacitus. According to these authors, soldiers were often so violently flogged or whipped that they fainted under the hands of the executioner; and the excessive abuse of the fustuarium supplicium was not seldom the cause of mutiny and riot—the more especially that the number of blows was not determined by law, but left to the will of arbitrary commanders. Most European nations have, in more modern times, resorted to flagellation for the maintenance of military discipline. It is on record that during the thirty years' war the greatest generals were generally the greatest floggers.

The French were the first to abolish the using of the lash as a military punishment: that they never flogged their soldiers, as has been stated, is untrue, but for a long time flogging has been unknown among them. Their punishments, so far as the army is concerned, are now death and imprisonment. In their military code no less than forty-five offences are punishable by death; twenty-six are punishable with imprisonment for periods of five to twelve years, with or without what is called the *boulet,* which is a cannon ball attached by a chain to the leg or body; and nineteen offences are punished by imprisonment in the *travaux forcés,* or galleys, not exceeding three years.

The following examples will shew the severity of punishments in the French army:- For desertion the punishment is three years of the *boulet:* the culprit is kept constantly dragging an eight-pound ball by a chain, working ten hours in summer and eight in winter, and when not working he is kept chained in his cell. Ten years of the *boulet* is awarded for a second desertion; and if he deserted while on duty, two years is added to the sentence; if he mutinies, the double *boulet* is his fate. Six months in prison is the punishment for disobedience in time of peace; one year in irons for threatening a superior without striking him, or, if with arms in his hand, two years; death, or ten years in irons, for actually striking a superior, two years in irons for selling or pawning his arms and equipments; and five years for selling military stores. These are a few of the punishments in the French army.

In the Prussian army there are two classes of men. The soldier enlists in the first class, and he cannot be struck or sworn at or abused by his officer or non commissioned officer; but if, by the sentence of a court-martial, he has been degraded into the second class, then he can be struck and corporally punished with such severity as the offence may require. In the field, corporal punishment is inflicted by blows with the flat of the sword. In execution of a regular sentence, the flogging is inflicted with small canes by a non-commissioned officer, and never in public, but in a separate place, such as the guard-room or barrack, and in presence of his comrades. Punishment in a private room, and without the appointed witnesses, is particularly prohibited. Every commanding officer has the power to inflict corporal punishment on a soldier degraded to the second military class, to the extent of forty lashes (maximum) at once; a prisoner, however, may receive as one punishment, but at different periods, the number of one hundred lashes. The prisoner is not undressed, but keeps his shirt and working jacket on during the infliction of the lashes. In Prussia, when a soldier who has been degraded to the second class for misdemeanour, has behaved well for a certain time, he is reinstalled in the first class with many gratifying ceremonies: the colours of the regiment being waved over his head, and the national cockade restored to him. In Prussian cadet-houses it is now strictly prohibited to beat the cadets: no master or officer dare touch them, for a stroke is thought dishonouring. Thirty and forty years ago exception were made in rare cases, and cadets in Potsdam where they remain from the age of eleven to fourteen were occasionally punished with birch rods. A general who attempted to punish a cadet in Berlin, where the youths are from fourteen to eighteen years of age, in a similar manner, met with determined resistance. The cadet fortified himself in his bedroom armed with his sword. When the room was forced open he wounded a lieutenant in the arm, and the general himself entering, received a sharp stroke over his cocked hat. Another cadet in Berlin, threatened in the same manner, jumped out of the window from the third storey, and was killed on the spot.

In the Russian army, minor offences are punished with the stick and running the gauntlet; but the latter punishment, being described in a previous chapter, need not be again referred to. Flogging and running the gauntlet are parts of the discipline of the Austrian army. When flogging is deemed necessary, the number of strokes is determined by the bodily constitution of the individual, and never exceeds fifty. In running the gauntlet, six turns up and down between one hundred men is the utmost punishment. No individual above the rank of a common soldier can be sentenced to be flogged, or to run the gauntlet, unless he be first broken. Flogging is not inflicted upon a criminal without his clothes, and not with the point but with the full length of the stick, which is of hazel wood, not thicker than the bore of the musket, and free from ferule and knots. Flogging is very prevalent among the Bohemians, Hungarians, and Wallachians.

In the Hungarian army, the officer enjoys the right of inflicting corporal punishment according to his discretion; if a buckle is rusty, a horse ill cleaned, or the soldier a few minutes late on parade, the officer can order him to be laid down and flogged on the spot. Even the youngest subaltern may at any time, and for very trivial faults, flog the men under his command. A young lieutenant of hussars was once reprimanded by his superior officer for the bad condition of a detachment under his care. He replied that, if his superior did not object to his flogging a little more than common, he would have them in excellent order within two months' time. Consent was readily given and he kept his word: but during that period he had not a moment's rest, nor did a day pass without several punishments, and ultimately he had them flogged up to the highest pitch of discipline. A recent traveller mentions an example of this summary way of dealing with offenders in the Hungarian army. He was travelling early in the morning over a plain, where a regiment of dragoons had been exercising: the greater part were wheeling off, but one troop remained on the ground; and when the traveller approached he found the officer in front of his corps, and a man in uniform stretched on the sand, receiving the stick for some offence at drill.

In the Belgian army corporal punishment has not been in use since the accession of Leopold to the throne.

In the Portuguese army it was usual to punish by strokes of the sword. The punishment was inflicted by a corporal seizing the culprit and striking him with the flat of the sword upon the back. It was necessary to be done with the utmost caution, for it shook the chest so severely that sometimes consumption or other lingering complaints were the consequence. The punishment was a dangerous one, because the injury was often more real than apparent.

The United States code does not include flogging, but they have a punishment called the "ball and chain," which inflicts severe corporal suffering. In time of war flogging is sometimes necessary.

In the British army flagellation was, for a long series of years, the principal punishment for military offences—indeed, the application of the lash has been legally authorised from the passing of the first Mutiny Act in the year 1689. This Act, annually renewed, with the exception of three years in the time of William III, is the foundation of all measures for the preservation of discipline. It originally gave courts martial the power of inflicting corporal punishment to any extent; and the courts not seldom flogged the victim to within an inch of his life. Sentence ordering from five to eight hundred lashes were by no means unfrequently given towards the end of the last century, and the general discipline of the army was at the same time very harsh. Sir Charles Napier states, in his "Remarks on Military Law," that forty years before the time at which he wrote (1837) he frequently saw from 600 to 1000 lashes inflicted in consequence of sentences of regimental courts martial only; and in those days a man who had suffered a part of the punishment was often brought from an hospital, when the wounds were barely healed, to receive the remainder. Officers and non-commissioned officers carried rattans or "supplejacks," and frequently the private soldiers were struck by them upon parade for momentary unsteadiness, or for not appearing critically dressed, or for any other real or imaginary fault, however trivial, that a petty superior might see or fancy. In 1792, a Sergeant Grant was sentenced to receive one thousand lashes for enlisting two drummers of the Coldstream Guards into the East India Company's service. In fact, at that time there was no limitation whatever of the power of regimental or other courts martial of awarding corporal punishment.

The agitation in Parliament which has ended in the abolition of flogging in the army during a time of peace was begun in 1811. On the 25th of May of that year, Sir Francis Burdett called the attention of the House of Commons to a recent instance of flogging a private in the Liverpool local militia, who had been condemned to receive two hundred lashes, merely for complaining, along with others, of the inferior quality of the bread served out to the regiment, and afterwards writing a song upon the subject! The punishment had afterwards been mitigated to fifty lashes, which were duly inflicted.

The subject of flogging in the army was at that time adjourned, but came up again on the 17th June following, when, after a long speech, in which he detailed many shocking cases of the abuse of this power, Sir Francis Burdett moved an address to the Regent, praying him to issue such orders to the commanders of regiments as would restrain and finally abolish the flogging of soldiers. The motion being seconded by Mr. Brougham, was opposed by Mr. Manners Sutton, who explained that in the case of the Liverpool militia man, cited by Sir Francis, the man had been punished, not for writing a song, but for being a ringleader of a drunken and dangerous riot, on the unfounded pretence of the bread of the regiment not being good, and that the man himself acknowledged the mildness of his punishment. After some discussion, the motion was negatived by a majority of ninety-four to ten.

Next year Sir Francis renewed his attack, and, on the motion for the third reading of the Mutiny Bill, strongly advocated the abolition of flogging in the British army. He said that "many persons died in consequence of its infliction by sentence of a regimental court martial, whose sufferings never met the public eye;" and instanced, on good

PUNISHMENT OF POLITICAL OFFENDERS IN COLDBATH FIELDS PRISON
—Caricature by Gillray

THE NAVY—TIED TO THE GRATING

OLD CARVED WHIPPING BLOCK
Preserved in the crypt of St. Martin's
Church, London

THE ARMY—TIED TO THE TRIANGLES

authority, the case of a soldier at the Cape of Good Hope, who being sentenced to receive one thousand lashes, had two hundred and fifty inflicted, when, the surgeon interposing, he was taken from the halberts, and died a few days after. The amendment was negatived; but bore fruit so far that in the same year, the Duke of York issued a memorandum to restrain the immoderate use of the "cat." Shortly afterwards, the Mutiny Act contained a clause limiting the awards of regimental courts martial to three hundred lashes, which practically (except for great crimes) reduced the punishment to that amount: for almost all crimes were at that time taken cognizance of by such a tribunal under an Article Of War commonly known as the devil's article, by which all charges, not capital, were referred to a regimental court martial.

In 1825, a soldier at Dinapore was sentenced for insubordination to receive nineteen hundred lashes, and it was considered weak of Sir Edward Paget to remit 750 of the stripes. In 1829 district courts martial were forbidden to give more than three hundred, and in 1832, regimental ones were restricted to two hundred lashes. In 1836 the death of a marine at Portsmouth, after undergoing 134 stripes, led to the appointment of a commission, but the only change made in consequence was a general restriction of the number of stripes awarded by courts martial. In 1847 the number of lashes inflicted by order of any court martial was reduced to fifty, and in 1859 crimes were classified, with the object of subjecting the perpetrators of the more serious offences alone to the punishment of flogging, and that only on the second commission of the offence. In 1867 the arguments urged against flogging—that it is inhuman and degrading; that it is unnecessary for the maintenance of discipline; that it exerts no reforming influence; and that it hinders recruiting—prevailed in Parliament, and an Act was passed by which flogging in the army in time of peace was abolished.

CHAPTER XXXV

MILITARY PUNISHMENTS—THE FLOGGING OF SOMERVILLE, OF THE SCOTS GREYS.

ACCORDING to a circular issued from the Horse Guards in 1833, the application of flogging was limited to certain offences—viz., Mutiny, insubordination and violence, or using, or offering to use, violence to superior officers; drunkenness on duty; sale of or making away with arms, ammunition, accoutrements, or necessaries; stealing from comrades, or other disgraceful conduct. In the annual returns which were ordered to be made, offences were arranged under classes—viz., Violence to superiors, insubordination, disobedience, disgraceful conduct, making away with necessaries, and desertion. Offences against morality were classed under the heads "disgraceful conduct" and "making away with necessaries."

The gradual decrease, or the reluctance to use, corporal punishment of late years, is seen from the returns. In the years from 1821 to 1823, of those who were tried by courts martial one man out of two was flogged. From the years 1825 to 1828, the proportion was one out of five; and from 1829 to 1832 it was reduced to one out of six. In 1863 the number tried by court martial was 18,659, of whom 518 were flogged, or one out of thirty-six. In 1864 there were 18,028 men tried by court martial, of whom 528 were flogged, or one out of thirty-four. In 1865 the proportion was only one out of fifty-four. The majority of flogging cases took place in distant dependencies, such as New Zealand, India, and in Canada for desertion, where there was a great temptation for soldiers to pass over the border to the United States. This is easily proved by an examination of the returns. In 1863 the 70th Regiment was at home, and no more than two floggings took place in it, while next year, having been sent to New Zealand, the floggings were thirty five, and in 1865 fifteen. In 1863 the 65th Regiment was located in New Zealand, and twenty-three men were flogged. The

14th was there in 1864, and had actually seventy-two flogged, whereas next year it appears to have been at home, when the floggings were reduced to five. In 1863 the 68th Regiment had only one man flogged, but the following year it was sent to New Zealand, and the floggings were nineteen; it came home, and the next year the floggings were nil. The 31st was abroad in 1863, when thirty were flogged: when it came home the flogging ceased for a time, so that within two years only three men were flogged. The 40th was once known as a flogging regiment. In 1863 it had twenty-one, the following year twenty-two, and in the next year fifteen exhibitions at the halberts—but all in Australia or New Zealand. A battalion of the 12th in New Zealand gave eight to the lash in 1863, while the other battalion at home gave but one. Next year it gave none. But in 1865 the regiment was in New Zealand, and thirty-three men in it were flogged.

The instrument of flagellation in the British army was the cat-o'-nine-tails, described in James's "Military Dictionary" as "a whip with nine knotted cords with which the public soldiers and sailors are punished—sometimes it has only five cords." Tradition assigns this penal device to William III, before whose arrival the whip used for the punishment of British soldiers is said to have had only three thongs. The military "cat" was a weapon about eighteen inches in length armed with nine thongs of the same length, each thong bearing five or six knots, compressed and hardened into sharp edges till each had acquired the consistency of horn.

Somerville, in his "Autobiography of a Working Man," has given his experience of the lash, while a private in the Scots Greys. He was tried before a court martial on the 29th of May, 1832, "for highly unsoldier-like conduct on the morning of the 28th inst., in dismounting without leave, when taking his lessons in the riding school, and absolutely refusing to remount his horse when ordered to do so." It is unnecessary here to enter into the question of the justice of the sentence pronounced on Somerville, which was afterwards the subject of an investigation. The court found him guilty, and by virtue of the Articles of War sentenced him to receive 200 lashes in the usual manner of the regiment, at such time and place as the commanding officer might see fit. The sentence was carried into effect the same afternoon. The regiment was formed four deep round the walls of the riding school. The officers stood in an oblong space within the lines of the men. The regimental surgeon was also there, the hospital sergeant, and two hospital orderlies. The sergeant of the band stood with the green bag (containing the "cats"), and Farrier Simpson and a trumpeter each stood with a "cat" in his hand. The sergeant had two more in the bag, to be ready in case these should give way. The handles were of wood or whalebone, about two feet long, the tails about the same length, each tail two, or perhaps three, times the thickness of ordinary whipcord, with six hard knots upon it. A form and a chair stood close by, and on the form a pail full of water, with some towels in the water to apply to the back of the culprit, and a basin of water to give him a drink in case he became faint. These were in charge of the hospital sergeant and the two orderlies. A ladder was placed upright against the wall, and several strong looking ropes, half an inch thick or thereabouts, with nooses on them, hung about the ladder and lay on the ground. When Somerville was led into the square, the Commanding Officer read the minutes of the court martial, after which he said to the prisoner, "You will take your punishment; strip, sir." He accordingly stripped to his trousers, and was fastened by the wrists and ankles to the ladder, so that his arms stretched outwards and his breast and face were brought tightly against the ladder, and so firmly that he could not move. The Regimental Sergeant-Major, who stood behind with a book and pencil to count each lash and write its number, gave the command, "Farrier Simpson, you will do your duty." The manner of doing that duty was to swing the cat twice round the head, give a stroke, draw the tails of the cat through the fingers of the left hand to rid them of skin, or flesh, or blood: again swing the instrument twice round the head slowly, and come on, and so forth. In the words of the narrator, "Simpson took the cat as ordered; at least, I believe so; I did not see him, but I felt an astounding sensation between the shoulders under my neck which went to my toe nails in one direction, my finger nails in another, and stung me to the heart as if a knife had gone through my body. The Sergeant-Major called in a loud voice, 'One, ' and I felt as if it would be kind of Simpson not to strike me on the same place again. He came on a second time, a few inches lower, and then I thought the former stroke was sweet and agreeable when compared with that one. The Sergeant-Major counted 'Two.' The cat was swung twice round the farrier's head again, and he came on some where about the right shoulder blade, and the loud voice of the reckoner said 'Three.' The shoulder blade was as sensitive as any other part of the body, and when he came again on the left shoulder, and the voice cried ' Four, ' I felt my flesh quiver in every nerve, from the scalp of my head to my toe nails. The time between each stroke seemed so long as to be agonising, and yet the next came too soon. It was lower down, and felt to be the severest. The word 'Five' made me betake myself to mental arithmetic; this, thought I, is only the fortieth part of what I am to get. 'Six' followed, so on up to twenty-five. The Sergeant-Major then said 'Halt!' Simpson stood back, and a young trumpeter, who had not flogged before, took his cat and began. He had practised often at a stable-post or a sack of sawdust, and could handle the instrument as scientifically as any one. He gave me some dreadful cuts about the ribs, first on one side and then on the other. Some one bade him hit higher up, I do not know whom. He then gave them upon the blistered and swollen places where Simpson had been practising. The pain in my lungs was now more severe, I thought, than on my back. I felt as if I would burst in the internal parts of my body. I detected myself once giving something like a groan, and to prevent its utterance again I put my tongue between my teeth, held it there, and bit it almost in two pieces. What with the blood from my tongue and my lips, which I had also bitten, and the blood from my lungs or some other internal part ruptured by the writhing agony, I was almost choked, and became black in the face. It now became Simpson's second turn to give twenty-five. Only fifty had been inflicted, and the time since they began was like a long period of life; I felt as if I had lived all the time of my real life in pain and torture, and that the time when existence had pleasure in it was a dream, long, long gone by. Simpson got up amongst the old sores: the strokes were not so sharp as at first: they were like blows of heavy weights, but more painful than the fresh ones. It was now that he, probably more inclined to remember that he was my friend than a farrier, was commanded in a loud voice in these words, 'Farrier Simpson, do your duty.' He travelled downwards, and came on heavier than before but, as I thought, slower. It seemed a weary slowness for the Sergeant-Major to be only counting the fifteenth and sixteenth of the third twenty-five. When the other youngster had reached his first five-and-twenty, which made a hundred, the Commanding Officer said, "Stop, take him down; he is a young soldier." The prisoner was then unbound, a wet towel spread on his back, his jacket laid loosely over that, and he was led to the hospital between two men. There a cloth dipped in a lotion was put on the skin, and the patient laid on his back. His back became so stiff that it seemed an impossibility to rise, and when the lotions were changed he had to be lifted up.

Soldiers have always had various flagellating customs for the punishment of offenders among themselves. The *Scots Magazine* for 1780 gives a case in point, on 28th February, at Salisbury; it is recorded thus:- "On Thursday we were entertained with an uncommon military tribunal under our council-house. Two of the dragoons now quartered in this city had been guilty of petty thefts or frauds on their comrades, and instead of a court martial the officers left the conviction and punishment of this trivial offence to the men. Accordingly they were drawn up; one of them, dressed as formal as a judge, with a knapsack round his head, came escorted by a guard, took his seat in an elbow chair with his clerk attending to take minutes; the two culprits brought by a file of musketeers—a jury of twelve collected indifferently from the men—and a charge given—the evidence then heard: and on conviction the judge, with great solemnity, after observing on the evils of the offences to their society, sentenced them to undergo the punishment of booting and bottling, which was immediately inflicted by each juryman giving a dozen blows with a bootjack on the posteriors of the criminal, and then pouring bottles of cold water through the sleeves of his coat, the arms being extended, which produced something equivalent to a fit of an ague from the trickling of the cold water down his sides."

In infantry regiments it was customary to sling-belt offenders. The criminal was extended and forcibly held down on a bench, while the jurymen in turn gave him so many lashes with the sling of a fire lock. In the cavalry service a portion of the bridle is used for the private flagellation of those persons who render themselves disagreeable to their comrades. Happily such "horse-play" is becoming very rare, and as the army becomes increasingly recruited with respectable men the practice will probably cease altogether.

Wearing oak-apples—a practice, we are told, now quite extinct—on the 25th of May, became a military offence under the first of the Georges. For a soldier to "sport" this emblem was to manifest a love for the Stuarts, and a hatred for the House of Brunswick. As a military offence, soldiers who ventured to show but an oak leaf in their fingers were flogged almost to death in the bloody corner of Hyde Park. Civilians were also amenable to the law if they thus offended on the anniversary of the Restoration; and the punishment for the offence were imprisonment, whipping, and fine.

CHAPTER XXXVI

FLOGGING IN THE NAVY.

THE British navy has now been long afloat: a thousand years at least "its flag has braved the battle and the breeze," and all through these ten centuries there has been flogging on board, and plenty of it too; for although the "cat" has had a vigorous enough life on land, it seems to have found its native element when at sea. In the army, there is but one Act for the government and discipline of its separate corps. In the navy, there are the original Articles of War of 1749, then enacted for severe discipline and summary punishments, in order to govern the unruly and insubordinate spirit of sailors of all nations, pressed from all quarters to form the crews of British ships of war, and several acts to amend those laws and ameliorate their severity, especially as regarded the many sentences of death.

In the palmy days of flogging, as we may term them, about the end of the last century, the system of corporal punishment in the naval service was much more severe than it ever was in the army, because the Captain of a man-of-war was at once judge and jury. No monarch on his throne had ever more power over the backs of his subjects than the Captain even of the smallest craft in the navy had over the people on board of his ship. He could scarify their backs to his heart's content, without a soul under him—except the surgeon, who might save the sufferer by testifying that he was not in a sufficiently robust state of health to bear flogging—without an individual on board daring to say, "it is wrong you do." Marryat, in one of his novels, describes a Captain of an eighteen gun brig of this period giving five dozen lashes to a seaman for spitting on the quarter deck, and it is by no means an overdrawn story. A Post-Captain, as much famed for his reckless gallantry as for his love of the cat, always flogged the last man down the rigging after reefing top sails, if the operation was not performed in an incredibly short space of time. In those days, boatswains carried rattans, and boatswains' mates colts, the latter standing at the hatchway, to start the men from below, when turning the hands up. "Rope's ending" was also much practised, and old seamen might be beaten severely by "youngsters" as a matter of course.

A story is told of a horrible revenge taken upon a petty officer, who was constantly in the habit of reporting men, and getting them flogged. The vessel to which he belonged was chasing a privateer, a fast sailing ship, that had captured several English merchantmen; and on this occasion, in order to get the Ship into good sailing trim, gratings loaded with eighteen-pound shot had been slung in different parts. One of these was over the main hatchway, and as the man in question was descending in the dead of night, this heavy weight of metal was let down upon his head, crushing him like a spider.

Here is another case. A man was placed on the look-out on the bowsprit of a ship which was off the coast of Norway, and was almost blinded by a bitter storm of sleet and hail driving in his face. In this state he, of course, failed to see as well as the officer on deck, who had the use of a powerful glass, which protected his eye; and, as a punishment for not seeing the land, he was ordered to sit for four hours on the crosstrees. At the end of that time he was ordered down, but being immovable as a statue, with every joint stiff, his flesh numbed and without feeling, he had to be lowered to the deck by means of tackle got ready for the occasion. He died from the exposure.

When Sir Ralph Abercrombie's force was on its voyage to Egypt, a Captain, who commanded a detachment on board a small brig-transport, armed each of his two drummers with colts (that is, platted rope yarns), and the first question he asked the drummer on duty every morning was, had he his colt? If he was deficient, the other drummer was called to colt him. As the two drummers were sworn enemies, it was said that each used to purloin the other's colt for the pleasure of colting him under the Captain's eye.

Seventy-three years ago, in Lord St. Vincent's fleet off Cadiz, the discipline of the severe code was diversified on the Sabbath by "flogging and fighting, hanging and preaching," each essential point of duty suited to the times going on as regularly as clockwork: and not so many years have passed since dozens of blockade men, of notoriously bad character, were in one day flogged in the Downs, about a mile and a-half from the town of Deal.

"Young gentlemen" did not escape the lash in the days we are endeavouring to picture, and were quite as often designated "young blackguards" as by any other title of honour. Ensign O'Donoghue records an instance of an officer being flogged. Admiral Cornwallis, well known by the nickname of Billy Blue, because he always hoisted a "blue-peter" (signal for sailing) whenever he cast anchor in any port, had been severely wounded in the head, and was ever afterwards subject to fits of mental aberration. If he indulged in a single glass of wine beyond his usual quantity, his brain was sure to get out of order. In this state, one evening, he came out of his cabin while his ship was at sea. Catching sight of an officer whom he was supposed to dislike, he immediately ordered the hands to be turned up for punishment. A grating was rigged, the ship's company mustered aft, and while each was wondering who was to suffer, the admiral, who shewed no outward signs of mental derangement, pointed out the individual whom he intended to punish. On board ship "to hear is to obey;" and so without ceremony the astonished officer found himself, naked from the waist upwards, firmly lashed by wrist and ankle to the grating, and a boatswain's mate, cat in hand, ready to flog him. Before the officers could so far recover from their astonishment as to remonstrate, the admiral himself gave the signal, and two dozen were rapidly given, "Billy Blue" looking calmly on, as if every-thing was quite *en regle*. After punishment the fastenings were cast loose, the sufferer handed over to the care of the surgeon, and the admiral went back to his cabin. Next morning no one was more astonished than the admiral when he was informed of the last night's proceedings, and he refused to believe it till the fact was brought so circumstantially before him that it was impossible to doubt any longer. All hands were again mustered as for punishment, and the officer who had been flogged brought on deck. Then the admiral appeared on the quarter deck, with a cane in his hand, and walking up to the astonished officer, addressed him nearly as follows:-

"I am told that yesterday evening I ordered you, sir, to be flogged, and that my orders were carried into execution on this quarter deck; but, upon my word of honour, I have not the remotest recollection of the circumstances. It appears to be true, however, and therefore this morning I have assembled together those who saw you punished; and, in their presence, I have to tell you that I don't come here to make an apology for what I have done, because no British officer could receive an apology from any one after being struck: if I did not strike you myself, I caused another to do so. I won't ask your pardon, sir, because, as a man of honour, you could not in this way pardon an unpardonable offence. Nor, sir, will I waive my rank to give you personal satisfaction on shore, because by receiving your fire or firing at you, I could not obliterate the stain I have laid upon your shoulders. But I ask a favour of you before the ship's company; which is, that you will take this cane, and use it on my back as long as it will hold together. By —, I would do so to any one that served me as I did you. Mr —, you may thrash me if you please, and as much as you like, and, as I am a living man, it shall not interfere with your future promotion." Here he presented the handle of the cane to the officer. Mr —, however, took his revenge another way. He took the cane, snapped it in two across his knee, flung the pieces overboard, and, extending his hand towards the admiral, told him that he forgave him with all his heart. The ship's company burst into a cheer when they saw them shake hands. The officer had no reason afterwards to complain of his taste of the cat, for he finished his naval career that voyage, and obtained a capital appointment on shore under the patronage of the admiral's brother—an appointment for which he might have sighed in vain but for his luck in tasting "Billy Blue's" discipline.

The punishment at sea similar to the whipping at the cart's tail on land was a flogging round the fleet; but the latter was, as may be supposed, immeasurably more severe. A man sentenced to be flogged round the fleet received an equal part of the whole number of lashes awarded alongside of each ship composing it. For instance, if he was sentenced to three hundred lashes in a fleet composed of ten sail, he would receive thirty stripes alongside of each ship. When such a ceremony was to be performed, a launch was fitted up with a platform and shears. It was occupied by the unfortunate individual, the provost-marshal, the boatswain and his mates, with their implements of office, armed marines being stationed as guards at the bow and stern. On the signal being made for punishment, all the ships in the fleet sent one or two boats, each manned by crews cleanly dressed, the officers in full uniform, and the marines being under arms. These boats were collected at the side of the ship where the launch was lying with the prisoner; the hands were turned up, and the ship's company ordered to mount the rigging to witness that portion of the whole punishment which, after the sentence had been read, was inflicted upon the prisoner. When he had received the allotted number of lashes, he was for the time released, and permitted to sit down with a blanket over his shoulders. The boats which attended the execution of the sentence were then made fast to the launch, their duty being to tow it to the next ship in the fleet, where the same number of lashes was inflicted, with corresponding ceremony: and thus the condemned one was towed from ship to ship until he had received the whole of his flogging. The severity of such punishment consisted not only in the number of lashes, but in the peculiar manner in which they were inflicted, as, after the unfortunate individual had received the first batch of stripes alongside one ship, the blood was allowed to congeal, and the wounds partially to close, during the interval which took place previous to his arrival alongside of the next, when the cat opened them afresh, and again subjected him to renewed and increased pain. During the latter part of the punishment the suffering was dreadful; and the man who had acted as principal during this weary voyage, and received the full number of stripes, was usually broken down in constitution, if not in spirits, for the remainder of his life.

One lash in the navy was considered equivalent in severity to several in the army; and although the lashes were numbered by dozens instead of hundreds, twelve stripes afloat were fully equal to a hundred on shore. This was partly owing to the make and material of the cat, and also to the mode of flogging. The naval cat-o'-nine-tails was altogether more formidable than the military one, being made out of a piece of rope, thicker than a man's wrist, five feet in length all over, three of which were stiff and solid stuff, and the remaining two feet ravelled into hard twisted and knotted ends. Such was the old-fashioned cat; but even when wooden handles were substituted for the rope ones, it was generally heavier than the military instrument. There was also a vast difference in the mode of inflicting the punishment. In the army, the drummer stood on one spot, waved the cat round his head, and brought it down on the culprit's back with the strength of his arm alone; while, in the navy, the boatswain's mate whose duty it was to perform, stood fully two strides from the delinquent, then combing out the tails of the cat, he swung it over his head, made a step forward, and bending his body to give more force to the blow, delivered the stroke at the full sweep of his arm. Marryat describes one huge, raw-boned boatswain's mate who flogged left-handed, and had also a peculiar jerk in his manner of laying on the cat-o'-nine-tails that always brought away with it little knobs of flesh wherever the knots fell, so neatly that blood would spout at every blow from the wounds as from the puncture of a lancet. Besides, the torture was also doubled by first scoring over the back in one direction, and the right-handed floggers coming after, it was then scored in another, thus cutting the skin into lozenges.

But the days of reckless and indiscriminate infliction of the lash at sea are past: no sailor may now be flogged without a council of inquiry being held by the Captain and his two lieutenants. The checks on the undue exercise of the authority of flogging are many and various. The actual orders and regulations of the Admiralty absolutely prohibit the hasty infliction of punishment, and restrict the amount of it in all cases. Then, the knowledge that a Captain sending an immoderate return of punishments is looked upon unfavourably at the Admiralty, and also the certainty that he will be held up in the public journals as a brute who gloats over and enjoys the spectacle of a flogging, help to curb the use of the lash. By a circular issued in 1854, on punishments in the navy, it was enjoined that corporal punishment should only be inflicted for insubordination or other heinous crime, and only for second and future offences. In the same circular was a clause to the effect that, as it is essential to check inattention or dirty habits in boys, the custom of punishing them on the hand with a slight cane may be resorted to with moderation, in such cases as the Captain may direct.

In 1856 sailors serving in the coast guard were made liable to flogging the same as their brethren at sea; and a determined officer of the navy, in order to support discipline within his district, might, by Act of Parliament, order the summary infliction of lashes on the bare back of an offending seaman, fastened to the flagstaff of the coast guard station.

In 1858 special regulations were issued for the punishment of naval cadets. They were not to be flogged according to the Mutiny Act, but simply with a birch rod, such as is used in public schools. Four cadets of the "Illustrious" having been guilty of such gross misconduct as would justify their dismissal from the service, the admiral in command suggested that they should be flogged with a birch rod, as a milder alternative, and the Admiralty sanctioned that course. In the circular issued from Whitehall to all Commanders in Chief, Captains, and other commanding officers, it was enjoined that boys should not be flogged as formerly with a cat, but that in all cases where the offences could not be lightly passed over they should be punished in a similar manner to that which is in use at our large public schools—viz., by birching—and that in no case should more than twenty-four cuts be inflicted. Officers were also requested to avoid as much as they possibly could having recourse to this extreme step for a first offence; but the birch was to be held *in terrorem* over such youngsters as were addicted to lying, swearing, thieving, smoking, and drinking. About the same time there was a proposal to reduce the maximum punishment of four dozen lashes, to which seamen and marines are now liable, to two dozen.

Sailors have a punishment among themselves similar to the sling-belting of the soldiers. It is called *cobbing*. According to Grose, *cob* or *cobbing* is a punishment used by seamen for petty offences or irregularities among themselves: it consists in bastinading the offender on the posteriors with a cobbing stick or pipe staff: the number of blows which is usually inflicted is a dozen. At the first stroke the executioner repeats the word *watch*, on which all persons are to take off their hats on pain of like punishment; the last stroke is always given as hard as possible, and is called the *purse*. This piece of discipline, we are told, is also inflicted in Ireland by the schoolboys on persons coming into the school without taking off their hats; it is there called *school butter*.

The punishment of flogging was abolished in the United States navy by a vote of Congress in 1850, but the result appears to have been not quite so satisfactory as the opponents of flogging could desire.

CHAPTER XXXVII

ANECDOTES OF DOMESTIC FLAGELLATION IN FOREIGN COUNTRIES.

IF WE are to accept the Rabbinical interpretation of the account of the fall of man, flagellation as domestic discipline commenced in the garden of Eden, and the mother of all mankind was the first to apply the Rod. The rabbis declare that when Adam pleaded that the woman gave him of the tree and he did eat, he means that she gave it him palpably—that, in fact, she laid it on so energetically that he was forced to give in, and "did eat" under compulsion; and many ladies, we know, have followed her example and assumed a right to correct their husbands. Butler, in his "Hudibras," gives a notable instance:-

> "Did not a certain Lady whip
> Of late her husband's own Lordship?
> And, though a Grandee of the House,
> Clawed him with fundamental blows,
> Tied him stark-naked to a bed-post
> And firked his hide as if sh' had rid post;
> And after, in the Sessions Court,
> Where whipping's judged, had honour for't."

The noble person thus alluded to was Lord Munson, who lived at Bury St Edmunds, and was one of the King's judges. To shew her disapprobation of his conduct in changing his political principles, his lady, with the assistance of her maids, tied him to a bed post, and gave him flagellation till he promised to behave better in future; and for this salutary discipline Lady Munson received thanks in open court.

On the other hand, the majority of lawgivers have been extraordinarily liberal towards men in the question of domestic discipline. The case has often been argued whether a man may honourably fustigate his wife, and the point has usually been settled that his right to do so depends on the behaviour and temper of the wife. Steele remarks in the *Spectator* that there are undeniably perverse jades that fall to men's lot with whom it requires more than common proficiency in philosophy to be able to live. When they are joined to men of warm spirits without temper or learning, they are frequently corrected with stripes. It has been argued that woman was created to be the helpmeet of man, to be his ministering angel, and to be good, quiet, and orderly, and when she is really such she readily submits to the authority of her husband, and is perfectly docile under his government. When, however, she is the opposite of all this, there is need for the Rod, and she must be dealt with. according to the advice of the poet:-

> "Thou wilt be constrained her head to punch,
> And let not thine eye then spare her
> Grasp the first weapon that comes to hand,
> Horsewhip, or cudgel, or walking stick
> Or batter her well with the warming pan;
> Dread not to fling her down on the earth
> Nerve well thine arm, let thy heart be stout
> As iron, as brass, or stone, or steel."

Or the advice of the Roman oracle given in such a case may be followed with advantage. A man had a wife full of bad temper. He went to consult the oracle, and asked what should be done with a garment which had moths in it. "Dust it," replied the oracle. "And," added the man, "I have a wife who is full of her nasty little tempers; should not she be treated in a similar manner?" "To be sure," was the reply, "dust her daily."

The Arabians have a tradition that Job once threatened to give his wife a severe flagellation. When Job, says the tradition, was in so loathsome a condition that he lay on the ground, and none could bear to come near him, his wife alone attended him dutifully with great patience, and supported him with what she earned by her labour. One day the devil appearing to her, reminded her of their former prosperity, and promised to restore all they had lost if she would worship him. He had overcome Eve by a less temptation. The wife of Job did not yield like the mother of all living, but neither did she withstand it; she took a middle course, and going to her husband, repeated to him the proposal, and asked his consent: whereat he was so indignant that he swore, if he recovered, that he would give her a hundred stripes; then, according to the Koran, he cried, "Verily, evil hath afflicted me," or, "Verily, Satan hath afflicted me with calamity and pain;" immediately after which exclamation the Lord sent Gabriel, who took him by the hand, and raised him up. A fountain sprang up at his feet; he drank of it, and washed and refreshed himself. His disease disappeared, and his health, riches, and family were restored unto him; and, in order that he might keep his oath with regard to chastising his wife, he was directed to give her a blow with a palm branch having a hundred leaves. There are various other reasons given for the threatened chastisement. Some say that Job swore to punish her with stripes because she stayed too long on an errand. His wrath is accounted for by another legend thus:- What Job's wife provided for her husband during his misery Satan stole, until he had deprived her at last of all means of supporting him, and thus rendered him utterly destitute. As soon as the tempter had effected this, he appeared to Rasima (so she was called) in the form of a bald old woman, and offered, if she would give him the two locks which hung down upon her neck, to supply her every day with whatever she wanted for her husband. Rasima joyfully accepted the proposal, cut off her locks, and gave them to the false old woman. No sooner was Satan possessed of them than he went to Job, told him that his wife had been detected in dishonouring herself and him, and that she had been ignominiously shorn in consequence, in proof of which he produced the locks. Job, when he saw that his wife had indeed been shorn of her tresses, believed the story; and not doubting that she had allowed the devil to prevail over her, swore, if ever he recovered his health, to punish her severely. How he was to fulfil his oath the Koran says: "It was said to Job, take a handful of rods in thy hand, and strike thy wife therewith, and break not thine oath." Commentators differ about this handful of rods: some supposing it to be dry grass, others rushes, and others (as we have mentioned) a palm branch.

Several passages from holy writ, alluding to the use of the Rod, have been quoted in an earlier part of this work. Here are a few more. The writings of Solomon and Sirach abound with injunctions to use the Rod in youth—and, indeed, at other periods of life; and the following passages relating to this subject have been literally translated:-The fool despises the chastisement of his father, but he who receives stripes will be wise: chastise thy son until there is hope, but let not thy soul be moved to kill him: let one beat the profane, so will the fool become wise; let one punish one of understanding, so will he become wise. Stripes for the profane, and a rod for the fool's back: the young man's strength is his praise; one must retain the wicked with hard punishment, and with sore stripes which one may feel; folly dwells in the heart of a child, but the rod of correction will drive it far from him. Open chastisement is better than secret love: the chastisements of a friend are well meant, but the kisses of a sycophant are dainty; rods and punishment give wisdom, but a boy given up to himself shames his mother: chastise thy son, so will he delight thee, and will do good to thy soul; the whip makes stripes, but an evil tongue breaks bones and all: he who loves his child holds it continually under the Rod, that he may afterwards experience joy in him; he who restrains his child will delight himself in him, and cannot be ashamed among his friends; he is weak towards his child who mourns his stripes and is terrified when he shakes; bow his neck while he is yet young, make blue his back whilst he is yet little, that he may not become stiff-necked and disobedient to thee. Cease not to chastise thy boy, for though thou strikest him with the Rod thou wilt not kill him; thou beatest him with the Rod, but thou preservest his soul from hell.

The Mohammedans were in plain terms advised to beat their wives in case of stubborn disobedience, but not in a violent or dangerous manner. The Prophet had no doubt found the system answer from his own experience, which led him to pen the injunction contained in the fourth chapter of the Koran, "But those whose perverseness ye shall be apprehensive of, rebuke, and remove them into separate apartments, and chastise them."

In France, and in other parts of the Continent, the instrument for correcting a wife was the old-fashioned scholastic birch. The old French poems and romances furnish many edifying examples of matrimonial correction. In the "Cent Nouvelles Nouvelles" is a story of this kind. A jealous husband had suspicions that his wife was very complaisant to a neighbouring parson. At any rate, he discovered the cleric in his house partaking, with great relish, of a stew of lampreys, an especially favourite dish with him; which had been prepared by the unfaithful one. Being determined to revenge himself, he made no remark at the time, but immediately procured a powerful birch, which he concealed in the bedroom occupied by his wife till he should require it. The lady, however, had watched his operations, and seeing the birch, had a shrewd fear that it was intended to be exercised on her own tender body. She therefore went to one of her female friends, and inventing some plausible reason that she required to be absent from home all night, requested her friend, as a great favour, to sleep in her house that night. The good lady, suspecting no evil, willingly consented. So, when the husband believed that his wife was safely in bed, he glided into the room, seized the rod that he had prepared, and, drawing aside the curtains, commanded his wife to prepare for punishment, at the same time pointing out her past transgressions, and the necessity for the course which he was now pursuing. Being quite panic-struck at her position, the poor woman was afraid to discover herself, and being brought into an appropriate position, the husband exercised the birch very severely, and then left his supposed wife to her own reflections. Next morning the deluded lady complained bitterly to her faithless friend of the treatment that she had undergone. The wife made all sorts of friendly condolences for the unfortunate mistake, and, as soon as she was certain that the coast was clear, returned home to put in order the scene of devastation and cruelty, invested the bed in fresh sheets, and quietly slipping into it, went to sleep, or at least pretended to do so, until her husband returned in the forenoon. He was of course very much surprised to see his wife, whom he had, as he supposed, belaboured so unmercifully, calmly and comfortably asleep, and asked her jeeringly if she did not think it was time to get up. Expressing her surprise that she had slept so long, and had not perceived her husband rise, she explained that it was doubtless the profound dream that she had. Her husband tauntingly said she was probably dreaming of the parson and the lampreys, and also of the little refreshment that he himself had given her. She looked at him with surprise, saying that she did not understand him. At length he ascertained the state of the bed and of his wife's body, by ocular demonstration, and then began to believe that all he had done had been only a mocking dream. His wife, having thus put him in the wrong, took the opportunity to read him a sharp lecture on his conduct, and to make him promise amendment in the future.

Wives were not always so successful in thus getting whipped by proxy. Once upon a time there was a French lady who kept most unreasonable hours; her very head ran upon nothing but balls and masquerades and she never concerned herself about her husband's ill concealed chagrin, so that in time he became quite discontented with her proceedings, and determined to be very explicit. One day therefore he said to her, "My dear, are the days not sufficiently long, but that the nights too must be devoted to your pleasure? I must insist that you return home at a certain hour; if you do not mind this injunction, I have a most infallible method to bring you to reason; and of this matter I will be judge as well as accuser." The fair lady, conscious that her pleasures were founded on innocence, paid no regard to his remonstrances, and returned home that evening at her usual late hour, little dreaming of the infallible method of cure which her husband had in store. He had three days before prepared a most rare collection of green birch twigs; and that they might tickle madam to some purpose, he had soaked them well in brine. Waiting for the appearance of his lady, as soon as she entered the apartment he ran and seized her in his arms, the lady thinking he did so only by way of frolic; but a shower of blows from the birch, wielded by the arm of her indignant husband, soon convinced her of her mistake. In vain she screamed and cried for help, and all in vain resisted his superior strength, for he continued flagellating her until she was in a thoroughly penitent state of mind. The next day she made grievous complaints to her female friends, who only laughed at the serio-comic adventure. At last, being apprehensive of another whipping, and not desirous of again tasting her husband's infallible cure, she thought it prudent to be silent and to reform her mode of life.

Madam Roland protested fiercely against the indignity of a whipping, and communicates in her memoirs one or two remarkable personal anecdotes. Her father, being a choleric man, used to beat her often. When a girl, she more than once bit the thigh across which she was laid for the purpose of undergoing a flagellation. Refusing one day to take some medicine, she was sentenced to be whipped. Being again asked to take it, and refusing, she was whipped a second time with still greater severity. Another day, when a similar punishment was about to be inflicted, she became fierce in her opposition, and thereby excited her father; but seeing her mother in tears, she yielded, and received her chastisement for that time with humility. But she was determined to carry her point—to die rather than give in—and so she was never whipped again.

In a south German town, not very many years ago, there lived a doctor who administered the Rod to his pretty wife on the slightest occasion. He was very jealous, and thought proper to practise flagellation on the body of his wife so often, that she at last complained to her friends, and on their advice obtained a divorce. We have heard of a case in the same country, where the husband did not give the correction with his own hand, but handed the matter over to the ecclesiastical authorities, who inflicted it quite as efficiently. This lady was of great beauty, and had many admirers. In consequence of instructions received from the husband, she was one night dragged out of bed, carried out of the house, put into a close carriage, and brought to an unknown place. There she was examined, and commanded to give up the names of her adorers, but as she persisted in refusing to do so, she received a violent whipping with a rod, and after some days was taken back to her husband, when her admirers collected for her a valuable present, as a reward for her fidelity and silence. In a somewhat milder way, but likewise with the Rod (although we are not aware that the husbands sanctioned or ordered the proceeding), did a canon at Limburg punish the transgressions of the pretty married women who came to him to make confession. They naturally could make no resistance, and had to endure their punishment with patience.

The father of Frederick the Great of Prussia was noted for his severe domestic rule. The young Frederick was repeatedly caned during his boyhood. He was kept very meanly, and when he procured for his table three-pronged silver forks instead of two-pronged iron ones, he was beaten. The King, until the year 1729, allowed him six hundred dollars a-year, every penny of which had to be accounted for. This income was quite insufficient for Frederick, who ran into debt, and his father, on hearing of this, flogged him unmercifully with his cane. The Prince was forbidden to learn Latin. One day the King came upon Frederick and his tutor actually engaged in learning Latin, with books, dictionaries, grammars on the table, and, among others, a copy of the Golden Bull of Kaiser IV. The scene that followed, according to Carlyle, was this:- "What is that that you are venturing on here?" exclaims Paternal Vigilance, in an astonished, dangerous tone. "Your Majesty, I am explaining *Aurea Bulla* (Golden Bull) to the Prince!" "Dog, I will Golden Bull you," said his Majesty, flourishing his rattan, which sent the terrified wretch off at the top of his speed, and ended Latin for that time. In December 1729, the Prince wrote to his mother:- "I am in the uttermost despair. What I always apprehend has at last came on me. The King has entirely forgotten that I am his son. This morning I came into his room as usual. At first sight of me he sprang forward, seized me by the collar, and struck me a shower of cruel blows with his rattan. I tried in vain to screen myself. He was in a terrible rage—almost out of himself. It was only weariness, not my

THE MOTHER'S CORRECTION
From Hans Holbein's Illustration to Erasmus' "Praise of Folly"

SCHOOL SCENE IN THE MIDDLE AGES
From a carving on a stall in Sherborne Minster. "The flogging scene at school appears to have been rather a favourite subject among the early caricaturists, for the scourge was looked upon as a grand stimulant to scholarship. In these good old times, when a man recalled to memory his schoolboy days, he did not say, 'When I was at school', but 'When I was under the rod.'"—*History of Caricature, p. 120.*

superior strength, that made him give up. I am driven to extremity. I have too much honour to endure such treatment, and I am resolved to put an end to it one way or another."

The Prince had shown some little civility to Doris Ritter, daughter of a Potsdam precentor; and his Majesty, believing that there was much more than mere civility, ordered the poor girl to be whipped by the Beadle, and to beat hemp for three years. Frederick the Great in after years was inclined to think well of all this strictness, for he is reported to have said to Sir Andrew Mitchell that he deemed it a great mercy not to have been brought up as a prince, but as a private person; at the same time expressing his conviction that the great harmony between his mother and the younger members of his family had indirectly been the effect of the severe domestic rule of his father.

The following particulars of domestic discipline in the islands of the Pacific will add to the interest of this chapter:- In New Ireland the people are divided into petty tribes, each governed by a chief whose power is absolute. The chief often interferes in matters of a domestic nature. If a native has a wife or two and a few children, and through his love for fishing, dancing, and loitering idly about, neglects to bring in the necessary supplies for his family, a complaint is laid before the chief. He makes a personal visitation, and if he sees just grounds for punishment, he orders out the whole population of the village—men, women, and children. These arm themselves with a stiff rod made of small canes, and forming into a long double line, about six feet apart, wait, with anxious glee, the approach of the delinquent. At last he is placed at the end of the lines, the word is given by the chief, and away he speeds through the ranks, every one endeavouring to hit him as he passes. According to his deserts he may get off with running the line once, or he may have to do so twice or thrice. For a month after, his family are provided for by the public at large, under the superintendence of the chief. At the end of that time, if he has all his domestic matters in perfect order, he is allowed to resume his place in society; and shortly afterwards, perhaps, helps with an experienced hand to flagellate some one else.

The ladies of the New World appear to have been favoured with the power of the whip by law. Such a law prevailed among the Mozcas, one of the tribes of New Granada, and was seen exemplified one day by the Spanish general Quesada. Happening to call on the chief of a place named Suesca, the general found him writhing under a discipline inflicted by all his nine wives; his crime being that he had got drunk the previous night with some Spaniards. His affectionate executioners had carried him to bed that he might sleep himself sober, and awoke him in the morning to receive the rigour of the law.

We have read in an American newspaper that the Mormon ladies have to suffer flagellation at the will of their lords, but have not been able to get this assertion confirmed.

CHAPTER XXXVIII

ANECDOTES OF DOMESTIC BIRCH AT HOME.

As will have been gathered from previous chapters, the birch has played its part in "the government of the family" from a very early period. A hundred years ago the Rod was in extensive use among all classes. Hogg, the Ettrick shepherd, mentions a story of a small laird, who not only whipped his daughter severely, but turned her out of the house, because she had fallen in love with a tailor. Not very many years ago, a farmer in Wilts ordered his daughter to give up the company of her lover. He discovered one day that she had not obeyed his commands, and he forthwith gave her a horsewhipping, whereupon she went to her room and committed suicide.

In the correction of children by their parents, the Rod has always borne a part, not only when the children were of tender years, but even as they approached the years of maturity. Boys and girls of the present time have happy days of it. It is not easy for them to conceive a period when whipping was almost never ceasing. Yet it is certain that sixty years since, and for twice sixty years before that, children of all growths passed a large portion of their time, when they were between two and seventeen years of age, over the knees of their mammas or governesses. To spare the Rod was to spoil the child; and if whipping could make good children, then the boys and girls of a hundred years ago must have been good indeed, for they were very frequently whipped. And it was not merely young boys and girls who were flogged, but old boys and girls as well. The young ladies of many families were sometimes birched by their mammas even after they had become marriageable—that is, when they were seventeen or eighteen years old! What would our young ladies of to-day think if they were to be birched at that age, as their great-grandmothers were birched a hundred years ago?

An illustration of domestic birching occurs in Fen's *Paston Letters,* referring to the middle of the fifteenth century. Elizabeth Clere writes to her cousin, John Paston, to advise him to get some suitable husband for his sister, she being then of marriageable age, because "she never was in so great a sorrow as now a-days, for she may not speak with no man, whosoever come, neither with any man nor servants of her mother, but that she beareth her an hand other than she meaneth, and hath, since Easter, the most part been beaten once in the week, or twice, and some times twice a-day, and her head broken in two or three places." The same mother, Agnes Paston, enters among her errands in London a commission to her son's tutor, Greenfield, to "belash" his charge till he amend, he being then fifteen and having been some time at Cambridge.

In Vanburgh's "Relapse," Amanda, a widow, asked by Berinthia why she did not refuse to marry a man whom she disliked, replies, "Because my mother would have whipped me." Hoyden, on being told that her intended husband has arrived, says to her nurse "I'll go and put on my laced smock, though I be whipped till the blood run over my heels."

Dr. Johnson, upon all occasions, expressed his approbation of the Rod, not only in schools, as a means of enforcing instruction, but in the domestic circle. Boswell records that when he (the Doctor) saw some young ladies in Lincolnshire who were remarkably well behaved, and was told that their good manners were owing to their mother's strict discipline and severe correction, he exclaimed in one of Shakespere's lines, a little varied:-

"Rod I will honour thee for this thy duty."

Johnson was a competent authority on the matter of whipping: if he did not get it at home according to his own confession he had plenty of it at school. Mr. Langton one day complimented him on his accurate knowledge of Latin, saying that he was one of the best Latin scholars of the day. Johnson replied, "My master whipt me well; without that, sir, I should have done nothing."

With regard to "the proper government of a man's own wife," it may be mentioned that among other rights which the husband possessed over his wife, during the whole Anglo-Saxon period in this country, was that of beating her. The civil law allowed the husband, for some misdemeanours, *Flagellis et fustibus acriter verberare uxorem*, for others only *modicam castigationem adhibere*. "But," says Blackstone in his Commentaries, "with us, in the politer reign of Charles II, this power of correction began to be doubted, and a wife may now have security of the peace against her husband. Yet the lower rank of people, who were always fond of the old common law, still claim and exert their ancient privilege."

Authorities are not agreed as to what constituted a "moderate castigation," or the instrument wherewith it was to be inflicted. A Welsh law fixes as a proper allowance "Three blows with a broomstick on any part of the person except the head:" and another fixes the size of the stick at the length of the husband's arm, and the thickness of his middle finger. Another says a man may lawfully correct his wife with a stick no bigger than his thumb. A man used to tell his wife that, though a husband might not by law beat his spouse with a stick of a certain size, he might safely do so with a switch or with his hand. Some men, not inclined to be severe, used to restrict the size of the thickness of the rod to the little finger. On one of the seats of the chancel of Holy Trinity Church, at Stratford-on-Avon, is a carving representing a man administering somewhat more than *modicam castigationem* to his wife, who figures in a very novel and uncomfortable position.

The following passages are from Pepys's Diary:-

12th May, 1667.—At home my wife finds Barker (servant) to have been abroad, and telling her so many lies about it, struck her, and the wench said she would not stay with her; so I examined the wench, and found her in so many lies myself, that I was glad to be rid of her, and so resolved having her go away to-morrow."

— *Vol. iv. p. 41.*

10th June, 1667. Down to Greenwich, where I find the stairs full of people, there being a great riding there to-day for a man, the constable of the town, whose wife beat him."

Note.—It was an ancient custom in Berkshire, when a man had beaten his wife, for the neighbours to parade in front of his house for the purpose of serenading him with kettles, and horns, and handbells, and every species of "rough music," by which name the ceremony was designated. Perhaps the riding mentioned by Pepys was a punishment somewhat similar.—*Vol. iv. p. 66.*

Note.—Malcolm ("Manners of London") quotes from the *Protestent Mercury*, about the close of the seventeenth century, that a porter's lady, who resided near Strand Lane, beat her husband with so much violence and perseverance that the poor man was compelled to leap out of the window to escape her fury. Exasperated at this virago, the neighbours made a "riding" i.e., a pedestrian procession, headed by a drum, and accompanied by a chemise displayed for a banner. The manual musician sounded the tune of "Ye round headed cuckolds, come dig, come dig," and nearly seventy coalheavers, carmen, and porters, adorned with large horns fastened to their heads, followed. The public seemed highly pleased with the nature of the punishment, and gave liberally to the vindicators of injured manhood.—*Vol. v. p. 259.*

5th August, 1665.—And so away by water, having ordered in the yard six or eight bargemen to be whipped who had last night stolen some of the King's cordage from out of the yard." —Vol. iii p. 66.*

In connection with the subject of domestic discipline may be mentioned a curious custom that, until lately, prevailed in the rural districts of the south of England—in Hampshire, Surrey, Sussex, and Somersetshire. When a husband had made himself notorious by beating his wife, or a wife was known to wear the breeches, he or she was treated by the neighbours to the punishment known in this part as the "badger's band:" a practice said to have been quite as effectual in reforming the parties as the present remedy of appealing to the police magistrate. In Hogarth's prints from "Hudibras" there is an illustra-

---

*Grose mentions a sport formerly common at fairs, vis:- "To whip the cock is a piece of sport practised at wakes, horse races, and fairs in Leicestershire. A cock being tied or fastened into a hat or basket, half-a-dozen carters, blindfolded, and armed with their cartwhips, are placed around it, who, after being turned thrice about, begin to whip the cock, which, if any one strikes so as to make it cry out, it becomes his property. The joke is, that, instead of whipping the cock, they flog each other heartily."

tion of a similar scene, where a woman and a man are sitting astride, back to back, on a horse; the woman from time to time belabouring the man over her shoulder with a ladle or skimming dish. In the custom of the "badger's band," however, the delinquent is not called on to appear in public, but is made to listen inside his house to the noise made by his neighbours outside, who collect in great numbers, with pots, pans, kettles, horns, and anything, in fact, with which plenty of noise can be made. In some parts the music would be kept up for half-an-hour, and then the orator of the party made a speech recommending the individual to conduct himself better in future, and hoping that they would not be obliged to pay such a visit again.

In the "Lives of the Lindsays" may be found a most amusing illustration of the severe domestic discipline of which we speak, and it will be seen that the manners of the time were somewhat free in other things as well as in the matter of whipping. It is thus narrated:- "Our governess, Henrietta C—, amidst many faults, was passionately fond of her [one of the Lindsay children], but did not spare her when she was wrong. On a certain occasion, I forget what, said she, "If you do so again, Lady Margaret, devil take me if I do not whip you severely," adding, "You do not mind what I say, and therefore I swear to it." Margaret, at no great distance of time, committed the same sin. "I see now you have not attended to what I told you," said Henrietta. "If this happens once more, I positively must whip you." "I do remember what you told me," said Margaret, "and you are bound to whip me." "I certainly shall the very first time you do so." "No, Miss C—, you must whip me now; you swore to it, and said, Devil take you if you would not whip me severely." Henrietta acknowledged it, but said this once she would excuse her. "And will God excuse you? No," said Margaret, "I insist upon it that you whip me directly." Henrietta remonstrated, Margaret cried, expecting every moment to see the devil take away the governess. At last she carried the point, and was laid on her knee; but Henrietta feeling no anger, and being full of admiration of the culprit, who was insisting on a flogging to save her soul, instead of inflicting the punishment quietly, bellowed so loudly herself at every stroke as to bring my mother into the room, who soon settled the business.

Margaret was to receive four lashes only; for though Henrietta had sworn to whip her severely, she had not said what number of lashes she was to give her."

In the age of family birching, servants and apprentices were not forgotten. Some of the Puritan writers, treating of the duties of masters towards their servants, include correction among the number: and one of them adds, "I have heard experience say, that in these punishments it is most meet and acceptable to the offender that the man should correct his men, and the woman her maids; for a man's nature scorneth to be beaten of a woman, and a maid's nature is corrupted with the stripes of a man." From Tusser's "Poem on Husbandry" we learn the correct fashion of administering the discipline. One verse in a poem describing the occupation of each hour at a farmhouse is:-

"Past five o'clock, hillo! maid sleeping beware,
Lest quickly your mistress uncover you bare:
Maids up, I beseech ye,
Lest mistress do breach ye!"

Apropos of the flogging of apprentices, there is a good story told of the Linlithgow shoe-making boys, but we do not vouch for its truth. Linlithgow, in Scotland, is famed as a seat of the boot and shoe manufacture at which trade a large number of apprentices were at one time employed. A number of the lads were parish children, and many of them were well disciplined by their mistresses in the orthodox fashion, indeed, the ladies of Linlithgow were adepts at using the strap: one buxom dame in particular was so good at it that she could untruss and polish off half a dozen of her husband's apprentices in less than ten minutes! Others of the Linlithgow ladies were also adepts at flogging. After a time some of the boys began to object to being so often laid over their mistresses' knees. They occasionally met together, and murmured their complaints to each other, determining that some day they would have a great revenge, and so they had. Four of the masters, it was known, were to proceed on a particular occasion to Edinburgh, on business, and as these were just the men whose lads were oftenest licked by the mistress, the day in question was chosen as the day of revenge. At a given moment, the mistresses of the ill-used boys were seized, each in her own house, and being made ready by willing hands, were treated to a dose of the "oil of strap," as flogging was then called, each lad laying on a few stripes with all his might. Dire threats of retribution were uttered, but when it was found, upon inquiry, that more than one mistress had suffered a similar fate, prudence dictated silence, and it was not till some time after the event that the masters came to know how their apprentices had served their wives while they were absent at Edinburgh. A similar story is told of some weaver boys of Kilmarnock. The mistresses in that town, we believe, were always greater floggers than the masters, and were constantly having the 'prentices over their knees for even very slight offences.

Apprentices in this country were often flogged—some of them very cruelly. In London, a woman of the name of Brownrigg was hanged for the murder of her female apprentices: —

"She whipped two female 'prentices to death,
And hid them in the coal-hole,"

says the "Anti-Jacobin" of Mother Brownrigg, but the account is not quite correct. Mrs. Brownrigg was a parish nurse, employed to attend lying-in women at St. Dunstan's Workhouse, during the early part of the reign of George the Third. She lived in Flower-de-luce Court, on the east side of Fetter Lane, and, besides her business in the workhouse, received women to nurse in her own house. She made a great profession of religion, was very regular in her attendance at church, and altogether appeared to her neighbours a sober, religious, industrious, and most commendable woman. She had three parish girls with her as apprentice servants—Mary Mitchell, Mary Jones, and Mary Clifford. Parish apprentices were not models of good servants, and Mrs. Brownrigg set herself to train up those under her in a proper way. The process was simply beating them—unlimited flagellation. She beat the children as a drunken costermonger would his donkey. She often laid Mary Jones across two kitchen chairs, and whipped her till too tired to lift the stick. She then threw water over her, and thrust her head in a pail. The girl was soon covered with wounds and bruises on the head, shoulders, and back. One morning she made her escape, and found her way back to the Foundling Hospital, where she was admitted and cared for. The governors of the hospital wrote to Brownrigg, threatening to prosecute him for the bad treatment of the girl, but Brownrigg took no notice of the letter. Meanwhile Mrs. Brownrigg turned her attention to the other two girls. Mary Mitchell tried to run away, but she was caught by a son of Mrs. Brownrigg and brought back. Mary Clifford, the other apprentice, was kept constantly stripped, and beaten now and then with a cane, a hearth broom, or a horse whip. She was made to sleep in a cellar used for a coal-hole, with straw for her bed, and bread and water for food. When they tore their clothes, the two girls were tied up, and kept naked for several days. The elder son also flogged the apprentices, and continued the punishment when his mother was wearied. One day Mary Clifford was stripped and tied up five times, and beaten with the butt end of a whip, and her fellow-servant compelled to look on. The neighbours at length interfered, and communicated their suspicions to the authorities. Mr. Brownrigg was apprehended; the girl Clifford was taken to the hospital, where she died a few days after; but Mrs. Brownrigg and her son fled, and managed to conceal themselves for about a month. They were at last taken by the police, and conveyed to prison. As soon as it was known that she had been found, there was great excitement about her trial, and most improbable stories circulated: that she had made away with fourteen other parish apprentice girls, and that, in her capacity as a midwife, she used to kill children at their birth, and throw the bodies to the pigs. At the Old Bailey sessions, the father, mother, and son were indicted. The father and son got off with six months' imprisonment, but Mrs. Brownrigg was sentenced to be hanged, which sentence was duly carried into execution at Tyburn, amid the fury of the mob, who never ceased to howl and curse her all the way from the prison to the place of execution.

A straw-plait manufacturer at a village in Bedfordshire, who had been in the habit of whipping the young females in his employment, was upon one occasion, much to his astonishment, sentenced to six months' imprisonment for indecently birching a girl who was in his service. We were recently told a story of a parish girl who obtained a coronet through being whipped by her mistress, a lady's shoemaker. The girl had been sent to wait upon a lady of rank with some ball shoes, and had behaved so awkwardly in fitting them that the lady was greatly offended. She sent her son with a note to the shop threatening to withdraw her custom, which so incensed the girl's mistress that she began to punish her before the astonished messenger had time to withdraw. The boy, being struck with the personal appearance of the girl, sent her to be educated, and afterwards made her his wife; and the husband succeeding to a title she became a countess!

The girls employed by milliners, mantle makers, stay makers, straw bonnet makers, and in other kinds of workrooms were all liable to the Rod, and many of them were severely birched during their periods of apprenticeship. A fashionable milliner in Pall Mall who had a very large establishment, was noted a hundred years ago for her severity as a mistress. She had learned how to use the Rod whilst living in Paris as an abigail in a family of rank.

A very curious old English custom may be briefly alluded to before closing this chapter. In London and many other towns it was at one time the practice to birch all the children of a family at the time of an execution; and as executions were very frequent a century ago, the children suffered the oftener in consequence. An old lady told us about the practice and said she had been more than once birched in the early part of the present century, to keep her in mind of the awful lesson of the gallows.

Coming down to modern times in England, we find in the *London Examiner* for October 11, 1856, quite a recent illustration of the right of chastising wives. It is there stated: "A very large number of wife-beating cases have recently been brought before the magistrates of Whitehaven, where there exists a sect of professing Christians, who propagate the opinion that the practice is in accordance with the word of God. The Rev. Geo. Bird, formerly Rector of Cumberworth, near Huddersfield, has established himself there, and drawn together a congregation, and within the last few weeks it has transpired he holds the doctrine that it is perfectly scriptural for a man to beat his wife. About six weeks ago, James Scott, a member of Mr. Bird's congregation, was summoned by his wife for brutally beating her, because she refused to attend the same place of worship that he did. When before the magistrates, Mrs. Scott said she had no wish that her husband should be punished, if he would promise not to ill-use her badly again. When asked by the magistrates whether he would make the requisite promise, he refused, saying, "Am I to obey the laws of God or the laws of man?" As he would not give the promise, the magistrates committed him to prison for a month, with hard labour. The Rev. Mr. Bird has since delivered a course of lectures on the subject of Scott's conviction. He contends that it is a man's duty to rule his own household; and if his wife refuse to obey his orders, he is justified, according to the law of God, in beating her in order to enforce obedience."

Before concluding this chapter, we must mention the case of a clergyman living in London, who "gave the correction of a schoolboy to his servant maid," and who, when sued at Westminster, made an eloquent defence, asserting his right to do what he had done. He likewise appealed to the public "in print concerning the lawfulness of the flagellation he inflicted."

In our next chapter, the subject of Domestic Flagellation in England is further illustrated by some extracts from an old diary, which contains numerous allusions to the subject of the whipping of children and servants. The extracts are given as written, with the exception of a few alterations which have been made in the phraseology.

CHAPTER XXXIX

EXTRACTS FROM THE DIARY OF A LADY OF QUALITY.

THE following are extracts from the diary of the Lady Frances Pennoyer of Bullingham Court, Herefordshire:-

Dec. 15th, 1759. —My lord hath just returned from London, after a journey of three days, performed in safety by the fast coach. When we were young there were no fast coaches, but our children must go flying about, forsooth, much quicker than their fathers, and my lord brings word that there is a coach projected which will convey travellers from London to Bath in *two* days. My lord hath seen all the sights of London during his stay: he hath been to Ranelagh, where all the wits and beaux assemble, and listen to music, and promenade; and he was taken by his friend, Lord Mounteagle, to the play, where he saw the great actor, Mr. Garrick, play Macbeth. Mr. Garrick is a very little man, but wondrously witty and obliging. My lord went to the green-room, and was introduced to Mrs. Prichard, whom he thinks monstrously handsome and affable. He bought a picture of her as Lady Macbeth, in a red satin sacque, over a white brocaded petticoat and a hoop. Her wig is in flowing curls, and her shoes high-heeled, with diamond buckles. I asked my lord if that was the mode in London now, but he could only tell me about gentlemen's dress, and certainly he hath taken the opportunity to get himself tricked out like a man of fashion. A parcel of new stuffs for me and the girls is amongst his luggage, but I should like to know something about the style of making them up. Mistress Bodinham's new French governess was at church last Sunday with a new hat of white chip quite flat on the head, and trimmed with little pink roses. Her ruffles, too, were of immense width, and I heard her tell the doctor's wife that her dress was in the latest mode. I thought it vastly becoming, but I shall not let my girls copy fashions from a person like that, who cannot speak a word of English, and whose only accomplishments seem to be to dress finer than her mistress, and to whip her pupils in all sorts of fashions. She may be a papist in disguise—a Jacobite, perhaps. Who knows? Heaven save us from all ill! Mem., to make dear Dr. Aubrey preach a sermon on vanity in persons of inferior station.

Jan. 1st, 1760.—Began the year by seeing that everything was right in the servants' hall. My new maid not nearly respectful enough in her demeanour. Talked to her seriously about it, and told her I should have her whipt if she continued so ill-mannered. "Whipt, my lady!" she said; "I never was whipped since I was at school!" Always thought there was but lax discipline kept in my Lady Combermere's household, from whence she came to me. At breakfast had to reprove my youngest girl Maria for too great familiarity with the tutor: he is a worthy young man, and hath a pleasant manner, but must be taught his place. Mem., to look out that black velvet suit of my lord's, and see if the tailor can cut it down for him: his clothes look threadbare. After breakfast saw the girls practise the new reverence they have learned from their dancing master, which appears to be mightily polite and elegant. Left them sitting with their feet in the stocks and their backboards at their shoulders and went out. Down to the village to see my poor people. Farmer Probert's wife very self-willed about her baby. She wants to bring it up bare headed, and with no support to its back beyond a roll of linen. Lectured her severely upon her neglect of her motherly duties, and promised to send her some proper garments and caps for it. Called at Ploughman Hodges' and left some orders on the butcher and the grocer. They are an ill-doing family, but in trouble: the mother is sick, and the eldest daughter near to her lying-in, and she refuses to name the father of her child. Told her plainly what I thought of her. She seems penitent, so bid her come up to the housekeeper's room for some old linen. My mind misgives me that the other half of the sin lies at our door. Mem., to write to my son George about it: I think he will tell his mother the truth. "Spare the Rod and spoil the child," Solomon says; and Dr. Aubrey, who met me on my route, commented on the passage as applicable to this sad case. Had Goody Hodges corrected her daughter in her youth with the Rod, as I corrected mine, and as every good mother doth, she would not now be mourning over her indiscretion. Dr. Aubrey to dinner, who praised the cooking and complimented me on my new crimson paduasoy. A very pleasant new-year's day this hath been. The children at the schools behaved very well, and answered the good Dr.'s catechising cleverly. Two of the girls are to be whipped tomorrow for insubordination and unseemly conduct during prayers. As the mistress is a new hand, I shall go and see to the whipping myself.

Jan. 2nd, 1760—Went to the school as I purposed: met Dr. Aubrey on my way. Found the school girls all prepared, and the mistress looking rather frightened. She is a deserving young woman, and will do well if she is careful, though I misdoubt she is too pretty for her place. The doctor entered with me; he assures me that he hath been present at many whippings in fashionable ladies' schools, and he was rather pleased than otherwise to see the scholars blush at his presence. "It argued a becoming modesty," he said. The two girls to be whipped had been well instructed by the governess, and knelt and begged pardon in a very becoming fashion. I was pleased to see with what a good grace they took their punishment, which I inflicted myself, to shew the governess the proper way of wielding the Rod. Went into her living rooms afterwards—was hardly so well pleased with what I found there. A jar of confections and a bottle of orange-flower water in the cupboard (says she had these from the landlady of the Blue Boar), a new chintz, far too smart and fashionably made, in her bedroom; and a volume of Mr. Richardson's new novel, "Clarissa Harlowe," stuffed under the cushion of the chair. Spoke to her seriously about it—strove to make her understand that novels were not compatible with her station and its duties; but failed to make any deep impression on her. She said Mrs. Aubrey lent her the book, and hath promised her the rest. Of course, it is not for me to say a word about anything done at the parsonage, but I think it is indiscreet. At home we found my Lady Catherwood and her son waiting for us: he is a vastly proper young man, and as I think, hath an eye on my eldest girl. Told her ladyship what we had been doing, who said there was nothing to be done without a liberal use of the Rod She spends more time and money on her school than I am able to do, and hath a greater celebrity for the servants sent out from it. The Hon. Horace, her son, talked greatly to my Maria, calling her attention to the new liveries of the servants and the trappings of the new chariot in which they came. One so light hath not been seen in this neighbourhood. My lord says he thinks it will not stand our heavy roads Took particular notice of my lady's gown and mantle—the former is very long in the waist and short in the sleeves, with the new fashion of panier skirts, which seems to me more inconvenient than hoops: the latter was just one round piece, scarce reaching below the waist, and trimmed with rich lace. Her son's suit was of plum-coloured velvet, with a furred greatcoat and top-boots of the finest Russia leather; his wig was tied with the newest bag, and his hat was cocked in the very latest mode. They have just returned from London, and assured us that the fashions have but little altered. The young gentleman talked much to the girls of the sights of London— more than I liked about the play-houses and such places but with a young man of such family and fortune it would not do to interfere. They left cards for us for the ball next March, when the Hon. Horace comes of age.

Jan. 30th, 1760—My lord made a rude remark to me this morning. I lay late, having a raging headache, and he said the sun ought never to shine on an old woman till she is out of her night gear. I could have told him that an old man without his wig, and in a red night-cap, was equally uncomely; but I have learned from experience it is better to bridle my tongue where he is in one of his saturnine moods. I must acknowledge his rudeness was not without some excuse, for a lady with her head-dress swathed in linen, and her face anointed with unguents to preserve her complexion, is not a pretty sight. Goody Hodges came at dinner-time to say her daughter hath been brought to bed of a fine boy, and to beg some cordial for her, as she is very ill. Sent the things, but spoke severely to the woman for not bringing up her child to a better end. Was shocked to hear my youngest boy say that my woman had said, in the housekeeper's room, that George was the father of the child.

Jan. 31th, 1760—Thought much of what Harry said yesterday, and feel perplexed what to do. Think I will do as my revered mother did, and whip the girl, or send her away. What she said may be true; I fear me much it is; but I cannot have the backslidings of my son, and the sinful frailty of a village wench, made subject of comment in the servants' hall. Dearlove must be made to know her place, and keep it. "Whoso thinketh he standeth, take heed lest he fall." She hath a pretty face, and should not be too ready to speak ill of those above her in station. I should be sorry to turn her adrift upon the world, and she hath but a poor home. Sent for her to my room, and gave her choice, either to be well whipt, or to leave the house instantly. She chose wisely, I think, and, with many tears, said I might do what I liked. I bade her attend me in my chamber to-morrow at twelve. She says the girl Hodges herself accused George—not maliciously, she thinks, but in a passion of terror and grief which seized her when first found out. Am distressed about it. Something must be done, and I hardly dare speak to my lord. He is angry with George for his extravagance already, and this will make him doubly so.

Feb. 2nd, 1760—A terrible accident hath happened, and I write this by the bedside of my wilful boy Harry, who hath had a grievous lesson on the sin of undue curiosity. Dearlove, my maid, came to my room as I bade her. I bade her fetch the rod from what was my mother-in-law's rod-closet, and kneel, asking pardon, which she did with tears. I made her prepare, and I whipped her well. The girl's flesh is plump and firm, and she is a cleanly person—such a one, not excepting my own daughters, who are thin, and one of them, Charlotte, rather sallow, as I have not whipped for a long time. She hath never been whipped before, she says, since she was a child (what can her mother and her late lady have been about, I wonder?), and she cried out a great deal. Before I had finished, there was a smothered laugh outside the window, and Charlotte, rushing in, said, "That is Harry's voice, madam." Before I had time to remonstrate with her on the absurdity of the remark, and her indecorous entrance there was a heavy fall outside, and a crash of broken glass. We all rushed to the window, and there, on the ground below, lay my Harry, bleeding. The girls forgot all the decorum they usually observe in my presence, and ran to his help; and I forgot Dearlove and her punishment in the terrible sight. The dear boy had suspected (so he says now) what was going on upstairs, and had taken advantage of the gardener's ladder to climb up. The window-ledge being slippery with the frost, it slid away, and he fell upon the new-fangled glass box my lord had made in Hereford for the protection of choice roots. He was abroad when it happened, and was more furious at the mischief than concerned about the boy, who, he says, deserves a good sound whipping. Luckily there are no bones broken though my darling's hands are badly cut, and he is much bruised. Dearlove has behaved very well, bringing me the distilled waters and balsams I required from the still-room, and assisting to wait upon Harry (who, I must say, is very fractious) with right good will.

Feb. 16th, 1760—My lord hath not forgotten his threat to Harry, and he being quite well again hath determined to whip him for his transgression. I ventured to say that I thought the consequences of his curiosity had been punishment enough, but my lord would not hear me; nay, he even went so far as to remind me of the Apostle's injunction, "Wives submit yourselves to your husbands," &c. I thought it rude, but said nothing, Dr. Aubrey hath been up to the house and talked to Harry, who behaved with much discretion, and promised to consent to whatever his father chooses to do, without opposition.

Feb. 17th, 1760—This morning my lord whipped Harry. He sent for the girls and ordered them to be present, as well as myself; Charlotte flatly refused, speaking firmly, but I must say, not rudely, to her father, who thereupon flew into a great passion and threatened to whip her too. I am puzzled at Charlotte; there is something in her manner lately I cannot make out—a sort of defiance, which sits ill upon her. Harry took his punishment very well; he hath sense enough to see that to anger his father further would be no use, and he knelt and begged pardon in a very becoming fashion. I thought my lord very severe; it seemed as tho' every stroke cut into my own flesh, but I thought it best not to remonstrate any more. My boy tried hard to keep down his feelings, and only cried out once or twice; but he had much ado to keep from throwing himself on the floor and rolling when it was over. Dr. Aubrey called him a brave fellow to me afterwards, and gave him a pretty riding whip in the evening, when he came upon him in the grounds.

Mar. 10th, 1760—The ball at Catherwood House is over; and though it cost me many anxieties, and much contrivance, I feel that my girls' appearance was a great success. The new ornaments for their hair, and the trinkets I begged my brother to send, arrived in time, and the like have not been seen here before. Charlotte's hair was drawn up over a high cushion in front, and was dressed at the back in bows, on which rested butterflies made of spangles. Maria's was not quite so high, and she had a nest of young birds of the same bright material, over which the mother bird hovered, supported by a cunningly concealed wire. My head was dressed exceedingly high with cushions, and delicately powdered, and shaded with lace lappets, fastened by small gold doves—the dove being the crest of my lord's family. We were fortunate in getting the hairdresser, who came at two o'clock. My gown was a brocade of my mother's altered as near to the fashion as the stuff would allow and my ruffles were those in which my grandmother stood beside Queen Anne at her coronation. They are real Venetian point, and are of the true coffee tint. I had the new panier, and was not at all comfortable in it, though I flatter myself I did not look awkward. The girls were in taffeta, which is a new stuff here—Charlotte in pink and Maria in blue, as became their complexions. They had white shoes, with red heels very high, in the new French style, in the middle of the foot, to walk in which cost them a great deal of practice. The dancing-master and music master from Hereford have been in attendance for a week, to see them go through their steps and to hear their performances on the harpsichord, which are pronounced vastly fine by those who are judges. At Catherwood, Maria walked through a minuet with the heir in a manner which was greatly commented upon. I do hope that more than mere compliments will come out of it. Charlotte performed a song, written by Mr. Pope to the harpsichord, which was much applauded by the company; and certainly the dear girl hath a voice of a fine quality. My lord says it is all "humbug," which is a new word much in favour in London. It soundeth vulgar, but as it hath been introduced by the wise Lord Chesterfield, I suppose it must be considered fashionable.

Jun. 6th, 1760—My diary hath lain idle a long time, for indeed my mind has been filled with other matters than those of home. The King hath had a fit, and news thereof hath been sent to the Prince of Wales. Also an expedition is fitting out for America, to be under the command of General James Wolfe, who, though a weakly little man, seems to be a great soldier and a noble commander. Maria is in great grief, for the young heir of Catherwood is appointed aide-de-camp to him, and will leave this in four days to join him in London. My lord laughs at her pale face and red eyes, but time will shew; and if the young man does speak, none will be more pleased than he, for, though the Catherwood family is not so old as our own, there is more money in it, and it is only ourselves who know how badly we want it. Some one serenaded the girls under their window last night. They were too discreet to look out in their night gear, but felt sure it was Mr. Horace, or some one sent by him, as the song was all to Maria, comparing her to a rose, &c. They told me of it at breakfast, and my lord burst into a great laugh, and asked them, did they not know the voice, or the twanging of the ill-tuned guitar? It was no Hon. Horace, but the tutor, who hath made a confidant of Harry, it seems, and frequently bewails the hopelessness of his passion. My lord bantered her so unmercifully that she had an attack of the nerves, but she is better now. I shall have that young man dismissed.

Jun. 8th, 1760—My surmises were not wrong: the Hon. Horace Catherwood hath spoken, and formally demanded the hand of my daughter in marriage. He came with his mother, previously demanding an interview through a mounted messenger, who brought a splendid posy of flowers, and a note to Maria, which she immediately handed to me, requesting permission to read it. I could see the dear child was in a flutter of delight, though she was quite composed; and when her lover and his mother arrived, she received them with all the true dignity of a Pennoyer. The affair is quite settled. The young man spoke very prettily of his hopes and his affection; and if the American campaign ends well they will be married on his return. My lord is delighted, though he conceals his pleasure under his accustomed churlishness, and teases Charlotte disagreeably about her younger sister being married before her. I cannot make her out: she takes his badinage in such an odd fashion.

Jun. 9th, 1760—Drove over to Catherwood to bid farewell to my son-in-law that is to be. Charlote very unwell, so left her at home. Maria behaved as a young lady should, and gave great satisfaction to my lady and her husband, who is but a poor sickly creature. However, he gave her a diamond ring, and my lady some fine old pearls, and from her lover she hath a set of turquoises and a Chinese fan. To me the young gentleman made a very acceptable present—no other than a little negro boy to be my page. These creatures are very fashionable among the quality in London, and Lady Catherwood brought down two of them, to hand her chocolate and stand behind her chair. I rather suspect they became quarrelsome, and she deemed it better to part them. My new page hath been at court, and in the service of my Lady Yarmouth, and is a perfect adept at all the ways of fashionable life.

Aug. 2th, 1760—Roused from my sleep by roars of laughter, and found my Lord and Harry in the library amusing themselves with Cæsar, whom they were making imitate my Lady Yarmouth. I could scarcely forbear joining in their mirth as I saw the boy pucker his black face into a hundred wrinkles, and shake his fist at an imaginary king. The imp declares that she boxes the ears of our gracious sovereign, and mimics the way in which he rubs his head with his august hands, and then coaxes his elderly favourite into a good temper again. I cannot have such doings under my roof. Shall our anointed King be mocked by my servants? And as for Lady Yarmouth—but enough of her in my diary: the nation hath had enough already. I took the boy to my room, calling Dearlove to help me, and I made her give him a sound whipping. I had never seen a black boy whipped before. The effects of the punishment are not so easily seen on his skin as on a white one, but, judging from his cries, it was pretty severe. I think the girl's arm ached before she had finished.

Sep. 20th, 1760—We are in great distress. For days I have not been able to write, and have had fit after fit of the nerves. My daughter Charlotte hath eloped with the tutor! We were all wrong in supposing the misguided young man fancied Maria: even that dear girl herself thought so for a time. My lord is furious. Charlotte was his favourite, and he swears they may starve for any help they shall have from him. They are in Bath, from whence my unhappy girl wrote to me begging forgiveness. How she got away is too long a tale to write down here; but I suspect they bribed Cæsar to carry messages, and assist them off. I have questioned him, and whipped him to make him confess, but he is dumb. It matters little now; it is done and cannot be amended. I dread to think what Lady Catherwood will say. My poor Maria! How will it affect her.

Oct. 1st, 1760—I have writ to Lady Catherwood, who is at Bath for to take the waters, and she hath sent me a very kind reply. She hath seen Charlotte, whose pride is not yet humbled in the least, and hath spoken to her seriously. She declares they both mean to work, and ask nobody for anything. I commend her spirit, and shall send her clothes, though my lord will not allow me to write. Lady Catherwood assures me it will make no difference to her son, which hath mollified my lord a little.

Oct. 27th, 1760—One woe doth tread upon another's heels, Shakespeare says somewhere. No sooner hath the excitement of General Wolfe's death died away than news comes that the King is dead. He died on the 25th; and we have today been into Hereford to hear King George the Third proclaimed in front of the Town Hall there. The sight was very fine, and there was a great crowd promenading. We left the chariot, and walked through the town, with Cæsar at our heels. Meeting the party from Catherwood, I heard the depraved little wretch say to one of their men, "What will become of the old witch now?" —meaning, of course, my Lady Yarmouth. Indeed he was not the only person who expressed the same curiosity, though in different words. My lord is rather elated: he fancies, with a new king, new ways will come in, and he may stand a chance at court. I wish he may, but I have too much to occupy my attention. I must see to our mourning: many of our stuffs will dye, and the school children must be provided with proper garments. Dr. Aubrey, who had been a great comfort to me in my affliction, hath hung the church with black, and already sees to the boys being fitted with their new suits. The poor ignorant children seem to think the King's death a matter for rejoicing. Who shall say whether it is or no?

Dec. 24th. 1760—Another year is drawing to a close, and its ending sees me a happy woman. I have seen my child again, and her father hath in some sort relented. Perhaps his new appointment about the person of the King, which will take him away from Bullingham to London, hath had something to do with it. Of course he is enraged that his daughter should only be plain Mistress Gibson instead of marrying a lord; but the young man hath accepted his reproaches with meekness, and owned his fault so humbly that it would be malicious to hold out any longer. They are to come to Bullingham during our absence, and an appointment of some sort is to be found for our son-in-law. From America we have good news. Horace Catherwood has been badly wounded, but is recovering, and will be home in the spring, when the marriage will take place: a happy prediction to write down, as the Christmas bells break out into cheerful music from the old church tower.

CHAPTER XL

DISCIPLINE IN AN ENGLISH CHARITY SCHOOL
A HUNDRED YEARS AGO.

THIS is a genuine narrative of the discipline of a private charity school, as conducted in an English county a hundred years ago. The exact situation of the school, and the name of the noble family who supported the institution, are, by request of the lady who has contributed the narrative, hidden under a nom de plume.

The charity school of East Barkham was the care—indeed, I may say the property—of the Ladies Royston. They provided and regulated everything necessary, ruled the teachers, and assisted with both head and hands, in enforcing the laws laid down for our guidance—indeed, they were very ready with their hands, the younger lady—the Lady Maria—superintending all the punishments, doing a great deal of whipping herself. The Lady Marjory did not care to flog us, but delighted to make her maid do it; and I have seen her stand by and look on till the poor girl was quite exhausted by the exercise of flogging a number of kicking, squalling youngsters, both boys and girls, for the ladies flogged indiscriminately, and, it seemed to me, took a pleasure in so doing. The school was in the grounds, about a mile from the house, which was a splendid mansion—one of the finest in the county. From the windows we could see the great doors upon which the arms of the family were emblazoned—two leopards with golden crowns upon their heads, supporting a shield. It was a very splendid place inside, and twice in the year we were taken in to see my lord and my lady the countess, who was a very handsome woman, always dressed in the last Paris fashion. We had cake and wine on those days in the great hall, a magnificent place, with painted windows, and a roof decorated like a cathedral all in gold and colours. My lady would speak very kindly to us, and generally tell one or other of us that she had found a place for her, as we were trained to be ladies' own women, still-room maids, &c.; and very well some of the girls did when they were put out in the world. Her ladyship's maid had been trained in the school, and a good one she was, though short tempered, and inclined to be tyrannical to us when she had the chance. We were very much afraid of my lady; she whipped without mercy; and just before I went to the school, she had taken her old place in the punishment hour, and once ordered the whole forty children up for correction, which she and her maid then and there administered. Joan—that was the maid's name—has many a time laughed at me when I was crying after a whipping, and told me to wait till I was the Lady Marjory's maid, and I should then learn what flogging really meant. She said Lady Marjory, for all her apparent mildness now, was a regular Tartar, and I should catch it if ever she was my mistress. I used to tremble a little at the prospect, but it was the fashion for ladies sometimes to use the Rod, and I thought but little of it: indeed, I think they were better servants then than they are now.

The school was an old building called the Hermitage, built in the hollow of a hill, and looking right down into the gardens. It had been built by a wicked earl for his mistress, and was beautifully fitted and furnished. It had been unused for a long time, and on the present earl's marriage (I speak of the year 1763, and the earl that lived then) his lady had taken a fancy to establish a school there for the sons and daughters of some of the tenantry and orphans, who were to be clothed and educated at her expense, and put out into the world afterwards fit to earn their own living. And an excellent school it was, and very well we were done by in it. There was accommodation in it for forty children, twenty boys and twenty girls. We were dressed in uniform, which was the most disagreeable part of our experiences, for my lady had chosen it as being extremely ugly, though sufficiently warm and comfortable. Our shifts and the boys' shirts were made of a material half cotton half linen, which was very harsh to a tender skin, and afflicted us sorely; then we had grey flannel petticoats, very thick and coarse yellow-stuff skirts, and parti-coloured gowns. This was a whim of my lady's, who said that her girls should not be like those of any other school; so our gowns were blue and red—the bodies and the skirts to the knee were blue, and the sleeves and the bottom of the dress bright scarlet. Our stays were made of leather, very long-waisted and hard, but there was no mercy in the matter of lacing: one of the teachers superintended that operation every morning, for my lady would not suffer the least stoop or looseness about the waist of any of us, and her daughters were just the same; they were the mistresses when I was there, for when they grew up their mother gave it up to them, and they proved themselves worthy successors to her, I can tell you. We had white kerchiefs, with a chain border of scarlet and blue, crossed over our bosoms, and pinned down so tight as to tear them often, for my lady said that it helped to give us a proper set of the breast and improved the fall in our shoulders. We had little calico caps, with round crowns and crimped borders, with a piece of muslin, bordered like our kerchiefs, twisted round it instead of ribbon. The ladies were very particular about these caps, and the girls who did the laundry work got many a whipping and other punishments if they were not ironed to their taste. One way of punishment for negligent laundry work was to pin all the ill-ironed caps and kerchiefs to the culprit's back, and make her stand upon a stool in the dining room, where she could be seen by every one who passed the front of the house, and was visible to the boys from their play-ground. We didn't like that—we even preferred to receive a whipping. Our gloves were of nankeen, with the earl's coronet worked on the backs in red and blue in stripes; and our shoes of strong leather, with high heels, pointed toes, and flat steel buckles. For going out we had large round camlet cloaks (black, bound with red), with hoods fitting tight to the heads; and as our hair was all cut off, they were not becoming, I can assure you. The boys wore knee-breeches of leather, stockings and shoes similar to ours, waistcoats of red cloth, with large pockets and flaps reaching nearly to their knees, loose blue coats with large buttons having the earl's crest on them, and calico cravats with the same bordering as our kerchiefs. Their cocked hats were of very heavy coarse felt, and had neither buckle nor trimming. No child was admitted into the school under seven years of age, and the time they remained in it was from seven to nine years, so that we were quite young women when we left. The training was excellent, and we were in request in all the families round about as ladies' maids and still-room maids.

The discipline of the school was very strict. We rose at six, summer and winter, half-an-hour only being allowed for dressing; at the end of which time we were inspected by the teacher on duty for the day, and if we had so much as a fold or a pin out of place, we were marked down for punishment. Then we had a piece of bread, after which we went to prayers, and then to an hour's early school. At half-past eight we breakfasted, and at nine we returned to school till a quarter to eleven; then another piece of bread, and a quarter of an hour's play; then school till twelve; then dinner and recreation till two; then school till five, supper at six, and bed at eight, after prayers.

The great event of the day was what we called "punishment hour," which was from four till five in the afternoon, when the ladies attended in person when they were at Saltire, bringing their friends with them to inspect the school. We used to regard that hour with very mingled feelings. Sometimes—especially when they had gentleman visitors living with them—they would come in good temper, and with pleasant faces; sometimes they would be very cross, and ready to vent upon us all the annoyances they might have met with at home. There was a great contrast between the two ladies. The Lady Marjory was fat and sleepy-looking, like her father, with fair hair and blue eyes, that seemed as though they could not flash; and the Lady Maria was slight and dark, with eyes like a hawk, the picture of her mother in features as well as temper. Both ladies had copied the French mode of dressing from their cousin, and used to come to the school daily in toilets that were to our eyes like the draperies in a fairy tale. Their feathers and flowers, their sparkling jewellery, and the huge scented fans they carried, were subjects of daily and hourly admiration amongst us. All the bad marks against any girl or boy were laid before their ladyships, who would appoint the punishments and see them carried out—the Lady Maria and her cousin, Mdlle. Burgoyne from Paris, who was staying at the castle, wielding the Rod with much grace and dignity. Lady Marjory used to bring her mother's maid with her to do the whipping, taking her to task severely for the awkward manner in which she some times managed the business. I remember one afternoon very well, her giving the girl two or three sharp cuts with the rod before us all for not administering punishment in a sufficiently smart manner. We were all mustered in school, and among the long list of black marks against many of us there were three to one girl who was a great trouble to the teachers. There was a laundry mark, a talking mark, and a mark for "want of respect to my lady:" any omission of the ceremonies of duly curtseying to, or saluting, our teachers was called by that name: the school belonging to her, we were considered to have insulted her personally. For the laundry mark, she was to have six stripes of the rod, and stand with the spoiled caps pinned about her on the stool; for the second offence she was not to speak or be spoken to, except in school hours, for a week; and, for the third, she was to be "well whipped." Lady Marjory wrote these down on a piece of paper, for it was her day, and gave them to the governess, who read them aloud; and Lady Maria and her cousin smiled, and said it was only proper punishment.

Mdlle. Burgoyne would like to have taken some of the whipping into her own hands, being just fresh from a French school, with the full remembrance of her own experiences in her mind, but the ladies would not give up their privileges, and she had to be content with offering some suggestions, for which we did not thank her. It was at her prompting that a slender whalebone rod was substituted for the old-fashioned birch, which, though it looked more formidable, did not hurt half so much, nor leave such weals upon one's skin. She was the pink of fashion, this young lady, and used perfectly to bewilder us with the elegance of her attire. She would come to the school in the most elegant brocade sacques over satin petticoats, with beautiful high-heeled satin shoes and clogs, and her hair dressed so that her head looked as large as a peck measure. But I am digressing from my story of how Lady Marjory whipped Joan in the school. Betty Brown, the girl to be whipped, was ordered to stand out, which she did, looking very shamefaced. She was a big, tall girl in appearance, far more robust than either the Lady Maria or her cousin. She was going to be still-room maid at Lord Royston's, a fine house in the next county, for she was a clever girl, though careless and troublesome at times. Betty stood before the party, till Miss Thomas, the school mistress, rose, and curtseying, read out the punishment. "Betty Brown will fetch the rod," my lady said; and the girl went, colouring crimson, and ready to cry. When she came back, she knelt, and presented it, as was the fashion, and then Mademoiselle said sharply—"Kiss it." That was one of the new notions she had brought from France, and we didn't like it—we never had to do it before she came. Betty kissed it, looking dreadfully terrified while she was prepared for flogging. Joan stripped her, and she was made to fold up her clothes, one by one, as though she were going to bed, while we all sat in our places looking on, not allowed to move or speak. When she stood ready for the rod, the bell was rung for the dairywoman—a great, stout person, who had the enviable task of horsing us when we were birched. Joan tucked up her sleeves and receiving the rod from the Lady Marjory with a profound curtsey, prepared for business. But Betty was not going to be flogged without opposition: she was a big, strong girl, and it took a good many pairs of hands to get her fairly established on Dorothy's back, who did not like her office at all. Once there, and the girl's hands pinioned by her brawny arms, there was little chance of the culprit escaping, however she might kick, for Dorothy was as strong as a man, and it was currently reported that she smacked her liege lord in the privacy of her own home.

"Hold that girl's feet," was Lady Marjory's next order, "or Joan will never be able to get at her."

So Miss Thomas made the feet fast, and then Joan began. The dreaded rod fell swiftly and surely on the white flesh, raising red weals in all directions. If Joan was clumsy, she was energetic, and Betty Brown roared and wrestled under the operation most lustily but, for all that, the performance did not please the three ladies.

"What a clumsy creature!" said Mademoiselle; "she hasn't an atom of grace." "Marjory should do it herself," said Lady Maria. "One can't expect everything from servants."

"I hate such violent exercise," said her sister; and then, turning to Joan, "You clumsy, awkward creature, you! Have I not shewn you how to use the rod a hundred times? Has not my mother shewn you?"

"Yes, and made me feel it, too," said the girl, sulkily; "the brat kicks so, there's no doing anything properly."

Lady Marjory had risen from her seat, and come nearer to the girl and her punisher as she spoke; and whether by accident or design did not appear, but Joan, in raising her arm to give an effective blow, happened to touch her ladyship's face. My lady forgot that she didn't like exercise then; she snatched the rod from her servant's hand, and posing herself in an attitude, commenced heartily lashing the astonished girl on her arms and neck, and wherever she could get an opportunity to hit her. For a minute Joan was too astonished to resist; but when she recovered her scattered wits, she rushed round the room, with the lady in full pursuit, leaving Betty Brown shivering and smarting on her uncomfortable elevation.

The ladies not only whipped us, but they whipped the boys too, at least the Lady Maria and her French cousin did—Lady Marjory had scruples of modesty about it, and declined. Mademoiselle Burgoyne introduced a good many new customs into our school. Before she came, the whipping used to be entirely optional, and the ladies used to whip with short, sharp blows, without any method; but she recommended the French fashion of long, regular, sharp blows, counted and applied in a measured manner; so that, when we were sentenced to a whipping, we knelt and said, "May it please your ladyship to give me so many blows on account of my great fault;" and when we returned the rod, the formula was—"I thank your ladyship humbly for the whipping I have received;" and we had to say it without any sobbing or stuttering either. She was a regular Tartar, that young French lady; any one fonder of using the rod I never did see. After a whipping at school, we had to carry the rod fastened upright on our backs the most of the day, no matter who came to see the school, or where we went, and I have been sent with a message to my lady with the rod at my back before now. It seems strange to tell of these things now, when it is rare even for children to be flogged; but when I was young, it was part of everybody's education. Nobody thought of correcting children in any other way, and servants were equally amenable to the punishment. My lady whipped her maids and her pages, and my lord thrashed his valet or his grooms. Mothers whipped their grown-up daughters, who submitted to the discipline without a murmur; for in my day a mother's will was law. I don't know that we grew up any worse for it; indeed, I sometimes think, though maybe that is an old woman's fancy, that there are no better wives and mothers under the present free and easy system of education than there were when mothers ruled their children only by the Rod.

CHAPTER XLI

SCHOOL PUNISHMENTS.

SOLOMON has said, "He that spareth the Rod hateth his son; but he that loves him chastises him betimes," and the maxim has been considered indisputable in all ages. Schoolmasters have regarded the Rod as absolutely indispensable in the education of the young. The first flogging schoolmaster that we meet with in our reading is Toilus, who used to whip Homer, and who, after performing that operation effectually, assumed the title of *Homeromastix*. This worthy man received no other reward for his enterprise than crucifixion, which he suffered by the orders of King Ptolemy. Horace calls his schoolmaster, who was fond of this discipline, "the flogging Orbilius" (*plagosus Orbilius*); Quintilian denounces the practice of whipping schoolboys on account of its severity and its degrading tendency; and Plutarch, in his "Treatise on Education," says: "I am of opinion that youth should be impelled to the pursuit of liberal and laudable studies by exhortations and discourses, certainly not by blows and stripes. These are methods of incitement far more suitable to slaves than to the free, on whom they can produce no other effect than to induce torpor of mind and disgust for exertion, from a recollection of the pain and insult of the inflictions endured."

An ancient philosopher, named Superanus, who began his studies after he was thirty years of age, so firmly believed that whipping was necessary in education, that "he never grudged himself either the rod or sharp lectures, in order to learn all that schoolmasters and tutors teach their pupils. He was seen more than once in the public baths to inflict on himself the severest corrections." Loyola, as we have elsewhere mentioned, was treated in the same way at an advanced age. Moliere has brought his power of ridicule to bear on such a character

Plate XVIII.

SCHOOL IN THE LAST CENTURY. "TAKE DOWN HIS BREECHES"—*Thackeray*

in his play "Le Bourgeois Gentilhomme." M. Jourdain, utterly illiterate, although of middle age, resolves that he will be a gentleman and a learned man; and to carry out his purpose procures masters in music, fencing, dancing, philosophy—everything, in short, that he could think of. Madame Jourdain, as ignorant as her husband, but gifted with a little more common sense, rebels against this, and on one occasion sarcastically asks him—" N'irez vous point, un de ces jours, vous faire donner le fouët, à votre age?" ("Do you mean, at your age, to get yourself whipped one of these days?") To which M. Jourdain fervently replies—"Pourquoi non. Plût à Dieu d'avoir tout à l'heure le fouët devant tout le monde, et savoir ce qu'on apprend au collège." ("Why not? Would to God I were whipped this very moment before all the world; and knew what it is to be learned at school.")

"Rods and sticks," writes a pedagogic author, "are school swords, which God after the fall committed to the hands of teachers, who ought not to wield them in vain, but chastise the wicked with them." Rods and sticks, he further says, are school sceptres before which the crowd of children ought to bow their heads. Even among heathen nations, who never heard of Solomon's wise saying, we learn that whipping was held in high esteem in training the young. The Peruvians whipped the rising generation plentifully, and the aborigines of Brazil gave children the bastinado on the soles of their feet. Two boys held the delinquent, while the *molla* beat his feet with a stick, often so severely that the blood spirted from under the nails. The Carribeans also applied the Rod. But it is in European schools that we find the birch most systematically used. In German schools the Rod was at one time plied industriously: the operator was called the "blue man." Not only boys, but youths up to the age of eighteen or twenty years, were subjected to the Rod. Some professors preferred to inflict the punishment with their own hands; but in general it was inflicted by a man wearing a mask, and having his instrument concealed under a blue cloak (whence the name, the "blue man"), in the passage before the schoolroom, and in the presence of the professor; and very few youths could boast, on leaving the gymnasium, of having never been under the care of the "blue man."

It is recorded of a Suabian schoolmaster that, during his fifty-one years' superintendence of a large school, he had given 911,500 canings, 121,000 floggings, 209,000 custodes, 136,000 tips with the ruler, 10,200 boxes on the ear, and 22,700 tasks by heart. It was further calculated that he had made 700 boys stand on peas, 6000 kneel on a sharp edge of wood, 5000 wear the fool's-cap, and 1700 hold the rod. The same system as has been mentioned prevailed in France. Ravisius Textor, who was rector of the University of Paris, in one of his epistles, writes thus concerning the treatment of boys:- "If they offend, if they are detected in falsehood, if they slip from the yoke, if they murmur against it, or complain in ever so little a degree, let them be severely whipt; and spare neither the scourge nor mitigate the punishment till the proud heart shall evidently be subdued, and they shall have become smoother than oil, and softer than a pumpkin. And if they endeavour by mollifying speeches to disarm the preceptor's anger, let all their words be given to the wind."

In England the schoolboy has been, time out of mind, subject to the birch. In the middle ages, we read of children running to the shrines of saints, in the hope of there obtaining protection against the cruelty of their masters. A boy, in that hope, once clung to the tomb of St. Adrian, at Canterbury, and the master, notwithstanding the sanctity of the place, proceeded to inflict chastisement. The first and second strokes were allowed to be given with impunity, but the outraged saint stiffened the master's arm as he was about to inflict the third; and it was only when he had implored forgiveness of the boy, and the boy had interceded for him, that the use of his arm was restored! Another legend is related where the miracle was still more surprising:- An ill-used boy having fled, as usual, to the shrine, the master declared that not even although the Saviour of mankind interfered would he escape punishment. Upon this a beautiful white dove is said to have alighted on the tomb, and, by bending its head and fluttering its wings, as if in the attitude of supplication, disarmed the schoolmaster's anger, and made him fall on his knees and beg forgiveness. St. Ermenilda was in the same way the patroness of the Ely schoolboys. Some boys had fled to her shrine for protection, but the schoolmaster dragged them from their place of refuge, and flogged them to his heart's content (*usque ad animi satietatem verberat*). The following night the saint appeared to him, and completely paralysed his limbs; and their use was not restored until his pupils had carried him to the shrine as a repentant sinner.

Tusser, in his rude rhymes, complains of the severity of the scholastic discipline in his day. He says:-

"From Paul's I went to Eton, sent
To learn straightways the Latin phrase;
Where fifty-three stripes given to me
    At once I had,
For fault but small, or none at all,
It came to pass thus beat I was
See, Udall, see the mercy of thee
    To me, poor lad!"

In those days it would appear that boys were flogged, not for any offence, or omission, or unwillingness or incapacity to learn, but upon the abstract theory that they ought to be flogged. Erasmus bears witness that this was the principle upon which he was flogged. He was a favourite with his master, who had good hopes of his disposition and abilities, but flogged him to see how he could bear the pain, the result being that the Rod nearly spoiled the child: his health and spirits were broken by it, and he began to dislike his studies. He describes, without naming, another schoolmaster who was of a similar disposition. This is thought to be Colet, Dean of St. Paul's, who, although he delighted in children, and was a good man, thought no discipline could be too severe in his school; and whenever he dined there, one or two boys were served up to be flogged by way of dessert. On one of these flogging occasions, when Erasmus was present, he called up a meek, gentle boy of ten years old, who had lately been earnestly commended to his care by a tender mother—ordered him to be flogged for some pretended fault, and saw him flogged till the victim was fainting under the scourge: "not that he deserved this," said the dean to

Erasmus, while it was going on, but it was fit to humble him."

So necessary was the Rod considered in education that in the case of princes whose delicate skins could not be ruffled, whipping boys were provided, on whom the offences of their royal masters were unsparingly visited. There is an old play, published in 1632, in which a prince (supposed to be Edward VI) holds a dialogue with his whipping-boy:-

Prince—"Why, how now, Browne: what's the matter?"

Browne—"Your Grace loyters; and will not plye your booke and your tutors have whipped me for it."

Prince—"Alas, poor Ned! I am sorry for it. I'll take the more paines and entreate my tutors for thee."

James the Fourth of Scotland had for his whipping boy Sir David Lindsay of the Mount.

William Murray, father of the Countess of Dysart, was page and whipping-boy to Charles I in his young days. Le Sage introduces an example of a whipping boy into his life of Gil Blas. Don Raphael, in relating his history to the hero, tells that at twelve years of age he was appointed companion to the young Marquis Leganez, who was very backward in his education and who did not care to improve. One of the masters at length thought of the capital expedient of whipping Don Raphael for the deficiencies of his master, and this was done so emphatically that Don Raphael was impelled to take French leave. Modern princes had not this immunity from the Rod. George III, when asked by the tutor how the young princes were to be treated, promptly replied, "If they deserve it, let them be flogged. Do as you used to do at Westminster." Pity that these whipping-boys, whom we have mentioned, were not of the humour of that youth who used to take a flogging for diversion; and, as a joke, this boy, named Smith, as we have been told, did not care a pin for a flogging, and would put him self in the way of being whipped, for mere amusement for himself and others. "Smith again!" the master usually called out at flogging time, and, with a groan, Smith was always ready, affected to kneel down, then rose again, and said facetiously, "Allow me, sir, to put my handkerchief under my knees—these breeches cost my father five-and-twenty shillings, and he gave me particular charge not to soil them." Then would he begin only to kneel down, the master all the while vociferating—"Take him up, take him up." "Sir," Smith would say, "be so kind as to hit high and gentle." Then, when fairly down, he would look round, and at every stroke make horrible faces, as if in dreadful agony, and when the matter was over, jump up with alacrity, make his bow, and say, "I thank you, sir."

Most of the schools of England have their stories of flogging, and of masters who were proficient in the art. To many of them the words of Crabbe's schoolmaster were quite applicable:-

> *"Students," he said, "like horses on the road,*
> *Must be well lash'd before they take the load;*
> *They may be willing for a time to run,*
> *But you must whip them ere the work be done:*
> *To tell a boy, that if he will improve*
> *His friends whill praise him, and his parents love,*
> *Is doing nothing—he has not a doubt*
> *But they will love him, nay, applaud without;*
> *Let no fond sire a boy's ambition trust,*
> *To make him study, let him see he must.*

The mode of providing rods in the 16th century for the grammar school at Uttoxeter, and the spirit in which the punishment was required to be received, are set forth in the "Orders" of the founder. These consist of seventeen items, and those relating to the Rod are as follows:-

"*Item.* I will that all my scholars shall love and reverence my school-master, and gently receive punishment of him for their faults, *sub pœna expulsionis.*

Item. I will that all my scholars at their first entrance into my school shall give twopence apiece to a poor scholar, appointed by the master to keep the school cleane and to provide rods."

An amusing story is told of Richard Mulcaster of Merchant Taylors' school. "He beeinge one day whippinge a boy, his breeches beeinge doune, and he ready to inflict punishment uppon him, out of his insultinge humour, he stood pausinge a while over his breech; and there a merry conceit taking him, he sayd, 'I aske ye bannes of matrymony between this boy, his buttockes, of such a parish, on ye one side; and Lady Burch of ye parish, on ye other side; and if any man can shew any lawfull cause why yey should not be joyned together, let ym speake, for yis is ye last time of askinge!' A good sturdy boy and of a quick conceypt stood up and sayd, 'Master, I forbid ye banes!' The master takinge this in dudgeon sayd, 'Yea, sirrah, and why so?' The boy answered, "Because all partyes are no agreed, whereat the master likinge that witty aunswer, spared the one's fault and the other's presumption." The same story is related of Dr. Busby of Westminster, whose name has passed into a proverb or scholastic severity. His rod, he used to say, was the sieve which sifted the wheat of scholarship from chaff. It is related of him and one of his scholars, that during the doctor's absence from his study the boy found some plums in it, which he began to eat. First, however, he waggishly cried out, "I publish the banns of matrimony between my mouth and these plums; if any here present know just cause or impediment why they should not be united, you are to declare it, or hereafter hold your peace."

The doctor having overheard the proclamation, determined to chastise for it, but said nothing till next morning; when causing the boy to be brought up and disposed for punishment, he grasped the well-known instrument and said, "I publish the banns of matrimony between this rod and this boy; if any of you know just cause or impediment why they should not be united, you are to declare it." The boy himself called out, "I forbid the banns." "For what cause?" inquired the doctor. "Because," said the boy, "the parties are not agreed." The doctor enjoyed the validity of the objection, and the boy escaped.

Some of Busby's successors were not far behind him in the severity of discipline. Dr. Vincent's rule nearly equalled "Busby's awful reign." Of him it is recorded that he was not satisfied with the regulation punishment, but boxed the boys' ears and pinched them in addition. Coleman protested against this, saying that a pedagogue was privileged to make his pupil red in the proper place, but had no right to squeeze him black and blue with his fingers. During Vincent's mastership the older boys started a periodical called *The Flagellant*, which so roused Vincent's wrath that he began an action against the publisher, and Southey, who wrote an article caricaturing the doctor, came forward and avowed the authorship, and had to leave the school in consequence.

The boys of Westminster once administered the "discipline of the school" on Curll the bookseller. Pope mentions in one of his letters that Mr. Edmund Curll was exercised in a blanket and whipped at Westminster School by the boys. He had incurred the resentment of the Westminster scholars thus:- In 1716, Robert South, prebendary of Westminster School, died. At his funeral a Latin oration was pronounced over the body by Mr. John Barber, then Captain of the King's Scholars, Westminster. Curll, by some means, obtained and printed a copy of the oration without the author's consent, and the boys determined to take vengeance. Under pretence of giving him a correct copy, they decoyed him into the Dean's yard, and what followed is stated by the *St. James' Post.*—

"Being on Thursday last fortunately nabbed within the limits of the Dean's Yard by the King's Scholars, there he met with a college salutation; for he was first presented with the ceremony of the blanket, in which, when the skeleton had been well shook, he was carried in triumph to the school: and, after receiving a grammatical construction for his false concords, he was reconducted to the Dean's Yard, and, on his knees asking pardon of the aforesaid Mr. Barber for his offence, he was kicked out of the yard and left to the huzzas of the rabble." The incident was commemorated in a pamphlet entitled "Neck or Nothing," with the unfortunate Curll figuring prominently in a series of tableaux, first "being presented with the ceremony of the blanket," then stretched in a table undergoing a flagellation on the breech, and lastly, on his knees between two files of Westminster scholars, asking pardon of Mr. Barber.

The rod in use at Winchester school is not of birch but is composed of four apple-tree twigs, set in a wooden handle, and provided by two juniors who hold the office of rod-makers under the orders of the

Prefect of Hall. The invention of this instrument is ascribed to Dr. John Baker, who was warder of the school for thirty-three years, from 1454-87. The mode of application was specially prescribed. The delinquent knelt down to the block or bench, and two boys "took him up" —that is, removed the shirt between the waist-band of his trousers and his waistcoat—and then the master inflicted four cuts called a "scrubbing," or six cuts called a "bibling," on which occasion the Bible clerk introduced the victim. Queen Elizabeth visited Winchester in 1570. Her Majesty asked a young scholar if he had ever made acquaintance with the celebrated Winton Rod, and he replied, with more readiness than was to be expected, by an apt quotation from Virgil:-

"Infandum, Regina, jubes renovrare dolorem."

"Great Queen, what you command me to relate
Renews the sad remembrance of our fate." —*Dryden*

Shrewsbury School, about the beginning of the present century, was presided over by a great flogger, in the person of Dr. Butler. The whippings which he administered with his left hand are not yet forgotten. At this school there was a small room lighted by one narrow loophole, a receptacle for the flogging block and birch, where delinquents were confined. It was called the Blackhole, or sometimes "Rowe's Hole," from a youth who is said to have been a very regular occupant.

Dr. Parr deserves mention in the annals of school flagellation. He had a firm belief in the utility of the birch. At his school in Norwich there was usually a flogging levée before the classes were dismissed. His rod-maker was a man who had been sentenced to be hanged, but had been cut down and resuscitated by the surgeons; and from the hands of this amiable character, according to the account of a pupil, Parr "used to receive the birches with a complacent expression of countenance." Another pupil speaks feelingly of "the lightning of his eye, the thunder of his voice, and the weight of his arm." One of the under-masters told him one day that a certain pupil appeared to show signs of genius. "Say you so?" said Parr, "then begin to flog him to-morrow morning"

Flogging went on briskly at Rugby in Dr. James's time, about 1780; and there was, in addition, plenty of caning on the hand. During the mastership of Dr. Wooll in 1813, a memorable scene occurred. One day the whole of the lower fourth class, except the boy who was up at lesson by the master's side, rushed out before the usual time. The matter was at once reported to the doctor, who sent notice that every boy in the form was to be flogged at three o'clock, before the third lesson commenced. A few minutes before that hour the rod-bearer made his appearance, and preparations for the doleful ceremony were soon made. Punctually at the time Dr. Wooll entered the class room, and calling for the list, began with the head boy, and went regularly through the thirty-eight, including, unfortunately, the boy who had not run out with the rest. The whole thirty-eight were finished off in a quarter of an hour. The late Lord Lyttelton was being shown by Dr. Wooll the room at Rugby in which the flogging was usually inflicted. "What motto would be appropriate?" asked the doctor. "Great cry and little wool," replied the other, looking at the diminutive form of the master.

The following note to a letter written by Mrs. Piozzi to Sir James Fellowes, from Bath, 30th March, 1819, is curious:- "I had met Mr. Wickens a few days before at Mrs. Piozzi's. As we were brother Rugbyans, the conversation took place about the mode of punishing the boys in Dr. James's time, when Mrs, Piozzi related the story of Vandyke, who, when a boy, first evinced his genius in a remarkable manner by painting the exact likeness of the master upon the person of a schoolfellow about to be flogged, which so astonished and amused the pedagogue that he burst out a-laughing, and excused the boy the punishment that awaited him. Mrs. Piozzi's manner and humour in relating this anecdote of Vandyke was remarkably comical."

An anecdote, illustrative of how boys took their birch long ago, is given in "The Guide to Eton:" —Sir Henry B—n, some seventy years since (at which period collegers always held down boys who were being flogged), calmly looked up at his two supporters, who were still holding him down, instead of releasing him, though his flogging was over, and said, "Gentlemen of the black robe, I believe the ceremony is over."

Birching is a time-honoured practice at Eton. We say is, because, on the appointment of the last new head-master, the Rev. Mr. Hornby, he was presented by the "Captain" of the school, in the name of his fellows, with an elegant birch rod, tied with a blue riband. The usual rod at Eton consisted of three long birchen twigs (no branches), bound with string for about a quarter of their length, and a charge of half-a-guinea for birch was made in every boy's bill, whether he was flogged or not. Dr. Keate was among the most remarkable of the Eton floggers. He was celebrated for the celerity with which he despatched those who were down in the "bill" or flogging list. According to the Eton boys' code of propriety, there was not the least disgrace attached to a flogging; there might, indeed, be some reproach in never having tasted birch, to avoid which lads have been known to get themselves flogged on purpose. A few years ago, a youth of eighteen years of age was condemned to be flogged for smoking, but, acting on his father's orders, he refused to take his punishment, for which contumacy he was dismissed from the school. In the olden time, that ill-omened day, Friday, was the only flogging day at Eton.

The most noted flagellator in Eton annals, as has already been mentioned, was Dr. Keate, whose reign began in 1809 and lasted for a quarter of a century, and many amusing reminiscences of his mania for the birch have been preserved. The author of "Eothen" gives the following portrait of the doctor:- "He was little more, if more at all, than five feet in height, and was not very great in girth; but within this space was concentrated the pluck of ten battalions. He had a really noble voice, and this he could modulate with great skill; but he had also the power of quacking like an angry duck, and he almost always adopted this mode of communication in order to inspire respect. He was a capital scholar, but his 'ingenuous learning' had not 'softened his manners,' and had 'permitted them to be fierce' —tremendously fierce. He had such a complete command over his temper—I mean over his good temper—that he scarcely ever allowed it to appear; you

WINCHESTER ROD AND CAP

Formerly the Rod consisted of a wooden handle, about two and a half feet long, with four grooves at one end, into which were inserted four apple twigs. As these branched off at a considerable angle, it was the "Rod maker's" duty to twist them together to form one combined stick. At present, the twigs are so cut as to lie in a straight line with the rod, which is considered a disadvantage to the person being flogged.

ETON FLOGGING "BLOCK" AND ROD.

could not put him out of humour—that is, out of the ill humour which he thought to be befitting for a head-master. His red, shaggy eyebrows were so prominent that he habitually used them as arms and hands, for the purpose of pointing out any object towards which he wished to direct attention; the rest of his features were equally striking in their way, and were all and all his own. He wore a fancy dress, partly resembling the costume of Napoleon and partly that of a widow woman."

Of Keate's flogging exploits one very good story is told. On one occasion, when a confirmation was to be held for the school, each master was requested to make out a list of the candidates in his own form. A master wrote down the names on the first piece of paper which came to hand, which happened unluckily to be one of the slips, of well-known size and shape, used as flogging bills, and sent up regularly with the names of delinquents for execution. The list being put into Keate's hands without explanation, he sent for the boys in the regular course, and, in spite of all protestations on their part, pointing to the master's signature to the fatal "bill," he flogged them all.

Another day, a culprit who was due for punishment could not be found, and the doctor was kept waiting on the scene of action, but a namesake of the missing one happened to pass the door: he was at once seized by Keate's orders, and brought to the block as a vicarious sacrifice. Absence from roll-call was punished by flogging. Keate had imposed on one division an additional roll-call as a punishment. They held a consultation, and resolved that none of them should attend. The doctor came and found himself alone. He had just left a dinner party at his own house. He collected his assistants, and waited until the whole division was brought into his presence. He then went to work and flogged them all—about eighty—and returned to his guests as placid and agreeable as usual.

Only one instance is on record of a condemned culprit having escaped the birch of Dr. Keate. A boy who had got into trouble was looking forward to his first flogging with considerable nervousness. Some mischievous schoolfellows recommended a preparation of gall-nuts as an infallible recipe for making the surface to which it was applied insensible to pain. The result was one of those cases better imagined than described. It was impossible for the boy to put in an appearance before the doctor in that (ink-stained) state; and a strictly private conversation with his tutor ended in that gentleman's waiting upon Keate, in order to explain the impossibility of the impending operation being performed without great risk to the gravity of both head-master and attendant collegers: a "pœna" of some hundred lines was therefore accepted in commutation.

Among the many good stories told of "Old Keate," says the *Saturday Review*, perhaps the best is that of the boy who called on him to take leave. "You seem to know me very well," said the great head-master; "but I have no remembrance of ever having seen your face before." "You were better acquainted, sir, with my other end," was the unblushing reply.

A similar anecdote has been versified as follows:-

An old Etonian once met Keate abroad
And seized his hand; but he was rather floored
To see the Doctor seemed to know him not:
"Doctor," quoth he, "you've flogged me oft I wot,
And yet it seems that me you've quite forgot."
E'en now," says Keate, "I cannot guess your name—
Boys' b—s are so very much the same."

A hundred years since, and, indeed, up till within a quarter of a century ago, the punishments at Christ's Hospital were heavy and frequent. The monitors or heads of wards had a licence to chastise their inferiors, which they used freely. Writing of them, Charles Lamb says: "I have been called out of my bed, and waked for the purpose, in the coldest winter nights—and this not once, but night after night— in my shirt, to receive the discipline of a leathern thong, with eleven other sufferers, because it pleased my callow overseer, when there had been any talking heard after we were gone to bed, to make the six last beds in the dormitory, where the youngest children slept, answerable for an offence they neither dared to commit nor had any power to hinder." The King's boys, or those intended for the sea, who studied navigation under William Wales, had peculiarly hard lines of it; as, in order to inure them to the hardships of a sailor's life, Wales brought up his boys with Spartan severity, using the lash on every occasion, and dealing out his punishments with an unsparing hand. These chastisements were expected to be borne with patience, and the training, whatever might be its effects in after times, had the immediate result of rendering the youths hardy but brutal, and, as a consequence, mercilessly severe on their younger companions. They were the mortal terror of the young boys; but, at the same time, it must be confessed that they maintained the prowess of the school outside: the apprentices and butchers' boys of the neighbourhood stood in considerable awe of their fighting powers. The formal punishment for runaways was, in the first instance, fetters. For a second offence the culprit was confined in a cell, large enough for him to lie at full length upon straw and a blanket, a glimmer of light being admitted through a small window. The confinement was solitary—the prisoner only seeing the porter who brought his bread and water, or the Beadle who came twice a week to take him out for an airing and a whipping. A third attempt at flight was usually the last, because the offender was, after certain formalities, expelled. The culprit, divested of the school uniform and clad in a penitential robe, was brought from his cell into the hall, where were assembled the whole of his school fellows, the steward of the hospital, the Beadle, who was the executioner, and, as befitting, was clad in state for the occasion; two of the governors were also present, to certify that the extreme rigour of the law was inflicted. The culprit being hoisted, was slowly flogged round the hall by the Beadle, and then formally handed over to his friends, if he had any, or to his parish officer, who was stationed outside the gate.

CHAPTER XLII

ADDITIONAL ANECDOTES OF SCHOOL PUNISHMENTS

IN "THE good old times" flogging was permitted by the statutes of many colleges, and was a favourite recreation of the deans, tutors, and censors of the day. Dr. Potter, of Trinity College, flogged a collegian, though arrived at man's state and wearing a sword by his side, and Dr. Bathurst, president of that College, used to surprise the undergraduates, if walking in the grove at unseasonable hours, with a whip in his hand. Dr. Johnson, in his "Memoir of Milton," says: "I am ashamed to relate, what I fear is true, that Milton was one of the last students in either University that suffered the public indignity of corporal correction." Aubrey mentions the story of Milton being whipped by Dr. Chappell at Cambridge, and afterwards being transferred to the tuition of one Dr. Tovell. But there is a tradition that Dr. Johnson himself was scourged over the buttery hatch at Oxford. There is, however, no authoritative statement on the matter, and it must remain a moot point whether Milton or Johnson was the last student on whom the Rod was inflicted at the Universities. In the *Dublin College Journal*, the fact of such and such a pupil having been trained in that seminary is recorded in the words, *educatus erat sub ferula*—that is, "was educated under the Rod," from which it may be inferred that the teaching was fostered by the birch.

The excessive use of the Rod in schools, at the time we speak of, led to the custom of "barring out," an attempt on the part of the boys to exclude the schoolmaster from the scene of his usual labours. The custom was very general in the schools of burgh towns and large villages, and usually took place at Christmas. If the boys were successful in keeping out the master for three days, the vanquished pedagogue was obliged to sign articles of agreement, relating to the number of holidays, hours of play, and matters of discipline. If, on the contrary, the attempt was unsuccessful, the pupils were compelled to submit to his dictation in these matters, and likewise to undergo an unlimited amount of flagellation.

It is said Joseph Addison was, one day, the leader of a barring out at the grammar school of Lichfield, about 1684 or 1685. Quite a modern attempt is recorded in the *Gentleman's Magazine* for 1828. It happened, probably, about the beginning of the present century at the grammar school of Ormskirk, in Lancashire. A few days before the Christmas holidays the older scholars resolved to revive the ancient custom of barring out the master. Many years had elapsed since the attempt had succeeded. The scholars had heard of the glorious feats of their forefathers, when they set the lash of the master at defiance for days together. The head of the Greek class took the leadership, and assembling his schoolfellows around him, he addressed them in heroic style: "My boys, to-morrow morning we are to bar out the flogging parson, and to make him promise that he will not flog us hereafter without cause, or set us long tasks, or deprive us of our holidays. The boys of the Greek form will be your captains, and I am to be general. Those who are cowards had better retire, and be satisfied with future floggings; but you who have courage, and know what it is to be flogged for nothing, come here and sign your names."

The proposal was carried out next day; and when the master appeared, he found the door of the school shut and barricaded, and the boys within armed with sticks, pokers, old pistols, &c., determined to defend the place to the last. The master, after vainly at tempting to force an entrance, and getting his head broken, went for the constable. On the arrival of the civil authorities, the boys got frightened, and proposed to surrender. A few escaped by the back windows; the others ranged themselves in two lines, weapon in hand. The door was thrown open—the master entered, denouncing vengeance on all concerned. As he walked in, however, the files walked out, and he was left with an empty school. It was afterwards resolved that the leaders should not come to school until sent for, and a free pardon granted; indeed, so many stayed away, that the master deemed it prudent to remit the promised flogging.

With regard to flagellation as now practised in schools in England, the reports of the Schools Inquiry Commission furnish some particulars. From Mr. Giffard's report on the schools of Surrey and Sussex, we find that in sixteen out of twenty-two boarding schools, or about 73 per cent., corporal punishment of some kind is in use, but in almost every case the use of the cane or the birch is said to be very rare, and no assistant, we are told, is allowed to inflict the punishment, which is the correction for lying, indecent conduct, swearing, insolence, and moral offences. Impositions, fines, and stoppages of pocket money are the other punishments. In all endowed schools the cane or birch is in use. Mr. Giffard reports that the accounts given by schoolmasters of the efficacy of corporal punishment differ very widely. Dr. Lowe, of Hurstpierpoint says, "It is a positive kindness to the boys." A private schoolmaster in Sussex said the discipline of the school had been "ruined by the exclusion of the cane." On the other hand, the commissioner was told that it was "degrading and unnecessary." But in general, both masters and boys seem to prefer the "short and sharp remedy of the birch to impositions or confinement." The parents are the chief objectors, and private schools have been forced to yield to their opinions. Two cases were cited in this district of schoolmasters who had been known to abuse their licence to inflict corporal punishment. One was Hopley, whose case made so great a sensation some years ago; the other was an under-master of an endowed school, who had been summoned before a magistrate and fined for cruelty to a boy. Such cases as these, however, are happily very rare.

In reporting on the schools in Flint, Denbigh, Montgomery, Glamorgan, and Hereford, Mr. Bompas says there is almost no corporal punishment: no birching at all and very little caning. In the girls' schools of this quarter there is a novel punishment said to be very efficacious—namely, sending the delinquent to bed! In Northumberland, according to Mr. Hammond's report, tasks, impositions, and corporal punishment are the means of enforcing discipline, but the last, inflicted either with the taws or the cane, is the most common mode of correcting the boys. Happily for the children, there is not a birch in the county, and flogging in the old-fashioned style is quite unknown! It is much the same in the schools of Lancashire: the cane is the last remedy for vice or insubordination, and so far as the commissioner, Mr. Bryce, has seen, there is only one birch in regular use in the county. At the Liverpool Institute Schools, flogging is tolerated, but only from the hands of the headmaster. The gentleman who was examined on these schools said at first the system of gentle admonitions was tried, but it turned out a complete failure, so that the Rod was ultimately introduced. Mr. Mason, of the Denmark Hill School, uses the cane and the birch, the first as most suitable for the older boys, and the latter for the younger pupils. He reserves to himself the exclusive right to administer either of these punishments. Mr. C. H. Pinches, proprietor of Clarendon House School, a private boarding school, said to the Commissioners, "I object to the accompaniments of the Rod—that is, taking the trousers down, and so on; although it perhaps would surprise you to know that I refused two boarders the other day because I declined to use the birch in the way suggested by the lady who wished to place them with me. I think, as far as the punishment itself is concerned, the birch is preferable, but I do not like the adjuncts."

The French Commissioners remark that the English schools have "a kind of punishment which we do not think we ought to envy—the corporal punishment which is reserved among us to children in the nursery." The conclusion at which they arrive in their report is that— "The Rod is one of those ancient English traditions which survive because they have survived. A foreigner can hardly conceive the perseverance with which English teachers cling to this old and degrading custom. We have read in Dr. Arnold's works an eloquent dissertation in favour of flogging, which has not at all convinced us. One is astonished at seeing English masters remove a garment which the prudery of their language hesitates to name."

Many anecdotes are told of schoolmasters who have been flogged by their pupils. In most cases of the kind, the elder boys, led on by one who has frequently been subjected to the punishment, have seized the unfortunate dominie at some unwary moment, and overpowered him by superior numbers. Then, prostrate on a table, or horsed on the flogging block, he has been treated to a most vigorous sample of his own birch.

In Scotland scholastic flagellation was carried to as great an extent as in England, only the instrument in use was more commonly "the taws," a long strap of tolerably stout leather, with the ends cut into stripes. The orders for the discipline of the school at the Kirk of Dundonald in Ayrshire for the year 1640 have been preserved, and they indicate the manner in which flagellation was to be performed. After the regulations for prayers, &c., the master is enjoined to teach his scholars good manners, "how to carry themselves fashionably and courteously towards all—superiors, inferiors, or equals." Then he was to appoint a clandestine censor, who should secretly acquaint the master with everything that concerned the scholars and, "according to the quality of the faults, the master shall inflict punishment, striking some on the hand with a birk wand or pair of taws, others on the hips as their faults deserve, but none at any time or in any case on the head or cheeks." The master is further counselled to repress insolence, and enforce duty rather by a grave and authoritative manner than by strokes, yet he is by no means to neglect the Rod when it is needful.

The Rod was not always in Scotland administered in this serious mood. In the High School of Edinburgh, one of the masters, named Nicol, would occasionally have a dozen culprits to whip at once, arranging them in a row for that purpose. When all was ready, he would send a polite message to his colleague, Mr. Cruickshank, "to come and hear his organ." Cruickshank having responded to the summons, Mr. Nicol would proceed to inflict a rapid cursory flagellation up and down the row, producing a variety of notes from the patients. Mr. Cruickshank was sure to take an early opportunity to return the compliment by inviting his friend to assist at a similar operation.

The master of a grammar school in the central district of Scotland, some ninety years ago, was a vigorous upholder of flagellation. This worthy, named Hacket, practised all the varieties of flagellation then in vogue. Heavy applications of the taws to the hands of the offenders were the mildest operations. Many times the culprit was stretched on a table, held down with one hand and thrashed with the other. Sometimes the boy was made to stride between two boards, while the master applied the rod behind. The dull boys were birched for their own demerits, and the bright lads suffered for the deficiencies of their fellows. Belonging to the former class was a boy, named Anderson, who had many a bitter taste of the birch to stimulate his faculties. His punishments were so many and unjust that he conceived the most deadly sentiments of revenge against his master. He left the school, went to India, acquired a competency, and returned to spend his days in Scotland. During his long residence in India he never forgot his floggings at school, or his determination to be revenged on Hacket. On his arrival in Scotland he purchased a whip, travelled to the town where he had been educated, and having ordered dinner for two at an inn, sent a message to Hacket (who had retired from his profession), inviting him to dine with an old pupil. Old Hacket accepted the invitation, dressed himself in his best, and went to the inn. He was ushered into the room, where he saw a gentleman, who, as soon as he entered, locked the door; then, taking down the whip, introduced himself, and informed the astonished Hacket that he was now about to punish him for the many flagellations he had inflicted on him at school. So saying, he ordered him to strip and receive the punishment. Hacket's presence of mind did not desert him in such untoward circumstances. He acknowledged that, perhaps, he was a little too severe with his boys in old times, but if he was to be punished he would prefer having dinner first and the flogging afterwards. Anderson could not but assent to such a reasonable proposal, although inwardly resolving that the flogging should be none the lighter for the waiting. So they sat down to dinner, which proved excellent and old Hacket's conversation was so fascinating and agreeable that gradually Anderson found his purpose of revenge growing weaker. At last he gave up all thoughts of his whip and the intended flagellation. Hacket got home in perfect safety, for his host insisted upon escorting him to his own door.

We are in possession of a large collection of anecdotes of school punishments in Scotland; but they are so similar in character that we shall not give more than one or two by way of sample. Even at the present day the old-fashioned style of whipping boys and girls still prevails in some remote districts of Scotland; and forty years ago, "houpsy doubsy" (being laid over the master's knee), as it was called, was practised even at schools in Edinburgh. A present dignitary of the Scottish dissenting church, who at the date indicated was master of a small village school, regularly whipped his pupils, male and female, in the mode indicated, and he did so with the full knowledge of their parents. At one time he punished his scholars without removing their clothes, but finding that a lad had placed within his trousers a skin of soft leather with a view to lessen the pain of the "skelping" he ever after insisted upon laying on the taws after the orthodox mode. The boy who had so imposed upon his master was immediately saluted by his schoolfellows with the nickname of "leather doub," which has stuck to him ever since.

An old-fashioned Scottish dominie used to punish the boys of his school by fastening the culprit over a desk at the door, and his clothes being removed, it was the rule for every one of his schoolfellows to give him a skelp with the "taws." Another Scottish schoolmaster had an odd way of chastising his pupils; he made them take down or raise up their clothes, and caused them to sit upon a large block of marble that had been brought to the parish in order to be hewn into a statue of some local magnate. In some of the schools in Edinburgh "horsing" was practised—one boy being flogged on the back of another boy. In English schools "horsing" was also prevalent.

The skins of eels, we are told, were in ancient times used in schools as whips to correct the pupils. In a fishing village near Edinburgh, the schoolmaster, forty years ago, used such skins with which to flog his pupils; and it is said that the "wives" of the village, "once upon a time," treated a town gallant, who came a-wooing to one of the lasses of the village, to a good hiding—it being a rule that fisher folk should only marry fisher folk: the instrument used was a bundle of dried eel skins.

An eccentric Scottish nobleman who had, when a child, been frequently whipped at a dame's school which he attended at a time when he had no expectation of being a man of title, insisted upon being flogged by his old schoolmistress, shortly after coming to his estate! For her "kindness" on this occasion, It is said he gave the old dame a present of one hundred pounds.

Quite recently there was an attempt at legislation in the matter of scholastic and domestic flagellation. The Marquis of Townsend introduced into the House of Lords a bill for the better protection of children, servants, and apprentices, by which it should be enacted that no schoolmaster, usher, or tutor, having the charge of children under sixteen years of age, should be allowed to inflict corporal punishment except by a birch rod, and further that there should be no corporal punishment whatever for inattention to, or inaccuracy in, their studies. It was also to be illegal for a master or mistress to strike an apprentice or servant. This last provision was quite superfluous, because the law, as it stands at present, is sufficient to meet such cases. In the discussion, that was followed by the withdrawal of the bill, it was pointed out that the safe and efficient instrument of school discipline in Scotland, the taws would be illegal, and since Scotch boys are not birched, no kind of corporal chastisement would remain by which a schoolmaster, or even an uncle or aunt, could correct a refractory lad.

CHAPTER XLIII

ON THE WHIPPING OF YOUNG LADIES

THE reader will have noted, in the perusal of preceding portions of this work, that ladies, both old and young, have had to submit themselves with humiliation to the birch. In ladies' boarding schools a century ago, the Rod was unsparingly used, and even up till about the year 1830, young ladies were whipt at school. In order that we may be as chronological as possible, we insert here an account of boarding-school discipline at the end of the last century. It is taken from a letter written twelve years ago, and which is brimful of information on the subject:-

MY DEAR LITTLE GRANDDAUGHTER —Though, I suppose, I ought not to call you *little* (young ladies of twelve years old consider themselves women now, I hear), I send with this the parcel of good and pretty things I promised you to take to school with you. Ah, my dear, schools were very different in my day! And I send you, too, what you and your sisters have so often asked me to tell you some particulars about, what going to school was like when I was young. I haven't written it down myself. No, no, I couldn't do that, but I've made Martha, my maid, do it. I can remember a good deal yet, thank God, though I am eighty years old and better; but I've got a good many memoranda of things gone by, and letters, which have helped me.

My dear, it is seventy-two years since I went to school—only think of that!—and I was twelve years old at the time. It was to Regent House, Bath, I was to be sent, and the journey from here, including a short stay in London, occupied a week. There's not much trouble now in fitting girls out for school, but it was very different then. My mother had all the old stores of the house turned out, and passed in review, to see what could be made up for me; for gowns were gowns in those days, and descended from mother to daughter not like the flimsy things made now-a-days, which are worn once or twice, and never seen any more, except in the windows of second-hand shops, or on the backs of poor wretches not to be named here. And my mother had a wardrobe which was the envy of all the neighbourhood. I was a young person of quality, and my outfit was proportionably good. I had six gowns; young ladies would think that nothing now, but then it was a great deal. I had a chintz gown of white with red spots, the newest style, and made in the first fashion, with the short waist, which had become so fashionable. Two inches from the arm-pits was the mode, and it was quite out of fashion to have the sash lower. There was another of the same material, with a pattern of lace running over it in many stripes, which was considered very genteel. Both these dresses (we never used that word in those days) were made very open in front and almost down to the waist, and the skirt of moderate width, almost always fastened up on one side. To wear with these there were elaborately trimmed petticoats, not at all unlike some of those you are going to take to school with you, and the proper out-door finish of the costume was a long, straight scarf, and gloves reaching up to the elbows to meet the sleeves. A lady might exercise her taste in the colour of her gloves. I had several pairs, white and coloured, all trimmed and embroidered; one pair, especially, of fine lawn, beautifully trimmed with lace and embroidered with silk, cost a great deal of money. The hair was worn frizzed and curled, and bonnets were small: they were made to sit quite on the top of the head, and had a great deal of trimming. I dare say young girls now-a-days would think them ugly, but as I remember them I can't see that they were uglier or more inconvenient than the things women put on their heads now; but it is all fashion, my dear—fashion: *la mode* is a very tyrant—always was and always will be. The days were not very long past then when women used to dress their hair two feet high, and wear coaches, and ships, and animals, on their heads for ornament. My mother had a coach-and-four in blown glass, which she used to wear, when she was young, on great occasions. I had nothing of that sort, the fashions being simpler, to my mother's grief, who would fain have had me decked out in the style of her early days. She had a chip hat made in the shape that the lovely Misses Gunning made so fashionable, but it would not do for me, and my best bonnet was not at all unlike a coal-scuttle turned upside down, with three bands of pink ribbon on it, and little rosettes at the top. Hoops were not quite gone out, and I had one for full dress, for it was a fashionable school I was going to. The gown to wear with it was a white brocade covered all over with little moss rosebuds, and trimmed with fly fringe and bunches of red and green ribbon, the body cut very low, and the short sleeves trimmed with a fall of deep lace. Ah, my dear, hoops weren't a bit uglier than the hideously large crinolines that women wore till lately, although King George IV did abolish them by a royal edict. I had stockings of many colours, and all with clocks, and numbers of pairs of shoes of colours, to match my dresses. My poor mother was so sorry that the high heels and clogs had gone out; she wore them to the day of her death, and declared they were the most comfortable and proper things; but they were out, and all mine were made in the mode, low in the quarter and flat in the heel, like a modern dancing shoe. I had fans, too; one is enough for a young lady now-a-days, but it wasn't so then; we carried fans everywhere like the Japanese, and I had one for walking and one for morning, one for evening and another for full dress. I had a good many jewels, but you may see many like them in the shop windows now, for the old fashion of large earrings and showy jewellery is reviving again. I had to take with me a large stock of towels and sheets, and a knife, fork, spoon, and silver ring, on which my name was engraven. Our journey from Greshambury to London, only four-and-twenty miles as you know, took nearly the whole day in Mr. Burnet's fast coach, the coachman and guard going a round-about road, for there were many unsafe places to pass—Blackheath especially. We put up at the Salutation Inn in the Borough, and the next day I was shewn a good deal of London.

One evening we went to the play at Drury Lane, and saw "The Clandestine Marriage" and "The Virgin Unmasked," which were pieces much in fashion at that time.

We posted from London to Bath in my uncle's chariot, and performed the journey in two days, which was quick work then, and reached Regent House on the evening of the second. The Misses Pomeroy, who kept the school, were two maiden ladies of the greatest fashion, who enjoyed the reputation of sending out their pupils in a most finished style, and perfected in every grace of manner and deportment. My wardrobe was thoroughly inspected, and, for the most part, approved of, except my stays, which were immediately sent away to be made much stiffer, so that when they came back I could scarcely move; but Miss Pomeroy said that young ladies did not require to swing their bodies about like milkmaids. She never did, and we were trained to be as stiff and as upright as she was. Every morning when we had walked into the school room, and saluted our governess with the latest dancing master's courtesy, we were placed with our feet in the stocks, the backboard at our shoulders, and a large darning needle, point uppermost, stuck in our bodice, so that if we stooped in the least we scratched our chins. We were punished if we did prick ourselves: ah, many a severe whipping have I had for that and other offences as trivial. Whipping was at that time decreasing as a punishment in girls' schools, but the Misses Pomeroy believed in its efficacy, and practised it largely. When a culprit had committed an offence (and it would astonish you very much to hear what slight things were offences then), and was adjudged worthy of being whipped, she had to march up to the governess's desk, and curtseying very low, request permission to fetch the rod. The permission granted—and it was given with much ceremony—she retired and returned, without her gloves, bearing the rod on a cushion. Then she knelt down and presented it, and the governess, bidding her rise, administered a few cuts upon her bare arms and shoulders. The rods were of two kinds, one made of birchen twigs and the other of fine pieces of whalebone, wound round with waxed thread to keep them together. Either of them would give a stinging stroke, but the whalebone one which we called "Soko" amongst ourselves, was especially dreaded. Its fangs were like a cat-o'-nine-tails, spreading over our unfortunate flesh. "Soko" was reserved for grave offences, amongst which any sort of disrespect to our governesses (and the Misses Pomeroy were regular martinets in these matters) was reckoned. It was a very select school, not more than thirty young ladies being received, and these all of the first fashion. It was not at all an uncommon thing for a girl in those days to remain at school till she was nineteen or twenty years of age, only going from school when an eligible *parti* appeared for her to marry, or when the settling in life of an elder sister made way for her presentation to the gay world. But young or old, rich or noble though many of them were, none could 'scape whipping when it was the Misses Pomeroys' pleasure to whip. Enough castigation went on at Regent House to have satisfied the most strenuous upholders of the oft-quoted proverb "Spare the Rod and spoil the child."

There were two or three degrees of severe whipping: one was in private, with only the Misses Pomeroy and a servant present; another was being publicly prepared for the punishment before the whole school and then being forgiven; and lastly there was the public whipping fully carried out. The only time I was privately whipped I remember well, old woman though I am, as well as though it were only yesterday. I was formally bidden by the teacher in charge of the school room at the time to fetch the rod, and carry it into a room which the lady principals called their study. There I found the two ladies, before whom I knelt and presented the rod, which the elder took and drew through her fingers, caressingly, as it seemed to me. Then she rang a hand bell which stood upon the table beside her, and one of the maids entered and was bidden to prepare me. This was done by simply turning my clothes up and holding my hands, though in the public performances the preparatory ceremony was much more elaborate. I was terribly frightened; the shame of the proceeding—I had never been whipped in my life before—completely overcame me, and a violent fit of hysterics was the result of my first school flogging. Alas! I got used both to seeing and feeling them before I left Regent House. I have seen marriageable girls flogged for breaches of discipline, before all their schoolfellows, the necessary portion or their dress being removed. There was a dress put on for a public flogging, something like a night-gown, and in this the culprit was exhibited before all her school-mates, to receive her punishment. She was made to stoop forward over one of the desks, her hands being firmly held by an attendant, and her feet secured in the stocks on the floor. I remember well a young lady being chastised in this way only a few weeks before she left school to be married. I will call her Miss Darwin here. She was a bad girl—naturally bad, I do believe—and she was always pilfering; nothing was safe from her fingers. We lost all sorts of things—money, trinkets, and even clothes. It was what they call kleptomania now, but we had no grand names for crimes when I was young: stealing was stealing, and there was an end of it. I forget what particular theft caused the whipping I am going to tell you about, but I remember it very well. In the midst of the afternoon school Miss Pomeroy said:- "Young ladies, you will dress half-an-hour earlier than usual to-day, and be in the class-room at half past four instead of five o'clock."

We looked at one another, and Miss Darwin coloured a little, but made no other sign that she knew anything about the alteration, and we went to our rooms. Up stairs we found out what it meant, for the maid who dressed my hair had to make the rods, and a new one had been tied up that day, expressly for the coming ceremony. At the appointed time we were all in the class-room, and Miss Pomeroy took her place. Miss Darwin was ordered to stand in the middle of the room, and then our governess proceeded to tell what she had done, and what she was going to suffer. She was a very handsome girl, quite a woman in appearance and size; yet she stood there to take her whipping as a matter of course. She was very handsomely dressed in a gown of green brocade, with a frilled under-petticoat of white silk, silk stockings, and embroidered shoes to match her dress. Her hair, which was only confined by a red ribbon, was frizzed and curled, and she wore a handsome necklace and earrings. Miss Pomeroy rang for an attendant, who came and stood beside her with a deep courtesy.

"Prepare her," was the mandate, and the girl courtseyed again, and requested permission to remove the gloves. Miss Darwin bowed (that was the formula), and the process of disrobing went on. Then the punishment blouse was put on—it used to remind us of a shroud—and then the young lady, taking the rod, presented it, kneeling, to Miss Pomeroy. The governess took it and came down from the dais, where her chair was placed, while Miss Darwin, between two teachers, was led to the desk, and fastened over it in the manner I have described. Then the governess, with right good will, whipped her till red weals rose in all directions on her white posterior flesh. The castigation over, she now, trembling in every limb, and with blazing cheeks and sparkling eyes, returned the rod to the governess kneeling, and retired to make her toilet, a servant bearing her clothes in a basket

Another curious punishment was practised in our school, to subdue our pride, our teachers said. Any girl transgressing against the rules respecting cleanliness or order—and it was no easy task to remember them all—was stripped of her clothes and dressed up in the costume of a charity girl! The slightest deviation from the regulations, the most trivial neglect of our toilet duties, sentenced us to this most provoking degradation. The dress used at Regent House was the fac simile of that worn by the "Red Girls," a large charity school in Bristol, whose attire was composed entirely of scarlet serge with a white apron. Any thing more unbecoming or more uncomfortable could scarcely be imagined, and there was hardly one of us that would not have preferred a flogging. The same ceremony was observed as in the whippings: the culprit requested permission to fetch the clothes, and carried them in on a salver neatly folded, with the coarse shoes and stockings laid on the top. Then a servant was summoned, and her dress and ornaments were taken off, and she was attired in the gown, tippet, and cap. Then her fashionable shoes were removed, and the coarse leather ones put on, and in that dress she had to remain for the time prescribed. No matter who she was, or who came to see her, the garb must be worn: she attended the dancing-master, the different classes, and the drill-master in it, and stood upon a high stool during school hours, a mark for all our eyes. I am sure no such punishments are in vogue now, Katie, and that you won't be so strictly disciplined where you are going. What would you think of having your pretty mouth plastered up for letting your tongue run too freely? Yet that was the punishment for talking in improper hours at Regent House: a broad strip of sticking plaster put slanting across the lips, holding them fast together, and that kept on for many hours. It used to be one large piece put completely over the mouth and covering it, but one rather delicate girl was almost choked by the process, and it had to be discontinued. The number and manner of punishments for faults would make schoolmistresses of these days open their eyes. We had our hands tied behind us if we blotted our copies, and our elbows fastened back with straps if we stooped over our spinnets in practising. Our life was a hard one, and yet it was thought effectual in turning out graceful and finished ladies. I could tell you a great deal more of our school life—of our lessons, and meals, and recreations, such as they were—but I think this will do for this time. When your schoolmistress seems strict, my dear, think about what I have told you, and be thankful. You'll learn more, I dare say, than I ever did, for a lady's education then was limited compared to what it is now; she was not expected to understand all the ologies, and be able to hold her own with the best, whatever was talked about. If she could dance well, speak French, play the spinnet and read and write passably, her schooling was complete. I've got through the world with it, and I don't know that I've been any the worse wife or mother for not understanding half-a-dozen languages, or being able to talk to learned folk about all sorts of things out of the world and in it. I've sent you a long letter, little Katie—it may be the last you'll ever have from me, for eighty three years is a long while to live. If I don't see you come back from your first half, my love, don't quite forget me, but think sometimes of the loving old grandmother who talked to you sometimes of her own school days. You'll never be flogged, my dear: its not the fashion now. But Martha says I have made her write enough.—So believe me, your affectionate Grandmother.

CHAPTER XLIV

BIRCH ACCORDING TO THE "FAMILY HERALD"

ON the whipping of young ladies a perfect mine of information is to be found in that most popular of all periodicals, the *Family Herald*. As everybody knows, this journal is famed for its notices to correspondents, and among these we find a large number relating to discipline in ladies' schools, and also at home. Correspondence on this delicate subject has been going on in the *Herald* at various times during the last eighteen years. These controversies begin in the simplest possible way. A mother, for instance, who has an unmanageable daughter, writes to know if any correspondent can inform her of a training school of severe discipline for girls in any of the suburbs of London; or Emily desires to find a school at which to place the daughter of a friend, a spoiled child, where the discipline is very strict, and flogging is permitted. And Emily goes on to mention that she herself attended the school of the Misses Fulcher at Chiswick (now abroad), where the discipline was severe, and birching the invariable punishment for certain offences.

Such requests, it would seem, draw out a series of replies; for, to begin with, "Domina" writes a long letter full of delicately chosen words, in which she expresses horror at Emily's request "for a ladies' school in which flogging is practised." She rightly says that it is as much a physical as an ethical question, and quarrels with the verb "flog" when applied to a girl. "I even never heard of a girl being flogged since the days of the murderess, Brownrigg," and "Domina" is troubled at so "rough a proposal as we have suffered to be inserted in our widely-circulated pages." She trusts the *Family Herald* will supply the antidote, and express strong disapproval of so gross an impropriety. It was a *lapsus calami*, she would hope. "I am pedantic, perhaps, in the choice of expressions," she continues, "because words denote things and actions, and to substitute the gross Dutch-sounding word you have used for the elegant and soft English expression, 'chasten, ' appears to me a clear indication of character, such as Emily would doubtless disclaim, and yourself would indignantly repudiate. I confess that I am one of the most earnest advocates of corporal chastisement, gently and affectionately administered; but I have an utter horror of severity, such as you mention having been practised by the ladies of Chiswick, at whose emigration I heartily rejoice. I do wish that our feminine teachers could discriminate between the extremes of baneful indulgence and pernicious laxity of discipline on the one hand, and the more revolting, if less injurious, system of using the Rod with severity, on the other. For my part, I shall continue to inculcate the practice and principle so humorously paraphrased by Sir Robert Peel, with reference to the Temple Rifle Brigade, in the motto (which please address to Emily), "*In medio tutissima ibis.*".

Another correspondent of the same periodical sends an account of the discipline practised in a high-class ladies' school in Edinburgh, which is certainly curious if true, but we very much doubt its veracity. According to the communication, the ceremony attendant on a whipping is as follows:- "When an offence of sufficient magnitude takes place, the culprit enters it in the book herself, and carries the report to the lady superintendent, who writes under it the amount of punishment. For the first offence the delinquent is prepared for punishment, but is generally pardoned. For the second she is whipped privately. For all subsequent delinquencies, the punishment takes place in the schoolroom, on the 'horse;' and, in addition the pain it inflicts, it costs in money about 1 shilling in fees. This is the system: The girl proceeds to the housekeeper to procure the rod, a leather thong; she pays 2d. for the use of it. She has then to be partly undressed by the maid, and this costs 2d. The culprit has then to walk barefooted to another part of the house to be robed for punishment, a peculiar dress being used to add to the disgrace. It is a long linen blouse, short cotton hose, and list slippers. The young lady, thus dressed, proceeds to the drawing-room, to be exhibited to the lady superintendent. Having been approved, she is then conducted to the schoolroom, when she has to pay 6d. to the governess who inflicts the punishment awarded. A wooden horse, covered with soft leather, is the medium of castigation. The delinquent subsequently thanks the governess, kisses the rod, thanks the superintendent, and retires to her own room, to appear no more until prayer time next morning. The ceremony has more effect than the punishment." We should think so.

A different method of punishment is described by a gentleman, a teacher in numerous ladies' schools. It is by means of a strap, or, as it would be called in some places, a pair of "taws." The gentleman thus describes the instrument and the mode of using it:- "This strap is made of soft, pliable leather, and at the end is divided into a number of small strips, and when this instrument is applied to a young lady's hand the effect is marvellous. The pain it produces is no doubt rather severe, but in a short time it goes off; and there is not the least doubt that in this respect it is infinitely superior to the birch, as there can be nothing immodest or indecent in this mode of punishment, not the slightest fear of bruising or injuring the lady's person, and the pain it produces is quite sufficient to cause the young ladies to learn their lessons."

When the controversy carried on in the *Family Herald* begins to flag it is stimulated by some such letter as that of Miss Birch who, says the editor, "sends us one of those extraordinary letters, so many of which we cast aside, begging for a further explanation, dissertation on, and defence of flogging in girls' schools, which she declares is necessary, and without which no school can be well conducted."

We gather from his remarks that the editor is evidently very suspicious of his correspondents. In many of the answers he conveys the idea that he is dealing with some one who is not what he (or she) implies by the signature attached to the letter. In other words, we gather from some of the communications that men are engaging in the correspondence from purient or, at least, questionable motives. Many of the writers desire strongly to have particulars of the modus operandi—that is, whether the culprit is put over the knee, mounted on some person's back, laid over a chair, tied down on an ottoman, whipt in bed, or how the necessary chastisement is administered, also what amount of whipping is given for different offences. Some of the correspondents are very stupid, others not very truthful or inventive, for we find the whipping letters of early numbers repeated in late numbers, and so on, with accounts of schools which evidently never were in existence.

The point discussed by another class of correspondents is whether or not punishments at ladies' schools are indecent; but it is very properly held that for a girl to be birched by a woman is no more indecent than for a boy to be flogged on his naked person by a man, as is done every day at such schools as Eton, Rugby, Winchester, and others. The question whether or not females ought to be flogged is a different point. The tenderest of mothers will sometimes beat children, and with good effect. "He that spareth the Rod hateth his son:" such is Solomon's dictum. Latterly we have introduced too much softness and too much indulgence with children, and it will not surprise us if our pedagogues turn round to the opposite extreme. We prefer corporal punishment, says one editor. To deprive of food, of open air, to stigmatise by a fool's cap, to degrade and insult, to imprison and confine—all these methods of punishment are bad; at the same time, discipline must be kept, and example set of diligence and devotion to study. A smart castigation, corporally, given in the best and most decent way, is infinitely preferable to mental depredation. Neither women nor girls are such ethereal beings as many good men think.

That a great variety of opinions are prevalent as to the propriety of whipping girls, we know from what took place a few years ago at the Chelsea female school for the daughters of soldiers killed in the Crimean war. The authorities of this school—the secretary, chaplain, and lady superintendent—who was the daughter of a naval officer, and a woman of great respectability—approved of the old-fashioned mode of correction. The girls were whipped by the lady superintendent herself, and the older ones were not exempt from the Rod. The superintendent was of opinion that a girl of fifteen or sixteen required strict discipline to keep her in order when she was ill disposed, and also that the Rod had greater terrors for her than for a younger child. There was a committee of lady visitors, some of whom disapproved of the practice, and a keen controversy was carried on. The secretary and lady superintendent held that in a school of about three hundred girls, many of them sprung from the lower ranks, corporal punishment was absolutely necessary. The ladies who dissented from this opinion resigned, and the subject was at last brought before Parliament. The inquiry resulted in a compromise; the birch was abolished, and the mistress was authorised to inflict punishment with a cane on the palm of the hand.

CHAPTER XLV

"BIRCH IN THE BOUDOIR"

THE *Family Herald* is not the only journal that deals in birch. The *Queen*, a fashionable journal emanating from the great metropolis, opened its columns about five years ago to a controversy on the subject. The communications were at first only about the proper discipline for little children, and whether or not the Rod should be used in the nursery; but a good many letters were ultimately permitted, illustrating the punishment of children of larger growth. We need not quote from these, as they were similar to those which appeared in the *Family Herald* many of them being quite unreal—so unreal that we presume the following burlesque communication from "B." was intended to bring the controversy (which had to be stopped by the editor) into ridicule:-

"I think the public exposure and punishment of grown girls should be legally prohibited. A whipping to a child of seven or eight is one thing; such castigation as your correspondents describe is quite another. A few months ago I should have read their letters with incredulity, but my own recent experience furnishes confirmation.

"I am a bachelor. Many years ago my only sister died, leaving her daughter to my care. My niece is only eighteen, and is as modest and well-conducted a young lady as I know anywhere. Up to last September she attended a London ladies' college of the first rank, and gave extreme satisfaction, and was at the head of her classes. In that month I took a residence at a pleasant town on the Thames. My niece, who is fond of study, wished to attend certain classes at a large school in the neighbourhood, and the arrangement was made by me with the lady principal.

"One Saturday afternoon in the commencement of December, I returned from London just before dinner, and was met with a very distressed face from my old housekeeper. Her young mistress had come home from the school in a half-distracted state, and locked herself in her room. The old servant had, however, obtained admittance, and ascertained what was the matter.

"There was a class for English composition at the school that morning, the teacher being a visiting tutor. Lecturing rather glibly on English poetry this person attributed the line,

'We mortal millions live alone,'

to Mr. Tennyson. As I am occupied in literary pursuits, my niece had read more than many girls of her age; she at once corrected him, saying that the line was Mr. Matthew Arnold's. A governess, who sat in the class-room, sharply told her not to contradict or not to interrupt, and when the lecture concluded a bad mark was entered against her in the register. It is the custom of the schoolmistress to inflict corporal punishment for all the bad marks of a certain magnitude, and my niece had seen one or two of the younger children whipped, but her attendance being only on certain days, she did not know that the discipline was anything but infantile.

"To her surprise, when about to leave after her lessons she was ordered into the schoolroom. To her amazement and indignation, she found she was to be birched for impudence to a teacher. She protested and implored, but in vain. Her resistance was useless against force: she was held bending forwards across a desk, the clothing was completely removed from the lower part of her person, and the lady-principal gave her twelve sharp cuts with a birch.

"I am an Irishman, and you may imagine my indignation at such an outrage to a modest young lady, who is actually engaged to be married. My resolution was soon taken. That evening I consulted the wives of three of my friends, who approved of it. With much difficulty I induced my niece to return to the school on Monday. Luckily, it was not long to Christmas, and she escaped any further insult, except the occasional chaff of one or two younger girls. Early in January I wrote a polite note to the lady-principal, asking her to lunch at my house, and receive the amount due to her. She came, and was shewn into the library, where the three married ladies above mentioned awaited her. Causing her to be seated, I told her my opinion of her conduct; observed that for my niece's sake I desired to avoid the exposure attendant on legal proceedings, and added that, with the approval of the ladies present, I should punish her as she had punished my niece. Of course there was a tempestuous scene, but she submitted. I had ridden over to Eton and got a good stout birch from the man who makes for the College—it is a good appointment. It is only necessary to add that she was treated as my niece had been in the matter of apparel, and that I gave her twenty strokes, whose severity the state of her cuticle plainly attested. She was well able to bear them, being forty years old, unmarried, a tall, strong, stout woman. My niece declined to be present at the punishment, but I compelled the woman to apologise humbly to her afterwards. I have since heard a rumour that she intends to give up the school and leave the neighbourhood."

It might have been supposed that the discussions in the *Family Herald* and the *Queen* would have exhausted the subject of the birching of young ladies, but that it is not yet exhausted is evident from the fact that a controversy about household whipping "broke out" in a popular magazine a few years ago. "Birch in the Boudoir" was the title given to an article in the *Saturday Review*, in which the letters that appeared in the *Englishwoman's Domestic Magazine* (the periodical in question) were criticised. After making some very satirical remarks on the correspondence, the *Review* concluded by asking, "Is it possible that before long the only creatures in Europe, besides cattle, that are flogged will be English criminals and English girls. Or is the whole of this amazing correspondence fictitious? Is it nothing more than an elaborate and vulgar hoax?"

The editor of the *Englishwoman's Domestic Magazine* says he gave only a small portion of the letters he received on the subject of birching young ladies; some of the communications, indeed, were unfit for publication. The following is one of the letters reproduced in full, just as it was published:- "I have just been reading in your admirable magazine the remarks of your correspondents on the important subject of corporal chastisement for children, and as I have had some experience in that way, perhaps you will kindly allow me to relate it. I may then state that, in consequence of my wife dying about three years ago, I was left with the entire management of my children, two girls and four boys. The latter I sent to a boarding school, and employed a governess to superintend the education of the young ladies, who, until eighteen months ago, had been carefully trained under the no-personal-chastisement system; but their progress was so very unsatisfactory, and their general conduct so insubordinate and unladylike, that I yielded to the reiterated solicitations of the governess, and consented to her introducing the Rod. One was accordingly procured, and at her suggestion it was made of soft pliable leather, cut into long narrow thongs at one end, which she assured me produced intense pain but with little or no injury to the person. It was used for the first time on the occasion of the girls being detected in pilfering money, after I had examined them and found there was no doubt of their guilt. I directed the governess to inflict upon each of them a most severe whipping, which was arranged to take place in her boudoir immediately after evening prayers. The eldest was first taken to her dressing-room and prepared for the Rod, and then conveyed to the boudoir by the governess, who at once administered the discipline. The younger one was then prepared, and received a wholesome flagellation. These whippings were administered *supra dorsum nudum*, the delinquents being tightly strapped over an ottoman during the castigation, at the conclusion of which they had to kiss the rod and thank the governess, when they were permitted to retire. Since then there has been a marked improvement in their behaviour, and the progress made in their studies has been truly gratifying. It is now nearly nine months since one had to be corrected in the boudoir, although the Rod is yet occasionally applied to the palms of their hands when they are negligent. I have also used it with good effect on my boys, and find it far more efficient than the birch, which occasions considerable injury to the person after a severe application. This is not so where the leather rod is used, while at the same time the pain suffered by the delinquent is much more acute; and this, I think, should be the object of all whippings—to make them remembered. In conclusion, I would recommend your correspondents to obtain a rod such as I have described, and they will find that, after using it thoroughly once or twice, their children will become perfectly docile."

The following account of the discipline of a lady's school at Havanna, in Cuba, has been abridged from an old newspaper. The practices referred to are evidently of an oldish date, 1836 being the year in which the paper was published from which the extract was taken:- "The school of Madame De Berros was the finest institution of the kind in the city. It was very select, and madame's terms were very exorbitant, no young lady being admitted who could not afford to pay two hundred pounds per annum. As only thirty-two pupils were received in all, great interest was made to obtain the entrée of this institution. It was a finishing school in the highest sense of the term. No young lady was admitted till she was fourteen years of age, and the series of lessons embraced a period of three years. As I had the advantage of finishing my education in madame's house, I will detail, as briefly as I can, how the discipline was conducted, and the ceremonies which were the usual etiquette of the house.

"In consequence of having to wait for a vacancy, I was beyond the proper age when I was admitted—a fact, however, which my guardians were obliged to conceal from madame, as it was a strict rule that no young person above fourteen years of age could be admitted. There were many parents who resorted to a little fraud to obtain the entrance of their children; and I was contemporary with one young lady, rather a fragile creature, who was over seventeen at the period of her entrance, whom I saw birched by madame on her nineteenth birthday. Madame, of course, recognised only the nominal age of her pupils, and was not supposed to be aware of the little frauds of parents. Every parent was made aware of the rules of the school, and that whipping was one of the commonest chastisements; but, indeed, at the time whipping was so common in every household that even grown-up young ladies and gentlemen had to submit to the birch, and madame was a perfect adept in the administration of this punishment.

"Each young lady was obliged to have a very expensive outfit: underclothing of the finest description of linen and lace; satin slippers of different colours, black morocco shoes, bedroom slippers, &c.; also silk and lace stockings of fine textures. Underclothing richly trimmed, elegant dressing gowns, and a large supply of gloves, also formed a portion of the *trousseau* if I may so call it. I was taken to school by my aunt, and was received by madame in an elegant drawing-room. I had to courtesy to the ground on being presented to her, and was then sent to the first room to be introduced to my future companions, which was done by one of the governesses.

"The schoolhouse was a very large and elegant château, which had been built for the governor of the city. It contained four reception rooms and several minor drawing-rooms and boudoirs, all of which were richly furnished. Each set of eight pupils had a separate drawing room, bedroom, schoolroom, dressing-room, &c.; madame herself occupying the principal drawing room, in which were held the weekly dancing assemblies of the pupils, and where took place what we used to call the state flagellations of the pupils.

"I had not been an hour or two in the house till I learned what was in store for me. Novices, however, escaped a considerable time before they were flogged in state. Although it is anticipating a little, I may mention that upon one occasion I was sent to madame's boudoir with the awful black book, in which was entered my first crime. Madame was dressed in a beautiful morning robe of cashmere, and looked awfully grand. I had to courtesy very low on presenting the book, and after madame had looked at it she rang the bell and desired her maid to prepare me for the Rod! Oh, how I trembled. The young woman took off my frock and upper petticoats, and then, pinning up my underclothes, left me exposed before madame. I felt as if I could sink into the earth, but after enduring a severe lecture I was, much to my relief, let away with out being whipped.

"The first public flagellation that I witnessed was that of an exceedingly beautiful and very handsome and also clever young lady; but neither her beauty nor her accomplishments saved her from the common discipline of the house—the universal birch rod, which knew no respect for persons, as every young lady who was finished by madame very well knew. I had not been many days in the house before I saw this lady smarting under the well-applied birch of the mistress. This young lady, being a person of family, was haughty in her disposition, and negligent in observing the etiquette of the household, which were, in the eyes of madame, very unpardonable offences. Having three times in the course of the same day omitted to courtesy when entering what we used to call 'the presence chamber,' Madame De Berros became so offended that she resolved to whip the offender at once, although it was not the usual time; nor did she allow Miss B to change her dress, which was also usual.

"The time at which the flagellation I am about to describe took place was just after tea, when we had assembled to dance for an hour in the blue drawing room. Observing that her pupil was more than usually haughty, madame had evidently resolved to flog her; therefore, calling her up, she made a little speech about her arrogance and rudeness of manners, and quietly concluded by saying, 'Dorothy, I must whip you again.' Madame De Berros then clapped her hands, when two of the female attendants, who were always in waiting in the anteroom, came in through the folding doors and courtesied. 'Bring me a rod ' said madame to one of them. 'Prepare Miss B,' she motioned to the other. The culprit scarcely even changed colour, and, seeming to know that all resistance would be in vain, resigned herself at once to her fate. The maid having brought in a long birch rod of very slender twigs, handed it to madame from a salver, with a courtesy, and then proceeded to aid her *confrère* in the unrobing. Having courtesied to madame, and kissed the rod—a ceremony which was never omitted upon the occasion of a flagellation—one of the maids took her gently on her shoulders, turning round at a little distance from madame. It being my first appearance at a flagellation, I felt a mixture of emotions which I cannot describe.

"All being ready, madame, flinging back her arm, brought the rod down gently on the culprit, who at once uttered an exclamation as if she had been plunged in a cold bath. About a dozen stripes equally gentle followed, and then madame, as if warmed by the exercise, concluded in a way which brought the lady to tears. Being at length let down on an ottoman, her hands were released, when, after kneeling down and kissing the rod, Miss B—retired with a profound courtesy, the attendant carrying her petticoats and robe into the ante-room."

Many other instances and descriptions of the discipline bestowed on the pupils of ladies' schools at home and abroad might be added, but as they have all a family likeness we need not extend this chapter by quoting them.

CHAPTER XLVI

INSTRUMENTS OF WHIPPING, ETC.

THE important question, "What is the proper and most effective instrument for inflicting a whipping?" has long been a matter of controversy. Of the almost endless variety of instruments that, at various stages of the world's history, have been used for this purpose, some were no doubt the product of long and thoughtful invention; while others were improvised and suggested by the circumstances and urgency of the moment. Angry dominies, unable to lay their hands on the usual instrument of correction, have been known to seize their hat, towel, ruler, or, in fact, the first weapon that could by any possibility be applied. Among saints, Dominic Loricatus thrashed himself with besoms (birch, we presume); St. Dominic, the founder of the Dominican Order, used an iron chain; Gaulbert had his knotted leather thong; and others employed nettles and thistles. In the "Golden Legend" we read of a saint who had no discipline of his own, but who did not on that account neglect to perform the penance of flagellation his custom being to take the poker, or the tongs, or any like instrument that came handy. St. Bridget diciplined herself with a bunch of keys, and another female saint, commonly reported to perform remarkably severe flagellation on herself, was found to have inflicted the discipline with a bunch of feathers. Sancho, as every reader of Don Quixote knows, in strict conformity with the simplicity of his character, did his penance with the palms of his hands.

Aubrey informs us that in 1678 English gentlemen were in the habit of carrying huge fans, with handles half-a-yard long, serving not only for their protection and delectation, but coming into domestic use as instruments for correcting their grown-up daughters when troublesome or rebellious. Sir Thomas More used to whip his grown-up daughters with a rod made of peacocks' feathers; and some Newhaven fishwives, as we have seen, once chastised a gay Lothario

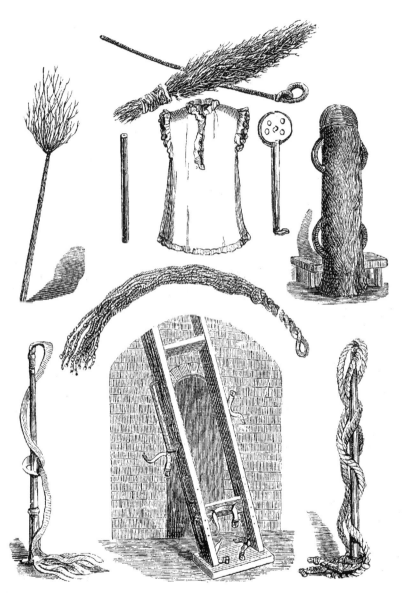

The figures in the upper half of this plate represent the Prison-Rod and Whipping-Post. The Rattan, Birch and Loose Garment belong to ladies' boarding schools in the last century. The Rule and Spatula (or "Jonathan") were used in boys' schools. The holes in the spatula raised blisters.

Beneath are the modern jesuit discipline with the Whipping-post or Hurdle in Wandsworth House of Correction. On either side are knouts of leather and of twisted cord.

with dried eel-skins; and we have heard of a mistress who inflicted a flagellation on her servant with a leg of mutton. A slipper has frequently been used as an instrument of punishment.

The Romans, who carried the art of whipping to a high degree of perfection, had a number of recognised instruments for different offences. Horace and Juvenal particularise three—namely, *scutica, ferula,* and *flagellum. Scutica* was a strap of leather or parchment, and *ferula* a rod or stick; both of these were employed as instruments of correction in schools, and, with several alterations and improvements, have been handed down to recent times. *Flagellum* was a whip or lash of leathern thongs or twisted cords tied to a wooden handle, and sharpened with knots, and sometimes with small bits of iron and lead. Some doubts exist as to the exact form of the *ferula* of ancient times whether it was a rod, or switch, or strap; but the means of determining its more modern shape are not so scanty. In the oak carvings of the cathedrals of the middle ages, the figure of a monkish schoolmaster, holding a rod ready to beat a boy on the breech, is quite frequent. The ferule of modern days was a more ingenious instrument, and was not used on the breech like the above mentioned, but only on the hand. It was made of wood, shaped somewhat like a small bat, and in many cases it was furnished with a small hole in the centre of the broad part, which raised a blister on the delinquent's hand and made the punishment very sharp. Thirty years ago the spatula used by London schoolmasters was known amongst the boys as "Jonathan."

The ferula in use at the school of Howgill some forty years ago is described as being of wood, shaped like a battledore; and the common seals of the grammar schools of Tewkesbury and Camberwell display a formidable battledore in the hands of the master. Lately, there was at Amsterdam, in Holland, an exhibition of objects either belonging or having belonged to school management and discipline. Among the relics exhibited was a ferula, and the figure of a bird. The mode of application was this: the bird was thrown to the offender, who had to take it back to the schoolmaster in order to receive his destined share of slaps on the palm of the hand. In Gerard Dow's picture of the Schoolmaster in the Fitzwilliam Museum, Cambridge, the master holds an instrument of this kind in one hand. The blows of the wooden ferule were called *pandies* in some parts, and were so far objectionable that they were liable to wound and bruise the hand. There was another form of the ferule, a less objectionable but equally effective instrument. This was a broad leather strap, about ten inches long, the end being rounded, and between four and five inches broad. The other end was tapered to a breadth of an inch and a half, and fastened to a wooden handle. The leather was thick and hammered hard without losing its flexibility. It was used for striking the palm of the hand, and produced a smart tingling sensation. The Scotch ferule or *taws* (toes, taes, taws) was simply a leather strap, with one end cut into strips and hardened in the fire. Sometimes it was furnished with a wooden handle, as in the case of the Edinburgh High School *taws*, but the usual form was a long strap, and although occasionally applied to the bare buttocks, was chiefly used on the hand; hence the word *palmy* from *palmæ*. Juvenal speaks of the Roman schoolboys "drawing back the hand from the *ferula*," *manum ferulæ subucimus*; and the modern schoolboy practises a similar dodge by pulling down the cuff of his jacket over his hand to catch the blow of the taws. The *virga*, a switch rod, was another instrument of whipping employed among the Romans, and seems to have suggested the use of the birch, which has long been in operation in large public schools. Following the opinion of Solomon that "a rod is for the back of him that is void of understanding," and "a whip for the horse, a bridle for the ass, and a rod for the fool's back," the punishment of the birch was in general inflicted on the bare posteriors of the offender. For the convenience of the flogger the delinquent was placed on a block or hoisted on the back of one of the older pupils (this last operation was called *horsing*), and there received his appointed punishment. The custom of *horsing* is of considerable antiquity, for a painting discovered at Pompeii, still preserved in the Royal Museum at Naples, represents one boy taken upon another boy's back, and suffering the infliction of a flogging. Another instance may be mentioned. The seal of the Louth Grammar School gives a representation of the punishment of the Rod, as applied to a schoolboy in the time of Edward VI, accompanied by the inscription:- "Qvi: Parcit: Virgâ: odit: filiv:" "He that spareth the Rod, hateth his son." In public schools there was an official whose duty it was to perform the operation of flagellation, and this custom has also been handed down from remote times. St. John, in his "Manners and Customs of the Ancient Greeks," mentions that in the Spartan Republic "regular floggers, as at our own great schools, always attended the inspectors of public instruction." In France, the flagellator in a school was called *cuistre*, which originally signified a cook, and this arose from the fact that in the houses of the nobility, as well as in public schools, the people of the kitchen were supposed to possess peculiar abilities and facilities for performing flagellation.

Excommunicated persons were formally restored to the Church, according to the old *Rituale Romanum*, by the ceremony of whipping their graves. When it was resolved that the dead party should be restored to the communion of saints, it was ordered that the body should be disentombed, but that the graves shall be whipped, and while the priest whip the grave he shall say, "By the authority which I have received, I free thee from the bond of excommunication, and restore thee to the communion of the faithful." This proceeding seems quite as rational as that of whipping the image of a saint. Many of the legends of the saints describe Jews and Pagans as having recourse to the agency of the saints with as much confidence in their miraculous powers as Christians themselves. St. Nicolas, the patron of Russia and Thieves, was much favoured in this way. One legend narrates that a Jew, who had witnessed the miracles of St. Nicolas, procured an image of the saint, which he kept in his house. When he went out, he used to entrust the image with the care of his property, saying, "Nicolas, these are all my goods; I leave them in your charge, and if you do not guard them well, I will take revenge by flogging you soundly when I return." One day while the Jew was absent, robbers came; they took away everything they could lay their hands on, leaving only the image behind. When the Jew came home, and saw his house completely plundered, he addressed the image, saying, "Master Nicolas, I placed you in my house to protect it from robbers, and why is it that you have not taken proper care of it? You shall be properly punished for your neglect. My losses shall be avenged by the tortures and beatings which I shall inflict, for on you I will vent all my rage." Then the Jew took the image, and beat it with whips and scourges most cruelly. But from this great marvels ensued; for the saint appeared to the robbers, in the place where they were concealing their booty, streaming with blood, and his whole body bruised and lacerated. Pointing to his wounds, he said, "Why have I been so cruelly beaten, and why have I endured so many tortures on your account? See how my body is lacerated, and how my blood gushes forth in streams! Go and restore all that you have stolen, or the anger of the Almighty God will burst upon you so fiercely that your crime will be universally known and you will all be hanged." The robbers asked, "Who are you that hold such language?" and he said, "I am Nicolas, the servant of the Lord, whom the Jew has thus cruelly beaten on account of the property which you have stolen." So terrified were the robbers that they immediately went to the house of the Jew, saw how he had treated his image, and restored all his property. Thenceforth the robbers led an honest life, and the Jew became a Christian. Whilst we are on the subject of legends, we may mention a tradition referring to St. Luke's day (18th Oct.). This day was known in York by the name of Whip-dog-day, from a strange custom that the schoolboys used of whipping all the dogs that were seen in the streets that day. The story goes that a priest was one day celebrating mass on St. Luke's festival in a church in York, and unfortunately dropped the pax after consecration, which was snatched up suddenly and swallowed by a dog that lay under the altar. The profanation occasioned the death of the dog, and a persecution began, and was for a long time severely carried on against the whole canine tribe.

CHAPTER XLVII

THE RODIAD AND OTHER POEMS.

The Rodiad.

THIS poem, said to have been written by George Coleman the younger, is by far the most elaborate defence of the Rod that we have met with. The author describes all the varieties of flagellation domestic, scholastic, penal, and eccentric—and is very enthusiastic in his praise of the Rod. Unfortunately it is impossible to give it entire, as many parts of it are altogether unsuitable for modern ears polite. The following extracts will give our readers a good idea the meaning and scope of the poem. Taking for his motto a line from an old ballad,.

"The Schoolmaster's joy is to flog,"

he begins:-

Schools without birch and all correction cruel
Beyond ten lines by heart—and water gruel,
All moral force—a nice look-out in truth
For us the teachers of ingenuous youth.

Far from participating in such sentiments, he exclaims —

But don't think me a sentimental fool:
I'm a schoolmaster of the good old school,
One to whose ears no sound such music seems
As when a bold big boy for mercy screams.

Whipping small boys across his knee is good sport, but he acknowledges a decided predilection for higher game:

But now for years my chief delight has been
To scourge the obnoxious stripling of sixteen,
Horsed at nice angle on the sturdy back
Of one whose faithful aid I never lack,
My John, who with his grip and grin enjoys
The bounds and twistings of rebellious boys.
Some masters love the wooden horse that holds
The fast-bound victim in its leathery folds.
But why this apparatus, which affrights
Ridiculous parents in their sleep o' nights,
Each fancying in his dreams his naughty whelp
There strapped and stripped, and yelling out for
     help?
Nor do I like the block—he never feels
The proper smart who there unharnessed kneels.
Or if the other lads must hold him down
It makes a scandal in the neighbouring town.
Stick to the living horse."

He then goes on to describe the flogging hour at noon, and the various unfortunate victims who are to feel his power. Then follows an account of the different offences which he considers proper to be rewarded by the birch, and in truth their name is legion. The most trifling fault is to form a pretext for flogging.

"Till the child learns the endurance of a man,"

and can take a whipping with cheerfulness and gratitude. During the vacation, when flogging material is scarce, he "keeps his hand in" by operating on the poor scholar, who at other times enjoys freedom from the birch:

"But when no other lad at school remains,
I read his bill of penalties and pains."

On rainy days, when there is nothing else to do, when he is in bad humour, or is ill with indigestion, a turn at the Rod relieves him at once. The parish apprentice also comes in for a share of the poor scholars entertainment, but his chastisement is in general left to the tender mercy of the "gods below," who certainly do not allow the privilege to lapse for want of use:

"Whatever maid her mistress calls a fool
Pinches and spanks him till her rage is cool:
Odd men and charwomen about the place
Punish his buttocks for their own disgrace:
"What's all that row downstairs?" I often cry,
"We're whipping Work'us, Sir,"'s the safe reply;
All right—the more the merrier, say I
The butler whips him when he's full of ale,
The footman whips him when the beer is stale,
The housemaids whip him their hot lust to slake,
The porter whips to keep himself awake;
There's not a groom nor horse-boy in the stable
But has a cut at Work'us when he's able;
The gardener, from this window, I can see
Whipping him now beneath the old birch tree.
He's licked for breakfast in the pantry small,
He's thrashed for dinner in the servants' hall,
The supper time's more beating time than all.

Flogging should by no means be confined to the school, for the poor-

est peasant may enjoy the pleasure of whipping his children—so our
author says:

"So live the Rod—let Spartan Dion rule
   Cottage and hall—the parlour and the school.
The rudest boor, who labours late and hard
To feed his children, finds his just reward
When he corrects them royally at night,
His honest face transparent with delight.
No nice scholastic rod can he display,
But picks up something on his homeward way,
Lithe willow—supple birch—or budded beech."

Then follows a description of whipping clubs, where children are corrected in an approved fashion, and where amateurs of the Rod may for
a trifling fee purchase the privilege of administering a flogging.
Whipping, according to our author, is sufficiently, appreciated among
the higher ranks, but not so among the middle class, where he is

     "Grieved to say
The Rod scarce holds its honourable sway.

The clergy, careless of the word of God,
Too often spoil the child and spare the Rod."

He is shocked at the discontinuance of the punishment in prisons, and
bewails the change:

"Time was—before the philanthropic trash —
When jails resounded with the hearty lash,
When any morning some known rogue you'd meet
At the cart's tail sent yelling through the street;
While the delighted crowd with jovial cries
Urged on the hangman's boisterous exercise,
When West End dandies paid a visit daily

To see strumpets well-whipped at the Old Bailey."

It is no less painful for him to reflect that

"In peace no drummer boy now fairly mangles
    The ruffian rascals lashed to the triangles.
    And only in the camp or bivouac
    Is the black deed paid off by purple back."

After this we are of course called upon to use every endeavour to keep
up the brave old custom.

"Oh ye, who still hold flagellation dear,
Maintain it bravely, each in his own sphere.
Parents—schoolmasters—guardians, do your best
Never to let the Rod in torpor rest.
Extend the practice, propagate the zest,
Flog at all times—in every novel mode,
Instruct your teachers in the Busby code."

We are enjoined to

"Make each nursery, in its form and rule,
A real preparatory ' Flogging School, '"

so that each urchin may take to the Rod as naturally as a duck to water.
In conclusion, our poet says:-

"Delightful sport whose never failing charm
Makes young blood tingle, and keeps old blood warm."

And the remaining lines of eulogy are too improper for quotation.

*

The Ancient Song of the Flagellants.

According to Massman's Edition, compared with the MS. by Professor Lachmann.

WHOE'ER to save his soul is fain,
   Must pay and render back again.
   His safety so shall he consult:
   Help us, good Lord, to this result
5 Ye that repent your crimes, draw nigh,
   From the burning hell we fly
   From Satan's wicked company
   Whom he leads
   With pitch he feeds.
10 If we be wise we this shall flee,
   Maria! Queen! we trust in thee
   To move thy Son to sympathy.
   Jesus Christ was captive led
   And to the cross was riveted.
15 The cross was reddened with his gore
   And we his martyrdom deplore.
   Sinner, canst thou to me atone,
   Three pointed nails, a thorny crown.
   The holy cross, a spear, a wound,
20 These are the cruel pangs I found.
   What wilt thou, sinner, bear for me?"
   Lord, with loud voice we answer thee,
   Accept our service in return
   And save us lest in hell we burn.
25 We, through thy death, to thee have sued,
   For God in heaven we shed our blood;
   This for our sins will work to good
   Blessed Maria! Mother! Queen!
   Through thy loved Son's redeeming mean.
30 Be all our wants to thee portrayed,

Aid us Mother! spotless maid!
Trembles the earth, the rocks are rent,
Fond heart of mine, thou must relent.
Tears from our sorrowing eyes we weep;
35 Therefore so firm our faith we keep.
With all our hearts—with all our senses,
Christ bore his pangs for our offences.
Ply well the scourge for Jesus' sake,
And God, through Christ, your sins shall take.
40 For love of God abandon sin,
To mend your vicious lives begin,
So shall we his mercy win.
Direful was Maria's pain
When she beheld her dear one slain
45 Pierced was her soul as with a dart:
Sinner, let this affect thy heart.
The time draws near
When God in anger shall appear.
Christ was refreshed with gall:
50 Prostrate crosswise let us fall.
Then with uplifted arms arise
That God with us may sympathise,
Jesus, by thy titles three
From our bondage set us free.
55 Jesus, by thy precious blood,
Save us from the fiery flood,
Lord, our helplessness defend,
And to our aid thy Spirit send.
If man and wife their vows should break,
60 God will on such his vengeance wreak.
Brimstone and pitch, and mingled gall,
Satan pours on such sinners all.
Truly the devil's scorn are they:
Therefore, O Lord, thine aid we pray.
65 Wedlock's an honourable tie

Which God himself doth sanctify.
By this warning, man, abide,
God shall surely punish pride.
Let your precious soul entreat you
70 Lay down pride lest vengeance meet you.
I do beseech ye, pride forsake,
So God on us shall pity take.
Christ in heaven, where he commands,
Thus addressed his angel bands:-
75 Christendom dishonours me,
Therefore her ruin I decree."
Then Mary thus implored her Son:-
"Penance to thee, loved child, be done;
That she repent be mine the care;
80 Stay then thy wrath, and hear my prayer."
Ye liars!
Ye that break your sacrament,
Shrive ye thoroughly and repent,
Your heinous sins sincerely rue,
85 So shall the Lord your hearts renew.
Woe! usurer, though your wealth abound,
For every ounce thou mak'st a pound,
Shall sink thee to the hell profound.
Ye murderers and ye robbers all,
90 The wrath of God on you shall fall,
Mercy ye ne'er to others shew,
None shall ye find—but endless woe
Had it not been for our contrition
All Christendom had met perdition.
95 Satan had bound her in his chain;
Mary had loosed her bonds again.
Glad news I bring thee, sinful mortal,
In heaven Saint Peter keeps the portal
Apply to him with suppliant mien,
100 He bringeth thee before thy Queen.

Benignant Michael, blessed saint,
Guardian of souls, receive our plaint.
Through thy Almighty Maker's death,
Preserve us from the hell beneath.

*

The Ingoldsby Penance.

"I'll devise thee brave punishments for him." —*Shakespeare.*

THIS legend narrates that Sir Ingoldsby Bray, while fighting in Palestine, heard that his lady had consoled herself in his absence with the Abbot of Abingdon. Sir Ingoldsby Bray took summary vengeance on all the parties concerned in the intrigue. He kicked the page, who acted as post-boy, down stairs, and broke his neck. He hacked the Abbot in pieces; and getting liberty to return to England for a time, he twisted his lady's head off. The penance imposed by the Pope for these crimes was very heavy, especially for the murder of the Abbot. Besides having to richly endow the abbey, it was decreed—

"That Sir Ingoldsby Bray, so bold and so brave,
Shall never wash himself, comb or shave,
            Nor adorn his body, nor drink gin-toddy,
            Nor indulge in a pipe, but shall dine upon tripe
And blackberries, gathered before they are ripe:
And for ever abhor, renounce, and abjure,
Rum, hollands, and brandy, wine, punch, and liqueur
            Sir Ingoldsby Bray here gave way
To a feeling which prompted a word profane
But he swallowed it down, by an effort, again,
And his holiness luckily fancied his gulp a
Mere repetition of *O, mea culpa!*).

Thrice three times upon Candlemas-day,

Between vespers and compline, Sir Ingoldsby Bray
Shall run round the abbey as best he may,
Subjecting his back to thump and to thwack,
Well and truly laid on by a barefooted friar,
With a stout cat-o'-nine tails of whipcord and wire.
So his qualms of conscience at length may cease,
And page, dame, and prior, shall rest in peace."

Sir Ingoldsby was further directed to collect the bones of his victim,
the Prior. The penance procession is next described. The monks and
nuns of Abingdon are drawn up in front of the abbey, when a funeral
procession appears:

"Palmers twelve, from a foreign strand,
Cockle in hat, and staff in hand,
Come marching in pairs, a holy band!
Little boys twelve, dress'd all in white,
Each with his brazen censer bright,
And singing away with all their might,
Follow the palmers—a goodly sight;
Next high in air twelve yeomen bear,
On their sturdy necks, with a good deal of care,
A patent sarcophagus, firmly rear'd
Of Spanish mahogany (not veneer'd),
And behind walks a knight with a very long beard.
Close by his side is a friar, supplied
With a stout cat-o'-nine-tails of tough cow-hide;
While all sorts of queer men bring up the rear—
Men-at-arms, nigger captives, and bowmen and spearmen.
It boots not to tell—what you'll guess very well—
How some sang the requiem, some toll'd the bell;
Suffice it to say, 'twas on Candlemas-day,
The procession I speak about reach'd the Sacellum;
And in lieu of a supper, the knight on his crupper
Received the first taste of the father's, fagellum;

That, as chronicles tell, he continued to dwell,
All the rest of his days in the abbey he'd founded,
By the pious of both sexes ever surrounded,
And partaking the fare of the monks and the nuns
Ate the cabbage alone, without touching the buns;
That year after year, having run round the Quad,
With his back, as enjoin'd him, exposed to the Rod,
Having not only kiss'd it, but bless'd it, and thank'd it, he
Died, as all thought, in the odour of sanctity.

Unfortunately, when the scattered limbs of the defunct Abbot were collected for burial, his head could not be found, and another was substituted in its stead, and the consequence was, that the first Candlemas Eve after the death of the knight, the monks and nuns were awakened by a terrible noise, and, looking out, saw:-

The form of a knight, with a beard like a Jew,
As black as if steeped in that "Matchless" of Hunts,
And so pushy it would not disgrace Mr. Muntz;
A barefooted friar stands behind him, and shakes
A *flagellum*, whose lashes appear to be snakes;
While, more terrible still, the astounded beholders
Perceive the said friar has no head on his shoulders,
But is holding his pate, in his left hand, out straight.

All gaze with surprise, scarce believing their eyes,
When the knight makes a start like a racehorse, and flies
From his headless tormentor, repeating his cries.
In vain—for the friar to his skirts closely sticks,
"Running after him" —so said the abbot—"like bricks!"
Thrice three times did the phantom knight
Course round the abbey as best he might,
Be-thwack'd and be-smack'd by the headless sprite,
While his shrieks, so piercing, made all hearts thrill,
Then a whoop and halloo—and all was still!

The ghost of Sir Ingoldsby *(ci-devant* Bray),
It is boldly affirmed by the folks great and small
About Milton and Chalk, and around Cobham Hall,
Still on Candlemas-day haunts the old ruin'd wall,
And that many have seen him, and more heard him squall.

Ingoldsby Legends.

*

The Hamburg Fishwife.

1.

In Hamburg town a fishwife dwells,
Whose venom'd words each neighbour fears;
Aye from her lips vile slander wells,
For lying tongue she has no peers.

2.

In a small court with single door
The victims of her tattling meet,
Intent to scourge her flesh right sore,
Could they but lure her from the street.

3.

One makes believe her fish to buy,
She comes—she's theirs—they shut the gate:
Eight or nine foes now meet her eye,
She has no hope to shun her fate.

4.

Smart as she may, between her lips
A sponge is thrust, t'impede her cries;
And, stoutly held by sturdy grips,
All motionless perforce she lies.

5.

Unhinder'd thus, with loud report
The rod exerts its stinging force;
Her quiv'ring body yields them sport,
And pain is dealt without remorse.

6.

And thronging to the windows round,
With curious eyes full many a head
Sees her stretched out upon the ground
And soundly whipp'd until she bled.

7.

Most wisely thus they strive to teach
The woman not to err again,
Their lesson wrote upon her breech,
Her blood their ink, a rod their pen.

CHAPTER XLVIII

THE ANTHOLOGY OF THE ROD.

Enigma.

Ye doughty physicians attend to my lure,
For I'm grown famous for many a cure,
And in reason and justice deserve more regard
Than the greatest performance of Taylor or Ward.
I'm as old a prescription as any on earth,
And Solomon often does speak of my worth;
And still I continue with the greatest success,
If with skill and discretion I'm used, you'll confess.
I'm known for dispelling the fumes in the head,
For correcting the humours, and sweet'ning the blood
For refining the intellect, clearing the brain,
With a long roll of maladies all in a train.
I'm an excellent cure, and a remedy tried,
But observe, I must always be outward applied.
I sometimes by sweating my virtues impart,
But bleeding's the top and the chief of my art.
Nay, once on a time I have bled a great prince,
And he—I much thank him—has remembered me since.
I could name you a doctor—in peace may he rest —
Stands famous on record for service confest,
Who by my assistance did more good I know,
Than all the physicians for ages ago —
Whose skill in his art was never disputed,
And neither a quack nor an upstart reputed.
There are constitutions and tempers I own,
That are to be modelled or mended by none;
Those soon I give over, because 'tis in vain

To strive where the cure will not answer the pain.
But to make all your labours to prosper and thrive
Apply me betimes, is the caution I give,
And then in all likelihood you'll find some relief
Against the most stubborn and obstinate grief.

The Birch Tree.

From "The Rod," a poem in three cantos, by Henry Layng.
Fellow of New College, Oxford.

A TREE there is, such was Apollo's will,
That grows uncultured on the Muses' Hill,
Its type in heaven the blest immortals know,
There called the Tree of Science, birch below.
These characters observed, thy guide shall be,
Unerring guide to the mysterious tree.
Smooth like its kindred poplar, to the skies
The trunk ascends, and quivering branches rise:
By teeming seeds it propagates its kind,
And with the year renew'd it casts the rind;
Pierc'd by the matron's hand, her bowl it fills,
Scarce yielding to the vine's nectareous rills.
Of this select, full in the moon's eclipse,
Of equal size thrice three coeval slips,
Around the osier's flexile band entwine,
And all their force in strictest union join.
Each muse shall o'er her favourite twig preside,
Sacred to Phœbus let their band be tied:
With this, when sloth and negligence provoke,
Thrice let thy vengeful arm impress the stroke,
Then shalt thou hear loud clamours rend the breast —
Attentive hear, and let the sound be blest:
So when the priestess at the Delphic shrine
Roar'd loud, the listening votary hail'd the sign.

Upon Fone, a Schoolmaster.

FONE says those mighty whiskers he does weare
Are twigs of birch and willow growing there:
If so, we'll think too (when he does condemne
Boyes to the lash) that he does whip with them.

Upon Paget, a Schoolboy.

PAGET, a schoolboy, got a sword, and then
He vow'd destruction both to birch and men:
Who would not think the younker fierce to fight?
Yet coming home, but somewhat late (last night),
"Untrusse," his master bade him, and that word
Made him take up his shirt, lay down his sword.

HERRICK

Parody on Sappho's celebrated Ode.

By Miss C., a child of eight years of age, but remarkably quick, now at
Mrs. D's boarding school, addressed to the Rod with which she had
just been corrected by her governess.

CURST as the meanest wretch is she,
The unlucky girl just whipt by thee,
Who sees and feels thy stinging rage
Which nought but time can e'er assuage

'Tis thou that plagu'st us ev'ry day,
To shame and smart mak'st us a prey;
Is ought misdone—straight on the knee,
Poor culprits, we are twigged by thee.

Thy shattered ends and shabby plight
Shew e'en thou sufferest by thy spite;
Judge then, thou ugly shaggy thing,
How my poor flesh can bear thy sting.

Guardian powers protect me then,
Let me ne'er taste fell birch again;
To naughty boys confine thy rage,
And not with tender chits engage.

An Ode.

To Miss L——y W——n, a beautiful girl, on finding her in tears, on having received just before from her mother the severe birch discipline for a small transgression, though fourteen years old.

My charming lady, tell me why
That blubbered face, that wat'ry eye?
Whom lately, like a lambkin gay,
I saw so wanton skip and play.

Is little Beau, thy goldfinch, flown?
Or playsome kitten sulky grown?
Has frolic squirrel broke his chain,
And been sad author of thy pain?

Has saucy Tommy snatched a kiss,
Or done still something more amiss?
Has he through keyhole dared to spy
Thy taper leg or wat'ry eye?

These would not make my fair one grieve,
Nor her of wonted smile bereave:
Far sharper evils cause her gloom,
A Rod has been poor Lydia's doom!

In vain at mamma's feet she knelt,
Not less the tingling birch she felt;
How hard, mamma, must be thy heart
To make that lovely skin to smart!

Hence, baleful twigs! from hence depart,
Curst birch, that caus'd my Lydia smart,
May'st thou prove food for honest fire,
And there, though late, thy stings expire!

Dear Molly.

THE following lines were the production of one of the boys in the upper form of a very large school where great severity was practised in the last century. The retaliation recorded was firmly credited by all the scholars, and affirmed by the servants

"The tables turned by 'Dear Molly,' the name of endearment used always by the Doctor to that vixen his wife.

"Our master, who, within his school,
Bears always most tyrannic rule,
And every day, to keep us jogging,
Gives four or five a good sound flogging,
Storming like any demi-god
Whilst he administers the Rod:
Of all his manlinness forsaken
At home can scarcely save his bacon,

Whilst his 'Dear Molly' with tongue pye
Scolds him all day confoundedly:
And oft at night with his own birch
Makes him pray louder than at church;
Until, 'Dear Molly's' wrath to appease,
He begs her pardon on his knees."

The Maister.

HE gied us Scripter names tae spell,
But what they meant we couldna tell;
He maybe didna ken his sel' —
    The maister.

What funny dogs we used tae draw
Upon our sklates, an' ships an' a',
Till, keekin' roond wi' fright, we saw
    The maister.

He gied oor lugs a fearfu' pu',
Said he wud skelp us black an' blue;
I doot he wudna try that noo —
    The maister.

We mind them weel, his lang black taws
They nippit sair like parten's claws;
A crabbit little man he was —
    The maister.

He birled me roond like Nanny's wheel,
Said he was tellt to lick me weel;
He seemed tae like tae hear me squeal —
    The maister.

His plump roond cheeks as red's the rose,
His twinklin' een an' redder nose,
Shewed that he suppit mair than brose —
    The maister.

He opened aye the schule wi' prayer,
An' psalms an' questions gied us mair
Than what we thocht was proper there
    The maister.

An' after time an' siller spent,
We left as wise as when we went;
It wasna muckle that he kent —
    The maister.

It's forty years noo since that day,
An' Time, whase besom's aye at play,
'Mang other things, has soopt away
    The maister.

JOSEPH TEENAN

Epigram on Busby.

AT a recent dinner of the "Old Westminsters," the Captain and Queen's scholars delivered their *Carmina et Epigrammata*. Among the latter was an English epigram, which convulsed even the Dons with laughter. It was in reference to the old "Birch Room" of Westminster School having been removed, with very pointed remarks to that Spartan disciplinarian, Dr. Busby. Two verses will shew the style in which it is written: —

"From time to time his watchful ear
Caught the old well-known notes of fear
    From hapless victims forced,
"Fetch me a rod!" this soothed his soul,
Recalling still his ancient *rôle*
    And maxims stern *endorsed.*

"But now the garish light of day
Let in, scares spirits all away;
    Hard, Busby, is thy lot!
For how, great doctor, can'st thou find
Ease and contentment to thy mind,
    Where birchen rods are not!"

The Terrors of the Rod.

THE following extract from a poem entitled "The Terrors of the Rod" is from a small collection of poems printed solely for private distribution in 1815, by the late Francis Newberry, Esq., the friend of Dr. Johnson, and Goldsmith's publisher: —

"The Muses smiled, and gave consent,
When, whisk, at once away I went!
And, what was still more odd and risible,
I found myself become invisible,
And slily seated on a stool,
Among a pack of girls at school! —
All tongues! as fast as they could chatter —
Sure never was there such a clatter
But one, much louder than the rest,
Amused them with a mighty jest —
A word!—she had picked up in the street
A word!—the bard will not repeat.
Now, hushed at once the little band,
Behold! the governess, so grand,
The schoolroom enters!—not a word,
Where all was riot, now is heard!
Each head, by her majestic look,
Bent down on sampler, or on book!
When, lo! the gloomy, lowering eye
Prognosticates a storm is nigh:
Too sure a presage! Says the dame,
"What girl, as down the stairs I came,
Dared utter that vile naughty word
Which never in my school was heard?
If now this instant you won't own
Who 'twas—I'll whip you every one."
All—all—were ready then to cry,
" 'Twas not me, ma'am—'twas Betsy Fry."

"Who! Betsy Fry?—I'm quite ashamed —
Such a great girl!—to hear her named;
But for this crime, a whipping ample
Shall be to others, good example.
Indecent wretch!—you, Sally Treacher,
Go run up stairs and tell the teacher
To bring that rod she made, just new,
And tied up with a ribbon blue:
Then such a punishment I'll give
As you'll remember while you live.
No begging, miss, will be of use,
For such a crime there's no excuse —
No further parley! Here Miss Glynn
With the grand instrument came in:
So smartly tied up with a bow,
It might be deemed a rod for show:
Yet though thus elegant the plan,
And wide expanded like a fan,
When well applied, each twig apart
Would tend to multiply the smart.
"You know, Miss Glynn, it is my rule,
When wicked words invade my school,
T' employ this instrument of pain
To whip and drive them out again:
So down with that vile hussy Fry,
That I may flog her instantly."
The ready teacher then, Miss Glynn
(A thorough friend to discipline),
Proceeds the culprit straight to seize,
Crying, and begging, on her knees:
But vain her tears, and vain her prayer! —
She laid her down across a chair.
The governess now takes her stand,
The birchen sceptre in her hand
With lofty air, inspiring awe,

And upraised arm to enforce the law,
She shakes the whistling twigs, and then,
Whip!—Whip!—Whip!—Whip!—inflicts the pain:
Now pauses—while Miss Fry roars aloud,
Sad warnings to the little crowd —
Crying, "Oh! dear Ma'am, pray give o'er,
I never will do so no more."
In vain: the rod's reiterations
Produce fresh pauses, fresh orations.
"These stripes I'm sorry to impart;
But 'tis for your own good you smart.
Who spares the Rod will spoil the child!
By me the proverb sha'n't be spoiled,"
This brought the conflict to a close;
When quick the smarting culprit rose.
The governess, with awful state,
And head erect, resumed her seat:
Then calling up her victim, Fry
(Sobbing and wiping either eye),
Descanted, with all due reflection,
On crimes provoking such correction:
But, still to heighten the impression
Of punishment for this transgression,
On a high stool she made her perch,
And in her bosom stuck the birch:
Warning the school 'gainst crimes and errors
By the grand triumph of its terrors."

The Birch.
A Poem. Written by a Youth of Thirteen.

THOUGH the *Oak* be the prince and the pride of the grove,
The emblem of power, and the fav'rite of Jove
Though Phœbus her temples with *Laurel* has bound,
And with chaplets of *Poplar* Alcides is crowned:

Though Pallas the *Olive* has graced with her choice,
And old mother Cybel in *Pines* may rejoice:
Yet the Muses declare—after diligent search —
That no tree can be found to compare with the *Birch*
The Birch, they affirm, is the true tree of knowledge.
Revered at each school, and remembered at college.
Though Virgil's famed tree might produce, as its fruit,
A crop of vain dreams and strange whims on each shoot,
Yet the Birch, on each bough, on the top of each switch,
Bears the essence of grammar and the eight parts of speech.
'Mongst the leaves are concealed more than memory can mention —
All cases, all genders, all forms of declension.
Nine branches, when cropp'd by the hands of the nine,
And duly arranged in a parallel line;
Tied up in nine folds of a mystical string,
And soak'd for nine days in cold Helicon spring—
Form a sceptre composed for a pedagogue's hand,
Like the Fasces of Rome, a true badge of command
The sceptre thus finish'd, like Moses's rod,
From flints could draw tears, and give life to a clod.
Should darkness Egyptian, or ignorance, spread
Their clouds o'er the mind or envelope the head,
The Rod, thrice applied, puts the darkness to flight,
Disperses the clouds, and restores us to light:
Like the *Virga Divina* 'twill find out the vein
Where lurks the rich metal, the ore of the brain.
Should Genius, a captive in sloth, be confined,
Or the witchcraft of pleasure prevail o'er the mind,
The magical wand but apply—with a stroke
The spell is dissolved, the enchantment is broke.
Like Hermes's Caduceus, these switches inspire
Rhetorical thunder, poetical fire:
And if Morpheus our temples in Lethe should steep,
Their touch will untie all the fetters of sleep.
Here dwells strong conviction—of logic the glory,

When applied with precision *à posteriori.*
I've known a short lecture most strangely prevail
When duly conveyed to the head through the tail:
Like an electrical shock in an instant 'tis spread,
And flies with a jerk, from the tail to the head:
Promotes circulation, and thrills through each vein,
The faculties quicken, and purges the brain.
By sympathy thus, and consent of the parts,
We are taught, *fundamentally*, classics and arts,
The Birch, *à priori*, applied to the palm,
Can settle disputes and a passion becalm.
Whatever disorders prevail in the blood
The Birch can correct them, like guaiacum wood:
It sweetens the juices, corrects our ill humours,
Bad habits removes, and disperses foul tumours.
When applied to the hand, it can cure with a switch,
Like the salve of old Molyneux, used in the itch!
As the famed rod of Circe to brutes could turn men,
So the twigs of the Birch can unbrute them again.
Like the wand of the Sybil, that branch of pure gold,
These sprays can the gates of Elysium unfold —
The Elysium of learning, where pleasures abound,
Those sweets that still flourish on classical ground
Prometheus's rod, which mythologists say
Fetched fire from the sun to give life to his clay,
Was a rod well applied, his men to inspire
With a taste for the arts and the genius to fire.
This bundle of rods may suggest one reflection —
That the arts with each other maintain a connexion.
Another good moral this bundle of switches
Points out to our notice, and silently teaches —
Of peace and good fellowship these are a token,
For the twigs, well united, can scarcely be broken.
Then if such are its virtues, we bow to the tree
And THE BIRCH, like the Muses, immortal shall be.

The Block.

"Infandum, regina, jubes renovare dolorem
Block loquitur."*

MOST people think, at least 'tis thought by some,
That a fat book is a "Gradus ad Parnassum;"
But these two steps called Block, you here behold
The real staircase Parnassian unfold:
The Library† my palace is; called so
Without a book; "Lucus a non lucendo;"
The bane and antidote of learning see
Filling both sides of this said Library.
The first a grim press, filled with betula,
Learning's sad tree (whence formed the ferula),
The tree of knowledge of the present day —
Of good, the masters—evil, younkers—say,
"The birch trees weep," so Scott, in "fragrant bloom,"
But here, they weeping cause, without perfume.
Opposed, in gilded letters names appear
Whom science crowns on each revolving year
As scholars, victors in Clintonian‡ race,
Or marked as medallists the old walls grace.
Heath, Ascot Heath§—so was he called, because
He wielded birch on fundamental laws —
Was the first high priest who, 'midst shrieks and noise,
Flogged on my altar hecatombs of boys.
Him followed Goodall, gentle, kind—too kind,
Of all my high priests I can bring to mind;

---

*The answer of an Etonian to Queen Elizabeth, who had asked him how often he had been flogged.
† The old, if not the present name for the flogging room.
‡ The scholarship founded by the late Duke of Newcastle.
§ Dr. Heath preceded Dr. Goodall as Head Master. Many of his poems are in the "Musæ Etonenses"

With boys least fit to cope: that savage race
Regards concession as a weakness base.
But e'en the boys at length to feel began
That 'twas a shame to plague so good a man.
As Eton provost he won general praise;
A lengthened sunset blessed his honoured days,
Keate, stern and resolute, who knew not fear,
And never, as a baby, shed a tear
(Though boys denied he'd been a baby e'er),
Came next, his name derived—the younkers said so —
Fromστη dolor, and fromcew fundo:
A man he was, austere and stern to view;
I knew him well, and every truant knew;"
Like Jove, with vengeful brand, the world he dares;
The robe ("Eothen" vide) which he wears
Half widow, half Napoleon, appears;
Yet he was fair—not "How divinely fair!"
But Just—a scholar;* and in this his lair
He quelled rebellion with Rod of birch —
With Rod cut those who cut their names in church
Here, here, boys lowly knelt to Block of wood;
Whilst, brandishing his sceptre, there he stood —
Down swept the birch, the boys who'd tried to shirk
Their books, resolved in future that they'd work.
'Twas in Keate's reign—one night, when flogging o'er,
(I think 'twas fourth of June) wide oped the door,
A band of miscreants upon me tore,
Headed by one† who, used to feats of arms,
And rows, and sprees, and all sorts of alarm
And rebel deeds—who often at my shrine
Had knelt unflinching to receive his nine —
Hard, unrepenting, when déculotté

---

* A most elegant Latin scholar.
† The late, alas! Marquis of W—d.

Seemed made of stone, whene'er Keate flogged away
Headed by him they bore me from the room
I hoped t' inhabit till the day of doom.

How boys were flogged during my absence brief;
Who 'twas who came at last to my relief;
What happened, where I went, is all unknown;
They say, there was confusion through the town,
Great, as when Helen in her Sunday gown
Was by that Paris helped the ladder down.
Such bangs and whacks I suffered and such noise,
I've almost since felt pity for the boys.
'Turas whispered that my captor's courage failed
(Though ne'er before nor since at aught he quailed),
And thought the *freehold* might some loss entail
Of what he'd been so oft *tenant in tail*.
Enough: again the Library I saw,
Again uplifted, Keate his sceptre bore,
Again boys knelt, as they had done of yore.
And all things went on "pleasant" as before;
Again my fatal room the old hands braved
And stammered "first fault" new boys scarcely saved.
When Keate "the bubble reputation" sought
By "cannon's mouth,"* and by his genius wrought,
Conviction, and by sermons gave alarm
To men, as erst to boys by lifted arm,
Hawtrey, another high priest, at my shrine
Began to serve; a scholar formed to shine
Wherever talent men of talent greet,
Where'er converse is made, by genius, sweet,
No pedant; he know that "dulce joco"
Sometimes "est desipere in loco."
Valued alike by woman, sage, or peer,

---

* Dr. Keate was made Canon of Windsor

Formed both the young to teach, the old to cheer.
In different tongues he wrote, or thought expressed,
The one he used seemed ever far the best.
The curse of Babel he was 'most excused,
And often proffered honours he refused.
The boys at once Hawtrey both loved and feared,
Their hearts spoke with their lips when him they cheered.
Scholar and gentleman at once was he,
Model of what Etonians should be.
Now full of years he fills the provost's chair,
Time but improves his brain, though grey his hair;
The tutors love to see him in his stall,
Though he, as boys, had doubtless flogged them all.
True son of Eton! where he's passed his life,
Eton to him is father, mother, wife!
Goodford now reigns, and through that good safe ford
Must wade some thousand boys, the hopeful hoard
Whence England will her future statesmen draw;
And those who in the Church, the army, law,
O'er surging waves, at home, abroad, in war,
In peace, shall spread old England's glories far.
Most of these thousands kneeling on the Block
Must rue the mysteries of hic, hæc, hoc.
'Tis for their good, although some modern Rads
"Non *taili* auxilio" say, "'Tis right our lads
Should form acquaintance with some crack jaw noun,
And flogging breaks the youthful spirit down;
And then to think of strengthening the brain
By giving the antipodes such pain!"
'Tis well for me that few talk in this strain
Like gunflints, else I should be thrown away,
Or, like stage coachmen, starve upon half pay.
Floreat Etona! floreat birchen wine,
Block floreat, floreant high priests mine!

CHAPTER XLIX

ECCENTRIC AND MISCELLANEOUS FLAGELLATION.

THE history of flagellation would be incomplete without some notice of the practice of whipping inflicted or received by persons of both sexes as a pleasurable sensation, which has at many periods of history been manifested, and which has been incidentally noticed and commented on in previous part; of this work. It is impossible, for obvious reasons, to enter at length into the philosophical and medical points involved in this question. Among the elements of the mania which some people have for flagellation there appears, according to an old commentator, to be "a feeling of gratification in the pain of another proceeding from that malignant principle which, in common with the good, is to be found in the heart of man; the close affinity between cruelty and voluptuousness, which, to the physical eye, produces sport from the ludicrous convulsions and gestures of the person under the Rod;" and, requesting the reader to study the following illustrations, that is all we need say on this part of the subject.

A striking example of this species of flagellation is to be found in the story of Peter Abelard and the beautiful Héloise. Fulbert, uncle of Héloise, committed the care of his niece to Abelard, and gave him full libert to chastise her according to his pleasure, whenever she was negligent or obstinate. At that time it was a universal custom for male and female scholars, without any hesitation about sex, or respect to age, to be chastised for school offences. The custom of the day led Abelard to use the Rod to his charming pupil, and she allowed herself to agree to it so willingly that, as he himself writes, "not schoolmaster's indignation, but love, often moved him from time to time to administer correction." No doubt there would be occasions when the obstinacy or disobedience of the pupil might lead to the infliction of punishment in full earnestness, but generally there was rather, we suspect, a feeling of voluptuousness in the matter than a desire to correct. At any rate, Abelard describes with poetic fire and pleasant recollection the sweetness of the discipline which he administered to Héloise.

In times when it was the fashion to correct pages and other dependents with the Rod, the mania was sometimes developed to an alarming extent, and more than one exalted mistress excelled in this point of house management. If of a serious turn of mind, the lady was no doubt deeply convinced of the utility of the punishment, while she was also possessed of an anatomical inquisitiveness and an undefined mental feeling. If, on the other hand, she was of an impure nature, she very likely sought in that manner the gratification of a voluptuous sensation. As may be guessed, disastrous consequences not unfrequently followed, and many a virtue was made shipwreck of in this way. Gentlemen also availed themselves of the same principle of house government, and many curious stories are extant of the flagellations that took place in palaces and other great houses. Brantôme, in his "Memoirs," mentions a lady, "a very great lady," who delighted in causing her female companions and dependants to strip, when she corrected them in nursery fashion with the palm of her hand. Those, however, who had committed grave faults she corrected in a more energetic manner using the Rod. She often amused herself in this way, and, according to her humour at the time varied the correction to produce laughter or tears. In this matter she may have been actuated by a desire to mete out justice among her dependants, or she may have meant it to be no more than a healthy exercise but, as Brantôme indeed says in so many words, she was most probably prompted to it by a wanton disposition.

Rousseau, in his "Confessions," discusses with great minuteness this penchant for the Rod. He shows that in his case, the frequent use of this means of correction towards him in his childhood created the desire to receive it in after years, a desire which was not at all momentary, but accompanied him through the greater part of his life. When a boy of eight years of age he was, with some others, entrusted to the care of a Miss Lambercier, a lady thirty years of age, who had a mother's care for her young charges, and sometimes exercised a mother's authority to inflict chastisement on them. After repeated warnings, Rousseau came under the punishment, and received the Rod while over her lap; but so far from experiencing only shame and pain, he tells us that he felt a strong desire to receive it again, and, in fact, wished for an occasion of a repetition of the punishment. Miss Lambercier was, however, an acute observer, and perceivin g that whipping did not answer her intention, which was entirely of a pedagogical nature, renounced the punishment for ever. The consequence of this taste of the Rod, administered by a woman's hand, was such that it is said he sought the company of young girls, and in their childish games the favourite one was where they figured as schoolmistresses and asserted their authority by whipping him. His imagination brooded over the satisaction of the senses which he had experienced under Miss Lambercier's rod, and he imagined every young woman to be a schoolmistress or stepmother. When he was afraid to commlmicate his ridiculous wish to be chastised, he revelled in thought under the lash of his mistress. He ardently desired the felicity of a flogging from the hand of Miss de Vulson, with whom he was enamoured, but was ashamed to ask foi it. IIe displays this absurd yet overpowering taste in his "Nouvelle Héloise," where, as St. Preux Julien, he prays for tormal chastisement for committed faults.

Domestic and scholastic flagellation sometimes rendered youth so familiar with the Rod that it was used in after years by way of sport and jest. Many incidents of the kind might be related. Youthful whipping clubs, where persons of both sexes joined in the game, we are told, were at one time common! Not many years ago, one of these clubs led to a lawsuit in Germany, and although the matter was kept secret it is known that a number of young women, from fourteen to seventeen years of age, were involved in it. In the relations of step-parents to the children entruste to their care this feature of sensuality often appears. The very idea of a stepfather or a stepmother is in many countries almost identical with that of much beating. There have been women who showed an especial pleasure in administering the Rod to their stepsons and daughters under the pretext of maternal discipline. We have the story of a celebrated officer, who, not only between his twelfth and fourteenth years, but after he was twenty years of age, received the Rod from his stepmother, who applied it passionately.

Another, who was frequently punished, and often saw his grown-up sisters and cousins chastised on account of love affairs, was excited to an inordinate love of whipping. In his later years he would bribe the officials in the Dutch houses of correction to allow him to perform the office of flagellator on such persons as were sentenced to receive it: and when he was not allowed to officiate, he took pleasure in looking on.

A story is told of a pretty milliner who almost daily received the Rod from her stepfather. Once the father caught her lover in the house. The lover was chastised vigorously on the spot, but the maiden was locked up for several days and treated to a double flagellation. In the whipping clubs that were formed, sisters and relatives whipped themselves in turn. Games of forfeits were sometimes introduced, in which the forfeit was an article of dress, and the game was continued until all was given up, when the forfeits were redeemed by so many strokes of the Rod!

It is related of a German lady, who was very fond of the exercise of whipping, that she was accustomed to rise early in the morning and make the tour of her servants' bedrooms, whipping all those that she caught in bed. She performed often on the maids with a slipper until they were black and blue. In consideration of the whippings, she made them presents from time to time. This lady was not content with the flagellation administered in her own house, but frequented the houses of correction in Holland, where women were flogged; and if the executioner did not appear to her to do his duty properly, she took the rod herself, and administered it heartily. The superintendent of police, who was himself an amateur of the Rod, readily granted her this liberty, and declared that her strokes should not be counted. The superintendent himself took great pleasure in flogging, a taste which he had acquired in Hungary.

Among the anecdotes of flagellation in our possession is one of a certain nobleman who flourished in the reign of George II. This singular character rented a house in St. James' Place, and made an elderly good looking woman his housekeeper. It was this woman's business, one day of each week, to provide every article for scrubbing out a room, and to engage two women to meet him there on the day: one to represent a housekeeper and the other a chambermaid. While he was scrubbing the room, he fancied himself a parish girl, and he did his work so very bad, that one or both of the women whipped him, as parish girls were wont to be whipped by their mistresses!

In the following case one application seems to have completely satisfied the craving for birch. A young lady of good family was married to a magistrate of great wealth and amiability, who was most studiously attentive to her. Her slightest desires were immediately satisfied; absolute mistress in the house, nothing was refused to her, and her husband made himself her submissive slave. In spite of all the happiness of this beautiful honeymoon, however, the young wife suddenly became melancholy and peevish; whereon the poor husband redoubled his attentions and caresses, and even supplicated her upon his knees to tell him what ailed her. She at last yielded to his entreaties so far as to reply that she had a longing so violent, ungovernable, and extraordinary, that she preferred to die rather than make it known. Of course, this had only the effect of heightening his eagerness to hear what this desire was, and if possible to gratify it; and after several more days of prayers and earnest beseechings, she owned that she wished to be beaten!—not with strokes from the fist or feet, but to be vigorously thrashed with a rod, sharp and quick, in a manner that would thoroughly satisfy this ridiculous longing. The husband regarded her in amazement, believing she had lost her reason; so that when she would not, do as he might, be content, he had her put to bed, and treated as for what might be a serious malady. A doctor was consulted, who relieved, yet still more surprised, the troubled husband, by at once falling in with the patient's desire, and prescribing the birch as the sole remedy of this vagary, only he recommended that she should be flogged on that part of her person least likely to be attended with any danger. The husband, as it were abandoning himself to his fate, then determined to execute the doctor's prescription, and, profiting one day by a turn of ill-humour on the part of his wife, seized a rod, and applied it in right good earnest to the region indicated. From that moment the young wife was completely satisfied and cured.

The penchant for flogging and for being flogged was exemplified in the case of Sir Eyre Coote in so extraordinary a way that we give, from a printed pamphlet of the period, a short narrative of its principal features.

On the 25th Nov. 1815, Lieut-Gen. Sir Eyre Coote appeared before the Lord Mayor of London to answer a charge of improper and indecent conduct, preferred by the officials of Christ's Hospital. The case was adjourned for investigation until the following Monday. The Lord Mayor then found, from the statements of Mr. Corp, the Chief Clerk of Christ's Hospital, that although the general had committed an act of egregious folly, there was not the slightest ground for supposing that it proceeded from any vicious or criminal intention or propensity; and his lordship accordingly dismissed the case. It was afterwards suggested by the President of the Hospital, Sir William Curtis, that Sir Eyre Coote should, in atonement for his folly and impropriety, present the institution with a thousand pounds. Sir Eyre Coote was induced to comply with this suggestion, and gave a cheque for the amount, which the Governors of the Hospital subsequently returned, as having been improperly demanded. Rumour magnified the facts that had come out before the Lord Mayor to such an extent, that His Royal Highness the Duke of York thought proper to institute an inquiry into the circumstances that had given rise to such reports, and applied to the Lord Mayor for copies of the minutes of evidence taken when the charge was before him. In the reply sent to the Commander-in-Chief, the Lord Mayor stated, that on the 25th Nov. Mr. Corp, Chief Clerk of Christ's Hospital, waited on him, and said that Lieut. Gen. Sir Eyre Coote had gone into the mathematical school, and conversed improperly with the boys asking them whether they liked flogging, and telling them they might flog him; and that for this extraordinary conduct the Lieutenant-General was taken by the porter of the lodge to the city compter. The result of this communication was that a Lieutenant-General and two Major-Generals met at the Mansion House to inquire into the charge that the Lord Mayor had seen proper to dismiss. From the evidence adduced before the court we give the following extracts:-

Edward Deane, aged fifteen years seven months, a scholar in Christ's Hospital (in the mathematical school):- "On a Saturday before Christmas, between two and three o'clock in the afternoon, the gentleman came into the school. He asked if we would let him flog us, and he would give us so much money. After he had asked me several questions, he asked if he should flog me. I consented. He said he would give me one shilling and sixpence for six stripes. I first let down my breeches, and then he flogged me. After flogging me, he flogged another boy. Then he asked if any more of us would be flogged; they said no, and he then asked if we would flog him. After his request some boys flogged him. I held his watch while he was flogged; he pulled down his breeches while the boys flogged him. The nurse came in, just as he was pulling up his breeches again. She sent me for the Beadle but I could not find him. Another boy found two of the Beadles; they took him to the steward. Seagrim was one that flogged him. I believe there were two others. He flogged us with a rod. He gave me one shilling and sixpence. I had seen him go into the school with other boys two years ago."

Henry Seagrim, aged fourteen years:- "I Remember the gentleman coming; I was in the school at my business. Bailey was sitting at second table, he was door boy. A gentleman came in, said this was one of the best schools for writing, and desired Bailey to let him look at his writing, and asked how often master flogged. If any of us would be flogged, he would give us some money. He asked Deane in particular; he is the biggest boy. Whilst he was talking to Deane, Mears came in, and asked him how he did, and shook hands with him. He asked Mears if he would be flogged and said he would give him one shilling and sixpence. Mears would not for less than two shillings. He flogged Mears and Deane. He asked me to flog him. Mears was on the table, Deane standing. Bailey did it first, Mears second, and myself third. We used the same rod. He took his breeches down and raised his shirt up behind. He held it up himself. He said he would give three shillings between us all. The nurse came in when he was buttoning up his breeches, and she asked what he came for. She thought he came for no good purpose, and sent a boy down for a Beadle, and locked the door, and locked him in. He asked her if she was the mother of a family. She said, Yes. And he asked her to let him go. Said several times, "Upon my word and honour I was doing no harm." He offered her something. She said, Take your detestable hand from me, and all its contents. The Beadles came and took him. I had never seen him, but heard of him before that he came to flog the boys, and give them money. He went by a number of names. Some boys said it was Sir Eyre Coote."

Several other boys gave similar evidence, and the Nurse said:- "One Saturday afternoon, in the month of November, I saw some of the boys upstairs. I asked them why they were not in school. They said they could not: there was a gentleman there. I went down. I Saw a gentleman uncovered as low as his knees from his breeches. He was closing his drawers. I asked him what he was doing there. "No harm, I assure you upon my honour—no harm." he repeated. I said, "That cannot be, Sir; I will have the Beadle." "Don't have the Beadle," he said. Again he repeated, "I am doing no harm, upon my honour: I was only flogging these boys." I said, "I am a mother: I will have a Beadle—fetch me a Beadle." "I am also a father, he said." "Worse and worse." I said. "Do let me go: you do not know who I am, nor what I am." I said, "Who you are I don't care, but what you are I plainly see." "I will go out side the door and stand, if you will not let me go." I said, "So you shall, and I will go with you." He stood a short time; then he said, "I will go in again, Ma'am." I said, "So you shall—I will go with you." He walked about agitated for a short time—then came near: said, "Hear me, Madam," and commanded me. He held his hand. There was paper in it. I said, "Take your detestable hand from me and its contents; your voice is dreadful to me and shocks me." He said, "Let me go before I make use of force." I said, "Don't talk to me of force; before you should go I would knock you down." Mr. Rigby, our porter, came, and I gave him into his custody."

Evidence was brought to prove that Sir Eyre Coote was not of sound mind, and that the unaccountable eccentricities and follies in his manner and conduct proceeded from insanity alone, and could not be imputed to any vicious or criminal intention or propensity whatever. The final report of the military court of inquiry concludes as follows:- "That although there is ample testimony of very eccentric and incoherent conduct, amounting perhaps to derangement of mind, yet, at the period when the aforesaid discovery occurred, he seems to have had such possession of himself as to he fully sensible of the indecency of the proceeding, and capable of adopting the most guarded and prudent means to avoid further disclosure."

The result of the inquiry was that Sir Eyre Coote was removed from the service by quietly gazetting his successor, without any explanation. All that the public could see was the announcement that on the 21st May, 1816, Lieutenant-General Sir G. Lowry-Cole was appointed Colonel of the 34th Regiment of Foot, vice Lieutenant-General Sir Eyre Coote.

There is still extant a comic opera in two acts, evidently written as a satire on this eccentric passion for the Rod. The characters are principally ladies, such as the Duchess of Pickle-rod, Lady Castigate, Countess of Green-birch, some children, and Miss Stout-back, whose rôle is to horse the culprits subjected to the birch. The scene is laid in Birch Grove, and the opera opens in a grand saloon, where a number of large branches of birch, tied together, represent a tree in the centre. The chief performers, each armed with a rod, make their appearance, and strike the key-note of the opera by singing a song in praise of the Rod, the first verse of which was as follows:-

> "All hail, lovely Rod I twigs of yonder Birch Tree,
> Which surely, dear Busby, was planted by thee,
> Enraptured I kiss it, and bow to the shrine:
> What comes from thy hand must be ever divine!
Chorus.—
> All shall yield to the lovely Birch Tree,
>> Bend to thee,
>> Immortal Tree,
>> None like thee
> The world agree,
> 'er gave such sweet felicity."

After much discourse on the advantages and felici ties of a good whipping, the children are set to learn the enigma which is given in the
chapter on the Anthology of the Rod. In order to impress its meaning
on their minds, the solution was written in legible charac ters on their
bodies. We have also a male votary of the birch introduced, and he
expresses great rapture at the sight of the performance. In the second
act, the proverbial fondness of stepmothers for chastising their children is satirised. One of the boys, however, is that rare character who
does not care a fig for the Rod, but rather thinks it a good joke to be
whipped. In the last scene there is a grand tableau, where some of the
performers are *horsed* on the back of Miss Stoutback, and made to taste
the delights of a whipping administered *con amore*.

Addendum

The following particulars were accidentally omitted to be placed in
the chapter on penal flogging. They are in regard to the whipping of
prostitutes:-

This practice has continued in some countries from very early times
among Pagan as well as Christian nations, and even among some of
the uncivilized peoples of the world. Such barbarous nations as held a
community of women would not recognise prostitution as an evil, and
among those there was, of course, no punishment awarded for it, while
some, backward in other respects with regard to morals, punished the
crime with great severity. Among the Romans, lenocinium, or the
keeping of female slaves to hire them out as prostitutes for profit, was,
during the reign of Theodosius and Valentinian, interdicted under
pain of the scourge, banishment, and other punishments. At other
times the matter was left to be regulated by public opinion.

The Anglo-Saxons of our own history enacted very severe laws
against adultery, but we do not find whipping adopted for the preven-
tion of prostitution. For the former crime the guilty creature was
whipped from village to village by a number of women, who tore off
her garments to the waist, and pierced her with their knives.

Among heathen nations the tone of morality is in general so low that there is very little shame or disgrace, far less punishment, attached to this crime. Some exceptions, however, occur. For instance, among the natives of New Zealand adultery is severely punished, and exposure of the person by a woman is a heinous offence. One girl at Kawaranga, on the river Thames, charged with this offence, was hung up by the heels, and ignominiously flogged before all the tribe. If we search among what may be called semi-civilized nations, we find flagellation a very common method of punishment for women. Polygamy is allowed in Persia, and, of course, the royal harem is well filled. Eunuchs are employed to keep order, and their favourite mode of chastising the female slaves is to strike them on the mouth with a slipper. When a girl refuses to accept a suitor who has obtained her parent's sanction, she is taken back to the recess of her parent's harem, and there whipped into compliance. In China and the surrounding countries, the bamboo is in constant requisition to discipline the women; and husbands are sometimes seen to fling their wives down in the open street, lay them on their faces, and flog them with a rattan. An unexpected virtue is related of one of the tribes inhabiting Arabia. Modesty among them is regarded as the finest grace of the female sex. It is genuine and unassailable.

In Sweden, parties guilty of adultery are punished; the male gets 120 blows with a stick, and the female 90 lashes with a whip. These punishments are in flicted in a public square at Stocknolm. In whipping females the breast and abdomen of the culprit are protected by a sheeting of copper.

According to the ancient German laws, any free woman who prostituted herself was, for the first offence punished with 300 strokes, and for the second reduced to slavery, given to some poor man, and prohibited from entering a town. Parents who connived at the vice of their children were flogged. If the offender was already in bonds, she was whipped, shorn of her hair, and returned to her master. Should he himself be the accomplice of her sin, he lost her, and suffered an equal penalty of the rod. Prostitutes who walked the streets and fields were thrown into prison. In France in early times, and down to 1756, it was usual to punish a procuress by mounting her on an ass, with her face towards its tail, a straw hat on her head, and an inscription on her back. In this state she was paraded through the streets, whipped, and sent to prison or exiled.

An edict of Charlemagne enacted that men found harbouring prostitutes were compelled to carry them on their shoulders to the place where they were to be whipped with rods. A refusal to do so was punished by whipping.

The laws of Naples were extremely severe. Any woman found practising prostitution was condemned to be burnt on the forehead with a hot iron whipped in the most humiliating manner, and exiled. The code of Alphonse IX, King of Castile, published about the latter half of the twelfth century, among other enactments, decreed that girls who supported Ruffiani should be publicly whipped, and also be deprived of the clothes they wore when arrested. The men themelves were to be flogged for the first offence, expelled the city for the second, and sent to the galleys for the third. Afterwards a severer law was passed against the Ruffiani, a first offence being punished by ten years chained at the oar, and a second by 200 blows and the galleys for life.

The master of a workhouse in England had to be dismissed for improperly whipping some of the female inmates who were under his charge. In 1841 it was complained to the magistrates of Rochester, in Kent, that James Miles, the master of the Hoo Union Workhouse, was in the habit of flogging the children, particularly girls of the age of twelve or thirteen years, with heavy birch rods. After several meetings had been held, and abundant testimony had been given that Miles carried on such a practice, the magistrates resolved to send him for trial at the next assizes. He was obliged to find bail in £100 for his appearance. In a letter written by Mr. Tuffnell, assistant Poor Law Commissioner, published shortly after this decision, we find the following:- "The master has, as yet, had no opportunity of putting in any defence, the proceedings having been purely ex parte, and it therefore might seriously prejudice him on his trial were I to call upon him at present for his answer to the charges brought against him. There is one chief point, however, in this investigation that I think may fairly be brought before you, as I understand that it has never been the master's intention to deny it, and, in fact, it was openly admitted by his attorney in the court. I have therefore thought myself justified in taking his admission on this simple point—viz., the fact of his whipping female children. It is thus: "I have been in the habit of whipping female children, but not often; I cannot say how often." Knowing your views on this point, I think you will consider this admission as decisive of the question: for although I cannot find one person in a hundred who will agree in my opinion, that no corporal punishment should be permitted in schools, and that the alleged necessity for its existence is only a proof of mismanagement, I think every one will allow that, at least, there is no small impropriety in the whipping of girls by the other sex."

We conclude our labours with the following anecdote:- A certain King Philip had lost a much valued falcon, on whose golden bells were engraved the *fleurs-de-lis*, and he offered two hundred francs to the fortunate finder and restorer. A peasant presented himself at the palace door with the hawk, but the porter would not allow him to enter till he had promised to give him half of his reward. Kings being easily accessible in those old days, the peasant soon came to speech with his Majesty. Having caressed the bird, and thanked the finder, Philip directed his treasurer to count out two hundred francs. "That is not the reward I desire, please your Majesty." said the pesant. "Then what else?" "Fifty lashes on my bare back." "You are jesting." "By no means: I will take no other reward." "Well, then call in the executioner and gratify him!" The peasant bared his back, and the lashes were steadily administered—not very severe ones, as may be supposed, the King having whispered to the officer to come down lightly. When twenty-five had been given, the patient cried out, "Stop your hand; I have a partner who is to get the rest," and he went on to tell of the porter's incivility and the bargain that had been made. The knave was brought in, and received his own twenty-five stripes, which were laid on with no light hand; and when all was over, it was an additional punishment to him to see the peasant passing out with his two hundred francs in a good canvas bag.

LIST OF AUTHORITIES.

Rather than burden each page of this work with a crowd of notes and references, it has been deemed advisable to give a separate list of the numerous authors referred to or extracted from (of which formal acknowledgment has not been made) in the course of this compilation:-

Arnold's Works: Dissertation on Flogging.
Baker's History of the Inquisition.
Bayle's Dictionary.
Blanc's (Louis) History of the French Revolution.
Boileau: Historia Flagellantium.
Boswell's Life of Johnson.
Brand's Popular Antiquities.
Brantôme's Memoirs.
British Essayists: World: Spectator.
Brooke's Fool of Quality.
Brown's Sixty Years' Gleanings from Life's Harvest.
Buckle's History of Civilization in England.
Burnet's History of his own Time.
Butler's Hudibras.
Campbell's Lives of the Lore Chancellors.
Carlyle's Frederick the Great.
Cent Nouvelles Nouvelles.
Chalmers's History of Dunfermline.
Chambers's Book of Days.
Chambers's (R) Domestic Annals of Scotland.
Coote (Sir Eyre), Plain Statement of Facts.
Coxes Travels in Russia.
Crabbe's Poetical Works; Tales of the Hall.
Cunningham's Handbook of London
Defoe's Works.
Dottings on the Roadside in Panama, &c., by Bedford Pim, Captain R.N.

Ellis's Embassy to China.
Empire of the Czar, by the Marquis de Custine.
Englishwoman in Russia.
Eversman's (Dr.) Journal of a Tour in Bokhara.
Flagellants, History of the; or, the Advantages of Discipline.
Foxe's Book of Martyrs.
Golovin's Russia under Nicholas.
Grant's Travels in Africa.
Grose's Antiquities.
Hallam's Middle Ages.
Haxthausen's Notes on Russia.
Hecklr's History of the Epidemics of the Middle Ages.
Helyot: Histoire des Ordres Monastiques.
Historie van B. Cornelis Adriansen van Dordrecht.
Huc's Chinese Empire.
Koran (The).
Lamb's (Charles) Works. Recollections of Christ's Hospital
Lanjuinais la Bastonnade et la Flagellation penales.
Les Mystères de la Russe.
Lives of the Lindsays.
Livingstone's Travels in South Africa.
Locke on Education.
Macaulay's History of England.
Mackenzie's Reminiscences of Glasgow.
Mackenzie's (Sir George) Works.
Madden's Phantasmata.
Manners of the Crim Tartars, by Mary Holderness.
Marryat's Works.
Mayhew's Prisons.
Medical Life in the Navy, by Stables.
Meibomius; de Usu flagrorum.
Memoirs of the Court of Russia, by Dr. Vehse.
Memoirs of the Empress Catherine II of Russia.
Millingen's Curiosities of Medical Experience.
Morellet's Translation of Beccaria's Crimes and Punishments.

Nicolim's History of the Jesuits.
Olmsted's Slave States of America.
Paget's Hungary and Transylvania.
Park's Travels in Africa.
Pinkerton's Collection of Travels.
Presbytery Display'd.
Plutarch's Works.
Public Schools (Blue Book).
Punishments of China.
Recollections of Russia, by a German Nobleman.
Report of the Commission on Military Punishments, 1836
Report of Schools Inquiry Commission, 15 vols.
Rousseau's Confessions.
Russia, by Count de Lagny.
Scotch Presbyterian Eloquence.
Scottish Annual for 1836.
Secondary Education in England, by J. Demogeot and Montucci.
Sewell's History of the Quakers.
Shenstone's Poems.
Smollet's Roderick Random.
Sommerville's Autobiography of a Working Man.
Southey's Doctor.
Speke's Travels in Africa.
Staunton's (Sir George) Penal Code of China.
Steinmetz's Noviciate.
Stephen's Travels in Greece, Russia, Turkey, and Poland.
Stowe's (Mrs.) Key to Uncle Tom's Cabin.
Taylor's Poems.
Timb's Curiosities of London.
Trelawney's Adventures of a Younger Son.
Tusser's Poems.
Voltaire's Works; Philosophical Dictionary.
Wilkinson's Manners and Customs of the Ancient Egyptians.
Wilson's Western Africa.
Wodrow's Collection upon the Lives of Ministers.

PERIODICALS CONSULTED.

All the Year Round.
Art Journal (Wright's Domestic Manners of the English during the Middle Ages).
Blackwood's Magazine.
Chambers's Journal. Nov. 11, 1843.
Cornhill Magazine (Notes on Hogarth).
Dublin University Magazine.
Edinburgh Review. Flogging at Eton. Vol. 51.
Frazer's Magazine (Ensign O'Doqoghue on Courts Martial 1836).
Gentleman's Miagazine.
Good Words. 1863.
Household Words.
Lancet (The).
New Monthly Magazine.
Notes and Queries
Once a Week.
Quarterly Review.
Scots Magazine.
United Service Magazine.